The *Sams Teach Yourself in 24 Hours* Series

Sams Teach Yourself in 24 Hours books provide quick and easy answers in a proven step-by-step approach that works for you. In just 24 sessions of one hour or less, you will tackle every task you need to get the results you want. Let our experienced authors present the most accurate information to get you reliable answers—fast!

This card is a quick reference for Samba's configuration file, `smb.conf`.

`smb.conf`'s *Sections*

Samba's configuration file has three built-in sections.

TABLE 1   BUILT-IN SECTIONS IN SAMBA'S `smb.conf` FILE

SECTION	DESCRIPTION
[global]	This section contains settings related to the overall configuration of the Samba server. For many service parameters, you can also specify a value in this section to be used as the default for all explicitly defined shares.
[homes]	If defined, this section instructs Samba to dynamically create a share using the username sent by the client. If a value has not been set for the path, Samba uses the user's home directory path defined in the system's /etc/passwd file.
[printers]	This section instructs Samba to create printers from the local /etc/printcap file in the same manner as the [homes] section is used. When Samba receives a connection, it attempts to locate the requested sharename in its smb.conf file. If the name is located, the associated definition is used. If it is not found and the [homes] service is defined, that section is used as specified above. The [printers] shares is used last. The requested sharename is searched for in the printcap file specified by the printcap name parameter. If located, Samba copies the settings from the [printers] service and creates a new share using the requested name.

`smb.conf`'s *Variables*

`smb.conf` provides variables that are expanded at connection time. These can be used in parameter values that accept a string value.

TABLE 2   `smb.conf` VARIABLES

VARIABLE	DESCRIPTION
%a	The architecture of the remote machine. Not guaranteed to be 100% reliable, but generally good enough in practice. Currently support values are `Samba`, `WfWg`, `WinNT`, and `Win95`. Windows 98 is returned as `Win95`. Windows 2000 is actually Windows NT 5.0 and so will be recognized as `WinNT`.
%d	The process ID of the current server process.
%g	The primary group of username `%u`.
%G	The primary group of username `%U`.
%h	The Internet hostname on which Samba is running.
%H	The home directory for the username `%u`.
%I	The IP address of the client machine in dotted decimal form.
%L	The NetBIOS name of the server.
%m	The NetBIOS name of the client machine.
%M	The Internet hostname of the client machine.
%N	The name of your NIS home directory server as specified in the `auto.home` map. If you have not compiled Samba with `AUTOMOUNT` support, this is the same as `%L`.
%p	The path to the user's home directory as specified in `auto.home`. The NIS map entry is assumed to be colon separated and is divided as `%N:%p`.
%P	The root directory of the current service.
%R	The protocol selected during the protocol negotiation phase of the connection setup. Valid values are `CORE`, `COREPLUS`, `LANMAN1`, `LANMAN2`, or `NT1`.
%S	The name of the current service.
%T	The current date and time.
%u	The username of the current service.
%U	The username the client requested in the session setup. This is not necessarily the same as the one that was used.
%v	Samba version number.

SAMS

Gerald Carter
with Richard Sharpe
Samba Team

SAMS
Teach Yourself

Samba
in 24 Hours

SAMS

201 West 103rd Street, Indianapolis, Indiana 46290

Sams Teach Yourself Samba in 24 Hours

Copyright © 1999 by Sams

International Standard Book Number: 0-672-31609-9

Library of Congress Catalog Card Number: 98-83129

Printed in the United States of America

First Printing: April 1999

01   00   99   4   3   2

Trademarks

Warning and Disclaimer

EXECUTIVE EDITOR
Jeff Koch

ACQUISITIONS EDITOR
Gretchen Ganser

DEVELOPMENT EDITOR
Hugh Vandivier

MANAGING EDITOR
Brice Gosnell

PROJECT EDITOR
Natalie Harris

COPY EDITOR
Michael Dietsch

INDEXER
Kevin Fulcher

PROOFREADER
Andrew Beaster

TECHNICAL EDITOR
Dylan Northrup

SOFTWARE DEVELOPMENT SPECIALIST
Michael Hunter

INTERIOR DESIGN
Gary Adair

COVER DESIGN
Aren Howell

LAYOUT TECHNICIANS
Brandon Allen
Steve Geiselman
Susan Geiselman
Staci Somers

Contents at a Glance

Contents

Foreword

People often complain to me that Samba can be hard to administer. I usually end up agreeing with them, but they often fail to grasp *why* Samba can be hard to administer. Samba is complicated to administer because it does complicated things. It makes a UNIX machine appear to be a Windows file and print server. It does such a good job that many Windows users don't even know the server they are saving their files on or printing their files to is running UNIX. To achieve this magic, Samba has to be the glue that holds these two very different systems together. It has to do that without breaking the assumptions that Windows clients make about their servers or breaking the robustness and security inherent in a UNIX system.

To master Samba, it helps to have guides who fundamentally understand the differences between Windows and UNIX and the ways in which Samba can bridge that gulf. Gerald Carter and Richard Sharpe are such guides. We made Gerald a member of the Samba Team after he took on and documented the early experimental code that was being written to support the Windows NT Domain protocols. Gerald is the author of the Samba NT-Domain Frequently Asked Questions (FAQ, for short) document and, even though the code is robust now, he still maintains it. Everyone who has worked with the Samba 2.0 code has seen Gerald patiently answering question after question on the Samba mailing lists, helping others gain the knowledge needed to make their systems work exactly the way they want.

Richard joined the Samba Team in 1995 and wrote the original *What Is SMB?* document that was for many people the first clear explanation of how Microsoft Networking actually works. He is the primary maintainer of the smbtar backup component of Samba and the maintainer of the SMBlib client library routines. Richard is a well-known presence on the Samba mailing lists, helping users with the deepest and darkest corners of Samba configuration and use.

I am very pleased to have been asked to write the foreword for Gerald and Richard's Samba book, *Sams Teach Yourself Samba in 24 Hours*. They truly are Samba experts in every sense. I might write lots of the code in Samba, but Gerald and Richard teach people to use that code, and for that I'd like to say a big thank you to them. Even though the Samba code itself is complicated, the book they have written enables you to set up Samba to bridge the Windows and UNIX worlds and make it look easy. For that, you have only Gerald and Richard to thank.

Jeremy Allison
Samba Team
February 1999

About the Authors

Gerald Carter is a network manager currently employed by the College of Engineering at Auburn University, Auburn, Alabama, where he works on PC clients and Solaris servers. He has been managing Samba servers since 1995 and is an active member of the Samba Team, a group of people who develop, test, and document Samba.

Jerry began his journey into computers in 1983 with a Commodore 64 and a copy of *Zork I: The Great Underground Empire*. In 1997, he received his master's degree in computer science from Auburn University where he is pursuing a doctorate, also in computer science.

Currently, he is an active Usenix member, particularly involved in the Large Scale Systems Installation of Windows NT (LISA-NT) conference, and also writes a monthly column on integrating Linux and Windows NT for the Web-based magazine *LinuxWorld*. His hobbies include running, hiking, and playing music. Jerry presently resides near Lake Martin, in Dadeville, Alabama, with his wife, Kristi. If you would like to contact him, Jerry's email address is `jerry@samba.org` and his Web page is located at `http://www.eng.auburn.edu/users/cartegw`.

Richard Sharpe is also a member of the Samba Team. Richard is a senior consultant at NS Computer Software and Services, a consulting firm in South Australia. He teaches TCP/IP and network security courses and has written several papers and articles on Samba-related topics.

Dedication

Gerald Carter

To God (1 Corinthians 10:31) and to my wife, Kristi. May I never take this gift for granted.

Richard Sharpe

To Natalie, Nicole, and Carole. Their understanding made my contribution possible.

Acknowledgments

Gerald Carter

I always pondered over the acknowledgements in a book. I now understand after having written my own. The time taken to author chapters in this book seems now to be a blur. I know most of all that my Heavenly Father helped me do this. I hope that He is proud. He also provided a wonderful, caring, and supportive wife who helped to keep the coffee warm and the smiles continual. Thank you, Kristi, for more than I can put into words. Thanks also need to be said to Gretchen Ganser and Hugh Vandivier at Sams who were always an encouragement.

I hope everyone enjoys reading this book as much as I enjoyed writing it. Finally, thanks to all the people on the Samba Team with whom I have become friends. Samba would not be without them. Thanks everyone for all your efforts.

Richard Sharpe

In helping to write this book on Samba, I have discovered how much work everyone has to put in to ensure a successful outcome. I would like to thank my development editor, Hugh Vandivier, and technical editor, Dylan Northrup, for their help in ensuring that my chapters covered the necessary material accurately and completely. The suggestions and comments they made were a great help and their patience was wonderful.

I would also like to thank my acquisitions editor, Gretchen Ganser, for being so patient and helpful to me, especially because we were working on almost opposite sides of the world, and certainly opposite extremes of weather. Also, my thanks goes to everyone at Sams who was involved in the production of this book. Without them, the book would not exist.

Of course, a book on Samba would not be possible without Andrew Tridgell, who started it all, and the help and assistance of all my fellow Samba Team members, so my thanks goes out to them as well. I must also thank Dan Shearer for getting me started with Samba and suggesting I help to maintain it.

Finally, I must offer an enormous thank you to Natalie, Nicole, and Carole for helping me complete my contribution, for understanding the long hours involved, and for supporting my desire to get it all done. I could not have done it without them.

Tell Us What You Think!

As the reader of this book, *you* are our most important critic and commentator. We value your opinion and want to know what we're doing right, what we could do better, what areas you'd like to see us publish in, and any other words of wisdom you're willing to pass our way.

As an associate publisher for Sams, I welcome your comments. You can fax, email, or write me directly to let me know what you did or didn't like about this book—as well as what we can do to make our books stronger.

Please note that I cannot help you with technical problems related to the topic of this book, and that due to the high volume of mail I receive, I might not be able to reply to every message.

When you write, please be sure to include this book's title and author as well as your name and phone or fax number. I will carefully review your comments and share them with the author and editors who worked on the book.

Fax: 317.581.4770

Email: opsys@mcp.com

Mail: Associate Publisher
          Sams Publishing
          201 West 103rd Street
          Indianapolis, IN 46290 USA

Introduction

Welcome to the world of Samba! We will spend the next 24 hours together learning about a tool that can help you integrate your UNIX servers and Windows clients. You can break the 24 hours up any way you like. You can even take longer if you prefer. This book contains 24 lessons on what I consider to the most important information you need to know about Samba.

Every lesson includes sample configurations to use, diagrams to illustrate concepts, and hands-on examples. There is even a section at the end of each chapter that summarizes things we've learned and provides answers to some common questions that you may ask.

After you work through all the lessons, you should find a place on your shelf for this book close to your desk or computer so that you can refer to it. In short, I believe that this book will be a good investment for you. The chapters contain information and examples that I use daily at my own job where I maintain multiple Samba servers. I hope that you'll find it useful.

What Is Samba?

Webster's Dictionary defines Samba as "a Brazilian dance of African origin characterized by a dip and a spring upward with a bending of the knee at each beat of the music." That is not the Samba I am going to talk about here. In fact, at no time in this book will you ever be asked to dance (unless of course you feel like it when something works!).

Samba is an implementation of a Server Message Block (SMB) protocol server that can be run on almost every variant of UNIX in existence. Microsoft clients can use this protocol to access files and printers located on your UNIX box just as though it were a native Windows server.

Samba is an open source project just like Linux (a UNIX-like operating systems for PCs). The source code, written in C, is always available to you to explore, test, or change. And it's free!

The implication of these items is that Samba is being installed in more and more server rooms in order to provide services to Microsoft Windows clients without installing a Windows NT Server or any other SMB server.

Offices of all sizes can benefit from Samba. My mother even uses Samba! (No joke!) Her small office network of three computers uses a bare-bones PC running Linux and Samba to offer home directories, group disk shares, and shared printers. It is a simple, cost-effective solution for her to use and me to support (we live about three hours apart).

Why Teach Yourself Samba?

There are many reasons to learn about Samba whether you are a full-time network administrator or just have a couple of PCs at your home:

- Samba enables you to share files and printers between your UNIX servers and your Microsoft Windows clients.
- Samba provides a way to authenticate PC logons.
- Samba is an efficient, stable, cost-effective replacement for some PC servers.
- There's a growing job market for Samba administrators.

Who Should Use This Book?

This book is designed for people who have some general knowledge of UNIX-based systems. Although you are not expected to be an expert, you should have a working knowledge of things like ps, grep, and kill. It is also helpful to know how to use the make utility and the gcc compiler.

What's Included on the CD-ROM?

Assuming that you have a UNIX system up and working on which to practice, the CD-ROM includes all that is necessary to compile, install, and configure Samba. The latest major release of Samba is included in source code form and as precompiled binaries. I've also included extra documentation in the form of FAQs, some useful Perl scripts, and additional GUI configuration tools for your enjoyment.

Conventions Used in This Book

Features in this book include the following:

> Notes give you comments and asides about the topic at hand, as well as full explanations of certain concepts.

> Tips provide great shortcuts and hints on how to program in shell more effectively.

Cautions warn you against making your life miserable and avoiding the pit-falls in programming.

 Paragraphs containing new terms feature the New Term icon. The new term appears in *italic*.

At the end of each chapter, you'll find handy Summary and Q&A sections. Many times, you'll also find a New Terms section.

In addition, you'll find various typographic conventions throughout this book:

- Commands, variables, directories, and files appear in text in a special `monospaced font`.
- Commands and such that you type appear in **boldface type**.
- Placeholders in syntax descriptions appear in a `monospaced italic` typeface. This indicates that you will replace the placeholder with the actual filename, parameter, or other element that it represents.

PART I

Installation and Initial Configuration

Hour

Hour 1

Introduction to Samba

This hour gives you an overview of what Samba is and what it does. In the past, I have received email messages from all types of people asking questions such as, "Can Samba authenticate http connections to a Windows NT Server against the NIS+ password database on a Solaris 2.6 machine?" and "Has Samba been ported to Windows NT?" This hour is designed to answer some of the questions that you might have about Samba, its capabilities, and its availability.

What Is Samba?

Samba is an Open Source Software (OSS) project first developed by Andrew Tridgell in 1991 at the Australian National University in Canberra, Australia. During that time, Andrew was a Ph.D. student in the computer science laboratory and was using PC-NFS to connect to files on Sun workstations. On the arrival of a beta copy of eXcursion from Digital, he began testing the client. To some disappointment, however, the servers to which the eXcursion client could connect were available only on VMS and Ultrix. Being curious, as most computer science graduate students are, Andrew began to think about implementing the file sharing protocol on nondigital workstations.

At the time, he had never heard of NetBIOS or SMB. In fact, this was his first venture into network socket programming. A short time later, Andrew had a somewhat working connection to the Sun using the eXcursion client. The initial implementation of his server had a lot of hard-coded "magic" values in it that simply replicated responses that the Ultrix server would make. After speaking to a person at Digital, Andrew was first introduced to the NetBIOS protocol. It was not until two years after his first implementation that he saw specifications for the SMB protocol and learned what all the "magic" values represented.

Andrew released his first implementation in January 1992. During the next two years, he mostly used an X terminal and had no need to further develop the pet project he began. During this time, Andrew was also introduced to Linux. When interest in his SMB server began to grow, development of Samba resumed, and the rest, as they say, is history.

One commonly asked question is "What does Samba mean?" The answer is fairly simple, to be honest. Andrew's original software was named SMBserver. Due to legal issues, the name had to be changed. One of the words that Andrew found after grepping through /usr/dict/words for s, m, and b was *samba*, and there you have it!

Samba is available for download from the primary distribution site in Australia. You can download and compile the source code for the suite, or you may download precompiled binaries for certain platforms. You should choose one of the several mirror sites around the world closest to you. You can find the complete list of mirror sites at the main Samba Web page located at the http://samba.org.

A simple description of Samba is a suite of programs that enables you to access files and printers on a non-Windows server using the Windows' client native support for accessing remote resources.

NEW TERM More specifically, Samba is a free implementation of an *SMB* (*Server Message Block protocol*) server primarily developed for UNIX-based machines. However, Samba has also been ported to other platforms. Many PC clients use the SMB protocol, recently renamed to *CIFS* (*Common Internet File System*), to access remote file systems and printers. These are referred to as *shares* or *services* in Windowspeak. For many sites, this is enough to sell the idea of Samba and might be all they ever use it for. However, some other capabilities of Samba add icing on the cake, so to speak. Here's a list of some of the things that Samba can do:

- Act as a NetBIOS name server (refer to Hour 18, "Resolving NetBIOS Names Without Using Broadcasts").
- Fully participate in NetBIOS browsing and browse master elections (refer to Hours 19, "Local Subnet Browsing," and 20, "Routed Networks and Browsing").

1

- Contains two SMB clients that allow UNIX boxes to access shares or printers on other SMB servers, PCs, or other Samba servers (covered in Hour 13, "UNIX (SMB client, SMBFs, SMB wrapper, and Various Utilities)").

- Contains extensions that allow UNIX machines to back up files on remote SMB shares, such as Windows file servers. (see Hour 23, "Tips and Tricks").

- Provides a command line utility for limited remote administrative functionality for Windows NT servers and Samba servers (refer to Hour 22, "Experimental PDC Support").

- Can act as a Domain Controller for Windows 9x and Windows for Workgroups clients. Development is underway to provide Domain Control for Windows NT 3.51/4.0 clients and has been partially implemented (see Hours 21, "Windows 9x Domain Control," and 22).

A Samba server can fit into existing networks in many ways. Here are some common examples:

- Replaces a Windows NT File/Print server for licensing cost reasons (refer to Hour 12, "Case Study: Replacing an NT File and Print Server").

- Provides a gateway for synchronizing UNIX and Windows NT passwords (covered in Hour 16, "Password Synchronization").

- Acts as a "home directory" server so that UNIX home directories and Windows home directories exist in a common space (see Hour 6, "Security Levels and Passwords").

- Act as a print gateway between PCs and UNIX networked printers (see Hour 7, "File Sharing").

- Allows UNIX machines access to NT files.

These are only a few examples. Only your own imagination and your ability as a programmer limit you.

Traditional Solutions

You might be familiar with some of the solutions used in the past to let Windows clients access remote files or printers. At one site where I worked, the only remote access to files was through FTP. Remote printing was done by saving your file to a floppy and going to the remote machine (which was affectionately known as "Sneakernet"). Although this sort of simplistic setup has its advantages (that is, it's simple), today's users need remote access that allows for work of a more collaborative nature.

During the late 1980s, several companies began to develop a Network File System client for PCs that became known as PC-NFS. Many sites embraced it as a way to integrate PCs with existing UNIX-based infrastructures.

Existing NFS servers required no software modifications to serve PC-NFS clients. Authentication of clients was performed by a daemon, usually called pcnfsd or rpc.pcnfsd, running on one server. The clients would send an authentication request to the pcnfsd server. If successful, the server would then send back the user's UNIX uid that could be used in all subsequent NFS requests.

Figure 1.1 illustrates how PCs can be connected to existing NFS servers. Only a single UNIX machine is necessary to handle the authentication of the PC clients. The PCs become somewhat of a second class citizen in this type of setup.

FIGURE 1.1

Existing NFS servers and single pcnfsd server topology.

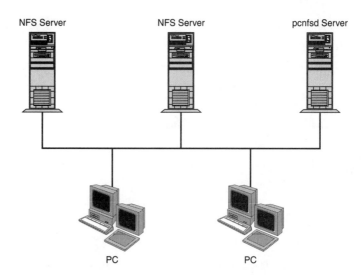

Two issues basically arose with PC-NFS software. The first was the limitations in the NFS protocol itself to handle things such as file locking. File locking was implemented differently on the Windows file systems and UNIX file systems (NFS' original target). NFS used a separate process to implement file locking that sometimes led to problems.

For example, if the lock daemon died or if the synchronization between the NFS daemon and the lock daemon were lost, the PC clients would be unable to do necessary file locking. Samba implements the SMB specifications for file locking and even opportunistic locking, commonly called *oplocks*. Silicon Graphics recently implemented oplock support in the Irix kernel so that data integrity is preserved even if Samba and another UNIX process access the file concurrently. The second problem was the lack of native support within PC operating systems. Microsoft has chosen the NetBIOS and SMB protocols to build its network model. As a result, no additional software is needed on the client to connect to a Samba server other than the operating system itself. To connect to an NFS server, extra client software was needed. In previous times when hard disks were smaller, this extra bulk was an issue.

The native SMB support has several advantages, one being that users are assured that the necessary client to connect to a Samba server will work correctly with new versions of the operating system. Also, on upgrading the operating system, users receive the latest network client software. In the case of NFS software, it is necessary to upgrade the PC-NFS client separately, which was sometimes problematic.

Perhaps one of the biggest advantages is financial. Licensing fees for NFS clients can add up quickly, especially for sites with large networks. And let's be honest, is there any-one who really likes tracking client licensing?

Using Samba eliminates these problems.

Today, many networks have already integrated PC servers into their infrastructures (if not replacing other operating systems altogether). The traditional solution this time is simply to add more Windows NT Servers. This is not always a cost-effective path for all sites. One solution—using Samba and one of the free PC UNIX operating systems such as Linux—enables administrators to leverage the advantage of low-cost, commodity hard-ware while still providing the stability and services necessary for their PC clients.

What Platforms Does It Run On?

Samba is distributed with full source code (written in C) and is available under the GNU General Public License. If you are unfamiliar with the GPL, read the section later in this hour that covers the details.

Because it is distributed with source, it can be compiled on just about any existing UNIX variant including

- Solaris 2.*x*
- SunOS 4.*x*
- Ultrix
- Linux
- Irix
- HP-UX
- OSF1

- AIX
- NetBSD, FreeBSD, and OpenBSD
- SCO
- DNIX

If Samba does not compile on your particular UNIX, report the problems via email to samba-bugs@samba.org, and someone will try to work things out. One of the wonderful things about OSS projects is fixing the problems yourself. "Luke, use the source!" If you do find or fix bugs in the source code, please report them as well to samba-bugs@samba.org.

In addition to the UNIX main distribution, Samba has been successfully ported to the following operating systems:

- Amiga
- VMS
- OS/2
- MVS
- Stratus-VOS
- MPE/iX

The GNU General Public License (GPL)

Many OSS projects are released under the GNU GPL developed by the Free Software Foundation. The spirit of the GPL is to allow software to be distributed and require that

- Any modifications to the software must be released under the same license as the original software (see section 2 of the GPL version 2).
- The source code, if not distributed with the binaries, is available by request (see section 3 of the GPL version 2).

Without stating the specific sections, the following excerpt from the GPL Preamble explains the intent of the license:

> When we speak of free software, we are referring to freedom, not price. Our General Public Licenses are designed to make sure that you have the freedom to distribute copies of free software (and charge for this service if you wish), that you receive source code or can get it if you want it, that you can change the software or use pieces of it in new free programs, and that you know you can do these things.

1

To protect your rights, we need to make restrictions that forbid anyone to deny you these rights or to ask you to surrender the rights. These restrictions translate to certain responsibilities for you if you distribute copies of the software or if you modify it.

The idea behind copying and distributing the free software is fairly self explanatory. The sections about modifying software licensed under the GPL might need a little more explaining.

2b) You must cause any work that you distribute or publish, that in whole or in part contains or is derived from the Program or any part thereof, to be licensed as a whole at no charge to all third parties under the terms of this License.

Section 2, part b of version 2 of the GPL states that any work derived from any other software licensed under the GPL must also be GPL. By doing this, the license ensures that software released under the GPL will always be free even if new changes are incorporated into existing code or the software is absorbed into another project.

The FSF has more information describing the philosophy behind free software and the GPL on its Web page at http://www.gnu.org/philosophy.

Samba is distributed under version 2 of the GPL. The full text of this license is included with the Samba distribution on the accompanying CD-ROM. For more information about the Free Software Foundation and the GNU project, contact the following:

Free Software Foundation
675 Mass Ave
Cambridge, MA 02139
USA
http://www.gnu.org

Summary

Samba has quite a few capabilities. Three points stand out:

- Samba is free.
- Samba allows UNIX boxes to serve as files and printers to PC clients.
- Samba can fully participate in NetBIOS browsing and name resolution.

In the following hours, you will learn how to install and configure Samba's specific capabilities.

Q&A

Q **Can Samba fully replace my Windows NT server (not PDC)?**

A Samba can completely serve files and printers to Windows, just as a Windows NT server would. I need to mention a few specifics here. Hour 12 contains a sample case study of replacing a Windows NT Server with a Linux box running Samba.

Q **Can Samba replace my Windows NT PDC?**

A Not completely. The Samba's domain control capabilities for a Windows 9x client are solid and complete, and so it would probably never know the difference. The domain control support for Windows NT clients is still being developed. Currently, enough has been implemented to allow a Windows NT client to join a Samba-controlled domain, but there is more to domain control than that. Samba's domain control capabilities are discussed more in Chapters 21 and 22.

Q **I didn't see my particular server's OS in the list of platforms on which Samba will compile. How can I find out whether Samba will compile on my server?**

A If I have not listed your particular version of UNIX (or other platform), you can do two things. First, simply try to compile Samba to see whether anything doesn't configure or compile. The second option is to check the Samba FAQ located on the Samba home page for an up-to-date listing of what platforms are supported and for any information specific to your operating system.

Q **How can I send Andrew a pizza to help support the development of Samba?**

A There are some possibilities if you would like to donate some brain food (a k a pizza) for development purposes. Here are the possible methods given from the Samba FAQ:

- Method 1   Call your local branch of an international pizza chain and see whether it honors its vouchers internationally. Pizza Hut does, which is how the entire Canberra Linux Users Group got to eat pizza one night, courtesy of someone in the United States.

- Method 2   Call a local pizza shop in Canberra, give the person your credit card number for a certain amount, and tell that person that Andrew will be collecting it. (Don't forget to tell him.) One kind soul from Germany did this.

- Method 3   Purchase a pizza voucher from your local pizza shop that has no international affiliations and send it to Andrew. It is completely useless but he can hang it on the wall next to the one he already has from Germany.

- Method 4   Send him a pizza via air freight with your favorite regional flavors. It will probably get stuck in customs or torn apart by hungry sniffer dogs, but it will have been a noble gesture.

Hour **2**

Windows Networking

Before continuing on to the details of configuring the inner workings of Samba, this hour briefs you on some of the concepts on which those details are based. The following sections explain the fundamental ideas behind the networking model that is used by Microsoft operating systems, from Windows for Workgroups to Windows NT. This hour is a view from 10,000 feet above the networking protocols which Microsoft (and other) clients use, but it provides the basis necessary to better understand and better configure your Samba servers in later hours.

NetBIOS Overview

NEW TERM   If you have worked with Intel-based machines for any length of time, you are probably familiar with the initial BIOS screen that appears when the machine first boots. *BIOS* stands for *basic input/output system*. During the mid-1980s, the concepts of a computer's BIOS were extended to emerging network concepts. The result was a programmer's *application programming interface (API)* called *NetBIOS* standing for *network basic input/output system*. The generally accepted definition of the NetBIOS API for this timeframe was the *IBM PC Network Technical Reference Manual* published by IBM in September 1994.

NEW TERM Shortly thereafter, in 1985, IBM developed a network protocol to encapsulate and extend the NetBIOS API. The resulting protocol was named *NetBEUI* for *NetBIOS extended user interface*. NetBEUI is optimized for small LANs but is not routable.

In addition to NetBEUI, NetBIOS can run over IPX. Presumably this would allow Novell networks and Microsoft networks to coexist.

In 1987, the Internet Engineering Task Force (IETF) standardized the interface over TCP and UDP in Request for Comments (RFC) 1001 and RFC 1002. NetBIOS over TCP/IP is commonly referred to as NBT.

RFC 1001/1002 defined three services that were to be provided by NetBIOS over TCP/IP:

- Name service
- Session service
- Datagram service

Name Service

NEW TERM A name service helps bridge the gap between how computers see and locate other machines and how humans see and locate them. People tend to remember names better than numbers, but numbers are smaller to store in computer memory. What is needed is some mechanism to match a number with a name.

That is what a name service does. If you are familiar with TCP/IP networking, you will remember that each IP host has a hostname, such as `bilbo`, and an associated IP address, such as `192.168.1.73`. When you type **telnet bilbo** from another machine, the local machine you are on has to match an IP address with the hostname `bilbo` before it can send any packets to the remote computer. The standard means of resolving an Internet hostname to an IP address is either by a local `/etc/hosts` file or by querying a domain name server.

The NetBIOS name service, defined in the RFCs 1001/1002, provides the same type of service to client as DNS. You can better understand the main difference between the two when I explain what a NetBIOS name is.

Names

NetBIOS names exist in a flat name space and consist of 16 alphanumeric characters (for example, a to z, A to Z, and 0 to 9) plus the following:

- !
- @

- #
- $
- %
- ^
- &
- (
-)
- -
- '
- {
- }
- .
- ~

Only 15 of the characters are available for naming the client machine. The sixteenth byte is a number from 0x00 to 0xFF representing the resource type of the name. Name ownership can be exclusive for user and machine names or shared for group names. For example, the NetBIOS name MYMACHINE<00> is an unique name representing the machine MYMACHINE. The name MYDOMAIN<1e> is a group name used by browsing clients to elect a master browser. If you have some background knowledge of TCP/IP, it might help you to think of NetBIOS resource types as being equivalent to TCP and UDP port numbers. Tables 2.1 and 2.2 list all the current NetBIOS resource tags with a short explanation.

TABLE 2.1 UNIQUE NETBIOS RESOURCE TYPES

Resource Byte	Description
<00>	Commonly referred to as the NetBIOS name, this byte refers to the Workstation service name
<03>	Messenger service name used for sending and receiving messages
<06>	RAS server service
<1b>	Domain master browser name used by a machine to contact a domain's Primary Domain Controller
<1f>	NetDDE service
<20>	Server service name to provide file sharing access points
<21>	RAS client
<be>	Network Monitor Agent
<bf>	Network Monitor utility

TABLE 2.2 GROUP NETBIOS RESOURCE TYPES

Resource Byte	Description
<1c>	A domain group name which is registered by the domain controller containing a list of computers which have registered this name
<1d>	Master browser name used by client to access the master browser (possibly a local master browser)
<1e>	Normal group name used in the election of browse masters
<20>	Internet group used to identify a group of machine for administrative purposes
MSBROWSE	Appended to the domain name and broadcast to announce to domain to other master browsers

If you want to see a practical use for these resource tags, examine the output given in Listing 2.1. from the nbtstat.exe command. The output was taken from a Windows 95 OSR2 machine and the machine being examined was a Windows NT 4.0 Workstation.

LISTING 2.1 OUTPUT FROM THE nbtstat.exe COMMAND

```
C:\users\jerry>nbtstat -a picante
        NetBIOS Remote Machine Name Table

    Name               Type         Status
    ------------------------------------------.
    PICANTE      <00>  UNIQUE       Registered
    SALSA        <00>  GROUP        Registered
    PICANTE      <03>  UNIQUE       Registered
    JERRYC       <03>  UNIQUE       Registered
    PICANTE      <20>  UNIQUE       Registered
    SALSA        <1E>  GROUP        Registered
    SALSA        <1D>  UNIQUE       Registered
    ..__MSBROWSE__.<01>  GROUP      Registered

    MAC Address = 00-60-97-40-CD-18
```

The listing in the Type column combined with the resource byte help determine what the name represents. For example, you can determine that the remote machine's name is PICANTE because it is a unique name with the <00> tag. Referring back to Table 2.1, you see the justification for this conclusion. You also can determine that for browsing purposes, the machine belongs to the SALSA workgroup because of the group entries. The <1e> tag is used to elect browse masters. The browsing process is discussed more in the section on Windows networking models later in this hour and in more detail in Hours 19, "Local Subnet Browsing," and 20, "Routed Networks and Browsing."

NEW TERM Previously I stated that NetBIOS names exist in a flat name space. Although this is true, it is possible to isolate one name space from another on the same logical subnet by using what is referred to as a *NetBIOS scope*. NetBIOS scope is a string of characters whose length plus the length of the NetBIOS name cannot exceed 256 characters.

Scope does not provide any hierarchical organization to the NetBIOS name space. It simply isolates names in one scope from machines in another. Unless you have a very good reason to set a NetBIOS scope, it is generally a good idea to simply leave it blank. Figure 2.1 illustrates the use of scope to segment machines on a network. Both machines, PICANTE and QUESO, are members of the same workgroup CHIPSNDIPS but have different scope ID settings that are appended to the machine names in the diagram. PICANTE has a scope ID of "" and QUESO has a one of "dept003". Neither one can communicate with the other as long as each has a different scope.

FIGURE 2.1

Using the NetBIOS scope ID to segment NetBIOS clients.

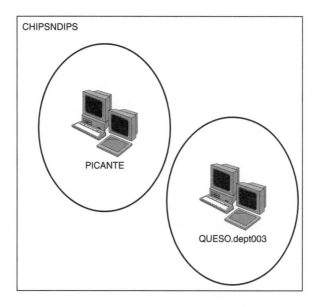

In Windows 95, you can set the scope ID by starting the Network control panel and viewing the WINS Configuration tab under the TCP/IP properties for your network adapter card. Figure 2.2 shows the scope ID field set to "dept003".

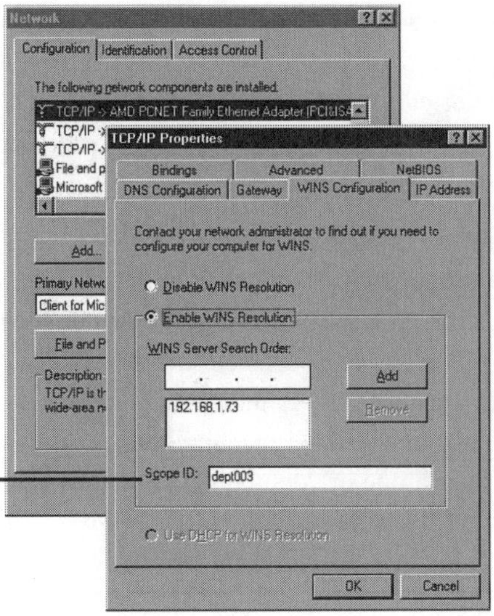

FIGURE 2.2

Setting the Scope ID in the Windows 95 Network control panel.

The Scope ID field ——————

Registration and Resolution

NEW TERM The NetBIOS name service provides a method for registering client machine names and for resolving those names. *Registering* a name means that the client machine made a successful bid and claimed the name so that any future request to that name will go to the client. During bootup, the client attempts to register the name by sending a request packet to the name service that can be either collaborative or singular in nature. Don't worry about the difference between the two types of name servers right now.

If another client already owns the name requested, it sends a response indicating that it has the name and wishes to keep it. When client #1 responds to a request by client #2 to register client #1's machine name, the first client is said to be defending its name, meaning that it wishes to keep the name. NetBIOS clients will always want to keep their name as long as they are functioning. Having to defend registered names is an important point because it provides a means of detecting hosts who have become inactive but did not gracefully release ownership of the name.

It might also be helpful to realize that when a NetBIOS interface is run over TCP/IP, NetBIOS names are mapped to a given IP address. Imagine the case where a client using DHCP to obtain an IP address successfully claims a name, then crashes without warning, and is unable to release the name gracefully. When the machine reboots, it attempts to reclaim the name even though it can potentially have a different IP address. Although IP addresses can be dynamically allocated, NetBIOS names are hard coded. In a Windows client, if the Client for Microsoft Networks is installed, you can find these by viewing the identification tab in the Network control panel (see Figure 2.3).

FIGURE 2.3

The NetBIOS machine name and workgroup settings in the Network Control panel under Windows 95.

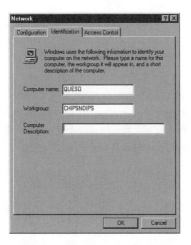

This might seem a little confusing if you are coming from a standard TCP/IP background where the host of a host is registered in DNS or a host's file and name clashes are avoided through good administration. I admit that it is a little strange to have a machine dynamically register names by requiring that they be statically recorded on the local host.

Having registered NetBIOS names, other clients must now be able to resolve the name to a network address. In this case, this is an IP address.

NEW TERM Two means are available for registration and resolution: *broadcast* and *point-to-point*. Broadcast registration or resolution means that the request packet is sent to all hosts on the same logical subnet with the same scope ID. Routers can be configured to forward broadcasts, but this is generally not a good idea because of the increase in traffic that is produced.

NEW TERM Point-to-point name registration and resolution is done by using a *NetBIOS name server (NBNS)*. The NBNS is also described in RFC 1001/1002. The NetBIOS RFCs allow the NBNS to accept varying degrees of responsibility with regards to the management and validation of names. Microsoft's implementation of the NBNS, the Windows Internet Name Service (WINS), acts as an agent to allow client to register as well as resolve names to an IP address. Samba is also able to function as a WINS server (see Hour 18, "Resolving NetBIOS Names Without Using Broadcasts").

The broadcast point-to-point registration and resolution creates the following taxonomy:

- *b-node*—b-nodes strictly use broadcasts for registering and resolving names.
- *p-node*—p-nodes unicast name registration and resolution requests to the NetBIOS Name Server (NBNS).

- *m-node*—m-nodes broadcast for name registration. If the registration is successful, NBNS is informed via unicast packets. Names are attempted to be resolved using broadcast first and unicast to the NBNS only on failure. In practice, this type of node is rarely used.

- *h-node*: h-nodes were added by Microsoft after RFCs 1001/1002 were written and are the logical inverse of m-nodes. h-nodes, or so-called "hybrid nodes" use the NBNS for all name registration and resolution and degrade to broadcasts only if the NBNS is unavailable or the requests fail respectively.

In practice, most NetBIOS clients are either b-nodes, meaning that they do not use a WINS server, or are h-nodes, meaning that they do use a WINS server. You can view the current node type in Windows 95 by running the Windows IP Configuration utility (`winipcfg.exe`) and clicking on the More Info button. Figure 2.4 shows the More Info that is displayed as a result.

FIGURE 2.4

Viewing the NetBIOS node type in the Windows IP Configuration utility.

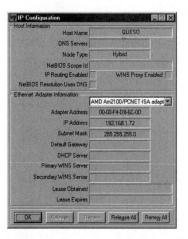

Session Service

NEW TERM
The NetBIOS session service provides a means of supporting reliable connections and exchange of messages between two clients. For any given connection, the sender has a *calling* name and the receiver has a *called* name. I mention these terms here only because they sometimes appear in error messages from Windows clients, as well as some of the utilities included with Samba.

Perhaps it will help to think of the relationship between the name server and the session service as a telephone connection. Before you can receive a call from your friend Pete, you need a phone number assigned by the phone company (obviously you have to have the phone unit first). This is the equivalent of registering your NetBIOS name. When both you and Pete have registered phone numbers, Pete can call you up.

His side of the connection is the NetBIOS calling name, and your side of the connection is the called name. The phone lines that connect you form the session service that carries the data (your conversation). Each phone call is its own session between you and Pete only (unless your phone has been tapped). If you move but don't tell Pete and he tries to call you, he will get someone by another name who would refuse the call. Hence the NetBIOS error message "Not listening on called name." This happens when you attempt to establish a session with another host but use the wrong name.

This service provides another capability to NetBIOS applications: the detection of failed sessions with other NetBIOS clients. I mention this more for completeness than technical reference. If you would like to find out more information about the NetBIOS session service, you will want to get a copy of RFCs 1001 and 1002.

Datagram Service

The datagram service is really the flip side of the session service. It provides a connectionless-oriented service for sending packets to a specific host or group of hosts within a workgroup (unicast/multicast) or sending to all hosts in a logical subnet or NetBIOS scope (broadcast). The datagram service allows for things such as locating the current browse master for a workgroup or domain by multicasting the request to the workgroup name.

 You might have heard the term *mailslots* used in place of datagrams. Mailslots are Microsoft's name for NetBIOS datagrams.

Let's return to the example using your friend Pete. Suppose that you don't have a phone anymore. How would Pete get in touch with you, assuming you don't live close to each other? Most likely, Pete would send you a letter in the mail. Now assume that you send Pete a letter in the mail before you receive his. In this example, your mailing address is the NetBIOS name, and the letters are packets. Next, Pete sends you another letter in response to the one you sent to him, but you never receive his first letter! This type of unreliable delivery method—I'm not criticizing the post office; this is just an example— is cheaper than a long distance phone call and is less bandwidth-intensive for the phone network (none).

Continuing to use the postal service example, suppose you want to send Christmas cards to all your friends. You send 25 cards, and all arrive safely, but you have no guarantee of the order in which people receive them. Do you ever get one of those sweepstakes entries that says, "If you're the first one to call in, you will the grand prize." This is the same type of thing. When the company sends out the notices, it has no way to control who receives the notice first, even if it mails each letter at different times. Now you get the idea of a datagram service.

CIFS Overview

CIFS stands for *Common Internet File System* and is often used interchangeably with the abbreviation *SMB*. In reality, CIFS is simply the next incarnation of the SMB protocol. Whatever you call it, don't let it get too confusing.

SMB was initially defined by a joint document between Microsoft and Intel in 1987 named "Microsoft Network/OpenNET-File sharing Protocol." Since then, the protocol has gone through many changes, and Paul Leach and Dilip Naik document its latest version in the CIFS 1.0 specification draft. Because it is a draft, the real documentation in practice is simply "how NT does it."

SMB over NBT

The Server Message Block protocol runs on top of NetBIOS (as seen in Figure 2.5). As discussed in the previous section, NetBIOS can run on top of NetBEUI, IPX/SPX, and TCP/IP. Samba only implements SMB over TCP/IP.

FIGURE 2.5

SMB over NetBIOS and possible transport layer protocols.

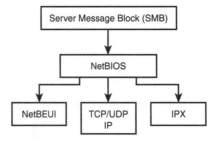

Connection-Oriented

SMB is a connection-oriented protocol meaning that all SMB packets occur within the context of virtual circuit (VC) between the client and server and are delivered in the order that they are sent. If the VC is broken, all the information contained within that circuit becomes invalid. Consider the following four things which represent an SMB connection environment: a virtual circuit between the client and the server, a session uid, a resource connection tree ID (tid), and a file identifier (fid) (as seen in Figure 2.6). The uid is described more in step 2 of the SMB protocol overview. The tid represents the shared resource and the fid represents individual file handles.

FIGURE 2.6

SMB connection environment.

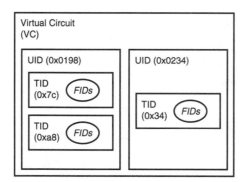

If any one part of the connection environment becomes invalid, everything contained within that portion of the environment is invalidated as well. The SMB protocol maintains no information about past connections, so that if a connection terminates, everything must be rebuilt from scratch. A session uid that a client obtained from a previous connection will not work with a new connection. All tree connection IDs and file handle IDs must be reopened as well. Any handles to files located on the network resource become useless when the connection is closed.

This is why PC applications that run from a network share crash if the connection terminates while the application is executing. The application attempts to use the file handles that were previously issued. Most clients silently attempt to reconnect the terminated session so that the share connection is available, but none of the file handles that the application is using are valid.

Figure 2.6 describes the environment for some fictitious connection. Now assume that the uid (0x0198) for some reason terminated. Both of the tree connections, x0x7c and 0xa8, would become invalid because they were contained within the uid's environment. Now suppose that the entire virtual circuit terminated. In this case, all the uids, tids, and fids would become invalid because they all occur within the context of the virtual circuit.

Protocol Overview

When a user connects to a share on a SMB server by, for example, using Explorer's Map Network Drive dialog box or browsing through the Network Neighborhood, three setup stages occur before he or she can access anything on the share. The steps described refer to file and file shares, but the same set of requests and responses is necessary for connecting to remote printers as well.

Figure 2.7 lists the steps in setting up an SMB connection between a client and a server. The chronological flow of the diagram is top to bottom and left to right.

FIGURE 2.7

Setting up an SMB connection to a shared resource.

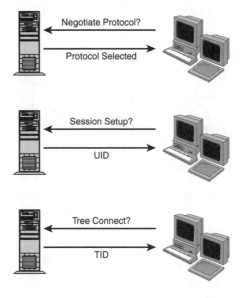

1. *Negprot*—The first step in connecting to an SMB share, shown in the top of Figure 2.7, is to negotiate the protocol dialect to use. In the request packet, the client sends a text listing off all the SMB dialects with which it is familiar. Each SMB dialect (or protocol level) supports certain functionality. The latest CIFS specification draft lists the different commands supported by each level. The server then selects the highest protocol it knows and responds to the client specifying the protocol number from the previous list.

2. *sessetup&X*—After the client and server have agreed on a protocol level that each will support, the next step is to create a session connection between the two. This step corresponds to the middle portion of Figure 2.7. The client sends a "sessions setup" request including a username and some proof of validity such as a password. The server attempts to validate the requesting user. If successful, the server then returns a session uid to the client. This uid is unique for each session and has no relation to the server internal representation of users. For example, the session uid is not the same thing as the user's UNIX uid or an NT user's security identifier (sid). As you will learn in Hour 6, "Security Levels and Passwords,"

this description is not entirely accurate. The SMB protocol can operate under different modes of security which affect steps 2 and 3. For the purposes at the moment however, this is a good enough description.

3. *tcon&X*—The final step necessary before allowing access to files on a remote share, which is depicted in the bottom on Figure 2.7, is to make a tree connection to the shared resource successfully. The client sends a "tree connect" request to the server including the uid issued by the server in the successful session setup. If the user has sufficient access to the share, the client is issued a tree connection ID (tid). The tid is used in all requests to access files contained with the resource referred to by the tid.

When these steps are complete, the user can perform operations on the share such as printing a document or opening a file contained in the share for writing.

Windows Networking Models

Peer Networking

Before PCs, the network model revolved around a central computer server and terminals that users could access. These terminals had no autonomous computing power of their own. They provided the user only with an interactive view of the server.

With the invasion of personal computers in the late 1980s, people began to store their files on the local hard drive space available on their PC. This however, proposed a problem to sharing files: something that was trivial when everyone was logging into the same machine (that is, mainframe) from their terminal. People wanted to store their files locally so that they would be accessible during a server outage (something which they had no control over) while still allowing other users to access the files from their own computer. This PC-centric distributed model was named *peer networking* because all the machines were equally likely to be clients and servers and could operate in both modes.

Workgroups

The idea of a workgroup goes hand in hand with the concept of peer networking. A workgroup is a unit of people who share responsibilities to achieve a common goal. Each one has to pull his or her own weight. A computer workgroup is no different. As you will see, a computer workgroup can be used in two contexts.

NEW TERM   The first concept of a workgroup is as an administrative group of machines that do not share user and group account information. Remember step 2 of the SMB protocol overview? That is when the client sends a username and some proof of identity. The question then becomes "Who will validate the request?" Each machine has a separate and local copy of an account database. Therefore, all validation is done locally. Remember that this is called *peer networking*, or sometimes *peer-to-peer networking*, because all machines are essentially equal. Each PC has the capability to serve files and printers as well as validate access requests. This equality does not mean that all machines perform the functions equally well, of course.

Figure 2.8 illustrates the idea of the workgroup authentication model. The client, shown on bottom, attempts to access the disk share on SERVER1. SERVER1 alone is responsible for validating the session setup against its local account database, whatever that might be. When the client attempts to access the printer share on SERVER2, that server is responsible for validating the connection. The outcome is entirely distinct from the outcome of the connection to SERVER1. Each server has a local distinct account database that is unrelated to the other's.

FIGURE 2.8

A sample workgroup networking model.

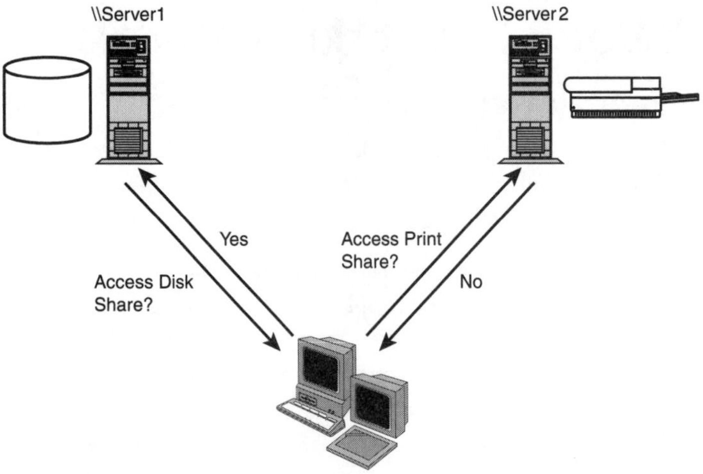

Another context for the concept of a computer workgroup is used in browsing which is covered more in Hours 19 and 20. The motivation for network browsing is the manner in which resources appear and disappear from the network as hosts start and stop. Unlike a central computing model, such as a mainframe or terminal solution, where everything is located on one machine, it is much more difficult to survey a large number of hosts that can come on and off the network at the whim of the PC's owner. Browsing allows users to view the current servers and resources available dynamically. In this context, a domain and a workgroup are equivalent.

Domains

A domain is similar to a workgroup with one major exception. In a domain, there is a central authentication server that maintains the domain's user and group accounts. Resources in the domain are accessed regardless of what machine they are located on by validating against the domain controller. This is still peer networking because all machines maintain the capability to serve files and printers and perform the necessary validation. The difference is that the validation is performed against a remote account database located on the domain controller.

Domains grew out of the need to get rid of the mass of passwords that was necessary when every machine had its own local account database. The solution provided users with one account that could allow access to all resources if so desired.

Figure 2.9 shows a sample connection to a server that is a member of some domain. First, the client sends the connection request containing the user information to SERVER1 asking to access some disk share. SERVER1 then sends a validation request to the domain controller (DC). The validation request contains the user information originally sent by the client. If the DC successfully validates the user, it sends a positive response to SERVER1 that then sends a positive connection response back to the client. This means, assuming that the access control mechanisms such as permission lists allow it, that a client can connect to any server in the domain using a single username and password. In Figure 2.8, the client needed a separate username and password to connect to each server.

FIGURE 2.9

Domain example.

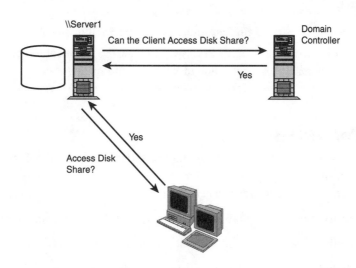

Summary

The NetBIOS and SMB protocols contain many implementation details that were not covered here. The main things to remember from this hour are

- NetBIOS offers three services to clients: a name service, a session service, and a datagram service.
- SMB is a connection-oriented service that uses the NetBIOS session service.
- A SMB connection requires three steps: negotiate the protocol level, establish a session connection, and establish a connection to a specific share.
- A workgroup name and a domain name are the same with regard to network browsing, but are different with respect to authentication models (see Figures 2.8 and 2.9)

Q&A

Q What TCP and UDP ports does NetBIOS over TCP/IP use?

A The NBT name service uses `port 137/udp`, the NBT session service uses `port 139/tcp`, and the NBT datagram service uses `port 138/udp`.

Q Where can I find the NetBIOS RFCs?

A The ASCII version of RFCs 1001 and 1002 are included on the CD-ROM that accompanies this book. Of course, you can always download them from the IETF's Web site (`http://www.ietf.org`).

Q. Where can I find out more about the SMB protocol?

A. Microsoft has pushed the SMB (a k a CIFS) protocol forward for obvious reasons. It maintains a collection of links and information at `http://www.microsoft.com/workshop/networking/cifs`.

New Terms

Broadcast name registration and resolution   Hosts use packets destined for the local network's broadcast address (for example, `aaa.bbb.ccc.255` for a standard class C subnet) to register and resolve names.

called name   The NetBIOS name of the server to contact in a connection request.

calling name   The NetBIOS name of the client in a NetBIOS connection request.

domain   A collection of machines where the ultimate authentication of connection requests to any shared resource on any machine is performed by a domain controller.

domain controller   A machine responsible for service authentication requests by servers in the domain.

NetBEUI   NetBIOS extended user interface. NetBEUI is a network protocol designed by IBM to encapsulate and extend the functionality of the NetBIOS API.

NetBIOS   Network basic input/output system. This is an API developed to allow programmers to write network applications.

NetBIOS scope   A character string used to segment the NetBIOS name space. Hosts in one NetBIOS scope are unable to see hosts in another NetBIOS scope.

Point-to-point name registration and resolution   Hosts use packets destined for a single host (unicast) that acts as a central name server to register and resolve names.

workgroup   A collection of machines where each machine validates client connection requests to its own shared resources.

2

Hour 3

Obtaining the Latest Source

Every once and a while I see a message posted to one of the Samba mailing lists or a newsgroup saying something such as, "I'm running Samba version 1.0 and I can't get _____ to work." Invariably the answer comes back, "Upgrade to the latest version and if it still doesn't work, post your question again." Now I might be exaggerating about the version (for reference sake, the latest distributed version is 2.0 at the time I'm writing this), but it is important to realize the rate at which code develops and changes, especially in an open source software project such as Samba. The problem the person was experiencing might have been due to a known bug that was already fixed.

Maybe you are installing Samba for the first time, or maybe the person who maintained the Samba server left to make five times as much money. For whatever reason, sooner or later you need to obtain a copy of the latest source code and compile it yourself. In fact, you might find that it's something you look forward to.

This hour provides the information necessary to download the latest source and set any specific compile-time options. You'll also take a look at the binary distributions that are available (in case you don't feel like compiling things on your own).

Finding Out What Version of Samba You Currently Have

If you already have Samba running and want to determine whether you have the latest version, read on! If you are installing Samba for the first time, feel free to save this section for later use.

There are two simple ways to determine the version of Samba that is installed on your system. The first method uses the log files that the smbd and nmbd daemons create and leave behind, whereas the second involves obtaining information from the processes themselves.

First, look at the log files. A Samba server comprises two daemon processes: smbd and nmbd, which create logs that are located in /usr/local/samba/var by default and are usually named log.smb and log.nmb, respectively. It is possible to override where Samba places these by specifying a value in the configuration file. If you find that the log files are not located in /usr/local/samba/var, the next step is to find the configuration file, which is normally named smb.conf.

Normally the configuration file is located in /usr/local/samba/lib. As with most other values and locations in Samba, it is possible to override the location and name of smb.conf by passing a command-line argument to smbd and nmbd using the -s switch. Samba can be started either from the inetd metadaemon or as a daemon itself. To determine the methods that your systems uses, first look in /etc/inetd.conf by

```
grep smbd /etc/inetd.conf
```

If your system uses System V init scripts, such as Solaris 2.x or RedHat Linux, you can go to the startup script directory which is normally similar /etc/init.d or /etc/rc.d and run the command

```
grep smbd *
```

If you notice that a filename follows an -l switch when starting smbd, this is your debug log file. Otherwise, run the following command:

```
grep "log file" smb.conf
```

The resulting output should give an absolute path to a file. Look in this directory for the Samba logs.

After you find the correct log files, you should be able to determine the version of the Samba daemon that created them by searching the file:

```
root# grep "smbd version" log.smb | tail -1
  smbd version 2.1.0-prealpha started.
```

If you do not see something similar to the output listed previously, most likely what happened was that the logs either were written over by a cron job on the system or were rotated out by Samba itself because of their size. In order to get Samba to reprint the information, you can remove the logs and restart the smbd and nmbd processes.

It's impossible to describe how to restart Samba on every system on which it runs. This example from a Slackware 3.5 Linux system should give you a general idea:

```
[root@bilbo /etc] killall smbd
[root@bilbo /etc] killall nmbd
[root@bilbo /etc] /etc/rc.d/rc.samba
```

If you forget to remove the logs, Samba simply appends the new entries to the existing logs.

> In Samba versions prior to 2.0, the default behavior for nmbd is to overwrite the old log.nmb file whereas smbd appends log entries. In version 2.0, both smbd and nmbd append log entries by default.

Another possible way to determine the version of Samba that is currently running is by using the smbclient utility that comes with the Samba distribution. Although this method is a lot simpler, it does require that smbclient be installed and that Samba is currently running. Locate the smbclient binary (usually in /usr/local/samba/bin) and run the following command:

```
smbclient -L localhost
```

As a result you should see something similar to the following (possibly mixed in with other text):

```
Added interface ip=aaa.bbb.ccc.ddd bcast=aaa.bbb.ccc.255
➥nmask=255.255.255.0
Domain=[CHIPSNDIPS] OS=[Unix] Server=[Samba 2.1.0-prealpha]
Sharename      Type     Comment
---------      ----     -------
...
```

The version information on the machine to which you are connected (the local machine) is printed in the brackets ([ ]) following the Server= label. This version in the previous example is "2.1.0-prealpha" (test code).

Download Sites and Methods

Now that you've determined that you need to get that latest Samba distribution, where do you go? The first place to start is to point your Web browser to http://samba.org (see Figure 3.1). This page contains links to all the Samba mirror Web sites and the FTP mirrors as well.

FIGURE 3.1

List of mirrors for http://samba.org.

If you are using HTTP to download the Samba distribution, first select the mirror closest to you. When you arrive at the mirror site home page, select the download link. The resulting page, which is shown in Figure 3.2, should have a link to download a file named samba-latest.tar.gz.

If you prefer to browse and see what is available, you can obtain a directory listing of files that can be downloaded (see Figure 3.3). Again you should see a file named samba-latest.tar.gz. If not, simply look for the samba-#####.tar.gz with the highest version number. The process of finding the latest distribution archive via FTP is similar to browsing the directory listing through HTTP.

FIGURE 3.2

Samba download page.

FIGURE 3.3

Folder listing of download archives from the Samba Web site.

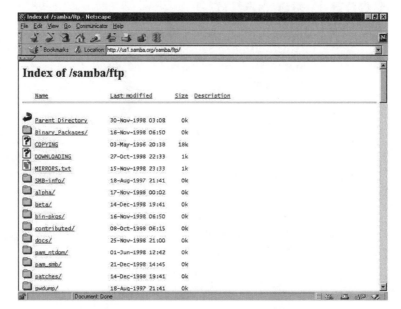

After you have downloaded the distribution, change to a good temporary directory where you won't overwrite anything when you extract the source files. I use a directory named ~/src as a working directory for compiling source code. If I want to save anything after I'm finished, I move the files to a more permanent location. To extract the files, you need a working version of GNU gzip and tar. If the file you download is named, for example, samba-latest.tar.gz, the following command will extract the files for you:

```
gzip -dc samba-latest.tar.gz | tar xvf -
```

Although the directory tree might change from time to time, three directories are common to all versions thus far:

- docs/   This directory contains various documentation such as man pages, HTML-formatted files, and ASCII HOWTO files.
- examples/   This directory contains various examples for many operating systems describing different setup possibilities. Mostly contains sample smb.conf files.
- source/   This directory contains the Samba source code tree for the distribution.

Compiling Samba

After you have the source code distribution of Samba, the next actions for compiling depend on what version of Samba you are installing. Things are done very differently in versions prior to 2.0 as compared to 2.0 and above. The reason is that 2.0 was reworked to use the GNU autoconf tests.

Pre-2.0

For some reason, you might not be able to upgrade to the latest version. Perhaps you have to support an inherited system and need to change one of the compile-time defaults. As I said before, the compiling versions prior to 2.0 are very different than the current method. To give you a frame of reference, the last version released prior to 2.0 was 1.9.18p10.

In the pre-2.0 code tree, all the source files are located in one directory with a make file that you have to slightly modify before compiling:

```
# The base directory for all samba files
BASEDIR = /usr/local/samba
```

One of the most common options to change is the base directory for the Samba binary tree after it's installed. The contents of this directory are discussed later in this hour. For now, think of it as the default location where Samba looks for and writes information. Most of these locations can be overridden using smb.conf options or command-line parameters. I prefer to explicitly tell Samba where things are at run time and not make assumptions, but that is my personal preference:

```
# The directories to put things in. If you use multiple
# architectures or share the samba binaries across NFS
# you will probably want to change this layout.
# Note: The SBINDIR is for files you do not want users to access
#       normally applies only to nmbd and smbd
#       SBINDIR implies a secure binary directory
BINDIR = $(BASEDIR)/bin
SBINDIR = $(BASEDIR)/bin
LIBDIR = $(BASEDIR)/lib
VARDIR = $(BASEDIR)/var
```

If you want to distribute the individual Samba directories outside of one tree, you can change the values of ${BINDIR}, ${SBINDIR}$, ${LIBDIR}, and {VARDIR}.

You can also override the default locations of individual files by changing any of the following make file variables. If you are unsure of exactly what the various files are, you can safely leave the defaults.

```
# set these to where to find various files
# These can be overridden by command line switches (see smbd(8))
# or in smb.conf (see smb.conf(5))
SMBLOGFILE = $(VARDIR)/log.smb
NMBLOGFILE = $(VARDIR)/log.nmb
```

Before continuing, I want to point out the convention of defining the section of the man pages where an entry occurs by adding *(number)*. In the make file excerpt listed here, the smbd(8) reference means that the smbd man page is located in section 8. Assuming the default install directories, the smbd man page is physically located in /usr/local/samba/mab/man8.

The log files are where the smbd and nmbd daemons write their logging information:

```
CONFIGFILE = $(LIBDIR)/smb.conf
LMHOSTSFILE = $(LIBDIR)/lmhosts
```

The smb.conf file has been mentioned already. The lmhosts file is the NetBIOS equivalent of an /etc/hosts file:

```
DRIVERFILE = $(LIBDIR)/printers.def
```

The printer.def file contains information about printer drivers which can be downloaded and installed by Windows 95 and 98 clients on-the-fly when connecting to the printers:

```
SMB_PASSWD = $(BINDIR)/smbpasswd
SMB_PASSWD_FILE = $(BASEDIR)/private/smbpasswd
```

These files are the Samba `passwd` utility and the `passwd` file respectively. They are discussed more in Hour 6, "Security Levels and Passwords."

```
# the directory where lock files go
LOCKDIR = $(VARDIR)/locks
```

The lock directory is where Samba places things such as its current browse list (see Hours 19, "Local Subnet Browsing," and 20, "Routed Networks and Browsing"), file lock information, and WINS database (see Hour 18, "Resolving NetBIOS Names Without Using Broadcasts").

One of the major advantages of the `autoconf` support is that it insulates you from having to specify many details about your operating system. In a pre-2.0 make file, you need to uncomment the flags in the section of the make file which refers to your OS. For example, the following section is for Linux installations that use shadow password but not `PAM`. The `FLAGSM` and `LIBSM` variables were previously commented out by a preceding # as are all the OS-specific sections:

```
# Use this for Linux with shadow passwords but not using PAM!
# contributed by Andrew.Tridgell@anu.edu.au
# add -DLINUX_BIGCRYPT is you have shadow passwords but don't have
# the right libraries and includes
FLAGSM = -DLINUX -DSHADOW_PWD -DFAST_SHARE_MODES
LIBSM = -lshadow
```

One last flag that is often useful to set is the `CC` variable. The default value for `CC` is to use the `cc` compiler. If you want to use the `gcc` compiler instead, you must uncomment the line that says `CC = gcc`.

Besides setting the make file variables, you might need to set some site-specific values in the `local.h` header, which is located in the `source/` directory. The file itself and the macros are fairly self explanatory. Unless you are sure you need to change something in this file, it is generally better to leave it alone.

However, one macro that I have regularly had to change was `MAX_OPEN_FILES`. The default value for this in pre-2.0 releases is `100`. Due to some code writes, the new Samba code has been made immensely more efficient with respect to file handles. The default in the 2.0 release is `10,000`.

One office I had to support used a shared database and the front end needed to open about 150 files simultaneously. Increasing the maximum to around 200 fixed my problem. Obviously this problem does not plague me with 2.0! Also a note of difference is that, in the 2.0 source code, this setting can also be set using a run time parameter in the `smb.conf` file.

After you have made the necessary changes to the make file and `local.h` (if any), you can create the binaries by typing **make**. If all goes well, the `smbd`, `nmbd`, and other utilities should be located in the same directory as the source files.

2.0's autoconf Support

In contrast to pre-2.0 makes, Samba 2.0 is very simple. There is a `configure` script located in the `source/` directory. To enable support for your operating system, simply change to the source directory and run the following command:

```
./configure
```

The script runs and creates the appropriate make file for you.

Although it is possible to edit the created make file manually and set variables, it is easier to simply specify some of the options as command-line parameters. To find out information about what options are available, type **./configure —help**.

I've included portions of the output in Listing 3.1. Where I've deleted lines for brevity, the change is noted by braces ({}).

LISTING 3.1 SAMPLE OUTPUT FROM `./configure --help`

```
01: Usage: configure [options] [host]
02: Options: [defaults in brackets after descriptions]
03: Configuration:
04: {lines deletd}
05: Directory and file names:
06:    --prefix=PREFIX        install architecture-independent files in
➥PREFIX
07:                           [/usr/local/samba]
08:    --exec-prefix=EPREFIX  install architecture-dependent files in
➥EPREFIX
09:                           [same as prefix]
10: {lines deletd}
11: Host type:{lines
12:   deletd}
13: Features and packages:
14: {lines deletd}
15: --enable and --with options recognized:
16:    --enable-maintainer-mode enable some make rules for maintainers
17:    --with-smbwrapper      Include SMB wrapper support
18:    --without-smbwrapper  Don't include SMB wrapper support
➥(default)
19:    --with-afs      Include AFS support
20:    --without-afs  Don't include AFS support (default)
21:    --with-dfs      Include DFS support
22:    --without-dfs  Don't include DFS support (default)
23:    --with-krb4=base-dir    Include Kerberos IV support
24:    --whithout-krb4          Don't include Kerbers IV support
➥(default)
25:    --with-automount    Include AUTOMOUNT support
26:    --without-automount  Don't include AUTOMOUNT support (default)
```

continues

LISTING 3.1 CONTINUED

```
27:   --with-smbmount      Include SMBMOUNT (Linux only) support
28:   --without-smbmount  Don't include SMBMOUNT support (default)
29:   --with-ldap      Include LDAP support
30:   --without-ldap  Don't include LDAP support (default)
31:   --with-nisplus      Include NISPLUS password database support
32:   --without-nisplus  Don't include NISPLUS password database
➥support (default)
33:   --with-nisplus-home      Include NISPLUS_HOME support
34:   --without-nisplus-home  Don't include NISPLUS_HOME support
➥(default)
35:   --with-ssl      Include SSL support
36:   --without-ssl  Don't include SSL support (default)
37:   --with-mmap      Include experimental MMAP support
38:   --without-mmap  Don't include MMAP support (default)
39:   --with-syslog      Include experimental SYSLOG support
40:   --without-syslog  Don't include SYSLOG support (default)
41:   --with-netatalk      Include experimental Netatalk support
42:   --without-netatalk  Don't include experimental Netatalk support
➥(default)
43:   --with-quotas      Include experimental disk-quota support
44:   --without-quotas  Don't include experimental disk-quota support
➥(default)
45:   --with-privatedir=DIR      Where to put smbpasswd
➥(/usr/local/samba/private)
46:   --with-swatdir=DIR      Where to put SWAT files
➥(/usr/local/samba/swat)
```

The list of options is quite long, but in reality, many of them come in pairs: one to enable the option and one to disable it. For example, look at the options in lines 25 and 26. The first enables automount support and the second disables it. You should also notice that Listing 3.1 indicates which options are enabled and disabled by default.

If you want to override the default location of the top-level install directory (/usr/local/samba by default) and use /usr/samba instead, pass

```
--prefix=/usr/samba
```

as a parameter when you execute the configure command. To create the make file accepting all the default options (which is usually fine), simply run

```
./configure
```

The configure script creates a make file in the source/ directory. All that remains in order to build the Samba binaries is to type **make**.

What Goes Where When I Type Make Install?

Whatever version of Samba you compile, when the binaries are ready, you can install the files to the directory specified by the `prefix` (or `BASEDIR`) variable in the make file by typing **make install**. I assume here, and for the rest of this book, that Samba has been installed to the default location of `/usr/local/samba/`.

This creates the Samba directory tree, if necessary, and copies over the binaries and other relevant files. When completed, the following directories should exist in the Samba install directory unless you have overridden the locations in the make file:

- `bin/` This directory contains the `smbd` and `nmbd` binaries and any other utilities included with Samba.

- `lib/` This directory contains the `smb.conf` and `lmhosts` files and the codepage support files in a `codepages/` subdirectory.

- `var/` This directory is empty until Samba is first run. At that time, the `smbd` and `nmbd` daemons create the lock files, shared memory files, browse list information file, and possibly the WINS databases. Under Samba 2.0, `smbd.pid` and `nmbd.pid` files are also contained along with the process ID of the currently running daemons. These are useful for easy restarting. This is also the default location for the Samba log files.

- `man/` The Samba man pages are located in various subdirectories here. If you want the pages located in your man page search path, you can either move the files to an existing man page location or add them to your `MANPATH` environment variable. For example, if the Samba man pages are located in `/usr/local/samba/man`, under the Bourne shell or bash, you can append this directory to the existing search path by setting

  `MANPATH=$MANPATH:/usr/local/samba/man`

- `swat/` This directory contains the files for the GUI `smb.conf` editor `SWAT`, which is discussed more in Hour 9, "GUI Administration Tools."

Binary Distribution Methods

If, for some reason, you choose not to compile the source code for yourself or are unable to on your system (say for a lack of a C compiler), now is good time to talk about availability of downloading only the binaries. In Hour 1, "Introduction to Samba," I discussed the basics of the GPL. One stipulation of the license is that the source code doesn't have to be distributed with the binaries, but it must be available on request.

The first job I ever worked as a network administrator was while working on my master's degree. I was flying by the seat of my pants and learning as I went. I had been given the responsibility of building a student-accessible PC lab. One of the things I purchased for the lab was a Sparc Ultra running Solaris 2.5.1. Imagine my surprise when I was getting ready to install software and realized that Sun didn't ship a C compiler with Solaris 2!

That said, binary distributions can be very helpful depending on what your needs are. If you do not plan to modify the compile-time defaults or don't have a particularly unique site, downloading the binaries probably saves you some time. Remember that the source is always available if you decide at a later time you need it.

> There is a mailing list specifically set up for posting notices about the Samba binary packages. The address is samba-binaries@samba.org. See http://samba.org/listproc for more information about Samba mailing lists.

Obtaining a Samba binary release is very similar to obtaining a source code release. The first place to look is the Samba home page (http://samba.org); select the FTP or HTTP site closest to you. If you use HTTP to download the files, again follow the download link off the Samba mirror home page and look for information on downloading binary packages. If you use FTP, look for a directory named bin-pkgs or Binary_Packages and then select your operating system.

Binary packages are not available for all platforms that Samba compiles on, nor are they always available for the latest source code release. The reason is the packages are compiled and uploaded on a volunteer basis. If possible, the binaries and associated files, such as an sample smb.conf files, are archived using the tools for the native OS. For example, RedHat binaries are stored using RPM and Solaris binaries and distributed using in the pkgtool format. Discussing the details of using the package distribution tools for various operating systems is beyond the scope of this book. If you need more information on the binary distribution tool for your operating system (for example, Solaris 2.x uses pkgadd and RedHat Linux systems use rpm), please read the man pages for the installation tool most appropriate to your system.

Now that you have the current version of Samba that you want to use and the binaries are ready to go, Hour 4, "Installing and Testing the Configuration," helps you get a sample installation up and running.

Summary

When installing Samba, you have two options. You can either download the source code and compile it yourself, or you can obtain a binary-only release if it is available for your platform.

Preparing to compile Samba 2.0 involves executing the configure script located in the source or directory of the distribution and specifying any options that you need. Versions of Samba prior to 2.0 require manually editing the make file and enabling the appropriate support for your OS. When the correct options have been set, both 2.0 and pre-2.0 distributions can be compiled by executing the `make` command. When the binaries have been created, they are installed to your local system by issuing `make install`.

Q&A

Q I downloaded Samba 2.0. I extracted the files and typed `make` but the system is complaining `make: Fatal error: No arguments to build`.

A You must run `configure` prior to executing make.

3

Hour 4

Installing and Testing the Configuration

During this hour, I'll walk through the preparation, configuration, and installation of a sample Samba server.

Imagine that my boss gives me the following orders:

Problem:

> "I need three things from you by lunchtime. First, I need some way to be able to share documents and project spreadsheets with Joe Underling down the hall. Second, my PC crashes all the time. This tape thingy-ma-watchit takes too long to reload all my important documents. I need a better way to protect my files. And finally, I need to be able to print to my secretary's printer located outside my office."

Scenario 1:

> "Hmmm...," I think. "Both machines are networked. I could set up an FTP server to solve the document-sharing problem. Because I'm thinking about using FTP, I could also show my boss how to upload all her files to

a disk on the server. That would be faster than a tape drive. To connect her PC to the printer, I guess I could get an automatic switcher box and run a long parallel cable up and over the wall to the secretary's desk. Oops. Too long for parallel. I guess I could use a serial cable. Nope. That would be too slow." Suddenly I walk away thinking I should start updating my résumé.

Scenario 2:

The first thing I do is make a note that all three PCs in question—the boss's, Joe's, and the secretary's—are connected to the local network. Next I go to my office and dig around for an external network interface box for the printer. Found it! Now I connect the printer to the network. The next thing to do is log in to my Linux box that I set up yesterday using my copy of *Sams Teach Yourself Linux in 24 Hours*. I've already downloaded and compiled the latest Samba source code over my morning cup of coffee (black, no sugar or cream).

Now I create a simple configuration file for Samba. First, I create a home directory on the server for the boss to store her precious files. Then I create a share that's accessible by Joe Underling and my boss so they can share documents. Finally, I create a share for the secretary's printer and head off to show the boss how to use it all.

After I mount the two shares on the boss's computer and show her how to access files on it, I print a sample test page to double-check the printer. The boss is so happy she doesn't have to learn anything new (other than to remember that there's an H: and a G: drive, for Home and Group respectively) that I get the rest of the week off and a raise!

Perhaps my account of my plight and victory is a little exaggerated, but you never know. It could happen!

What I'll do for the remaining sections in this hour is to walk you through the steps for configuring Samba to implement the solution described in scenario 2. The remarks regarding Linux were made only as an example. The solution will work as long as Samba will compile under the server's OS.

Figure 4.1 illustrates the access that each user will require. The dotted lines depict access by the secretary, the dashed lines represent my boss, and the solid lines are associated with Joe Underling. Thus the secretary should have access only to the shared printer, Joe should have access to the printer and the group network drive, and my boss should have access to both of the previous resources in addition to her home directory.

FIGURE 4.1

Samba solution to implement (a) a group share, (b) home directories, and (c) network printing.

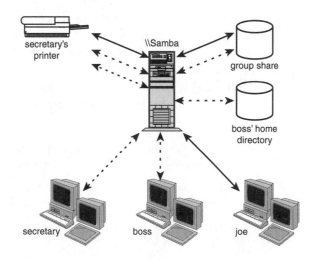

Which Processes?

If you remember from Hour 3, "Obtaining the Latest Source," I said that a Samba server comprises two main binaries. The first is smbd, normally located in /usr/local/samba/bin. smbd handles the file and print service requests. The second binary, nmbd, is normally located in the same directory as smbd. nmbd handles NetBIOS name service requests and network browsing functions.

Configuring the [global] Section of smb.conf

NEW TERM Before actually configuring any of the network shares needed to solve the problem, I must configure some initial settings to get Samba up and running. To provide some background, SMB shared resources, whether they are directories or printers, are often referred to as *shares*. This is the equivalent of an NFS-exported directory or remote printer made available via lpr. Sometimes an SMB share is also called a *service*. I use the terms interchangeably.

To begin, I must answer the following two questions:

- What will be the NetBIOS name of the Samba server?
- Of which workgroup will the Samba server be a member?

4

For this example, assume that the hostname of the server is `eagle` and, therefore, the NetBIOS name of the server has been chosen to be `EAGLE` as well. Although the names are not case sensitive, a convention I will follow through this book is to refer to DNS hostnames in lowercase and NetBIOS names in uppercase. The workgroup will be the same as the one of which the PCs are a member, which is `FOWLPLAY`. Hour 5, "The `smb.conf` File: Telling Samba What to Do," goes into more detail about these decisions and associated `smb.conf` parameters.

After these two choices have been made, I can configure the initial settings in the smb.conf file. Comments in smb.conf are preceded by a ; or a # character.

```
; smb.conf's global parameters section
[global]
    ; set the netbios machine name for the server
    netbios name = EAGLE
    ; set the workgroup membership
    workgroup =  FOWLPLAY
    ; set Samba to authenticate in user mode security
    security = user
```

The comments are fairly self explanatory. The line `security = user` determines the mode of security that Samba uses to validate users. More details about user authentication can be found in Hour 6, "Security Levels and Passwords."

If you remember from Hour 3, the default location for `smb.conf` is in `/usr/local/samba/lib/`, which is what I will use. Using my favorite text editor (`vi`), I create `/usr/local/samba/lib/smb.conf` and enter the text from the previous code listing.

Setting up the Shared Group Directory

The first part of the problem that I'll examine is how to configure a network drive to allow multiple users read and write access. Figure 4.2 gives an example of a situation where the users, `joe` and `boss`, need to access files from the disk share depicted on the right. The diagrams illustrate the capability of allowing both users to read a file at the same time, but I allow only one user at a time to open a file for writing.

Before I create the directory that will be accessed by Joe and your boss, I first must make sure that each one has a valid account in `/etc/passwd` (or the network equivalent in the case of NIS or NIS+). Next, I create a group in `/etc/group` (or the network equivalent map) and add the two accounts as members. For this example, I call the group `boss1` and use the usernames `joe` and `boss`.

FIGURE 4.2

Multiple users accessing files in a shared directory.

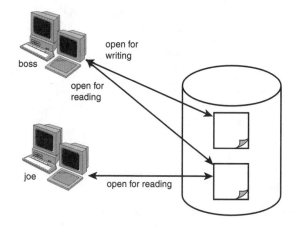

The step would be identical if I was setting up a shared directory for access via UNIX because Samba allows the underlying operating system to control access to the files. Therefore, I am able to use a model of security with which I am familiar even though the Windows clients have no notion of UNIX.

I generally use the /export/ directory for all disk shares, so I'll stick to that convention here. I'll create a directory named /export/smb/boss1/ to be the shared directory. Figure 4.3 displays a portion of the server's directory structure. The directory that will be shared via SMB has been circled.

FIGURE 4.3

UNIX directory tree and the portion which will be shared via Samba.

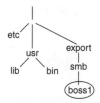

Next, set the group ownership and permissions using the following commands:

```
chgrp boss1 /export/boss1
chmod 770 /export/boss1
chmod g+s /export/boss1
```

The last step to perform is to define the share in Samba's configuration file by adding the following settings to smb.conf:

```
; share name
[boss1]
      ; text to list when browsing the share from a client
```

```
comment = Shared directory for group boss1
; absolute path to the disk directory
path = /export/boss1
; should the share be writeable?
writeable = yes
; user allowed to connect to the share
;   the '@' is used to designate a unix group
valid users = @boss1
; enforce file locking?
locking = yes
; default file creation permission mask
create mode = 0660
; default directory creation permission mask
directory mode = 0770
```

Again, I've included comments to describe the general meaning of each parameter. It is not necessary at the moment to understand exactly what function each one serves. Disk shares are discussed in depth in Hour 7, "File Sharing."

Setting Up a User's Home Directories

Setting up home directories in Samba is very similar to setting up the group share that was discussed in the previous section. The main difference is that I want to enforce the rule that only the owner is permitted to connect to a particular home directory. In other words, I don't want to allow Joe to connect to the boss's home directory. That would be bad.

When I set up the shared group directory, it was necessary to verify that the boss and Joe had valid UNIX accounts on the server. Under normal circumstances, these UNIX accounts also have some disk space allocated as the user's home directory. Rather than allocate new space, I configure Samba to share the user's home directory specified in the UNIX account database (that is, //passwd). Here are the parameters that need to be added to smb.conf to make the home directories available:

```
; share name
[homes]
    comment = Unix home directory space
    path = %H
    writeable = yes
    valid users = %S
    create mode = 0600
    directory mode = 0700
    locking = no
```

I've not included comments in this section because most of the settings are similar to the parameters used in definition of [boss1]. There are a few differences that should be noted.

The first is the name of the share or service, [homes]. Home directories are something of a special case. During a connection attempt from a client, the share name [homes] will be substituted with the username sent by the connecting client. This means that if my boss is attempting to connect to her home directory, she can specify either the network path \\EAGLE\homes or \\EAGLE\boss. Samba interprets both as the same share. Figure 4.4 illustrates how Samba creates the [homes] share for each user at connection time. If the user exists in /ect/passwd, Samba uses the home directory path defined in the user's entry for the location of the [homes] folder.

FIGURE 4.4

Samba creates and expands the %H variable from the home directory specified in /etc/passwd at run time.

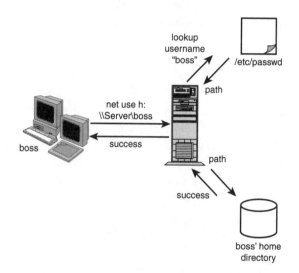

The second item is the valid users = %S entry. The %S variable is expanded at connection time to the name of the share. Remember that the [homes] share is renamed at run time to the username sent by the connecting client. By allowing only connections from a user who has the same username as the name of the share, Joe is prevented from accessing \\EAGLE\boss. This method works even if the permissions on the /home/boss are set to be world writeable (that is, rwxrwxrwx).

Setting Up the Printer

After setting up the disk shares, it's time to turn my attention to the printer. Continuing with the example, I have already set up the printer correctly on the Linux server. When I can successfully print from the Linux box to the network printer using the lpr command, the next step is to define a printer share:

```
[global]
     printing = bsd

[printer1]
     comment = printer located outside office
     printable = yes
     writeable = no
```

This definition causes Samba to search the /etc/printcap file for a printer named *printer1* and use the standard print command. Note that I also need to add the additional printing = bsd entry to the [global] section of the smb.conf file. There are other styles of UNIX printing systems. Samba works with these as well as you will see in Hour 8, "Printers."

Verifying smb.conf

I assume that the binaries you have are compiled correctly using the default locations. The next step is to verify that there are no syntax errors in smb.conf. If you installed all the Samba utilities (which is what happens when you type **make install**), you should find a tool named testparm in the /usr/local//samba/bin/ directory. The utility checks smb.conf and prints out all the default values which were not overridden. It can be very helpful to make sure Samba is seeing what you think it should see.

I purposely misspelled *netbios* in the [global] section of the following smb.conf file.

```
; smb.conf's global parameters section
[global]
        ; set the netbios machine name for the server

        netbis name = EAGLE
        ; set the workgroup membership
        workgroup =  FOWLPLAY
        ; set Samba to authenticate in user mode security
        security = user
        printing = bsd
```

I then ran it through the testparm tool. If you want testparm to examine an smb.conf file located somewhere other than the compile default, you can use the -s *filename* switch:

```
root# /usr/local/samba/bin/testparm -s smb.conf ¦ head -6
Load smb config files from smb.conf
Unknown parameter encountered: "netbis name"
Ignoring unknown parameter "netbis name"
Processing section "[boss1]"
Processing section "[homes]"
Processing section "[printer1]"
```

You'll notice that the output reports an unknown parameter: *netbis name*.

Another useful means of using `testparm` is to determine the default values of parameters. For example, the following output indicates that the default guest account is nobody.

```
root# /usr/local/samba/bin/testparm -s smb.conf ¦ grep "guest account"
         guest account = nobody
```

Starting `smbd` and `nmbd`

With the `smb.conf` file completed and with the Samba binaries (from either compiling the source code or downloading available binaries) obtained, the next step is to start the Samba daemons, `smbd` and `nmbd`. There are two methods of launching the processes. Which you choose depends on how many connections you expect to have to the Samba server, how frequent they will be, and how many resources you presently have to spare on the server.

Each client connection has its own `smbd` daemon; however, the `smbd` process responsible for a client can maintain many connections to shares. Each `smbd` process generally uses about 1MB of RAM in its working set but can allocate more total RAM. The working set of a process is the number of memory pages that it must keep in physical memory. You can calculate how much total memory Samba will generally require by multiplying 1.5 times the number of simultaneous users. Some operating systems use memory mapping to allow processes to share nonmodifiable code pages and thus reduce the amount actual memory that is used. This formula at least gives you a place to start for performing capacity planning on your particular server.

The two means of starting the Samba server process are through the `inetd` metadaemon or as standalone daemons. My experience has been that running `smbd` and `nmbd` as standalone daemons generally provides faster service on initial connections. However, if the server sits idle for long periods of time without any SMB connections, you can choose to run `smbd` and `nmbd` from `inetd.conf` to save a little on the overall memory usage of the system. You need to decide which is best for you, but you must choose one and only one method.

Starting from `inetd`

To run Samba from the `inetd` daemon, you must edit two files. I'm going to assume that the UNIX server is not using NIS or NIS+ to distribute system files.

First, I need to add the following entries in `/etc/services`. Make sure that there are no other entries for TCP port 139 and UDP port 137:

```
netbios-ssn      139/tcp
netbios-ns       137/udp
```

Next, using your favorite text editor, add the following entries to /etc/inetd.conf:

```
netbios-ssn stream tcp nowait root /usr/local/samba/bin/smbd smbd
netbios-ns  dgram  udp wait   root /usr/local/samba/bin/nmbd nmbd
```

After saving the changes, I need to tell the inetd daemon to reread the configuration file. Usually, I can accomplish this by sending a HUP signal to the process. Here are the commands I use on my Slackware 3.5 Linux installation:

```
root# ps -ax ¦ grep inetd
102  ?  S    0:00 /usr/sbin/inetd
root# kill -HUP 102
```

Running as a Daemon

If the Samba server will receive frequent connections, you might want to start smbd and nmbd as daemons to increase response time. You can accomplish this using the -D switch when you start smbd and nmbd.

UNIX variants today use two popular models to start processes at boot time. One is referred to as the System V init style and is used by operating systems such as Solaris and RedHat's Linux distribution. The second method is the older BSD style used by systems such as SunOS and Slackware's Linux distribution.

System V Init Scripts

First, I'll examine System V init scripts. These scripts are normally kept in /etc/rc3.d or /etc/init.d with links pointing from /etc/rc#.d where the # represents a particular run level. You should normally start Samba during run level 3. The scripts take a single command line argument of either start or stop which either starts or stops the service. Here is a sample System V–style Samba script:

```
#!/bin/sh
#
# this script should probably only be run at run level 3
#
cd /etc
PATH=/usr/bin:/bin:/usr/sbin

case $1 in
'start')
   if [ -x /usr/local/samba/bin/smbd -a -f /etc/smb.conf ]; then
      echo 'Starting Samba...'
      /usr/local/samba/bin/nmbd -D
      /usr/local/samba/bin/smbd -D
   fi
   ;;
'stop')
```

```
    pid=`/bin/ps -x ¦ egrep '(smbd¦nmbd)' ¦ sed -e 's/^  *//' -e
➥'s/ .*//'`
    if test "$pid"
    then
       kill $pid
       rm /usr/local/samba/var/locks/smbd.pid
       rm /usr/local/samba/var/locks/nmbd.pid
    fi
    ;;
*)
    echo "usage: /etc/init.d/samba {start¦stop}"
    ;;
esac
```

To start the Samba daemons, you would type **/etc/init.d/samba start.**

To stop the processes, you would reenter the command replacing the word **start** with
stop.

BSD-style Startup Scripts

The BSD style scripts do not provide the starting and stopping flexibility of the System
V init scripts, but they are probably a little easier to manage because there are fewer
total scripts.

When the system boots, it generally follows a process similar to the following:

1. Runs /etc/rc.S when starting single-user mode.

2. Runs /etc/rc.M when moving into multiuser mode.

3. /etc/rc.M will normally start /etc/rc.inet1 and rc.inet2 which are responsible
   for starting the network interface(s) and services.

4. Finally runs /etc/rc.local which contains all local system process startup.

Normally the Samba server process would be started from /etc/rc.local. Here's
an example:

```
#!/bin/sh
#
# /etc/rc.local:  Local system initialization script.
#
# Put any local setup commands in here:
if [ -x /usr/local/samba/bin/smbd -a -f /etc/smb.conf ]; then
   echo 'Starting Samba...'
   /usr/local/samba/bin/nmbd -D
   /usr/local/samba/bin/smbd -D
fi
```

4

There are slight variants to this, which attempt to merge System V startup and BSD scripts. You will most likely need to consult the man pages and other documentation for your system to determine exactly where you need to place the start commands.

Command-Line Arguments

In Hour 3, I made several mentions of overriding default behavior in Samba using either command-line arguments or parameters in smb.conf. Most of the smb.conf parameters will be covered in Hour 5. This section briefly covers some of the common command-line arguments that are available. The best references for current options are the smbd and nmbd man pages. The man pages for the Samba suite are installed if you did a make install to copy the binaries. If so, you can access the pages using the standard man command.

If you did not install them, the man pages should be included with the Samba distribution in docs/ for pre-2.0 Samba releases and docs/manpages/ for versions 2.0 and greater. To view the man pages, locate the files smbd.8 and nmbd.8 and use the nroff command to display them:

```
nroff -man smbd.8 ¦ more
```

TABLE 4.1 COMMON smbd/nmbd COMMAND-LINE ARGUMENTS

Option	Description
-D	Runs as a daemon, meaning that the process runs in the background servicing requests. This is the preferred way to run smbd for a file server that does more than replying to infrequent requests. The default behavior is to *not* run as a daemon.
-d *debuglevel*	Specifies the debug level at which the process should run. The debug level is an integer between 1 and 10.
-l *log file*	Path to the file where the process should write log entries.
-s *config file*	Path to the configuration file that the process should use.

Table 4.1 lists some common options for smbd and nmbd. For a complete list, please read the man pages on the respective process.

Testing the Installation

At this point in the game, I

- Have compiled binaries for Samba
- Have correctly set up the directories that will be shared
- Entered settings for a complete `smb.conf` configuration file
- Have chosen how I want to start the Samba server

The time has come to see whether I made any mistakes along the way. I'll highlight some common errors during setup, how to detect them, and how to correct them.

Samba includes a utility named `smbclient` that provides an FTP-like interface for accessing SMB servers. In fact, the original use for `smbclient` was to test Samba. In this case, it enables me to test the Samba server without locating extra PCs. Although it cannot guarantee zero glitches when the PCs are connected, it should enable me to find any obvious errors.

After verifying that the Samba daemons are running or that valid entries exist to start the processes from `inetd.conf`, I attempt to get a list of shares from the server. The `-L` *netbios name* switch tells `smbclient` to get a list of shares from the server specified by *netbios name*. I use the `-N` switch to suppress the prompting for a password because it is not needed if all I want is to see what shares are available:

```
root# /usr/local/samba/bin/smbclient -L EAGLE -N
Added interface ip=192.168.1.73 bcast=192.168.1.255 nmask=255.255.255.0
Domain=[FOWLPLAY] OS=[Unix] Server=[Samba 2.0.0beta4]

        Sharename      Type      Comment
        ---------      ----      -------
        boss1          Disk      Shared directory for group boss1
        homes          Disk      Unix home directory space
        printer1       Printer   printer located outside office
        IPC$           IPC       IPC Service (Samba 2.0.0beta4)

        Server                   Comment
        ---------                -------

        Workgroup                Master
        ---------                -------
        FOWLPLAY
```

4

All three shares that I defined (homes, boss1, and printer1) appear in the share list. The IPC$ share is created automatically and is used for browsing. I'll talk about this one more in later hours. Everything appears fine to this point.

The next step is to verify the individual disk shares. First, I'll connect to the [boss1] share as joe. When connecting to a share, the network path is written as //servername/sharename replacing servername and sharename with the appropriate values. In the bash shell, to connect using a username other than the one stored in the $USER environment variable, I'll need to use the -U username switch:

```
root# /usr/local/samba/bin/smbclient //eagle/boss1 -U joe
Added interface ip=192.168.1.73 bcast=192.168.1.255 nmask=255.255.255.0
Password:
Domain=[FOWLPLAY] OS=[Unix] Server=[Samba 2.0.0beta4]
tree connect failed: ERRSRV - ERRinvnetname (Invalid network name in
➡tree connect.)
```

After entering the correct password, smbclient returns with an error of an "Invalid network name in tree connect." If you remember from Hour 2, "Windows Networking," a tree connect occurs after the client has been authenticated and is attempting to connect to a specific resource. After some checking, I find that I misnamed the directory /export/boss instead of /export/boss1:

```
root# ls -l /export
total 1
drwxrws---   2 root      boss1       1024 Dec 29 09:50 boss/
root# mv /export/boss /export/boss1
root# ls -l /export
total 1
drwxrws---   2 root      boss1       1024 Dec 29 09:50 boss1/
```

After correcting my mistake, I try again. This time, I successfully connect. You will notice that the hosts file I uploaded was created with the correct permissions and group ownership as well. I can use a similar method for verifying the [homes] share:

```
root# smbclient //bilbo/boss1 -U joe
Added interface ip=192.168.1.73 bcast=192.168.1.255 nmask=255.255.255.0
Password:
Domain=[FOWLPLAY] OS=[Unix] Server=[Samba 2.0.0beta4]

smb: \> lcd /etc
the local directory is now /etc

smb: \> put hosts
putting file hosts as \hosts (101.073 kb/s) (average 101.074 kb/s)

smb: \> dir
  hosts                             621  Tue Dec 29 10:36:48 1998
```

```
                    61967 blocks of size 4096. 15359 blocks available

smb: \> quit

root# ls -l /export/boss1
total 1
-rw-rw----   1 joe      boss1          621 Dec 29 10:36 hosts
```

When I've tested the disk shares, the last item to verify is the network printer. The process is the same except I'll use the -P switch to tell smbclient to connect to the share as a printer rather than a network drive. Using the put command to upload a file to a printer informs smbclient to send the file to be printed. I can verify that Samba sent the file correctly by using the lpq command to view the appropriate print queue:

```
root# smbclient //bilbo/printer1 -P -U boss
Added interface ip=192.168.1.73 bcast=192.168.1.255 nmask=255.255.255.0
Password:
Domain=[FOWLPLAY] OS=[Unix] Server=[Samba 2.0.0beta4]

smb: \> lcd /etc
the local directory is now /etc

smb: \> put hosts
putting file hosts as \hosts (5.41469 kb/s) (average 5.41469 kb/s)

smb: \> quit

root# lpq -P printer1
waiting for printer1 to become ready (offline ?)
Rank   Owner    Job  Files                              Total Size
1st    boss     0    hosts                              621 bytes
```

Other Tools Included with Samba

In addition to the tools already mentioned, several other utilities are also included with Samba (see Table 4.2). These can be found in the /usr/local/samba/bin/ directory.

TABLE 4.2 OTHER TOOLS AND UTILITIES INCLUDED IN THE SAMBA SUITE

Tool name	Description
smbstatus	This tool reports on the current status of connections and locked files.
nmblookup	This utility queries NetBIOS name information over TCP/IP.
testprns	This simple utility verifies whether a printer name is valid for use as a service name. This means that the printer name can be found in the /etc/printcap specified.

continues

TABLE 4.2 CONTINUED

Tool name	Description
make_smbcodepage	This tool allows for the compiling or decompiling of code page files for use with the internationalization features of Samba.
smbtar	This shell script provides a means of backing up and restoring files on remote SMB shares to UNIX tape drives by using the smbclient utility. Backups are discussed more in Hour 23, "Tips and Tricks."
smbrun	This small glue program is used by smbd to execute shell commands. By *gl·ie* I mean that it acts as an interface to allow smbd to run some type of shell scripts or other command-line tools.
rpcclient	This command-line tool analogous to smbclient allows for performing DCE/RPC to Windows NT and Samba servers. This is discussed more in Hour 22, "Experimental PDC Support."
swat	This GUI administrative tool manages the smb.conf file. GUI administration tools are examined more in Hour 9, "GUI Administration Tools."
smbpasswd, addtosmbpass, convert_smbpasswd	These tools provide means of manipulating changing the LanMan and NT hashes stored in the private/smbpasswd file used by Samba when encrypted passwords have been enabled. Encryption is discussed more in Hour 6.

Two of the tools listed, which can be extremely useful, are smbstatus and nmblookup. You will look at both of these diagnostic tools here, beginning with smbstatus.

The smbd daemon for a connection runs as root until it is necessary to perform some operation on behalf of the user connected. At that time, the process uid becomes the user's UNIX uid and then switches back to root. This can result in some difficulty when trying to determine which smbd process belongs to which user. smbstatus displays information about currently connected users and currently locked files. The following output shows that I'm connected to my home directory and currently have a file open for editing:

```
root# smbstatus
Samba version 2.0.0beta4
Service     uid      gid      pid      machine
-------------------------------------------------
jerryc      jerryc   users    472      queso    (192.168.1.72) Tue
➥Dec 29 11:31:05 1998

Locked files:
Pid    DenyMode    R/W       Oplock         Name
-------------------------------------------------
```

```
472    DENY_NONE  RDONLY     EXCLUSIVE+BATCH  src/samba/source/
➥Makefile   Tue Dec 29 11:31:56 1998

Share mode memory usage (bytes):
   1048368(99%) free + 136(0%) used + 72(0%) overhead = 1048576(100%)
➥total
```

The second tool that I often use is nmblookup. This command-line utility provides a
means of querying NetBIOS names and returning the associated IP address:

```
root# /usr/local/samba/bin/nmblookup eagle
Sending queries to 192.168.1.255
192.168.1.73 eagle<00>
```

nmblookup defaults to locate the <00> type name. By appending #<xx> to the NetBIOS
name you querying, nmblookup can resolve a different resource type, such as the messenger server name type <03>:

```
root# /usr/local/samba/bin/nmblookup eagle#03
Sending queries to 192.168.1.255
192.168.1.73 eagle<03>
```

nmblookup can . also resolve group names:

```
root# /usr/local/samba/bin/nmblookup fowlplay
Sending queries to 192.168.1.255
192.168.1.73 fowlplay<00>
```

And finally, you can use the -S switch to perform a node status request on the name and
return output similar to the nbtstat.exe -a *netbios name* command run from a
Windows box:

```
root# /usr/local/samba/bin/nmblookup chipsndips -S
Sending queries to 192.168.1.255
192.168.1.72 chipsndips<00>
Looking up status of 192.168.1.72
received 8 names
        QUESO           <00> -          M <ACTIVE>
        CHIPSNDIPS      <00> - <GROUP> M <ACTIVE>
        QUESO           <03> -          M <ACTIVE>
        QUESO           <20> -          M <ACTIVE>
        CHIPSNDIPS      <1e> - <GROUP> M <ACTIVE>
        CARTEGW         <03> -          M <ACTIVE>
        CHIPSNDIPS      <1d> -          M <ACTIVE>
        ..__MSBROWSE__. <01> - <GROUP> M <ACTIVE>
num_good_sends=0 num_good_receives=0
```

4

Summary

Samba can effectively act as a file and printer server for PCs in a group environment. The access-control mechanisms are handled using the underlying OS model with which you are comfortable: namely, the standard lpr printing system (or others) and the basic UNIX file permission bits. Creating group shares and remote printer shares is very similar to do equivalent actions on UNIX.

First, you must make sure that the resource is available for access from the UNIX side. For example, users can print to the print by executing lpr -Pprintername somefile.txt and that users can successfully access files in the directory to be shared.

Next, the shares need to be defined in Samba's configuration file. As you will see in the upcoming hours, many parameters exist to define and control these services.

Samba also includes many tools for administering the server and diagnosing problems. Two of the diagnostic utilities that you examined were smbstatus and nmblookup.

Q&A

Q Is it possible for Samba to share file systems that have been mounted using NFS?

A Yes.

Q How many simultaneous connections can be supported by a Samba server?

A In theory, there is no limit. In practice, the limit is determined by the server's hardware, specifically the total amount of available RAM. It can also depend on the amount of activity that you expect from the smbd processes. One situation in which a smbd process grabs a large amount of CPU time is when a Windows client is running a Web browser and caching files to a network drive.

New Terms

share A share, sometime referred to as a *service*, is a resource, such as a directory or a printer, that has been made available via the SMB protocol to remote machines across a network.

PART II
Configuring Samba

Hour

HOUR 5

The `smb.conf` File: Telling Samba What to Do

The `smb.conf` file really lies at the heart of Samba. It is used by both `smbd` and `nmbd` as well as many of the other tools included in the Samba suite. And although it probably has more parameters than Godzilla has teeth, it is not extremely hard to understand. This hour provides an in-depth look at the `smb.conf` file. You'll look at the general layout of the file, variables that are available for use at run time, and some of the global parameters that control the overall behavior of Samba.

Layout

A standard `smb.conf` file can consist of multiple sections each containing multiple parameters. However, though true, this is not the most helpful description available.

The following definition might make more sense. A Samba configuration file is an ASCII text file logically divided by section headings, which are denoted by enclosing square brackets ([ ]). For example, [foobar] would be a valid section heading. The section names, parameters, and values are not case sensitive unless pertinent to the operating system, such as the case of a directory path. Each section continues until the next section heading. Samba's smb.conf has three built-in sections named [global], [homes], and [printers].

Figure 5.1 illustrates the three built-in sections and one sample section. Because section headings are not case sensitive, [global], [GLOBAL], and [Global] all represent the same section. The four settings—netbios name, workgroup, security, and printing—all represent global parameters. Therefore, they are all located in the [global] section, which ends at the next section header, [homes]. The final section [boss1] represents a disk share that has been configured for this server.

FIGURE 5.1

General layout of smb.conf.

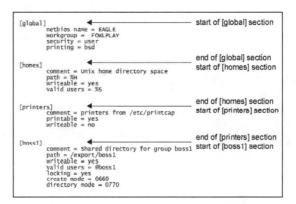

[global]

The [global] section contains parameters that relate to the overall functionality of the server. The netbios name and workgroup parameters, which were discussed briefly in Hour 4, "Installing and Testing the Configuration," are examples of [global] parameters. These parameters and others are discussed in more detail later in the hour.

[homes]

The [homes] section was briefly mentioned in the sample Samba server in Hour 4. This special share enables users to connect to their home directories without requiring that a specific share be defined for each user. The process works as follows:

1. Samba receives a connection request.
2. The smb.conf file is searched for the name of the requested service.
3. If the requested name is not found and the [homes] service has been configured, Samba searches the /etc/passwd file for a matching username.
4. If a matching username is found, a copy of the [homes] share is created, and the name is changed to the located username. Also, if no path is listed, it is set to the user's home directory as listed in the /etc/passwd entry.
5. If a matching username is not located, Samba returns an Invalid resource in tree connection request error message to the client.

[printers]

The third built-in section, [printers], is analogous to [homes]. The difference is the type of resource it makes available. [homes] creates home directories from /etc/passwd, whereas [printers] creates printer resources from /etc/printcap. If you use a printing system other than BSD, you need to create a dummy printcap file for Samba to verify printer names. This is covered more in Hour 8, "Printers."

The Remaining Parts of smb.conf

Any section other than [global] is considered a shared resource (*share*, for short); therefore, the section must follow general share naming conventions.

To create custom shares, you need to enter only a section header, such as [foo], and the necessary parameters, as discussed in Hours 6, "Security Levels and Passwords," and 7, "File Sharing." The SMB client is then able to access the share via the network path \\servername\FOO. Earlier, I said that smb.conf section headers were not case sensitive. Therefore [foo] and [FOO] refer to the same service. This is why the PC client can mount \\servername\FOO when the share is defined as [foo].

Depending on how much you like to document your work—I hope it's a great deal for the poor soul who arrives after you and must support your creation—you can insert comments liberally by placing a semicolon (;) or pound sign (#) as the first non–white space character on the line. Comments are terminated at the first carriage return:

```
; This is a comment
# and so is this
```

Table 5.1 lists a summary of the syntax for the smb.conf items that I have discussed.

5

TABLE 5.1   SUMMARY OF THE smb.conf FORMAT

Entry	Format
Section	Line containing a character string enclosed in brackets ([ ]). For example, [foo].
[global]	Special section containing parameters related to the general settings of Samba and default service settings.
[homes]	Dynamic share that obtains names from /etc/passwd.
[printers]	Dynamic share that obtains printer names from a specified printcap file.
Comment	Line whose first non–white space character is either a ; or a #.
Parameter	Configuration parameters followed by = and some value. For example, writeable = yes.

Variables

Several different variables are available to use in smb.conf. These macros, denoted by a % character, are replaced during the parsing on the configuration file at run time. For example, when user jdoe sends a session setup request, Samba parses smb.conf and replaces all occurrences of %U with jdoe. Table 5.2 contains a listing of the complete set of smb.conf variables that are available to you.

TABLE 5.2   smb.conf VARIABLES

Variable	Description
%a	The architecture of the remote machine. Not guaranteed to be 100% reliable, but generally good enough in practice. Currently supported values are Samba, WfWg, WinNT, and Win95. Windows 98 is returned as Win95. Windows 2000 is actually Windows NT 5.0 and so is recognized as WinNT.
%d	The process ID of the current server process.
%g	The primary group of username %u.
%G	The primary group of username %U.
%h	The Internet hostname on which Samba is running.
%H	The home directory for the username %u.
%I	The IP address of the client machine in dotted decimal form.
%L	The NetBIOS name of the server.
%m	The NetBIOS name of the client machine.
%M	The Internet hostname of the client machine.
%N	The name of your NIS home directory server as specified in the auto.home map. If you have not compiled Samba with AUTOMOUNT support, this is the same as %L.

Variable	Description
%p	The path to the user's home directory as specified in `auto.home`. The NIS map entry is assumed to be colon separated and is divided as `%N:%p`.
%P	The root directory of the current service.
%R	The protocol selected during the protocol negotiation phase of the connection setup. Valid values are `CORE`, `COREPLUS`, `LANMAN1`, `LANMAN2`, or `NT1`.
%S	The name of the current service.
%T	The current date and time.
%u	The username of the current service.
%U	The username the client requested in the session setup. This is not necessarily the same as the one that was used.
%v	Samba version number.

These variables can be used in many ways. A variable can be used in any location where a text string is valid. For example, the following `[global]` parameter entry would cause Samba to log connection information to a file named `/var/log/log.`*netbios name* replacing *netbios name* with the client's NetBIOS name.

```
log file = /var/log/log.%m
```

This can aid in debugging or monitoring certain clients.

Here's another example that tells Samba to use a different domain logon script depending on the connecting client's operating system:

```
logon script = %a.bat
```

The available logon scripts would be named `WfWg.bat`, `Win95.bat`, and `WinNT.bat`. Domain logons are covered in detail in Hours 21, "Windows 9x Domain Control," and 22, "Experimental PDC Support."

In light of the current explanation of variables, the `[homes]` share, which I used in Hour 4's example, is perhaps more sensible:

```
; share name
[homes]
    comment = Unix home directory space
    path = %H
    writeable = yes
    valid users = %S
    create mode = 0600
    directory mode = 0700
    locking = no
```

5

The `valid users = %S` entry restricts connections to the user whose username is the same as the name of the service. Remember the previous explanation of the `[homes]` share. If Samba can locate a match for the sharename in the `/etc/passwd` file, a share is created using the parameters from the `[homes]` definition, but is renamed using the matched username. Therefore, the only user allowed to connect is the owner of the home directory.

One last example before you move on. At work, I manage around 30 different Samba servers running on different operating systems. Generally, all servers are upgraded to the same version of Samba concurrently, but there are always a few exceptions. To determine the installed version on a server quickly, each `smb.conf` has an entry similar to the following in the `[global]` section:

```
server string = samba print server for administration [%v]
```

The server string parameter is used to set the text displayed next to the machine name in browse lists that are available through tools such as the Network Neighborhood. The `%v` is dynamically expanded to the version of the currently running `nmbd` process. Therefore, to determine what version of Samba a server is running, I simply use the `net view` `\\servername` command from a Windows box to examine the server's comment string.

Parameters

A quick `grep` through the `smb.conf` 2.0 man page reveals over 130 unique global parameters and approximately 100 parameters related to shares. The `smb.conf` man page for version 2.0 is around 8,500 lines in length. Needless to say, quite a few options are available for configuring your server. In this section, I'll mention some of the more common ones. I've deferred discussion of some `[global]` options until later hours where the context is more relevant to the parameter's functionality. For a complete listing of all current `[global]` parameters, as always, please read the `smb.conf` man page.

The values for parameters, with a few exceptions, fall into three categories:

- The first is a string of characters such as `jerryc` or `samba server`. Case is preserved in text strings.

- The second is a Boolean parameter value that accepts yes/no, true/false, or 1/0 conditions. Boolean values are not case sensitive so `YES`, `Yes`, and `yes` and all equivalent as far as Samba is concerned.

- The third type of parameter accepts a numeric value. You have to check each parameter to determine whether this is an integer or base such as a create mode which is an octal number.

Parameters are of the form *name* = *value* such as:

```
netbios name = EAGLE
```

Only the first = sign is used in the parsing of the parameter and value. The value begins at the first non–white space character following the equals sign and continues until it locates the first carriage return that is not preceded by a \ character. Therefore, the following setting is equivalent to the netbios name parameter example.

```
netbios name    =       EAGLE
```

netbios name

You have briefly seen the netbios name parameter, which enables you to set the NetBIOS machine name of the Samba server. As with most smb.conf parameters, it has a default value of the server's hostname. It is possible not to set this parameter and use the default value, but my personal preference is to define the machine name explicitly.

```
Default:     netbios name = machine's internet hostname
```

Without getting too much into name resolution and browsing issues, it has been my experience that unless you have a very good reason to use a different NetBIOS machine name than the current Internet hostname, it is generally easier to manage if both names are the same. As an example, if the server's hostname was eagle, I would explicitly set the NetBIOS name as

```
netbios name = EAGLE
```

> All valid DNS names under 15 characters in length are also valid NetBIOS names. The reverse is not true, though, because some characters, such as the tilde (~), can be used in machine names that are invalid as far as DNS is concerned.

netbios aliases

In Hour 2, "Windows Networking," in the section, "NetBIOS Overview," I mentioned that in a NetBIOS connection, there is a "calling" name held by the client and a "called" name requested by the client. A NetBIOS server answers only requests that match its called name. The netbios aliases parameter allows Samba to reply to multiple called names. In a particle sense, this means that you can see the same server under multiple names within a workgroup when browsing through the Network Neighborhood on a Windows client. Each server name could provide different services while still residing on the same physical machine. The default is to have no netbios aliases.

```
Default:      netbios aliases = empty string
```

Figure 5.2 displays one server viewed through the Windows 95 Network Neighborhood when using this setting:

```
netbios aliases = admin acct business
```

> The Samba server's primary NetBIOS name, BILBO, also appears in the listing. Be aware that only the primary name (that is, netbios name = ...) is used for responding to requests for domain logons or when configured as a browse server.

FIGURE 5.2

An example of a single Samba server using multiple NetBIOS aliases.

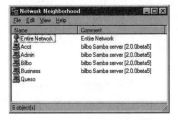

workgroup

The workgroup parameter decides what workgroup the server indicates that it is a member of when servicing requests to clients. Workgroup membership also affects other settings such as domain logons, domain membership, and browse services.

The default for this parameter is determined at compile time by the WORKGROUP macro defined in the make file.

```
Default:     workgoup = determined at compile
```

A workgroup name is a group NetBIOS name, and therefore must follow the standard naming conventions (see Hour 2). For example,

```
workgroup = FOWLPLAY
```

server string

The server string parameter determines the text string displayed in the printer comment section of the Windows print manager. It is also displayed with the machine's NetBIOS name when viewing during network browsing such as in the Network Neighborhood. The text string, as with others, accepts smb.conf variables. This provides an easy way to verify the currently running version of Samba by using the %v variable.

The default setting is

```
Default:    server string = Samba %v
```

I normally use a more descriptive string to help determine the physical location of a machine:

```
server string = Administrative Print Server in Blg #1 [%v]
```

Here's an example of viewing the servers in the current workgroup from a Windows NT 4.0 SP3 machine.

```
H:\>net view
Server Name            Remark

- - - - - - - - - - - - - - - - - - - - - - - - - - - - - - - - - - - - - - - - - - -
\\BURRITO        Administrative Print Server in Blg #1 [2.1.0-prealpha]
\\PIZZA               Samba [1.9.18p7]
```

log file

This parameter provides a means of overriding the compile time default location of the smbd log files.

```
Default:    log file = set at compile time
```

There are some caveats to this parameter. You need to be aware of the order in which things occur.

1. If a file is specified using the -l switch at startup, smbd writes the initial log entries to the filename on the command line. If no location is given at startup, the smbd logs initial information in the file set at compile time.

2. After the configuration file is parsed once and the log file parameter is encountered, all future log entries are written to the file specified by the parameter's value.

This means that because smbd cannot be aware of the log file location as defined in the smb.conf file, it writes some initial information in the log file that it is aware of at startup.

> The only way to override the compile default location for nmbd's log file is to use the -l switch at startup.

5

This example would create a separate log file for each user who connected (or attempted to connect) to the server.

```
log file = /var/log/log.%U
```

max log size

The max log size parameter takes an integer value that specifies the maximum size in kilobytes that the log size should be allowed to grow. Samba regularly checks the size of the log files. If a log file has exceeded the maximum size defined, Samba renames the file using the extension .old and creates a new one. If a file by the same name (*logfile*.old) exists, it is overwritten. The default value is set to 5MB.

```
Default:    max log size = 5000
```

You can, however, set this to whatever value you want. The following entry would set the maximum log file size to 2MB.

```
max log size = 2000
```

syslog

In order for this parameter to have any effect, you must set the compile-time option to enable syslog support:

```
./configure --with-syslog
```

The syslog parameter takes an integer value and maps Samba debug levels to syslog log levels. Table 5.3 lists the mappings. Only Samba debug messages with a level less than the integer specified are sent to the syslog daemon. Therefore, the default is to send only 0-level debug messages to syslog even though the value is set to 1:

```
Default:    syslog = 1
```

Table 5.3 lists how the various debug levels map to the syslog error levels.

TABLE 5.3 SAMBA DEBUG LEVEL TO syslog LEVEL MAPPING

Samba Debug Level	syslog Level
0	LOG_ERR
1	LOG_WARNING
2	LOG_NOTICE
3	LOG_INFO
>3	LOG_DEBUG

If I wanted to send all equivalent `LOG_NOTICE` messages to the `syslogd` process, I would add this entry in `smb.conf`:

```
syslog = 3
```

syslog only

This Boolean parameter determines whether messages are sent only to the `syslog` daemon and not to the normal debug log files. This parameter is used in conjunction with the `syslog` parameter and also requires that `syslog` support be enabled at compile time. The default is to log debug entry to the standard `smbd` and `nmbd` logs in addition to the `syslog` files. You can force Samba to send only logging information to the `syslogd` daemon by setting

```
syslog only = yes
```

debug level

The `debug level`, also named `log level`, parameter enables you to set the maximum level of debug messages to be written to disk. The parameter has a default integer value of 2.

```
Default:    debug level = 2
```

The `debug level` parameter sets the logging level for both `smbd` and `nmbd`. You use Samba's logs extensively for debugging purposes in later hours. Here is an example that sets the log level to 5:

```
debug level = 5
```

> If you specify a debug level from the command line using the `-d` option, it overrides the value set by the `debug level` parameter.

lock directory

This parameter takes a directory path that determines where Samba writes its shared memory file, status file, browse list, WINS database (if WINS support is enabled), and lock files that are used to implement the `max connections` parameter. Samba's `max connections` setting is discussed in Hour 7, when you examine how to configure Samba to share directories. The purpose of the parameters is to define a limit on the number of clients that are able to simultaneously connect to a service.

The default lock directory, determined at compile time, is normally
`/usr/local/samba/var/locks`:

Default: `lock directory = `*`determined at compile time`*

A practical example of why you would want to specify a lock directory other than the default would be in the case of allowing several servers to use the same set of Samba binaries by placing tools on an NFS-mounted file system. Many sites mount a file system at `/usr/local/` for the purpose of sharing tools and utilities unique to its network. Although you can share binaries among Samba servers, it is impossible to share a lock directory. Therefore, you would need to specify a directory local to each server where Samba could place the necessary files.

`lock directory = /var/spool/locks/samba`

name resolve order

The `name resolve order` parameter is analogous to the `/etc/nsswitch.conf` file on platforms such as Linux, Solaris, and IRIX. This parameter lets you control the order in which names are attempted to be resolved. The parameter value is a space-separated list of four possible words. Table 5.4 lists the possible values and any curiosities.

TABLE 5.4   VALID ENTRIES FOR THE `name resolve order` PARAMETER

Value	Description
lmhosts	The Samba `lmhosts` file is searched for a match to the requested name.
hosts	This value instructs Samba to perform a standard hostname-to-IP-address mapping using whatever means are available on the system such as `/etc/hosts` lookups, DNS queries, or NIS/NIS+ matches. Be aware that this method is used only if the NetBIOS name being resolved has the server resource tag (`<20>`).
wins	If a WINS server is specified by the `wins server` or `wins support` parameters (see Hour 18, "WINS"), attempt to resolve the NetBIOS name by querying the WINS server.
bcast	Perform normal NetBIOS broadcast name resolution, which requires that the host in question be located on the same broadcast subnet (or there's a WINS proxy server perhaps).

The default setting looks up the host first in the local `lmhosts` file. An `lmhosts` file is the NetBIOS equivalent to UNIX's `/etc/hosts` file. Next, Samba attempts to match the name with a hostname and resolve it using standard the standard means such as `/etc/hosts` lookups or DNS queries. If both of the two previous methods fail, the server contacts a WINS server if one has been specified in `smb.conf`. Finally Samba resorts to broadcast name queries.

```
Default:          name resolve order = lmhosts hosts wins bcast
```

If you want to configure Samba so it never uses broadcasts as a means of resolving a name, you would use the following settings:

```
name resolve order = lmhosts wins hosts
```

deadtime

This parameter enables you to set the number of minutes of inactivity before a connection (such as an smbd process) is considered to be dead and dropped. A connection is considered idle when there is no activity and it contains no open files. This can be helpful on a server that handles a large number of connections that are not always in use. My users have a tendency to log in and never log out, even when they go on vacation. Most modern clients have an automatic reconnect feature that makes this setting transparent to the user.

The default value of 0 indicates that the connection should never be dropped.

```
Default:    dead time = 0
```

On my servers at work, I use a dead time of fifteen minutes:

```
dead time = 15
```

smbrun

This parameter sets the absolute path to the smbrun binary, a small program used by the smbd daemon to execute shell commands. If you installed Samba using the standard make install, this parameter should not be needed. If you manually installed the Samba binaries to a location other than the $prefix defined in the make file, you need to set this parameter. If smbd cannot locate the smbrun binary, it logs appropriate debug messages in the log.smb file. The actual default value is determined by the $prefix make file variable.

```
Default:    smbrun = set at compile time
```

If you have installed the tool in another directory, such as /usr/bin, you need to set the path location.

```
smbrun = /usr/bin/smbrun
```

message command

The message command parameter sets the action that smbd takes when it receives a WinPopup-style message. From the discussion of NetBIOS names in Hour 2, you know that names with the <03> resource tag represent the messenger server. The WinPopup

messages are sent to this name. Figure 5.3 shows the WinPopup Windows 95 utility
preparing to send a message to the Samba servernamed BILBO.

FIGURE 5.3

Windows 95 OSR2
WinPopup.exe sends
and receives messages.

Samba's default action is to discard WinPopup style messages.

```
Default:     message command = none
```

Many possibilities can be used to send the message. The following example is one I used
to display the message sent by the WinPopup client (see Figure 5.3) on my Linux box
(see Figure 5.4).

```
message command = /bin/bash -c '/usr/X11R6/bin/xterm -T
➥"WinPopup Message" \
-e /usr/bin/vim %s; rm %s' &
```

FIGURE 5.4

Message command
executed on receipt of
a WinPopup message.

Another example would be to use a command-line mail utility such as /bin/mailx to
deliver the message using SMTP.

The WinPopup message is delivered as the global guest account (usually the nobody account). The command can contain additional variables besides the standard macros. These are listed in Table 5.5.

TABLE 5.5 ADDITIONAL VARIABLES AVAILABLE FOR THE MESSAGE COMMAND
PARAMETER VALUE.

Variable	Description
%s	The name of the file containing the message body.
%t	The destination name to which the message was sent. This is normally the name of the server.
%f	The name of the client who sent the message.

There are a few items to be aware of when setting a message command:

- Unless the commands you specify are in the default search path for the shell that is executed, you need to use absolute paths to the binaries.

- You must explicitly remove the received message, or else it remains after the message command has completed.

- The message command should return immediately, or else the sending client can hang until a timeout period occurs.

auto services

This parameter accepts a list of all the share names that you want to be automatically visible in the browse list for the Samba server. This is probably most useful with regard to dynamically created services such as [homes] and [printers]. The default action (no shares automatically visible) would not allow the expanded version of these services to be seen.

Default: auto services = *none*

The following setting would enable the home directories for users jerryc and peteh to be seen in a browse list. This parameter does not delegate any more access to the files contained in the shares than a user would normally have.

Assume that jerryc and peteh are usernames in the local /etc/passwd and that the [homes] share has been defined correctly. These services are not normally available until the user has made a connection to the server. The following sample setting causes the shares to be shown in the browse list no matter what user connects to the server.

auto services = jerryc peteh

This, however, does not mean that users are able to connect to those particular shares; only that they can see that they are available on the particular server.

protocol

During the negotiation phase of an SMB connection setup, the client sends a list of protocol dialects that it understands. The server then selects the highest one that it knows. See Hour 2 for a review of this if you need to.

The protocol parameter enables you to specify the highest SMB dialect that Samba can negotiate. Normally this option should be left alone so that Samba handles the protocol selection automatically. The default allows smbd to negotiate the highest possible SMB dialect, NT1.

```
Default:    protocol = NT1
```

The valid names and a short description of each one are listed in Table 5.6.

TABLE 5.6 SMB DIALECTS

Name	Description
CORE	This is the earliest version of SMB and has no concept of usernames.
COREPLUS	This version is basically a more efficient version of the CORE protocol.
LANMAN1 file names.	This is the first modern version of the protocol. It also contains support for long
LANMAN2	Version 2 is a enhanced version of the LANMAN1 protocol.
NT1	This is the most current version of the protocol implemented in Samba and is the version used by Windows NT 4.0 Service Pack 3. Version 2 of this protocol was released with Service Pack 4 for Windows NT. Windows NT SP4 clients still function correctly with Samba using version 1 of the protocol.

time server

Setting this parameter to true makes nmbd announce itself as a time server to Windows clients and thus enables you to execute the following command and attain the appropriate result.

```
C:\WINDOWS> net time
Current time at \\BILBO is 1-27-1999 9:39P.M.
The command was completed successfully.
```

Even if you do not set this parameter, you can always query a specific server for the current time by executing the following

```
C:\WINDOWS> net time \\<servername>
Default:            time server = no
```

The default is not to respond to `time server` requests.

```
Default:    time server = no
```

Summary

Although there are quite a few `smb.conf` parameters, you need to set only the ones you want to use or the ones you explicitly want to define if you're as overly cautious as I am. For example, this is probably the simplest working `smb.conf` file that I can imagine. It implements a simple home directory server:

```
[global]
    workgroup = MYGROUP
[homes]
    writeable = yes
```

How elaborate you make your `smb.conf` file is up to you and the needs of your network.

Q&A

Q **After I make a change to Samba configuration file, do I need to kill and restart the Samba daemons?**

A For most configuration changes, you do not need to do anything. Samba periodically checks to determine whether the configuration file has changed. If it has, it is reloaded. There are some subtleties to this. First, if you make changes to a share definition, any users currently connected to it can't see the changes until they disconnect and remount the share. Secondly, some changes require that Samba be restarted such as the `NetBIOS name` or the `workgroup` parameters.

Q **Can Samba be a member of more than one workgroup at the same time?**

A No. Samba can be a member of only one workgroup.

5

Hour **6**

Security Levels and Passwords

After my weeklong vacation in Hour 4, "Installing and Testing the Configuration," I arrived back at work, and the boss pulled me aside. "These network drive things you set up are great! Productivity has gone through the roof! I'd like to scale this setup company-wide, but before I can make the recommendation to management, I need some hard facts on the security of things. Can you explain to me how Samba checks my password when I log in?"

I stood there for a moment thinking. After a few silent moments, I said, "I'd be glad to sit down and explain how it all happens, but first I need an hour to get my morning cup of coffee and finish a few things."

"Sounds good," the boss replied. "I'll see you in an hour in my office."

I started down the hall toward the testing lab trying to remember where I left my favorite coffee cup and my copy of this book.

Would I be able to find the information in time? Would Samba be deployed company wide?

Stay tuned and find out more!

In the previous hour, I talked about the general layout of the Samba configuration file as well as some of the general and miscellaneous [global] parameters. In this hour, I'll examine the parameters that relate to the authentication methods that Samba uses to validate connections. In addition to that, I'll also talk about password security using encryption and a client's IP address to decide whether to attempt to validate the connection at all.

Security Levels and the `security` Parameter

The SMB protocol has two fundamental modes of validating connections. The mode that Samba uses is defined by setting the `security` parameter in the [global] section of the `smb.conf` file.

The `smb.conf` man page entry for the `security` parameter lists four possible strings which can be used, but I said that the SMB protocol has two basic levels of authentication. In reality, of the four modes that Samba supports—share, user, server, and domain—the only ones that are fundamentally different are share and user, which are the two SMB security levels. The other values supported by Samba are variations on user-mode security:

```
security = [share¦user¦server¦domain]
```

> Prior to version 2.0, the default settings for the security parameter was share. In version 2.0, the default was changed to user-mode security.

Samba 2.0 introduced a password database API to enable developers to plug in difference authentication by defining a set of functions. This means that there are several choices for you when deciding on how to store your user account information.

Figure 6.1 shows the possible back ends that are currently in use or in the process of being developed. The client requests a connection to the server and the server contacts the account database through a defined interface. It is not necessary to really know what back end is being used; as far as Samba is concerned, the database provides the user information needed.

FIGURE 6.1

Samba allows multiple, mutually exclusive, user account databases.

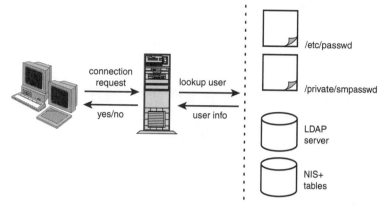

Experimental support is underway for accessing NIS+ tables as well as an Lightweight Directory Access Protocol (LDAP) server. Of the possibilities displayed in Figure 6.1, the two which are currently supported are Samba's `private/smbpasswd` file and the standard UNIX `/etc/passwd` file. Both of these are discussed in depth later in this hour. For now, you should be aware that each one requires a username and password for validation.

security = share

In share-level security, the client sends a password during the tree connection request. No associated username is required. This is slightly different from the description I gave in Hour 2, "Windows Networking," which more accurately represents user-level security. Figure 6.2 illustrates the two steps used in a connection to an SMB server in share-level security.

FIGURE 6.2

Password sent in share-level security with the tree connection request.

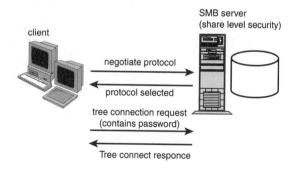

6

You might already be aware of a common example of a share-level SMB server. Share-level security is the default setting for a Windows 95 file or print server (see Figure 6.3). Figure 6.4 displays the page in the network control panel that enables you to change the security level.

FIGURE 6.3

Share-level security screen in Windows 95.

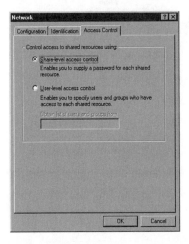

FIGURE 6.4

Choosing the security level in Windows 95.

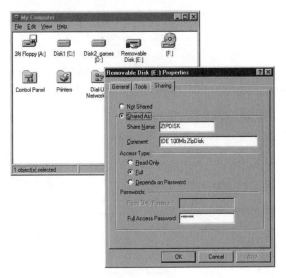

By now you might be thinking, "Share-level security seems to violate the UNIX username/password authentication model." You are correct. The concept of share-level security does not work well in a multiuser environment, such as UNIX, but Samba goes to great lengths to not compromise the UNIX security model.

Although the client expects the share-level SMB server to associate a password with each share, Samba uses the standard UNIX username/password scheme. In spite of the fact that clients connecting to a server in share-level security send the password in the tree connection request, many clients also send a session setup request containing a username. Samba adds this username to a list of names which it attempts to validate using the transmitted password. You can specify other usernames to be added to the list by using the user parameter in the service:

```
user = jerryc, smbguest, jdoe
```

Samba attempts to validate the connection by trying to validate each username with the password until a pair is successfully authenticated or all the possible pairs fail, in which case the tree connection is refused. Because Samba always attempts to validate a username/password pair anyway, share-level security is not recommended. It is generally better to use one of the forms of user-level security, which I will discuss next.

security = user

The SMB connection setup process in Hour 2 (see "Protocol Overview") describes a connection attempt to a server in user-level security. If plain text passwords are being used, the client sends a username and password during the session setup.

Because this is a book on using Samba and not on developing an SMB server, I won't bore you with packet dumps very often. But I think there is some value in displaying the account information transmitted during this portion of the connection. Here is a session setup request from a Windows 95 OSR2 client connecting to a Samba server. The packets were captured using an SMB-enabled version of tcpdump:

```
C:\WINDOWS> net use h: \\bilbo\boss
The command was completed successfully.
```

> tcpdump is a network packet sniffer that is distributed with source code. The SMB-enabled version is available for download from http://samba.org. More about packet sniffers can be found in Hour 11, "Troubleshooting."

6

After executing the previous command, tcpdump produces the following output:

```
SMB PACKET: SMBsesssetupX (REQUEST)
SMB Command   =   0x73
Error class   =   0x0
Error code    =   0
Flags1        =   0x10
Flags2        =   0x0
```

```
Tree ID       = 0
Proc ID       = 28754
UID           = 1
MID           = 3586
Word Count    = 13
Com2=0x75
Res1=0x0
Off2=125
MaxBuffer=2920
MaxMpx=50
VcNumber=0
SessionKey=0xBE
CaseInsensitivePasswordLength=
[000] 54 45 53 54 50 41 53 53  00 00 00 00 00 00 42 4F  TESTPASS ......BO
[010] 53 53 00 00 00 00 00 00  42 4F 53 53 00 43 48 49  SS...... BOSS.CHI
[020] 50 53 4E 44 49 50 53 00  57 69 6E 64 6F 77 73 20  PSNDIPS. Windows
[030] 34 2E 30 00 57 69 6E 64  6F 77 73 20 34 2E 30 00  4.0.Wind ows 4.0.
```

You can clearly see that the password testpass and the username boss are transmitted during the session setup request. If you look closely, you can also notice that the username and password are translated into uppercase letters. This can be annoying and is covered in the section, "Password Encryption," later in this hour.

When in user-level security, Samba accepts the username/password pair transmitted and attempts to validate them against its account database. This process is the same regardless of the user account backend (for example, encrypted passwords, LDAP, and /etc/passwd), although the proof of identity might be some derived value rather than the actual password itself. Please refer to the notes on the SMB challenge/response encryption under the "Password Encryption" section later in this hour. If the session setup validation succeeds, the client does not need to transmit user account information during subsequent tree connection requests.

The three steps for a connection to a user-level SMB server are shown in Figure 6.5. First the protocol level is selected, next a session is established between the client and server, and finally the connection to resource is configured.

security = server

Samba's server-level security is really a type of user-level security. Samba reports to the client that it is in user-level security and the client performs a normal session setup. Samba then takes the information and sends a session setup request to the machine designated as the password server. If the password server is in user-level security and accepts the session setup, Samba accepts the initial session setup request from the client.

FIGURE 6.5

Tree connection requests in user-mode security.

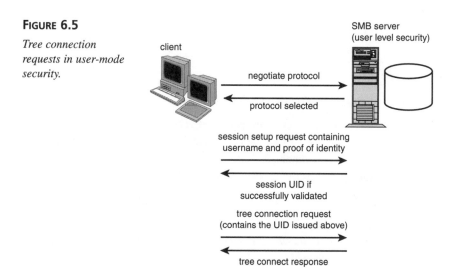

Figure 6.6 illustrates this process. The chronological flow of the diagram is from top to bottom. If you follow the arrows, you'll see that at the point where the client requests a session with the server, the latter machine sends a session request to the password server. Only after the server has received a response from the password server is the client's session request accepted or rejected.

FIGURE 6.6

A client connecting to a Samba server in server-level security.

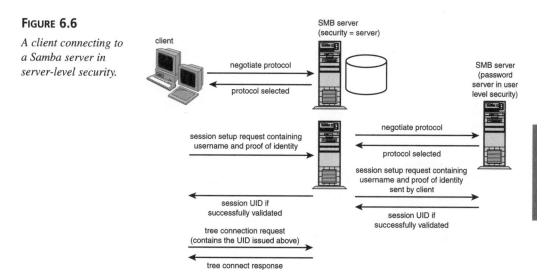

6

The `password server` parameter has the following syntax:

`password server = NetBIOS name of SMB server`

You can list multiple NetBIOS names in the list such as

`password server = DOMAINPDC DOMAINBDC1 DOMAINBDC2`

This allows Samba to attempt a session setup request to each machine in the list in order until a server is contacted. This means that the next machine on the list is contacted only if the previous machine was unreachable. This does not mean that Samba attempts to contact the other machines listed, if the session request to the first machine fails.

You must use the NetBIOS name of the password server (not the IP address), and Samba must have a way of resolving the name to an IP address in order to attempt the connection.

You can use any SMB server in user mode security as the password, but the security of your Samba server then becomes only as secure as the password server you select. You have been warned! Common choices for a password server are your Windows NT Primary Domain Controller (PDC) or another Samba box.

There is one fine point of using server-level security. After Samba has granted the session setup request to the client, it must then have some means of obtaining a UNIX uid for the user in order to control access to files. This means that although local accounts are not used to validate the connection, the user must have a uid on the local server. There are two possible solutions to this problem:

- You can create a local account for all users that access the Samba server and simply disable the password field in `/etc/passwd` (or whatever file in which the passwords are stored). Setting the `password` field to the asterisk character (*) normally does this.

- You can use one of the means of mapping usernames within a share, such as `force user`, which is described in Hour 7, "File Sharing." Or use the `username map` parameter, which I'll talk about shortly.

Figure 6.7 appears very similar to Figure 6.6; they do in fact represent the same process. Figure 6.7 has been expanded to describe the point at which Samba attempts to obtain a valid UNIX uid for the username specified in the session setup request. What is transparent, in a sense, is that the username lookup can be filtered through a `username map` before actually searching for a name in `/etc/passwd`.

FIGURE 6.7

Mapping a validated username to a UNIX uid.

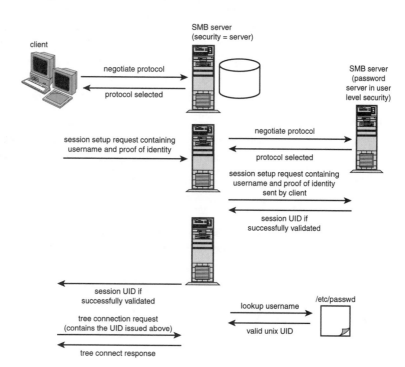

security = domain

Samba's domain security is basically the same concept as its server-level security, with the exception that the Samba server becomes a member of a Windows NT domain. This means that the Samba server can participate in things such as trust relationships. There are several other advantages to using `security = domain` rather than `security = server`. I would like to defer this discussion to Hour 12, "Case Study: Replacing an NT File and Print Server," where I'll look at how to replace a Windows NT File and Print Server with a Samba box running in domain-level security. For now, consider them equivalent.

6

Usernames and Passwords

Now that you understand how smbd authenticates connections, turn your attention to the details of usernames and passwords.

Username Level

As you have seen already in the packet dump from a session setup request, some clients send the username in all uppercase letters. By default, Samba attempts to look up this username in all lowercase and then with only the first letter capitalized, for example boss and Boss. If you have a strange UNIX username, such as BobAcct assigned to Bob in Accounting, Samba is unable to locate the username with this method.

What is provided is a parameter to specify the maximum number of capital letters in the username. Samba then attempts to discover the username using a brute force method of trying all permutations of capitalized letters from 1 to the value defined.

Set a username level of 4 and apply that to Bob's account name:

```
username level = 4
```

You can assume that BOBACCT is transmitted as the username in the session setup request. Samba attempts to locate the following names in the system password file (or whatever account back end is being used):

```
bobacct

Bobacct

bObacct

boBacct

bobAcct

bobaCct

bobacCt

bobaccT

BObacct

BoBacct

BobAcct
```

After the username is located, the search terminates. The greater the `username level`, the more combinations of uppercase/lowercase letters that are tried and hence the longer the delay before being able to report success or failure. If all the UNIX account names are in the standard format of all lowercase letters, this parameter becomes unnecessary.

Username Map

One of the main problems when integrating UNIX and PC operating systems is synchronizing user account information. Some variants of UNIX restrict use to eight characters or fewer for the username, whereas some Windows clients allow a free-form string including white space. Many times administrators find themselves attempting to integrate two already established systems, both with existing account names. The `username map` parameter enables you to specify a file that contains mappings from the username sent during the session setup to a local username.

This option is not enabled by default.

`Default:`   `username map = ` *`none`*

In order to use mapping, you need to specify the location of the file containing the mapping entries.

`Example:`   `username map = /usr/local/samba/lib/users.map`

Each entry in the map file looks like

`unix username = client username ...`

For example, if you want to map the Administrator or Admin username to the `sysadmin` account, you would define an entry as

`sysadmin = Administrator Admin`

When a user attempts to connect to a share as Administrator, he or she would need to supply the password for the `sysadmin` account.

> The mapping affects all instances of the client username with the exception of the session setup to a password server when `security = server`. Using the previous example, if a user attempts to connect to the Administrator's home directory (`\\server\Administrator`), the user would actually connect to `\\server\sysadmin`.

6

It is possible to map UNIX groups to a single account. This line would map any user in the staff group to the staffsmb account:

staffsmb = @staff

There is also a wildcard that enables you to match any username sent by the client. This entry maps all users to the guest account:

guest = *

There is a catch to beware of regarding substitutions: smbd parses the file line-by-line and carries out any substitutions to the end of the file. This can lead to multiple mapping from username to new_username1 to new_username2. If you want to stop parsing the file after a map is made, you should preface the line with an exclamation point (!). If no match is found in the file, Samba uses the original username.

Password Level

When plain-text passwords are used for authentication, the issues that arise are similar to the ones I mentioned in the section about usernames regarding case sensitivity. This snippet of the tcpdump output shown before reminds you that the password, testpass, is being sent in uppercase letters:

```
[000] 54 45 53 54 50 41 53 53   00 00 00 00 00 00 42 4F   TESTPASS ......BO
[010] 53 53 00 00 00 00 00 00   42 4F 53 53 00 43 48 49   SS...... BOSS.CHI
[020] 50 53 4E 44 49 50 53 00   57 69 6E 64 6F 77 73 20   PSNDIPS. Windows
[030] 34 2E 30 00 57 69 6E 64   6F 77 73 20 34 2E 30 00   4.0.Wind ows 4.0.
```

The password-level parameter acts analogously to the username parameter. The difference is that the default tries to use the password two ways, as it is sent from the client and in all lowercase letters.

The parameter takes an integer value that defines the maximum number of uppercase letters allowed in the password, as did the username-level parameter. Samba then attempts to validate the username using permutations of uppercase letters in the password.

The higher the value and the more combinations Samba tries, the longer delay in authentication attempts. You need to determine what is acceptable for your server. A password level of 8 on most systems means that the passwords are no longer case sensitive. I have found that using a level of 4 is generally acceptable, without causing too much trouble with existing passwords. However, it is also helpful to have a password change policy dictating that no more than four uppercase letters be used.

Password Encryption

Samba supports both the LanManager and Windows NT SMB password-encryption algorithms. This means that Samba can authenticate users in the same manner that Microsoft servers can.

If you are familiar with UNIX's encryption of password, some points might seem to be similar. For example, the LanMan and NT password hashes are irreversible, as are UNIX passwords stored in /etc/passwd (or /etc/shadow). *Irreversible* means that the only way to determine whether a user has entered the correct password is to encrypt the entered password and compare it against the encrypted version stored on disk. There is no means of decrypting a LanMan/NT password hash other than brute force methods, such as a dictionary attack.

NEW TERM　You should be aware of one major difference between UNIX and LanMan/NT password-encryption algorithms. The algorithm for generating a LanManager- or Windows NT–hashed password always produces the same result if given the same input. This means that if you encrypt the password testpass 200 times, the encrypted password is the same every time. This creates what is known as a *plain-text equivalent* password.

I hope that the following example will clarify this. You can follow along in Figure 6.8.

FIGURE 6.8

Sample challenge/response authentication between a client and server.

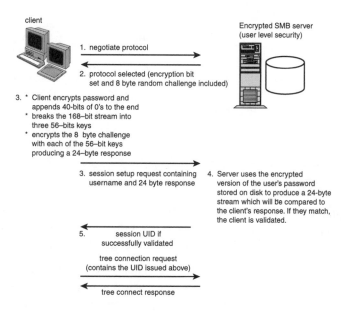

client

1. negotiate protocol

2. protocol selected (encryption bit set and 8 byte random challenge included)

Encrypted SMB server (user level security)

3. * Client encrypts password and appends 40-bits of 0's to the end
* breaks the 168–bit stream into three 56–bits keys
* encrypts the 8 byte challenge with each of the 56–bit keys producing a 24–byte response

3. session setup request containing username and 24 byte response

4. Server uses the encrypted version of the user's password stored on disk to produce a 24-byte stream which will be compared to the client's response. If they match, the client is validated.

5.　session UID if successfully validated

tree connection request (contains the UID issued above)

tree connect response

6

1. The client sends a negotiate protocol request to the server.

2. If the server supports password encryption, the appropriate bit to indicate this is set in the response packet and the server includes an 8-byte challenge in the packet. The challenge is randomly generated and is different for each client.

3. Figure 6.9 illustrates the generation of the client's response. The client then uses the encrypted password appropriate for the protocol level negotiated (either LanMan or NT) appended with five null bytes (this creates a 168-bit stream) to generate three different 56-bit DES keys which are each then used to encrypt the 8-byte challenge. The three 8-byte results are concatenated to form the 24-byte response. This response is then sent to the server.

FIGURE 6.9

Generating the 24-byte response.

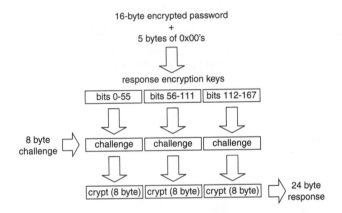

4. The server then performs the same steps using the encrypted version of the user's password stored on disk. The resulting 24-byte stream is compared to the one sent by the client to determine whether the client knew the correct password.

5. If the server's 24-byte stream and the response sent by the client match, the user session setup request is accepted (or tree connection request in the case of share-level security). If they don't match, that means that the client did not know the correct password.

Don't worry about being able to repeat the process verbatim. I've included it only to prove a point. The user's password is never transmitted across the network. The result is increased security! Only data generated from the password is sent.

Now back to my previous comment about plain-text equivalent passwords. The server must store the encrypted password somewhere to be able to produce the 24-byte value so that it can verify the client's response. Remember that the password is always encrypted to the same value. Therefore, if someone knows the encrypted version of the password, that person could participate in the previous scenario without ever knowing the password!

Does this seem like too much information to digest? Perhaps some of these points can help you to decide whether to use encrypted passwords or plain-text passwords:

- Plain-text passwords allow Samba to use the same password database (that is, /etc/passwd) as other UNIX services such as login and FTP. Often these services also transmit passwords in plain text across the network, so Samba is not transmitting user account information that is not already being sent across the network.

- When using plain-text passwords, there is no need for anything other than normal UNIX system files to be stored on disk.

- Windows NT does not like plain-text passwords and doesn't enable you to browse a server that does not support encryption. It also prompts for passwords to connect to nonencrypted shares which can get extremely annoying if you connect to a large number of shares.

- Keeping the smbpasswd and unix passwd synchronized can be difficult. See Hour 16, "Password Synchronization."

- Encrypted passwords cannot be viewed by anyone who has access to the packets between the client and server. If you are using plain-text passwords, the transmitted information can be viewed using simple network analyzing tools such as tcpdump.

If you decide to use password encryption, which is turned off by default, you must enable it in the smb.conf file by setting encrypt passwords to yes:

```
encrypt passwords = yes
```

After you enable password encryption, you must now keep track of a second user account file. This file, usually named smbpasswd and stored in a subdirectory named private located underneath the Samba install directory, is where Samba stores the LanMan and NT hashes of the user passwords. The format is very similar to /etc/passwd:

```
username:uid:XXXXXXXXXXXXXXXXXXXXXXXXXXXXXXXXX:
➥XXXXXXXXXXXXXXXXXXXXXXXXXXXXXXXXX:account flags:lastset:
```

The username and uid fields are self explanatory. The next two fields contain the two 16-byte LanMan and NT hashes of the user's password respectively. The account flags field determines the type of the account such as user account or a machine account (machine accounts are discussed more in Hour 22, "Experimental PDC Support"). The lastset field records the time of the last password change.

6

Here's a sample entry:

```
jerryc:1009:AAD3B435B51404EEAAD3B435B51404EE:
➥31D6CFE0D16AE931B73C59D7E0C089C0:[U          ]:LCT-36918AD9:
```

If you decide to locate or name the file containing the encrypted passwords in a location other than the default, you can define the encrypted password file using the `smb passwd file` parameter. The value should be an absolute path to the SMB password file:

```
smb password file = /etc/smbpasswd
```

Creating the initial SMB passwd file and setting passwords can be an extremely daunting task if you have a large number of existing UNIX accounts.

There are two common solutions to this. Both solutions require you first to create an initial `smbpasswd` entry for each user. Using one of the scripts included with the Samba distribution, this can easily be done:

```
cat /etc/passwd ¦ mksmbpasswd.sh > /usr/local/samba/private/smbpasswd
```

If the UNIX box obtains account information from NIS or NIS+, you can substitute the preceding `cat` command with either `ypcat` or `niscat` depending on your system. The `mksmbpasswd.sh` shell script is located in the `source/script/` subdirectory of the Samba distribution. The resulting `smbpasswd` file contains all the users from `/etc/passwd` with their LanMan and NT hashed passwords set to 32 X. Samba does not validate a user whose password entry is set to this value.

If you want to set the value to an empty password, you must change

```
XXXXXXXXXXXXXXXXXXXXXXXXXXXXXXXX:XXXXXXXXXXXXXXXXXXXXXXXXXXXXXXXX
```

to

```
NO PASSWORDXXXXXXXXXXXXXXXXXXXXX:XXXXXXXXXXXXXXXXXXXXXXXXXXXXXXXX
```

Issue the following command as root:

```
/usr/local/samba/bin/smbpasswd -n username
```

Replace *username* with the appropriate string. Samba stores the encrypted passwords in a file named `smbpasswd` and includes a utility also named `smbpasswd` to manipulate entries in the file. Don't let the common name confuse you.

Alternatively you could edit the `smbpasswd` file by hand using a text editor and change the string yourself. However, if you do edit the `smbpasswd` file by hand, make sure that the LanMan and NT password fields contain 32 characters, no more and no fewer. If the field does not have exactly 32 characters, Samba can never validate that user.

After changing the `smbpasswd` entry, you need to set the following `null passwords` parameter to `yes` in the `[global]` section of `smb.conf`:

```
null passwords = yes
```

```
null passwords = yes
```

After the `smbpasswd` file is created, the next question is "How do I populate the password field for each entry?"

Solution #1

If you are currently using Samba with plain-text passwords, you can gradually set the encrypted password fields for each user by using the Boolean `update encrypted` parameter The default value to this parameter is `no`. In order to enable support, you need to add the following entry to `smb.conf` in the `[global]` section:

```
update encrypted = yes
```

If you set the parameter's value to `yes`, you must make sure that the `encrypt passwords` parameter is set to `no`.

```
encrypt passwords = no
```

When `update encrypted` is set to `yes`, each time that a user successfully requests a session setup, Samba writes the encrypted version of the plain-text password that was transmitted for that user. The only requirement is that the user has a valid entry in the existing `smbpasswd` file. Whatever the previous value of the `passwd` field was, it is now set to the user's current password. Obviously, this method makes sense only when in user-level security.

This solution allows the Samba server to run for a few days or weeks, whatever length is necessary, capturing passwords and populating the `smbpassword` file. When the `smbpasswd` file contains enough entries to your satisfaction, you can simply change the following parameters in `smb.conf` and switch to using encrypted passwords:

```
encrypt passwords = yes
update encrypted = no
```

Most of your users will never know that anything has changed.

Figure 6.10 displays the process of how the `update encrypted` parameter works. First the client and server select the SMB protocol dialect to use and then the client sends the username and password in plain text contained in the sessions setup request. If the user can be successfully authenticated against `/etc/passwd`, `smbd` encrypts the password and writes the information to the `smbpasswd` file. You should be aware that the user's entry in `smbpasswd` at this point is never used in the validation process. It is used only as a storage facility for the encrypted password.

6

FIGURE 6.10

Gradually populating the smbpasswd file using the update encrypted parameter.

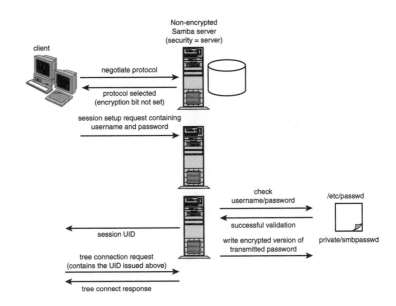

Solution #2

I mentioned before that Samba includes a utility named smbpasswd for manipulating entries in the smbpasswd file. This tool is located in the bin/ subdirectory and is the Samba equivalent of the UNIX /bin/passwd program.

When a user receives a new UNIX account, most sites assign a random password and then instruct the user on how to change it to something that is more memorable or personal. If you are beginning a Samba infrastructure—that's a word right out of Dilbert cartoon strip, isn't it?—you might simply assign users an SMB password at the same time that they are issued a UNIX account. Along with the standard instructions for using /bin/passwd to change their UNIX passwords, you would also include instruction for using the /usr/local/samba/bin/smbpasswd command to change their SMB passwords as well. This is certainly the easiest solution because the responsibility of keeping the password synchronized, if desired, has been handed over to the user. However, this could result in more help desk calls depending on the caliber of your users. It can be very easy to confuse which password goes with which logon if the accounts become out of sync; a user can be very adamant about her belief that she is entering the correct password for her account. You be the judge which solution is best for you.

Here's a sample session of changing my SMB password using the smbpasswd command. I've included comments regarding what was typed in angle brackets (< >). (You didn't really think I would show you my password, did you?)

```
[jerryc@bilbo jerryc]408: /usr/local/samba/bin/smbpasswd
Old SMB password: <enter old SMB password here>
New SMB password: <enter new SMB password here>
Retype new SMB password: <reenter new SMB password here>
..Password changed for user jerryc
```

Regarding Plain Text and Encrypted Passwords and Windows 9x and Windows NT Clients

I want to make a quick note about using plain-text passwords and newer Microsoft clients. This and other issues specific to the Microsoft 32-bit client are more fully covered in Hour 14, "Windows 9x and Windows NT."

Beginning with Service Pack 3 for Windows NT 4.0, Microsoft changed the default to use only encrypted passwords. Therefore if you attempt to connect to a unencrypted Samba server, you will see this error:

```
System error 1240 has occurred.
The account is not authorized to login from this station.
```

You'll see the same behavior in Windows 95 clients that have the SMB network redirector update (vrdrupd.exe). However, Windows 95 will simply keep asking for a password. This patch updates:

```
\windows\system\Vredir.vxd
\windows\system\Vnetsup.xvd
```

It is possible to use a unencrypted Samba server with these clients. It simply requires setting a value in the Windows system registry. If you want to see the details of this solution, you can get the full story in Hour 14.

Accessibility

Samba offers some additional options to control connection requests besides the standard username/password validation. These options allow you some control of connection based on the client's IP address, which can be very helpful if your network is connected to a larger LAN (or the Internet).

6

hosts allow

You can use the hosts allow parameter to define a list of hosts that are allowed to connect to a particular service. If the parameter is used in the [global] section, it applies to all services regardless of individual share settings.

The parameter takes a list of IP addresses in dotted decimal form, which can be a full address or a subnet network address. For example, `192.168.1.73` would allow a specific host to connect, whereas `192.168.1.` would allow connections from any host on the `192.168.1.` class C subnet. You can use hostnames rather than IP addresses as long as Samba can resolve the name. This usually means entering the *fully qualified domain name* (*FQDN*) as the value. It is also possible to exclude hosts by using the `EXCEPT` keyword. The default behavior accepts connections from any IP address. Here are some examples:

```
hosts allow = 192.168.1.73 queso.my.net 191.168. EXCEPT 191.168.2.
```

This setting allows connections from two specific hosts, `192.168.1.73` and `queso.my.net`, and connections from any host in the `191.168.` class B subnet, except ones located in the `191.168.2.` class C subnet.

Here's an example that uses an IP address/subnet mask pair:

```
hosts allow = 192.168.1.32/255.255.255.224
```

This allows connections from hosts in the range `192.168.1.33` to `192.168.1.63`. The broadcast address for the subnet is `192.168.1.64`.

hosts deny

The `hosts deny` parameter is the compliment of the `hosts allow` parameter. It provides the same functionality of the `EXCEPT` keyword in the `hosts allow` value but to a larger degree. The syntax is the same format as `hosts allow`. The default is not to deny connections from any host:

```
hosts deny = 192.168.3. 192.168.1.72
```

hosts equiv and user hosts

I mention the next two parameters only for completeness and do not recommend using them. The reason is that both provide a means of enabling users to connect to shares and authenticate without using a password. It can be a severs security hole in your server. Be careful!

The `hosts equiv` parameter enables you to specify the location of a file that contains a list of hosts or users, one per line, that are allowed to access services without specifying a password. The default disables this behavior entirely. Here is an example:

```
host equiv = /etc/hosts.equiv
```

The Boolean `user hosts` parameter causes Samba to use the UNIX user's `~/.rhosts` file to determine certain hosts that are allowed access to shares without specifying a password. As it was with the `hosts equiv` parameter, the default setting is to disable this capability. If you want to enable it, you need to add the following in the `[global]` section on `smb.conf`:

```
use rhosts = yes

use rhosts = yes
```

Miscellaneous

The last two parameters I'll present relate to security but do not fit into any of the subjects I've discussed so far.

map to guest

Without getting in over your heads in details, the `map to guest` parameter enables you to determine what Samba does when a session setup request contains invalid user authentication information (for example, the client sent a bad password). There are three possible responses:

- `Never` Samba rejects sessions with an invalid password. This is the default behavior.
- `Bad User` If the client sends an invalid password, the session is rejected unless the username is invalid. In this case, the connection is accepted and the user is mapped to the `guest account` specified in `smb.conf`.
- `Bad Password` This setting causes any invalid username/password pairs to be accepted as guest connections. However, the connecting user is not told this and might complain about being unable to access their files because they are connected as the guest account.

I would recommend that you leave the default settings unless you have a legitimate reason for changing them. If you cannot think of a legitimate reason on your own, that's probably a good rationale to leave it alone.

root directory

This is another parameter that is not commonly used. It instructs Samba to perform a `chroot()` to the specified directory similar to the way that anonymous FTP connections do. This is not strictly necessary, because Samba denies access to files outside the share by default. It does, however, add an extra level of security, but you must make sure that all necessary scripts, system files, and binaries are contained below the root directory. To override the default root directory of /, you can simply specify the directory of your choice:

```
root directory = /export/smb
```

```
root directory = /export/smb
```

Final Comments

I thought it would be better to leave you with this point rather than bury it within an hour. If you are separated from other networks by a firewall and you do not want to allow clients on the outside of the firewall to access your internal SMB servers, make sure you block incoming ports 137, 138, and 139. This is especially true if you have users who like to share their entire hard disk because "it's so convenient!"

In Hour 7, you'll move on to the nitty-gritty of configuring the shares so that your users can actually access their files. Oh! I forgot to finish the story I started at the beginning of the hour, didn't I?

After spending a little less than an hour, I finished the last gulp of coffee (which was lukewarm by then) and headed off to find my boss. After explaining my decision to use encrypted passwords and defining a strategic plan—another Dilbert word—for migrating existing users to encrypted passwords fairly painlessly, she congratulated me on another job well done. She then signed a purchase order for a new laptop so I could stay in touch on my company-paid vacation. (It could happen!)

Summary

The SMB protocol supports two modes of connection authentication. Samba supports both share-mode and user-mode security. In addition, Samba offers two other variations on user-level security: server and domain.

You can use either plain-text passwords or encrypted passwords in all the security options in Samba. Plain-text passwords are validated against the standard UNIX account database, /etc/passwd (or the network equivalent). Password encryption however, requires that Samba keep a separate file containing the password encryption hashes.

Q&A

Q Are there any external libraries needed to enable password encryption in Samba?

A Although it was true in older versions that the administrator had to obtain an external DES library to link against, newer versions of Samba do not need this. All the source code necessary is included with the Samba distribution.

Q Can a Samba server be configured to enable both plain-text passwords and encrypted passwords simultaneously?

A No. A single Samba server cannot be configured to use both plain-text and encrypted passwords to validate users. There is a way to work around this, but it involves using the `netbios aliases` parameter. The functionality necessary to implement a solution to this is discussed in Hour 10, "Server Side Automation."

Q Can some shares be configured to use share-level security and others on the same server be configured to use user-level security?

A No. Samba's `security` parameter is a `[global]` option.

New Terms

plain-text equivalent password   These are generated when the encryption algorithm used always generates the same byte string given the same input. In other words, a password always encrypts to the same value. Obtaining the encrypted version of the password enables an intruder to successfully take part in the challenge/response authentication scheme used by SMB servers such as Samba and Windows NT.

6

HOUR 7

File Sharing

by Richard Sharpe

In Hours 5, "The smb.conf File: Telling Samba What to Do," and 6, "Security Levels and Passwords," you looked at the basic format of the smb.conf file, security levels, and password handling parameters. Samba is designed to enable you to share files between machines and that is what you will explore now.

File sharing enables you to share files between machines, shown in Figure 7.1. Usually, a file server contains more disk space than any of the client workstations (Windows for Workgroups, Windows 95/98, Windows NT, and so on) that can use the server. The server can also have most of the printers connected to it, but I will leave a more complete discussion of printing until the next hour.

FIGURE 7.1

A file server sharing files and printers.

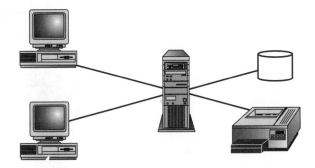

In this hour you'll go through all the steps necessary to set up file services on a Samba server. You will also explore most of the global and service parameters that affect the way in which files can be shared and accessed.

If you are following along in a step-by-step fashion, you should ensure that your clients are not using encrypted passwords, for they complicate matters unnecessarily. Please refer to Hours 6 and 14, "Windows 9x and Windows NT," for details on how to set up your clients to switch off the use of encrypted passwords. You should also log in to your client machine using the account boss. If your Samba server is your first SMB server on your network, you might get a message during logon that indicates that you could not be validated against a logon server. Ignore the message for now.

Building an `smb.conf` File

Before you can share files, you must have a working `smb.conf` file for Samba to use. In Hour 4, "Installing and Testing the Configuration," you looked at the `smb.conf` file; here you build one from scratch.

As I discussed, the `smb.conf` file has a global section and a shares section. In what follows, you use the following global section and add file share sections as you explore various ways of controlling and managing file shares:

```
[global]
  workgroup = FOWLPLAY
  netbios name =EAGLE
  server string = My first server
  guest account = pcguest
  security = user
  password level = 8
```

The first thing to notice about this `smb.conf` file is that it does not define any shares, but it still works. This `smb.conf` file sets the workgroup that Samba is in to FOWLPLAY, which you saw earlier in Hour 5, and your NetBIOS name is EAGLE.

If you install this `smb.conf` on your server and restart Samba (you need to log in to your Samba server as `root` to do this), you should be able to see the new server under Network Neighborhood in Windows 9x or Windows NT 4.0 (for Windows for Workgroups 3.11, use File Manager and select Drives, Connect Network Drive).

If you are already using Samba, do not replace your existing `smb.conf` file with the preceding. Make a backup copy first.

After you have restarted Samba (see Hour 4 for details of starting Samba on different platforms), you should see the Network Neighborhood on Windows 9x or Windows NT, shown in Figure 7.2.

FIGURE 7.2

Network Neighborhood for the FOWLPLAY workgroup.

Here, you see that your server shows up as EAGLE (which is what you called it in your `smb.conf` file) and that it is a Samba 2.0.0Beta4 Server. If you remove the `netbios name` parameter from the preceding `smb.conf` file, your server shows up with a name consisting of the first component of its DNS name. This might be what you want but will not match the examples in this hour.

If you now double-click the preceding server, you see the window in Figure 7.3.

FIGURE 7.3

Listing of shares on the Eagle file server.

This simply confirms that your Samba server has no shares, or at least none that are browsable (which I will discuss later).

Your next step is to set up a share and see what changes.

7

Setting Up a Share

To set up a share, you must add a section for the share to your smb.conf file in the share definitions area. Because Samba shares directories and the files under them, you must first find or create an appropriate directory on your server to share.

Here you are going to create a directory called /home/first-share that you tell Samba to share for you:

```
mkdir /home/first-share
```

If you are feeling adventurous, you can use a different name, but you have to make sure you change all the pathnames in what follows, and the examples in this book might be different from what you see.

Next, you add the following to the preceding smb.conf file:

```
[first-share]
    comment = My first share
    path = /home/first-share
    browsable = yes
```

Now that you have added a share to your smb.conf file, you can restart Samba, and (after a while) should be able to see the new share in Network Neighborhood, as shown in Figure 7.4.

FIGURE 7.4

Network Neighborhood shows your first share!

Great, now you can see a share on your Samba server. What else can you do? Well, before you go looking at the share, you had better put some files in it:

```
cat > /home/first-share/file-1.txt
Now is the time for all good men
To come to the aid of their country
^D
cat > /home/first-share/file-2.txt
The time has come the walrus said
To talk of many things
^D
todos /home/first-share/file-2.txt
```

Note that you might not have the `todos` utility on your server, in which case you should get a copy, or type the Perl script (on the CD accompanying this book), because you will need it.

Now that you have put some files in the share on your server, see what your client shows you. Double-click `first-share` in the Network Neighborhood window, and you see your files, as shown in Figure 7.5.

FIGURE 7.5

The first two files in your file share.

Now that you can see these files, have a look at them. Double clicking on `file-1.txt` should produce the display in Figure 7.6.

FIGURE 7.6

`file-1.txt` *has funny characters in it.*

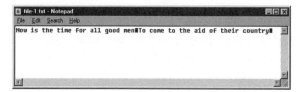

Close that window, and then double-click `file-2.txt`. You should see what appears in Figure 7.7.

FIGURE 7.7

`file-2.txt` *looks more normal.*

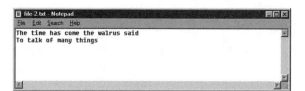

7

Why do these two files display so differently in Notepad? The problem is a consequence of the different ways in which Windows and UNIX store an end of line in text files. Under UNIX, end-of-line is represented with the newline, or NL, character (octal 012, hex 0x0A), whereas under Windows (and DOS), end-of-line is represented as a carriage return character, or CR (octal 015, hex 0x0C) followed by a newline character. When you created file-2.txt, you explicitly converted it to a DOS format text file (using todos) while leaving file-1.txt as a UNIX-format text file.

Now, although the purpose of each of the lines added to the smb.conf file might be obvious, I'll go through them and explain them in more detail.

[first-share]

This line introduces a new section that is for the share first-share. Each share is introduced as a new section, with its name in square brackets.

comment

This line provides a descriptive comment for the share. It serves to document the share in the smb.conf file and shows up in the Network Neighborhood listing.

path

This line tells Samba which part of the file system to share to clients. You should always specify a directory that exists or a file that is a symbolic link to a directory (see the following).

If the directory does not exist, Windows clients can give weird error messages when trying to access the share. For example,

```
Cannot access \\EAGLE\first-share: The network name is either
not found on the running network, or is incorrect.
```

browsable

Strictly speaking, you do not need to specify this entry, as the default is yes. You would normally use browsable only if you do not want clients to see particular shares. For those of you who cannot spell, *browsable* is a synonym for *browseable*.

To see the effect of the browsable setting, change it to

```
browsable = no
```

in your smb.conf file and restart Samba. Then go back to the FOWLPLAY Network Neighborhood window and double click the server EAGLE. Do you now see the share you have created when the window finally comes up?

Accessibility

Now that you have created a file share, you need to make it more usable. For example, browse the file share (after making it browsable again in your smb.conf file; don't forget to stop and restart Samba). Then try to copy a file into the file share, or create a new file or directory in the file share. You should find that you can't. You will now explore the reasons for that and how to change it.

The file share is great for sharing files that have been put into the file share directory by users with sufficient access rights, but client workstations cannot create files in the share. Even if you log in as root (the superuser under UNIX) you are unable to create files in the share as yet. As you will soon see, the share is read-only by default.

In order to allow clients access to the file share, you must tell Samba a few things about the file share. First, however, you must look at how Samba determines whether a client can have access to file shares.

In Hour 2, "Windows Networking," you looked at the way in which a CIFS/SMB client accesses a resource, or file share, on a server. To refresh your memory, the following steps occur, although some can be skipped:

1 The client negotiates a protocol variant to establish which variant of the CIFS/SMB protocol it understands.

2 The client might then do a logon to the network or server, depending on the protocol variant being used and the presence of logon servers. At this point the client provides a username and a password, but this step can be skipped, especially for old clients.

3 The client requests a connection to a tree, or share.

To process the client's request to connect to a share, Samba first determines whether the requested share exists. The following simple approach determines whether it does:

1 Scan the smb.conf file looking for a section that matches the requested share name. If one is found, use it.

2 If the share is not found, check to see whether it contains a [homes] section in the smb.conf file. If so, check the passwd file to see whether the share name matches a user name. If it does, the [homes] share is cloned (as detailed later in this hour), and the new share is used.

3 If the share is still not found, check to see whether the smb.conf file contains a [printers] section. If so, check whether the requested share matches a printer in the printcap file. If it does, clone the [printers] share and use the cloned share. The [printers] section is discussed in more detail in Hour 8, "Printers."

7

4 If the share is still not found, check whether a default service exists and, if so, change the default service name to match the requested service and use it.

5 If no share is found, Samba returns an invalid network name error to the client.

Next, Samba uses the following procedure to determine whether a client should be given access to the share found, and who they will be given access as. The steps are tried in order, with the process terminating successfully with the first step that succeeds. If all the steps fail, access to the share is denied.

1 If the client has submitted a username/password pair that validates, access is allowed to the share as the validated user. Some older clients can submit their user-names using the \\\server\\service%username syntax.

2 If the client has already submitted a valid username and now supplies a correct password (on the share request), access to the share is allowed as the validated username.

3 The client's NetBIOS name and any previously used usernames are validated using the operating system's standard mechanisms (or the smbpassword file) with the supplied password. If any validate successfully, access to the share is allowed as the validated username.

4 If the client has previously validated a username/password pair with the server (using a SessionSetupandX) and the client passed the validation token in the share access request, access to the share is allowed as the username indicated in the token. This step is skipped if the share specifies revalidation (revalidate = yes).

5 If a user = field has been specified on the share, the client has supplied a pass-word, and the combination of username specified in the share and password vali-dates, access to the share is allowed as the specified user.

However, if the service is a guest only service, access to the service is allowed as the username specified as the guest account without going through any of the preceding steps. Any supplied password is ignored.

If the user chosen as the accessing user is in an invalid user list (described later this hour), the request to connect to the share is rejected at this point.

This procedure allows Samba to determine under which account access to files in the share is allowed. However, access to shares and the mode of access to files allowed is further controlled by a number of parameters in the smb.conf file.

Share Accessibility Parameters

The following parameters affect access to shares by clients in one way or another. Most Samba administrators do not use many of these parameters. As always, the final list of such parameters and the final word on their function rests with the manual pages on smb.conf for the current version of Samba. You should use man smb.conf to check these parameters.

admin users

This share-level parameter sets the users who are granted administrative privileges for the share. When they access the share, they do all file operations as root.

Names starting with @ are interpreted as an NIS netgroup and then as a UNIX group if not found in NIS. Names starting with + are interpreted as UNIX groups, whereas names starting with & are interpreted as NIS groups.

This parameter can be very dangerous, as any user in the admin users list can do anything they want, including deleting all files in the share.

By default, there are no administrative users for a share. An example of using this parameter is

```
admin users = root, fred
```

which specifies that root and fred are admin users.

default service

This global parameter sets the name of the default service. The default service is used if the share requested by a client cannot be found. If the default service is used to satisfy a share connection request, its name is changed to match the requested share.

Typically, the default service would have the parameters guest ok and read only set.

This parameter has no default value. An example of using this parameter is

```
default service = lastchance
```

which sets the default service to the service called lastchance.

guest account

This global parameter sets the name of the guest account. It is often set to pcguest and must exist in whatever account database is used on the server (for example, passwd file, NIS, and so on). Typically, this account doesn't have a valid password, so no one can log in to it, either from UNIX or from a client. The account can be used only to control access to files.

7

This parameter can be set in the global section and in individual share sections. Guest accounts specified in a share section override any global one.

The default for this parameter is specified at compile time, and it set to *nobody* by default. An example of using this parameter is

```
guest account = pcguest
```

which specifies that the account called pcguest should be used as the guest account.

guest ok

This share-level parameter specifies whether access to a share can be obtained without submitting a username and password.

When clients are granted guest access, they access files under the share as the guest account.

A synonym for guest ok is public.

The default value for this parameter is no. An example of using this parameter is

```
guest ok = yes
```

which specifies that it is permissible to access the share using the guest account.

guest only

This share-level parameter specifies that only guest connections are allowed to a particular share. It must be used in conjunction with guest ok or public.

The default value for this parameter is no. An example of using this parameter is

```
guest only = yes
```

which specifies that this service can only be accessed using the guest account.

hosts allow

This parameter sets the list of hosts that are allowed to access services. If set in the global section, it applies to all services, regardless of any setting specified by individual services. If not set in the global section, it can be set for individual services.

Hosts can be specified by name or IP number. The full syntax for this parameter is the same as that in the TCP Wrappers hosts_allow file. Please check the man pages (man hosts_allow) for more details.

There is no default value for this parameter. An example of using this parameter is

```
hosts allow = 192.1.1. graham.goodies.com
```

which specifies that any host in the subnet 192.1.1.0/24 can access the share as well as the system called graham.goodies.com.

hosts deny

This parameter is the opposite of hosts allow. Hosts listed in this parameter are not allowed to access services unless a specific service overrides this list with their own list of allowed hosts. When the hosts deny and hosts allow parameters conflict, hosts allow takes precedence.

There is no default value for this parameter. An example of using this parameter is

```
Hosts deny 192.1.1. badhost.bad-company.com
```

which specifies that access to the share is not allowed for any host in the subnet 192.1.1.0/24 as well as badhost.bad-company.com.

invalid users

This share-level parameter specifies a list of users that should not be allowed to access the service. This parameter uses the same syntax as admin users preceding.

There is no default value for this parameter. An example of using this parameter is

```
invalid users = root fred @bin
```

which specifies that the users root, fred, and any user in the group bin are not allowed to access the share.

max connections

This share-level parameter specifies the maximum number of clients that can connect to the share. If set to a value greater than 0, no more clients are allowed to access the share after the specified maximum number of users has connected to the share. When the number of connected users drops below the specified value, new connections are allowed up to the specified maximum. If set to 0, no limits are placed on the number of connections that can be made.

This parameter can limit the load on a Samba server and can also provide a measure of license usage enforcement if you are sharing licensed software. Be aware that you are limiting the number of connected users, not the number of active users. Also a user who connects to the share at the beginning of the day and stays connected all day while doing nothing still consumes one of those max connections.

The default value for this parameter is 0, which, as stated before, allows unlimited connections to the share. An example of using the share is

7

```
max connections = 100
```

which specifies that no more than 100 connections are allowed to the share.

read list

This share-level parameter is a list of the users who are given read-only access to the share. That is, they are not given write access to the share, even if the share is writable.

There is no default for this parameter. An example of using this parameter is

```
read list = fred @guests
```

which specifies that fred and all the users in the group guests are given read-only access to the share. That is, they are unable to write it.

read only

This share-level parameter is the opposite of writable. When set, it indicates that clients may not write to a share.

By default, this parameter is yes, which means that the share is read-only. That is, if you do not provide a value for a share, it is read-only. An example of using this share is

```
read only = no
```

which means that the share can be written. An alternative way of specifying the same is

```
writable = yes
```

valid users

This share-level parameter lists the users who are allowed to access the file share. It uses the same syntax as admin users.

By default, this parameter is empty, which means that any user can access the share. An example of using this parameter is

```
valid users = fred @accounts
```

which specifies that the user fred and all users in the accounts group are the only ones allowed to access the share.

writable

This share-level parameter (and its synonym writeable for those who can't spell) indicates whether clients can write to the share. See also read only.

By default, this parameter is set to no, which means that a share is read-only by default. Examples of using this share are

```
writable = yes
writeable = yes
read only = no
```

which all specify that the share may be written to by anyone who has the permission write to the files and directories in the share.

write list

This share-level parameter specifies a list of users who are given read-write access to a share, despite the value of the read only parameter.

If a user is in both the read list and the write list, he is given write access.

By default, this parameter has no value, which means that all users are governed by the value of the read only parameter. An example of using this parameter is

```
write list = root @admin
```

which specifies that at least the user root and all the users of the admin group have write access to the share.

Making Your first-share More Accessible

Now that you have looked at the parameters that affect accessibility of shares, you are ready to fix the problems you encountered in accessibility earlier, where you could not write to your first-share.

This problem arose because, by default, a share has

```
writable = no
```

set. To see that neither file nor directory privileges are causing the problem, look at the UNIX privileges for the directory that is shared, and then change them to world RWX (0777 for simplicity). Unless you have changed your umask, /home/first-share on your Samba server looks like this:

```
ls -al /home/first-share
total 4
drwxr-xr-x   2 root      root          1024 Jan  5 14:23 .
drwxr-xr-x  17 root      root          1024 Jan  5 14:23 ..
-rw-r--r--   1 root      root            69 Jan  5 14:22 file-1.txt
-rw-r--r--   1 root      root            59 Jan  5 14:23 file-2.txt
```

Now, change the permissions on the directory to 0777 with

```
chmod 0777 /home/first-share
```

This should allow any UNIX user to write to the directory, as it sets group and world (other) read, write, and execute access.

7

But, when you try to create a file in the share from your client, you get what's shown in Figure 7.8.

FIGURE 7.8

Access is denied, despite the directory being wide open.

If you add the following to your first-share (and restart Samba), you can allow clients to write to the share:

```
writable = yes
```

Try it! You now can create directories and files in the share, as shown in Figure 7.9.

FIGURE 7.9

With the share writable, you can cre-ate folders in it.

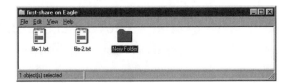

Over on the Samba server, your shared directory now looks like this:

```
ls -al /home/first-share
total 4
drwxrwxrwx   2 root     root         1024 Jan  5 14:23 .
drwxr-xr-x  17 root     root         1024 Jan  5 14:23 ..
drwxr-xr-x   2 boss     boss         1024 Jan  6 01:09 New Folder
-rw-r--r--   1 root     root           69 Jan  5 14:22 file-1.txt
-rw-r--r--   1 root     root           59 Jan  5 14:23 file-2.txt
```

Your New Folder has been created as a directory and is owned by you, with group owner as your group. But this is possible only because you set the directory /home/first-share to mode 0777, which is quite dangerous.

You could set many of the other parameters to affect access to first-share, including

- write list The list of users who have write access to the share
- valid users The list of users who are allowed to access the share

As an example, your share might become

```
[first-share]
comment = My first share
    path = /home/first-share
    browsable = yes
    writable = yes
    valid users = boss joe +users
    write list = root boss
```

This modifies first-share to specify that boss, joe, and any user in the UNIX group
users can access the share, whereas only boss and fred can write to the share.

Now you must look at how file permissions are handled by Samba, so you can see how
UNIX file permissions interact with requests to read or write files.

Permissions

As you saw in the previous section, Samba first applies large-grained access checks, such
as read or write and user-based access to shares. When a requested operation, such as
opening a file for read or write, has passed these access checks, it still has to satisfy normal operating system restrictions on file and directory access. These are based on the
user that Samba has determined is accessing the file share.

That is, normal UNIX permissions apply to all file operations after Samba has determined accessibility.

Recall that earlier you were able to bring up the files file-1.txt and file-2.txt in
Notepad. This was because they were world-readable and thus accessible by anyone.
Here is a detailed listing of the share directory again:

```
ls -al /home/first-share
total 4
drwxr-xr-x    2 root       root         1024 Jan  5 14:23 .
drwxr-xr-x   17 root       root         1024 Jan  5 14:23 ..
drwxr-xr-x    2 boss       boss         1024 Jan  6 01:09 New Folder
-rw-r--r--    1 root       root           69 Jan  5 14:22 file-1.txt
-rw-r--r--    1 root       root           59 Jan  5 14:23 file-2.txt
```

As you can see, the files file-1.txt and file-2.txt have mode 0644, meaning that
they are not group- or world-writable. If you try to modify those files from a client, you
will be unable to. Bring one of them up in Notepad and try to modify them. When do
you get an error message? It should happen when you try to save your changes.
Eventually, Notepad gives you the error message shown in Figure 7.10.

7

FIGURE 7.10

Notepad cannot save
file-1.txt.

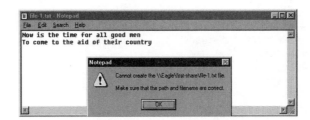

This happens because of the way Notepad tries to save the file. It tries to create the file file-1.txt in the file share, but that file already exists, and you do not have permission to write the file, so the operation fails.

If you were to try to save the file with a name that did not already exist in the directory (or share; the terms are interchangeable from the point of view of someone administering Samba), Notepad would be happy, and a new file would be created.

What you are seeing here is this: After all the accessibility checks that Samba applies, it also checks the normal file system permissions that the user (who Samba regards is connected to the file share) has to the files in the share!

In particular, if you do not have read access to directories, you will be unable to see their contents, despite being able to see the directories themselves. Typically, you get Access Denied messages when trying to browse such directories.

Now, when files and directories are created on a Samba share, who owns them, and what permissions do they inherit? Refer back to the long listing of the first-share directory, and look at the entry for New Folder. Here is that entry again:

```
drwxr-xr-x   2 boss      boss          1024 Jan  6 01:09 New Folder
```

You own the directory, which is in your primary group and has mode 0755.

Now you have to look at UNIX file modes a little, because Samba wants to use numbers such as the 0755 shown previously. Here is what they mean and how to construct them.

Every file in a UNIX file system has an owner, a group owner, and file modes (sometimes referred to as permissions) that consist of four parts:

- The SETUID, SETGID, and T bits.
- The user, or owner permissions, which can be any combination of read, write, and execute. They specify what access rights the owner has to the file.
- The group permissions, which can be any combination of read, write and execute. They specify what access rights anyone in the group that the file is in has to the file.

- The other, or world permissions, which can be any combination of read, write, or execute. They specify what access rights anyone who is not the owner and who is not in the owner's group has to the file.

A file's mode is usually displayed as the three letters RWX and dash (-). So, RWX means read, write, and execute, whereas R-X means read and execute. To change a mode, express it as a series of 12 bits in octal. Thus a file's mode is represented as four octal digits, where the first digit is encoded the following way:

4 = SETUID, 2 = SETGID, 1 = T or STICKY bit

The remaining three digits (the permissions bits proper) are encoded in the following way:

4 = read, 2 = write, 1 = execute

When you want to construct a particular mode for a file, you simply add together the encodings for the permissions you want. So, RWX adds up to octal 7, whereas RW- adds up to 6, R-X adds up to 5, and so on.

Thus, a mode of 1755 means

- The file has the T bit set, or the directory has the sticky bit set.
- The owner has read, write, and execute access.
- Members of the group that owns the file have read and execute access.
- Everyone else has read and execute access.

Finally, a mode of 0755 would be listed by *ls -al* as RWXR-XR-X.

Samba handles the creation modes of files and directories separately. A number of share-level parameters can be set to control both ownership and the mode of created files and directories.

File and Directory Creation Parameters

The following sections list many of the Samba share-level parameters that affect permissions and ownership of files and directories created by Samba. As always, the final list of such parameters and the final word on their function rests with the manual pages on smb.conf for the current version of Samba.

create mask, create mode

These share-level parameters are synonyms for each other, and they control the permissions that are set when files are created. The value given is a bit mask that is used to mask against the UNIX mask calculated from the DOS mode requested.

7

Any bit not set in the mask is removed from the permissions (modes) of the file when it is created.

By default the create mask has the value 0744, which specifies that for new files, the owner gets RWX permissions, whereas members of the group owner of the file and all other users get R-- permissions only.

An example of using this parameter is

```
create mask = 0755
```

which specifies that the owner (or user) gets RWX permissions, members of the group owner of the file get R-X permissions, and everyone else (world, or others) gets R-X permissions.

directory mask, directory mode

These share-level parameters are synonyms for each other, and they control the permissions that are set when directories are created. The value given is a bit mask that is used to mask against the UNIX mask calculated from the DOS mode requested.

Any bit not set in the mask is removed from the permissions (modes) of the file when it is created.

By default, the directory mask is set to 0755. An example of using this parameter is

```
directory mask = 0744
```

which specifies that the owner (or user) gets RWX permissions, whereas members of the group and everyone else (world, or others) get R-- permissions only.

> The execute bit has a special meaning for directories. It allows a user to change to that directory. Thus, if users do not have X access to a directory, they can open files in the directory if they have read access to the files, but they cannot change to the directory. However, because of the way Samba and Windows handle browsing folders, the X bit does not matter for access from Windows.

force create mode

This share-level parameter allows you to force certain permission (mode) bits on when files are created under a share. You can do this by performing a bitwise or of the bits specified here with the bits that are calculated from the create mask. Note that this means force create mode overrides create mask.

By default, this parameter has the value 0000, which means that no extra mode bits are forced into the `create mask/mode`. An example of using this parameter is

```
force create mode = 0755
```

which means that the created files have a mode of at least 0755 (or RWXR-XR-X).

force directory mode

This share-level parameter allows you to force certain permission (mode) bits on when directories are created under a share. You can do this by performing a bitwise or of the bits specified here with the bits that are calculated from the `directory mask`. Note that this means `force directory mode` overrides `directory mask`.

By default, this parameter has the value 0000, which means that no extra mode bits are forced into the `directory mask/mode`. An example of using this parameter is

```
force directory mode = 0755
```

which means that the created directories have a mode of at least 0755 (or RWXR-XR-X).

force group

This share-level parameter specifies a UNIX group name that is used as the default primary group for all users accessing the service.

By default, this parameter has no value, which means that all new files and directories are given in a group owner by applying the normal UNIX rules (if the SETGID bit is set on the parent directory, use that directory's group, otherwise use the creator's primary group).

An example of using this parameter is

```
force group = users
```

which means that all new files on the share are created with a group owner of users.

force user

This share-level parameter specifies a UNIX user name that is used as the default user for all users accessing the service.

By default, this parameter has no value, which means that all new files in the share are owned by the UNIX user that is deemed to have connected to the share (see the section "Accessibility" earlier this hour). An example of using this parameter is

```
force user = boss
```

which means that all new files in the share are owned by boss.

7

Some Examples

Now that you have seen many of the parameters that affect the way Samba handles the creation and accessing of files under file shares, how might you use them? Here are some ideas.

To force all files created in a particular directory to be owned by a particular group, use the force group parameter. For example, if you want all files and directories created under a particular share to be owned by the group accounts, use the following parameter for the share:

```
force group = accounts
```

To prevent all files and directories created under a particular share from having any world permissions (perhaps to prevent UNIX users from accessing files in the share), use the following parameters for the share:

```
create mask = 0750
directory mask = 0750
```

You have to use both of these parameters, because Samba handles file creation and directory creation separately.

Modify your first-share to include some of these changes:

```
[first-share]
comment = My first share
    path = /home/first-share
    browsable = yes
    writable = yes
    create mask = 0750
    create directory = 0750
    force group = users
```

After you modify your smb.conf to change first-share to the parameters noted previously and restart Samba, create the file new-file.txt and the directory another-new-folder from a client.

You should now see something such as the following when you do a full listing of the share directory:

```
ls -al /home/first-share
total 6
drwxrwxrwx   4 root     root         1024 Jan  6 16:58 .
drwxr-xr-x  17 root     root         1024 Jan  5 14:23 ..
drwxr-x---   2 boss     boss         1024 Jan  6 14:53 New Folder
drwxr-x---   2 boss     users        1024 Jan  6 16:58 another-new-folder
-rw-r--r--   1 root     root           69 Jan  5 14:22 file-1.txt
-rw-r--r--   1 root     root           59 Jan  5 14:23 file-2.txt
-rwxr-----   1 boss     users           0 Jan  6 16:58 new-file.txt
```

Notice that `new-file.txt` and `another-new-folder` both have a group owner of users, and neither of them have any world permissions.

Finally, you have set the directory `/home/first-share` to mode 0777, which is very dangerous. A better way to allow you to create files on the share from clients is to change the group owner of the directory to a group you are in.

To do this, you must find out which groups you are in on the UNIX machine. So, if you logged in as `boss` on your client, you must find out which groups `boss` is in:

```
groups boss
boss : boss wheel users
```

Then change the group owner of the directory `/home/first-share` to be one of those groups. `users` is a good candidate, especially if you plan to allow other people to access and share files on the share. You need to set the group write bit on the directory as well.

To affect these changes, use the following commands:

```
chgrp users /home/first-share
chmod 0775 /home/first-share
```

If you want to ensure that these changes occur for all files and directories under the share, include the `-R` flag with the `chgrp` and `chmod` commands.

Finally, this illustrates an aspect of Samba that is very useful: You can perform management of the files in your file shares from UNIX. This means that you have access to all the standard UNIX facilities, including scripting (even Perl) as well as `cron` files.

For example, in a student lab where students are required to submit their labwork (by copying it to the `\\eagle\labwork` share) by a particular date and time, the following shell script

1. Changes the ownership of the files to the instructor so that students cannot modify their submission after the deadline.

2. Sends mail to the instructor pointing out which students have not turned in their labwork.

```
#!/bin/sh
# Figure out who has not handed in their labwork and then change
# the owner so students cannot submit after the deadline.
# Finally send mail to the instructor about those who failed to
# hand in their work. Obviously, while this script is running,
# there is a small chance that someone can resubmit.  Could be
# fixed by shutting Samba down. First, stop any students from
# adding files to the directory from PCs.
chmod 1700 /home/labwork
# Next, figure out who owns the submitted work
```

7

```
ls -ld /shares/labwork ¦ tr -s " " " " ¦ cut -f3 -d" " >
➥/tmp/submitted.$$
# Now change the owner of all those files.
chown -R instructor /home/labwork/*
# Now figure out who has not submitted, based on a list of
# students in the course
diff -y /tmp/submitted.$$ /home/instructor/students ¦ grep \< ¦ \
mail -s "Students who did not submit their labwork on time"
➥instructor
rm -f /tmp/submitted.$$
```

This shell script is an example only. It needs modification for the real world where
instructors often have multiple classes, and so on.

Special File Services

Now that you have looked at how to create file services, how to control access to them,
and how to handle access permissions for services, it is time to look at some special services that Samba provides.

Clients like to access their home directories, and if Samba had to declare each user's
home directory as a separate file share, life would very difficult for administrators.
Imagine having to add a section to the smb.conf file for each new user you add to the
system, and then having to restart Samba.

To make life easier for all overworked administrators, Samba provides two special share
sections: a [homes] section and a [printers] section. I will discuss the [printers] section in the next hour and look at the [homes] section in detail here.

When a client requests a connection to a file share, the existing file shares are scanned. If
a match is found, that share is used. However, if no match is found, the requested share
is treated as a username and looked up in the password facility. If the name exists and
validates, a share is created by cloning the [homes] share. This means that the new share
takes most of its parameters from the [homes] share.

When the new share is created, its name is changed to the username, and the share's path
is set to the user's home directory if none is set in the [homes] section.

The following shows an example of a [homes] share in the smb.conf file:

```
[homes]
    comment = Home Directories
    browsable = no
     writable = yes
```

This is all you need to allow clients to access their home directories. Add the preceding to your smb.conf file, and restart Samba. You should then be able to bring up a DOS prompt under Windows, and issue the command

```
net use h: \\EAGLE\homes
```

after which you are able to access all the files in your home directory from your PC.

Filename Handling and Mangling

UNIX file names and DOS/Windows file names follow different rules.

UNIX allows almost any character in a filename, except for a directory separator (/) and escape, and distinguishes between uppercase and lowercase characters in names. It also allows filenames to be very long (up to 255 characters long). In addition, pathnames can be very long under UNIX, often up to 1,024 characters.

DOS (6.22 and below), on the other hand, has the 8.3 restriction, where the filename must be no longer than eight characters, and the extension can't be more than three characters long. In addition, DOS case folds characters to uppercase when dealing with file and directory names. DOS also has restrictions on pathname lengths that are considerably smaller than what most UNIX systems allow. Windows for Workgroups follows the DOS restrictions.

Windows 95 (with DOS 95) and Windows NT have removed many of these restrictions, allowing filenames to be longer than 11 characters, as well as allowing both uppercase and lowercase characters in files. However, both Windows 9x and Windows NT have restrictions on filename and pathname lengths that are lower than what UNIX allows. Windows 95 truncates file names to 127 characters. When the total pathname exceeds 255 characters (including the server and share names), it refuses to create any further files or folders. Windows NT has the same restrictions. However, both Windows 95 and Windows NT can deal with longer filenames and pathnames if they already exist on the Samba share (perhaps created under UNIX).

To provide for compatibility with older clients (DOS, Windows for Workgroups, PATH-WORKS, and so on), as well as applications that depend on 8.3 filenames Samba has many share-level parameters to control the way in which UNIX filenames and pathnames are reported to clients. It also has parameters that control the way in which case is handled when new files are created.

7

Samba refers to this as *name mangling*, and the following general approach is taken:

- The first five alphanumeric characters before the rightmost period are forced to uppercase and appear as the first five characters of the mangled name.
- A tilde (~) is appended to the first part of the mangled name, followed by a two-character hash of the original root name (that is, minus the final extension). However, the final extension is included in the hash calculation if it contains any uppercase characters or is longer than three characters. The tilde character can be changed to some other character (using the `mangling char` parameter) if users object or applications have problems with tildes.
- The first three alphanumeric characters of the final extension are forced to uppercase and appear as the extension of the mangled name. If there are no periods in the filename, the mangled name has no extension.
- Files which have UNIX names that begin with a period are treated as DOS hidden files. Their mangled names are similar to the others I've discussed, except the leading period is removed and an extension of ___ (that is, three underscores) is added, regardless of the original extension.

The following shows an example of name mangling done by a Windows 95 DOS box while listing your `first-share` after a couple of new files and folders have been added to it. The mangled names are shown in the left column, whereas the full names are shown in the right column.

```
E:\>dir
Volume in drive E is FIRST-SHARE
Directory of E:\
file-1   txt          69  01-05-99  2:22p  file-1.txt
file-2   txt          59  01-05-99  2:23p  file-2.txt
NEWFO~YX      <DIR>        01-06-99  2:53p  New Folder
File-1   txt          69  01-06-99  5:33p  File-1.txt
new-file txt           0  01-06-99  4:58p  new-file.txt
ANOTH~9Y      <DIR>        01-06-99  4:58p  another-new-folder
A-FIL~BH TXT          24  01-07-99 12:45a  a-file-with-a-long-name.txt
         5 file(s)         221 bytes
         2 dir(s)   33,488,896 bytes free
E:\>
```

By default, Samba 2.0 operates the same way as Windows NT server: it is not case sensitive but case preserving. That is, in opening files, it matches filenames in a way that's not case sensitive, but when new files are created, Samba preserves the case presented by the client.

In most cases the defaults applied by Samba are fine, but you might need to change some of them for specific clients or applications.

The following parameters control how names are handled. As always, the final list of such parameters and the final word on their function rests with the manual pages on smb.conf for the current version of Samba.

mangled names

This service-level parameter controls whether UNIX names that are not DOS compatible should be mapped to DOS-compatible names. By default, Samba mangles names for clients that cannot handle non-DOS names.

The default value for this parameter is yes. That is, by default, non-DOS names are mangled to their DOS-compatible forms.

Setting this parameter to no specifies that Samba should not provide DOS-compatible names for non–DOS-compatible files. If you do this, DOS clients and DOS command prompts simply see the name of the file truncated to the normal DOS rules.

mangle case

This service-level parameter controls whether names are mangled if they have characters not in the default case. If this parameter is set, names such as *Mail* would be mangled to the default case.

The default value for this parameter is no. This specifies that no mangling of mixed case names be performed.

mangling char

This service level parameter specifies the character that Samba uses as the mangling character when it mangles names. The default is the tilde character (~).

An example of using this parameter is

```
mangle char = ^
```

which specifies that Samba should use the caret (^) character rather than the tilde.

case sensitive

This service-level parameter controls whether Samba regards filenames as case sensitive. If set to no, Samba must do a case insensitive filename match for all filenames passed to it by clients.

By default, this parameter is set to no.

7

default case

This service-level parameter controls the default case of new files and should be used in conjunction with `preserve case`.

The default case is lowercase.

preserve case

This service-level parameter controls the behavior of Samba when files are created. If set to yes, the case that the client requests is used (including mixed case); otherwise, the case of new files is forced to that specified with the default case.

The default behavior is to preserve case.

short preserve case

This service-level parameter controls the behavior of Samba when files with DOS-compatible (that is, 8.3 and all in uppercase) names are created. If set to yes, such files are created with uppercase names; otherwise, their names are forced to the default case.

This parameter can be used with `preserve case = yes` to allow long filenames to retain their case, whereas short names are created in lowercase.

The default value of this parameter is yes.

File Locking

By default, Samba supports two types of file locking. These are share modes and opportunistic locks, or *oplocks*.

Share modes support the standard DOS/Windows file open sharing requests of `DENY_DOS`, `DENY_ALL`, `DENY_READ`, `DENY_WRITE`, `DENY_NONE`, and `DENY_FCB`.

Under versions of UNIX that support shared memory (most versions of UNIX), share modes support is implemented using shared memory, which is very fast. If your version of UNIX does not support shared memory, share modes support is implemented using lock files, which can be very slow.

You most likely never have to turn share modes off, but in the event that you do, they can be turned off on a per-share basis with the following command:

```
share modes = no
```

Oplocks are a performance enhancement introduced with Windows NT Server. They allow clients to cache many file operations as long as that client is the only one accessing a particular file. When another client opens the same file, the server has to send an oplock break to the client with the oplock, which forces that client to stop local caching.

When clients can obtain oplocks, performance enhancements of 30% or more are possible, because clients can do aggressive caching on file operations (including caching opens and closes and possibly reordering some operations).

With Samba, oplocks are enabled by default. In some cases, client programs fail to operate properly in the presence of oplocks, so you might want to switch them off. They can be switched off for individual shares with the `oplocks` command:

```
oplocks = false
```

They can also be switched off for individual files with the `veto oplock files` parameter:

```
veto oplocks files = /*.mbx/
```

To complete the picture, SGI's Irix 6.5.2f now has kernel-level oplock support, and Linux and FreeBSD might have it soon as well. Samba can detect the presence of kernel oplocks and use them if available. This allows oplocks to be broken whenever a local UNIX process or an NFS operation access a file that `smbd` has locked, thus providing more complete data consistency between SMB, NFS, and local file accesses.

Although you should never need to touch the parameter, `kernel oplocks` can be switched off with

```
kernel oplocks = off
```

Symbolic Links

By default, Samba follows symlinks in the UNIX file system that are contained within the shared directory tree, but doesn't follow symlinks to files/directories outside that directory.

Two share-level parameters control this behavior. They are `follow symlinks` and `wide links`.

By default, they are set to yes and no respectively.

Setting `follow symlinks` to no stops all symlinks being followed, with some slight loss in performance.

Setting `wide links` to yes allows links outside the shared directory tree to be followed.

7

Handling CD-ROMs

A problem with sharing CD-ROMs is that they have to be mounted into the file system on the Samba server. If a user changes the CD in a CD-ROM drive and wants to access the new CD, someone or something has to intervene on your Samba server and mount the CD. Wouldn't it be great if the CD could be mounted when the client accesses the CD-ROM file share?

Well, Samba has such a capability, with its preexec/postexec and root preexec/root postexec commands. These parameters allow specific UNIX commands to execute when a client connects to a file service and when a client disconnects from a file service, respectively. The root version simply executes the command as root.

A CD-ROM service might look like this:

```
[cdrom]
    comment = CDROM, automounts when connected to
    browsable = yes
    read only = yes
    path = /mnt/cdrom
    root preexec = /bin/mount /dev/hdd /mnt/cdrom
    root postexec = /bin/umount /mnt/cdrom
```

Now of course, the actual device used (/dev/hdd) is specific to your type of system (this one is for a Linux system with the CD on the second IDE controller as a slave device).

With such a service, users are able to change the CD in the CD-ROM on the server and simply remap it (for example, with net use /d v: and then net use v: \\EAGLE\cdrom).

Other Parameters

The following parameters are all related to file sharing in some way, but don't fit neatly into any of the preceding sections.

maxopenfiles

This global parameter controls the maximum number of open files that one smbd file-serving process may have open for a client. As of Samba 2.0.0, the default value for this parameter is 10,000 files, although smbd sets it to a more sensible value if the OS does not support that many open files. So, under Linux, **maxopenfiles** gets set by default to about 246.

Prior to the aforementioned version of Samba, maxopenfiles was a compile-time parameter.

nis homedir and homedir map

These global parameters tell Samba to hand out the location of home directories using NIS. They are used in situations where the user's home directory is located on a remote server and would be accessed via NFS by the Samba server.

As long as the actual home directory servers are running Samba as well, a logon server can return the home share as being on a different server. It does this by consulting the NIS map specified in homedir map. This works only when there is a working NIS server and Samba is running as a logon server.

The default values for nis homedir and homedir map are false and auto.home respectively.

ole locking compatibility

This global parameter allows you to turn off OLE compatibility byte range lock manipulation that Samba provides. Some UNIX lock managers can crash or have other problems when Samba does ole locking compatibility, which is why you might want to switch it off.

The default value for this parameter is yes.

strip dot

This global parameter controls whether Samba strips trailing periods (dots) from UNIX filenames. Some CD-ROMs have filenames ending with a single dot.

The default value for this parameter is no.

Summary

In this hour you looked at creating file shares and many of the parameters that control how file shares are made available to clients. You also looked at how files are created and accessed on those file shares, as well as how to perform more advanced functions with file shares.

Along the way, you looked in some detail at the steps Samba uses to determine whether shares exist, whether a particular client can access a requested share, and whether that client can read or write files in the requested share. With this information you are now in a position to debug many problems with the configuration of Samba.

In the next hour you will look at how to create printer shares, how to configure Samba to support automatic installation of printer drivers under Windows 9x, and how to print from UNIX systems to Windows clients that have printers connected to them.

7

Q&A

Q My `smb.conf` file has a file share called [docs] in it. This share is intended for document writers to save their documents in. The directory has a group owner of docs, which all the document writers are in, and the mode of the directory is 0770, but no one can write into the directory. What have I done wrong?

A Do you have one of the following parameters in the share definition?
```
writable = yes
writeable = yes
read only = no
```

Remember, a share is read-only by default, and you have to make it writable before writes are allowed, regardless of directory or file permissions in the share.

Q I have defined a new share called kits, but no one can connect to it. They keep getting a message: `The specified share directory cannot be found.` Other users get a dialog box saying `Cannot access \\server\kits ....` What could the problem be?

A Check the path statement in your [kits] share section. If the path does not exist or the users do not have access to it, they can get these sorts of messages.

Q What is the smallest [HOMES] section you can get away with? Hint, if the share is not browsable, it doesn't really need a comment.

A You need to make the share writable, so users can at least write into their home shares and so the smallest [HOMES] section has two lines, for example:
```
[homes]
  writable = yes
```

Q How would you stop files created in the [HOMES] share from being created world (other) readable?

A Here you have to use the create mode and directory mode parameters to ensure you handle files and directories correctly. So, simply add the following to your [HOMES] share:
```
Create mode = 0750
Directory mode = 0740
```

This takes away any world permissions.

Q How would you ensure that only machines A, B, and C can access the file share [DOCS]?

A To ensure that only machines A, B, and C can access any file share, simply add a hosts allow statement to the share. Remember, you can use names or IP addresses, netgroups, and so on. So add the following to the [DOCS] share:
```
Hosts allow = A B C
```

HOUR 8

Printers

by Richard Sharpe

In Hour 7, "File Sharing," you looked at file sharing and how to configure it. In this hour, you look at printing with Samba in some detail. Samba's printing philosophy is that if UNIX can print it, Samba can too.

Printing with Samba encompasses the areas of

- Printing styles
- Printer share configuration
- Automatic printer driver installation
- Printing from UNIX to Windows systems

Figure 8.1 shows how versatile Samba can be, in that it supports printing from Windows (and DOS) clients to printers attached to UNIX systems and enables UNIX systems to print to printers attached to Windows systems.

FIGURE 8.1

Printing with Samba in a diverse environment.

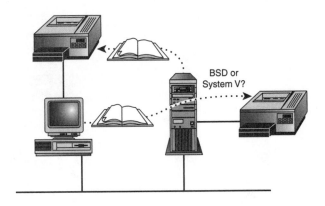

BSD or
System V?

I will explore each of these areas and configure printing on your Samba server.

If you have not yet read Hour 7, you should go back and do so, because I will build on many of the concepts presented in that hour.

Samba and Printing

From the point of view of a CIFS/SMB client, printing involves opening a file on a special file share, writing to it, and then closing that file. What happens to the file after it is closed by the client is of no concern to the client, but users generally would like such files to be printed. When you configure a print share under Samba, it takes care of getting files printed when they are closed. Figure 8.2 provides a more detailed look at printing from a CIFS/SMB client.

FIGURE 8.2

A more detailed view of printing from a client.

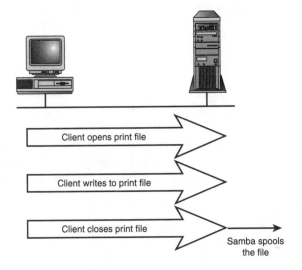

Client opens print file

Client writes to print file

Client closes print file

Samba spools
the file

As you see in Figure 8.2, the steps taken by a client in printing a file are as follows:

1. The client opens a file for writing on the printer share. Thus the server must provide file system space where the file can be stored

2. The client writes the print file. It can use any CIFS/SMB operations. A perverse client might write a lot of data, and then seek back to the beginning of the file and overwrite some data.

3. The client finally closes the file, at which point the server sends the print job to the printing system (spools the job).

Some clients, such as Windows 95, open print files on printer shares with blank (that is "") filenames. Don't be confused by this if you are poring through an smbd log file.

Apart from printing the files of course, clients also often want to be able to query the status of print queues. Samba supports this by returning print queue status information when a client requests that information.

So, because a print share is basically a file share with some extra attributes, you already know most of what you need to create a printer share. Almost all you need to add to a file share is the printable parameter. Here is a first try at a print share:

```
[first-printer]
    comment = My first printer
    path = /var/spool/samba
    printable = yes
```

Why does a print share need a path? Well, the files that the client prints need to go somewhere in the file system while they are being written. Typically, this directory is world writable and would have the sticky (t) bit set, so people cannot delete files they do not own.

Now when you restart Samba, what do you see? Figure 8.3 shows what you would see in Windows 9x or Windows NT if you bring up Network Neighborhood and double-click EAGLE.

FIGURE 8.3

Your first-printer shows up.

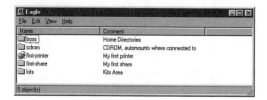

As you can see, your printer shows up. If you configure a printer on your client and print something to this share, what happens? You run into a couple of problems. The first is that Samba assumes that the printer associated with this share is called first-printer. Because this printer is unlikely to exist at this stage, the file you printed ends up in the directory specified in the path parameter and sits there. Here is a detailed listing of the directory /var/spool/samba after a file was printed to first-printer:

```
ls -al /var/log/samba
total 14
drwxrwxrwt   2 root      root      1024 Jan  8 12:09 .
drwxr-xr-x  14 root      root      1024 Dec 30 15:45 ..
-rwxr--r--   1 rsharpe   sharpe   12240 Jan  8 11:59 rjspc1.a00652
```

To fix this problem, you can add the printer parameter to tell Samba what printer to use. For example, to direct print jobs to lp, use the following parameter in the printer share:

```
printer = lp
```

If you add such a parameter to your first-printer share and the printer type is the same as you defined on your client (that is, the client has the correct driver) and you restart Samba, you should see your print jobs appear on the printer the next time you print to that queue.

Unfortunately, the first job you sent to the printer is never queued, because Samba spools a job only when it is closed. The first job sent simply sits in the directory specified by the path until you delete it.

To see that printing is indeed working, stop the queue on your Samba server; for example, if you have a BSD-derived printing system, try:

```
lpc stop lp
```

Then check the printer from your client. Under Windows 9x or Windows NT, you should see something like Figure 8.4.

FIGURE 8.4

*Print queue informa-
tion for your printer
share.*

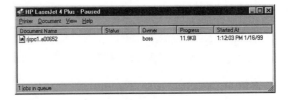

Remember to restart the `lp` queue so that future print jobs are printed.

Printing can be as easy as that, but printing can also be a complex issue. You might have to worry about the printing style used by your Samba server, printer drivers that generate PostScript with those infamous Ctrl-Ds (^D) on the front of them, or a myriad of other issues. You will explore many of them in subsequent sections.

Supported Printing Styles

Samba uses the native operating system's printing commands to print a file sent to a print share. It also uses the other commands provided by the printing system to query the status of print queues and print jobs, pause print queues, restart print queues, and so on.

However, there are many different printing styles under UNIX. Apart from the original BSD and System V, which have different commands for performing printing related tasks, there is also PLP (Portable Line Printer) and LPRNG, each of which take a BSD approach with improvements. Both PLP and LPRNG were developed by the same author, Patrick Powell.

As well as the printing styles, the popular UNIX variants AIX and HPUX have their own printing styles. In addition, Samba supports printing for QNX and SOFTQ.

When Samba is compiled, it sets the default printing style by checking for macros in the following way (see `$SRCDIR/include/includes.h`):

1. If an AIX system, it sets printing style to AIX.
2. If an HPUX system, it sets printing style to HPUX.
3. If a QNX system, it sets printing style to QNX.
4. If a System V system, it sets printing style to SYSV.
5. Otherwise, it sets the printing style to BSD.

This works for the majority of systems but needs to be changed if your system is not one of AIX, HPUX, QNX, or System V, but uses System V printing. It also must be changed if you are using PLP, LPRNG, or SOFTQ.

If you do need to change the default printing style, simply add the following parameter to the global section:

```
printing = <your printing selection>
```

If your system is truly bizarre and does not conform to one of the printing styles, you might need to set individual print commands to get printing to work correctly.

The [printers] Share

If you had to create a new printer share every time you added a new printer to your Samba server, administration of the Samba server could become complicated. To simplify life, Samba provides a scheme for printers similar to the [homes] share described in Hour 7. Briefly, when a client requests a connection to a share, Samba uses the following approach:

1. Searches for a share in the smb.conf; if found, returns the share.

2. If not found but a [homes] section is present, looks for a user in the passwd file with the same name as the requested share. If found, returns that as a share.

3. If still not found but a [printers] section exists, searches for a printer with the same name as the requested share and returns it as a share.

4. If still not found, looks for the default service, and if present, returns that as a share.

5. If still not found, returns an error indicating that the network name is not present.

The [printers] share looks like any other printer share. In fact, you can turn this one into a [printers] share:

```
[printers]
    comment = All printers on this machine, got from printcap
    path = /var/spool/samba
    printable = yes
```

When Samba uses the [printers] share because the requested share does not exist as a section and does not resolve as a [homes] share, the [printers] share is cloned and given the name of the requested share and printer name. This means that all such printers defined by the [printers] section take their parameters from the [printers] section.

Where does Samba get the list of printers? From the printcap file. If your system is based on BSD for printing or uses PLP or LPRNG, you have a printcap file in /etc/printcap. However, if your system uses System V printing, you can make a printcap file, or use the printcap name parameter as shown later in this chapter.

Printer-Related Parameters

The following parameters affect in one way or another the way in which printer shares work. Most Samba administrators do not use many of these parameters. As always, the final list of such parameters and the final word on their function rests with the manual pages on smb.conf for the current version of Samba. You should use man smb.conf to check these parameters.

Many of the parameters listed in the following sections take variables such as %p, %j, and so on, which are expanded with printing-related information when commands are executed. Table 8.1 supplies the meaning of many of these parameters.

TABLE 8.1   PRINTER VARIABLE SUBSTITUTIONS

Parameter	What It Does
%p	Replace with printer name
%j	Replace with job number
%s	Replace with spool file full pathname
%s	Replace with the spool filename (no path)

load printers

This global parameter controls whether Samba loads all printers in the printcap file for browsing.

The default value for this parameter is yes, which means that all printers in your printcap file are available for browsing by default. If you don't want this, simply use the following in the global section of your smb.conf file:

```
load printers = no
```

lppause command

This parameter specifies the command that Samba executes in order to stop printing a specific print job. It should be a command or script that takes a queue name and job number and pauses the job.

This parameter has no default unless using SysV or SOFTQ printing styles.

Please refer to the smb.conf man pages for more details.

lpq cache time

This global parameter controls how long lpq info is cached. It prevents the lpq command from being called too often. The value is expressed in seconds.

The default value for this parameter is 10 seconds.

lpq command

This parameter specifies the command that Samba executes in order to obtain printer queue status information for clients. It should be a program or script that takes a queue name and outputs printer status information.

The default value of this parameter depends on the value of the `printing` parameter.

lpresume command

This parameter specifies the command that Samba executes to restart or continue printing a job for clients. It should be a program or script that takes a printer name and job number to resume. This parameter does the opposite of `lppause command`.

This parameter has no default, unless the printing style is SysV or SOFTQ.

Please refer to the `smb.conf` man pages for more details.

lprm command

This parameter specifies the command that Samba executes to delete a job for clients. It should be a program or shell script that takes a printer name and job number to delete.

The default value of this parameter depends on the value of the `printing` parameter.

An example of using this parameter is

```
lprm command = /usr/bin/lprm -P%p %j
```

which specifies that the `lprm command` uses `/usr/bin/lprm` and is passed the queue name and the job number.

min print space

This parameter specifies the minimum amount of free disk space that must be available for clients to be able to spool print jobs. It is specified in kilobytes. A value of 0 (the default) means always spool jobs regardless of the amount of free space.

postscript

This parameter specifies that Samba should interpret print files as PostScript. Samba then adds a PostScript comment (`%!`) to the start of the print job, which enables you to overcome problems with PCs that insist on putting Ctrl-D characters at the start of print jobs. This confuses PostScript printers.

The default value of this parameter is false or no.

print command

This parameter specifies the command that Samba uses to spool a print job. It should be a program or script that takes a printer name and spool filename and spools the file to that printer.

The `print` `command` must contain at least one occurrence of `%s` or `%f` and can contain an occurrence of `%p`.

The default value of this parameter depends on the value of the printing parameter.

An example of using this parameter is

```
print command = /usr/local/samba/bin/localprintscrip %p %s
```

which specifies that a local program or shell script named `localprintscript` be called and passed the queue name and job number.

printable

This parameter specifies that a share is a print share, which enables clients to write spool files to the directory specified for the share. When a share is designated as printable, it is also `writable` by default. Any `read` `only` parameter only controls nonprinting access to the share.

The default value of this parameter is no, which means that by default, shares are not printable. That is, clients cannot connect to them as printer shares.

To make a share printable, simply add the following to the section for the share:

```
printable = yes
```

printcap name

This parameter (and its synonym `printcap`) is used to tell Samba the location of the `printcap` file used to find printers when the `[printers]` share is being used.

On System V systems that use `lpstat` to list available printers, you can set the `printcap` `name` to `lpstat` to obtain a list of available printers automatically.

The default value of this parameter is `/etc/printcap`.

An example of using this parameter is

```
printcap name = /etc/myprintcap
```

which specifies that the file `/etc/myprintcap` should be used when Samba needs to locate printers.

printer

This parameter tells Samba the name of the printer to send spooled jobs to when the spool file is closed by the client.

This parameter has no default value. Some examples of its use are

```
printer = lp
printer = hplj4
```

printer driver

This parameter tells Samba what driver name to give clients when they ask for the printer driver associated with a printer. It is used with auto install printer queues as discussed later this hour.

This parameter has no default value. An example of its use is

```
printer driver = HP LaserJet 4 Plus
```

printer driver file

This parameter tells Samba the location of the printer driver definition file, which is used when serving drivers to Windows 9x clients.

The file is created from a Windows 9x `msprint.def` file as described in the section "Automatic Printer Driver Installation."

The default value for this parameter is `SAMBA_INSTALL_DIRECTORY/lib/printers.def`.

printer driver location

This parameter tells Samba what share to return when clients ask for the location of printer driver files when automatically installing drivers on Windows 9x machines. This is described more fully in the section, "Automatic Printer Driver Installation."

This parameter has no default value. An example of using this parameter is

```
printer driver location = \\%h\printer$
```

printing

This parameter tells Samba the printing style to use on your server. In general, the printing style is determined at compile time, but if your system uses PLP, LPRNG, SOFTQ, or is perverse (that is, is SysV based but uses LPD), you have to set this parameter manually.

Currently, eight styles are supported:

> AIX

> BSD

> HPUX

LPRNG

PLP

QNX

SOFTQ

SYSV

The default value for this parameter is determined at compile time as specified above.

queuepause command

This parameter tells Samba what command to use to pause a queue. It should specify a program or script that takes a printer name and stops that queue.

The default value for this parameter depends on the printing style in effect.

queueresume command

This parameter tells Samba which command to use to resume printer queues. It should be a program or script that takes a queue name and resumes the queue.

The default value for this parameter depends on the printing style in effect.

Automatic Printer Driver Installation

Windows 95 and Windows 98 enable the automatic installation of printer driver files using Point and Print. Samba implements the functionality required to support such automatic installation.

Although the setup required to support Point and Print installation is described in detail in the Samba documentation directory (PRINTER_DRIVER.txt), I will explore it in some detail here.

First, you must set up a [printer$] share where all the driver files reside. This file share looks like this:

```
[printer$]
    path = /usr/local/samba/printer
    public=yes
    writable= no
    browsable=yes
```

Remember to create this directory so that the file share has somewhere to put files.

The next step is to create the printer definition file so that Windows 9x knows how to install the printers you have made available for automatic installation. To do this, you need to obtain the Windows INF files msprint.inf and msprint2.inf from the directory C:\WINDOWS\INF on one of your Windows machines. Sometimes these files might be located in a different directory. If you use unsupported or updated drivers, you must first install these drivers on your Windows 9X system, then copy the oemNN.inf file, and use it instead of msprint.inf.

> The file is not always exactly named oemNN.inf; rather, it might have a similar name. You can find which one you need by checking for the correct printer name within each such file.

When you have copied these files to your Samba server, you must use the make_printerdef program that comes with Samba to make an entry in the printers.def file for your printer. Find the exact name of the printer you are defining (the name Windows knows it as) by looking in the appropriate INF file. For printers with names starting from A to K, look in msprint.inf; otherwise, look in msprint2.inf. Here you assume a printer type of HP LaserJet 4 Plus. Create a new printers.def entry in the following way:

```
make_printerdef msprint.inf "HP LaserJet 4 Plus">> printers.def
```

Make sure that the new printers.def entry goes on the end of the printers.def file. In these examples, you put it in /usr/local/samba/lib.

When make_printerdef executes, it prints out on stderr the files required to be installed. All these files need to be out into the [printer$] share you have defined above. The files generally are all in the C:/WINDOWS/SYSTEM directory. In the case of the HP LaserJet 4 Plus, the following files are required:

```
FINSTALL.DLL, FINSTALL.HLP, HPPCL5MS.DRV, ICONLIB.DLL,
➥PJLMON.DLL, UNIDRV.DLL, UNIDRV.HLP
```

Lastly, you need to add some additional parameters to your smb.conf file. One of these goes in the global section and specifies the location of the printer definitions file:

```
[global]
    ...
    printer driver file = /usr/local/samba/lib/printers.def
    ...
```

This is the file where you put all the printer definition entries created with the
`make_printerdef` program.

The other parameters, `printer driver` and `printer driver location`, need to go in
each printer share where you want support for automatic installation. The following
shows your `first-printer` modified to support automatic installation:

```
[first-printer]
    comment = My first printer
    path = /var/spool/samba
    printable = yes
    printer driver = HP LaserJet 4 Plus
    printer driver location = \\%h\PRINTER$
```

Don't worry about the `%h` in the last line. It is one of the variable substitutions that
Samba can make in the `smb.conf` file. These will be explained in more detail in Hour 10,
"Server-Side Automation."

When you have made all these changes to your `smb.conf` file and restarted Samba, you
can try out automatic installation of the driver for the printer you defined. Bring up your
server in Network Neighborhood, as shown in Figure 8.5. Then double-click `first-printer`. This should start the installation of the printer. You are presented with the
following window.

FIGURE 8.5

*Your printer is about
to be installed.*

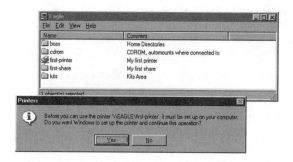

Click Yes to continue setting up the printer. This takes you through the Add Printer Wizard. Select Next and you are presented with the window in Figure 8.6.

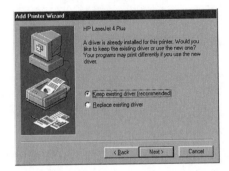

Here you can see that the Add Printer Wizard knows that it is dealing with an HP LaserJet 4 Plus. This is because Samba has told it so. If you complete the printer setup and print a test page, you should eventually see the test page print out on your printer.

Automatic installation can be enormously time saving on a medium to large installation, because it makes installing new printers a breeze for Windows 9x systems.

Printing from UNIX to Windows

In some situations, you might want to print from your UNIX servers to a printer that is connected to a Windows client. Samba can accomplish this. To set this up, you need to configure an appropriate print filter for the printing system under UNIX.

This section covers doing this for Berkeley-style printing (LPD, PLP, and LPRNG) as well as System V–style printing.

Samba comes with a small shell script called `smbprint` (or `smbprint.sysv` for System V systems). You can use this program to accept print jobs and queue them to printers shared on remote Windows systems. You do this in different ways, depending on whether your UNIX system uses BSD-style printing or System V–style printing.

In either case, the printer must be shared on the Windows machine. You do this with the Sharing menu item when you right-click a printer in Windows 9x or Windows NT. See Hour 14, "Windows 9x and Windows NT," for more details.

The `smbprint` (or `smbprint.sysv`) script uses `smbclient` to copy the print file from UNIX to Windows (perhaps with end-of-line translation if required) on a printer share. The `smbclient` utility is described in Hour 13, "UNIX (`smbclient`, `smbfs`, `smbwrapper`, and Various Utilities)."

Printing to Windows with BSD-Style Printing

BSD-style printing uses LPD and is controlled from a file called /etc/printcap. All printers are defined in the printcap file. To specify that a particular printer should send its print jobs to a shared printer on a remote Windows 9x system, perform the following steps:

1. Define the printer; that is, build a printcap entry either manually or with your favorite tool.

2. In the spool directory created for the printer, usually /var/spool/<printer-name>, create a file called .config (make sure that the name starts with a period) and place the following lines in the file:

   ```
   server=<server name>
   service=<printer share name>
   password=<password>
   ```

3. Change (or add) the input filter in the printcap entry for your printer to:

   ```
   :if=<directory path to smbprint>/smbprint:\
   ```

4. Restart the printer.

For example, if the local printer's name is hawk_print, the remote server is HAWK, the printer share is called MY_PRINTER, and no password is required to access the share, your .config file would look like:

```
server=HAWK
service=MY_PRINTER
password=""
```

On a Red Hat Linux system, you would create this file in the directory /var/spool/lpd/hawk_print, and the entry in the printcap file would look like

```
:if=/usr/bin/smbprint:\
```

You generally do not need to do this for printers located on Windows NT systems, because you can install LPD on Windows NT. Please refer to the printcap man page for more information on configuring remote LPD printers.

Printing to Windows with System V–Style Printing

System V–style printing is different from BSD-style printing and uses lp. Samba supports printing to Windows machines from System V systems using the script smbprint.sysv located in the examples/printing directory under the Samba source tree.

This script is a modified version of the BSD-style script. To use it, make a modified version of the script to specify the Windows server, service, and service password. These are located in a block in the program:

```
server=admin
service=hplj2
password=""
```

Change each of these to the correct values, and then install the script as an interface script for your queue and start printing using

```
lpadmin -punixprintername -v/dev/null -i./smbprint.sysv
enable unixprintername
accept unixprintername
```

For example, if the local printer's name is hawk_print, the remote server is HAWK, the printer share is called MY_PRINTER, and no password is required to access the remote share, the changes to smbprint.sysv required would look like:

```
server=HAWK
service=MY_PRINTER
password=""
```

The commands required to set up and enable this printer would be

```
lpadmin -phawk_print -v /dev/null -i./smbprint.sysv
enable hawk_print
accept hawk_print
```

You would generally not need to do this for Windows NT systems, because Windows NT supports LPD, and lpadmin can configure a remote BSD-based printer. Please refer to the lpadmin man page for more information.

Summary

In this hour you have looked at printing with Samba. You have explored how to create print shares and many of the parameters that control them. You have also looked at automatic printer installation for Windows 9x as well as printing from UNIX to Windows machines.

Along the way, you have explored in some detail many of the processes Samba uses in supporting printing for printing and the numerous printing styles that Samba supports. This information should enable you to debug many of the Samba printer configuration problems that arise.

In the next hour you will explore some of the GUI administration tools that are available for Samba.

Q&A

Q My users are printing to a PostScript printer, but the PostScript is being printed rather than the actual page. How do I fix this?

A Many UNIX systems have a PostScript printer that converts text files into PostScript (for example, enscript). The filter is smart enough to leave PostScript alone so it prints correctly. However, some Windows printer drivers place a Ctrl-D (^D) at the beginning of the file. This confuses the filter, which is usually looking for %!, and the PostScript in the print job is converted to PostScript and you get pages and pages of rubbish. You can fix this by adding the parameter postscript = yes to the printer share.

Q We print from our Windows clients to Samba printer shares, which are then sent to HP LaserJet printers or Lexmark printers using network printing cards (such as the JetDirect or MarkNet cards). Some print jobs seem to mess up badly, especially those with graphics in them. How do we fix this?

A This probably has to do with the way these types of network printers handle end-of-line sequences. Both of the types mentioned previously provide a raw queue (RAW in the case of HP, printer in the case of Lexmark), which simply takes the data provided and prints it. However, they both also provide a queue that converts standard UNIX text files into something printers can deal with. These queues (TEXT in the case of HP and printer_cr in the case of Lexmark) add a carriage return every time they see a newline character. This ensures that UNIX text files are printed correctly. However, if you send a binary from a PC, chances are you will corrupt the binary.

What you need to do is to provide two queues in your printcap file. One for the PCs to print to (perhaps specified with the printer parameter in the smb.conf file) and one for UNIX users and programs to print to. Samba should print to the raw style queue, whereas UNIX should print to the text style queue.

Q We have a System V machine. How do we tell Samba about all the print queues we have so our clients can browse them?

A Here you should add the following parameter to the global section of your smb.conf file:

```
printcap name = lpstat
```

HOUR 9

GUI Administration Tools

by Richard Sharpe

In the previous four hours, you have looked at configuring Samba in some detail. However, this took the form of delving through many of the configuration parameters that can appear in your smb.conf file and required that you be able to edit that file with your favorite editor.

Those who are experts in Samba configuration no doubt find that directly editing the smb.conf file is the quickest way to add new shares or change settings. For many people, though, a simple GUI interface to the smb.conf file would be a boon. Such a facility is even more useful if you need to make only a simple change, and you are not physically logged onto the Samba server.

In this hour you explore the following GUI configuration tools for Samba, some in more detail than others:

- The Samba Web Administration Tool, SWAT
- SMBedit, a Windows 9x–based admin tool
- Webmin, another Web-based admin tool

- smbconftool, a Java-based admin tool
- smb-mode.el, an Emacs mode for editing the smb.conf file

These tools can be broadly divided into three groups:

- Those that use CGI scripts and thus can be used from a browser on any platform, including Windows machines, UNIX machines, VMS machines, and so on
- Those that are Windows applications and thus only work on Windows systems
- Those that are UNIX applications or must run on the server that has the smb.conf file on it and thus can run only on a UNIX machine

In the following sections, you will explore the installation and use of most of these tools and discuss the advantages and drawbacks of each.

SWAT

The Samba Web Administration Tool (SWAT) is a new facility with Samba 2.0.0. It is a miniature Web server and CGI scripting application designed to run from inetd that provides access to the smb.conf file on the system that SWAT is running on. inetd is the daemon that handles the startup of most network servers under UNIX and is controlled by the file /etc/inetd.conf. (For more details on inetd, try man inetd.)

SWAT enables a suitably authorized person (with the root password) to configure all aspects of Samba via Web pages. SWAT also places help links to all configurable smb.conf options on every page, which lets administrators easily understand the effect of any changes.

SWAT is built and installed by default under Samba 2.0.0, but depending on the system you are on and the installation method, you might have to do some additional configuration to use SWAT.

If you are installing Samba from RPM on a Linux system, RPM does all the necessary configuration (including the changes mentioned later). However, if you use more manual methods, you need to complete the following steps:

1. Configure Samba:
   ```
   configure
   ```
2. Build Samba:
   ```
   make
   ```
3. Install Samba:
   ```
   make install
   ```

4. Add a line to /etc/services such as the following:

```
swat            901/tcp
```

> If you use NIS, you probably need to rebuild your NIS service maps.

5. Add a line to /etc/inetd.conf like the following:

```
swat    stream    tcp        nowait.400        root
➥/usr/local/samba/bin/swat swat
```

> If you have installed your Samba binaries somewhere else, you need to change this directory to the appropriate directory.

6. When you have finished steps 1–5, you can restart inetd by sending a HUP signal to it. This causes inetd to re-read its confile file (/etc/inetd.conf) and SWAT is ready for use. To do this, you can use a variety of methods. The most portable is kill -HUP *PID* where *PID* is the process ID of the inetd daemon.

When you have completed these steps, you should be able to use your favorite browser to access SWAT. To do this, visit your Samba server on port 901 by going to http://*your-server*:901/.

When your browser has contacted SWAT, you are presented with an authorization dialog box asking for your username and password. You must enter a sufficiently privileged user here, such as root. Figure 9.1 shows how you would use a browser to access SWAT on EAGLE.

> In using SWAT you are sending your username and password in plain text over the network. It is not a very good idea to enable people to use SWAT to administer your Samba server remotely over the Internet, as they must send usernames and passwords in the clear over the Internet.

9

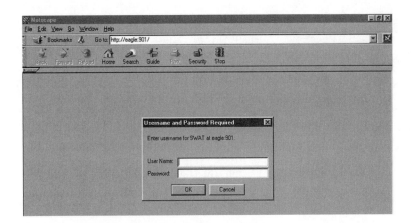

FIGURE 9.1

Accessing SWAT from a browser.

When you have logged in, you are presented with the main SWAT page, shown in Figure 9.2, which enables you to choose from among the following areas:

- Home, which takes you back to the SWAT home page
- Globals, where you can manage the Samba [global] section of this Samba server
- Shares, where you can manage file shares for this Samba server
- Printers, where you can manage printers shares for this Samba server
- Status, where you can obtain status information about Samba on this server
- View, where you can view the current smb.conf file
- Password, where you can manage your password on your Samba server or on a remote machine

At any time you can return to the SWAT home page by clicking on the Home icon.

SWAT should work on any operating system that Samba runs on, whereas some of the other configuration tools mentioned in this hour are more restrictive.

The following sections discuss each of the configuration pages you can access.

Managing the [global] Section

When you select the Globals icon, SWAT returns with a Web page that enables you to modify many of the most relevant Samba global parameters. The Web page returned is shown in Figure 9.3. The Samba global variables are grouped into related options.

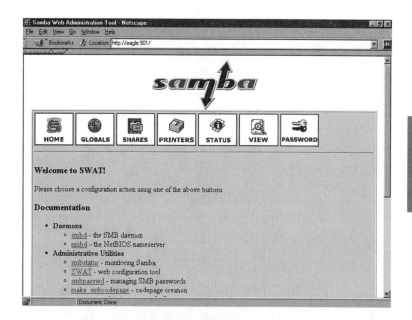

FIGURE 9.2

The SWAT home page.

FIGURE 9.3

SWAT enables you to modify parameters in the Globals section.

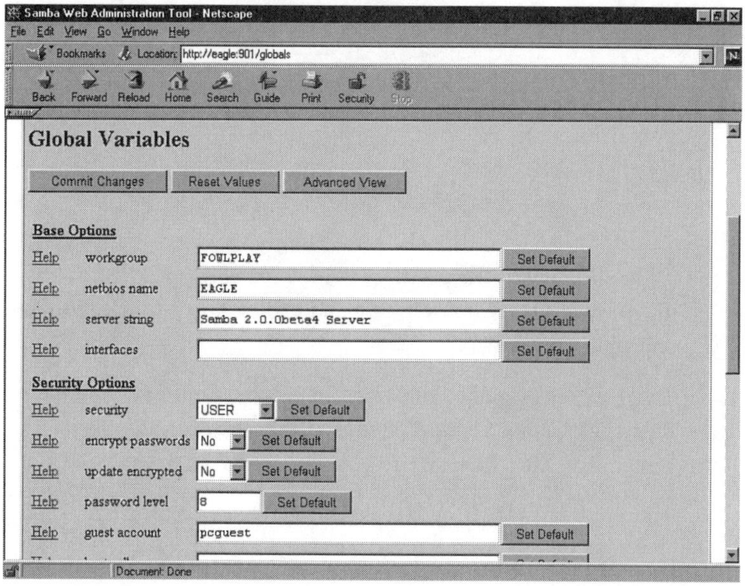

Clicking the Advanced View button brings up the same set of groups of related options, but you can now edit all of them.

To make a change, simply scroll down to the parameter you want to change, enter the new value, and then click the Commit Changes button.

Managing File Shares

When you select the Shares icon, SWAT returns a Web page that enables you to create new shares and modify existing shares. The page returned is shown in Figure 9.4.

FIGURE 9.4

Creating and modifying shares with SWAT.

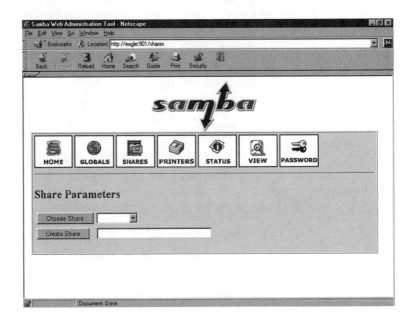

To modify any of the parameters of an existing share, select the share from the drop-down list next to Choose Share and click Choose Share. You are presented with the page shown in Figure 9.5.

To create a new share, enter its name in the field next to the Create Share button and then click Create Share. You then are presented with a page similar to that shown in Figure 9.5, with the name of your new share as the choice in the first field.

You should notice that Figures 9.4 and 9.5 contain the same fields at the top of the page. That is, they both contain the Choose Share and Create Share buttons. These enable you to choose a new share to view or create a new share without going back to the SWAT home page. Simply enter the name of the share you want to view and click Choose Share.

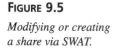

FIGURE 9.5

Modifying or creating a share via SWAT.

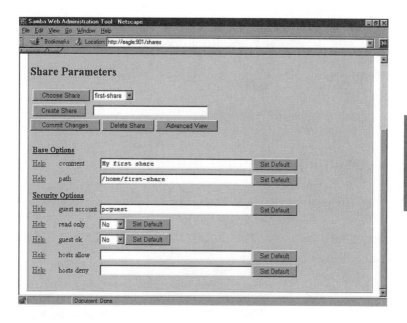

9

From this page you can

- Choose another share, by selecting it and clicking on Choose Share
- Create a new share, by entering its name in the appropriate field and clicking on Create Share
- Commit all your changes made so far, by clicking on Commit Changes
- Delete the share by clicking on Delete Share

If you need to modify parameters not shown on this page, click the Advanced View button and modify the appropriate parameters.

The Advanced View page shows all the parameters related to the selected share, grouped in the following sections:

- Base Options, such as Comment and Path
- Security Options, such as Username, Guest Account, and so on
- Logging Options, such as Status
- Tuning Options, such as Maximum Connections, Sync Always, and so on

- Filename Handling, such as Case-Handling Parameters, and so on
- Browse Options, such as Browsable
- Locking Options, such as Oplocks and Strict Locking, and so on
- Miscellaneous Options

When you have made all the changes you need, click Commit Changes, and they are made to the share. Samba immediately makes the changes you choose.

Managing Printer Shares

When you select the Printers icon, SWAT returns a Web page that enables you to create new printers and modify existing printers. The page returned is shown in Figure 9.6.

FIGURE 9.6

Creating and modifying printers with SWAT.

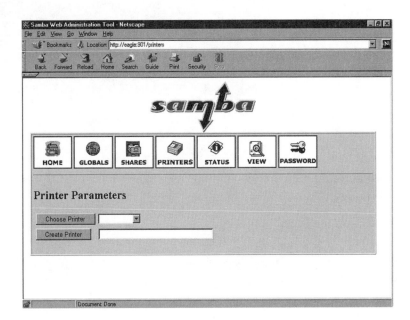

To modify an existing printer, select it from the dropdown list next to Choose Printer and then click Choose Printer. You are presented with the page shown in Figure 9.7.

To create a new printer, enter the name of the printer in the field next to Create Printer and click Create Printer. You are presented with a page similar to that shown in Figure 9.7 with the name of your new printer in the first field.

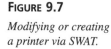

FIGURE 9.7

*Modifying or creating
a printer via SWAT.*

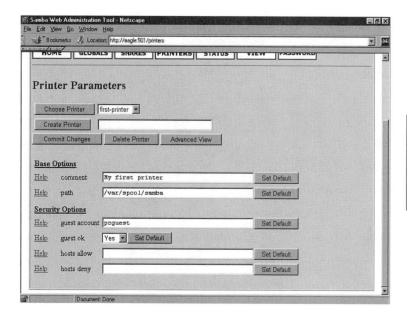

From this page you can

- Choose another printer, by selecting it and clicking on Choose Printer
- Create a new printer, by entering its name in the appropriate field and clicking on Create Printer
- Commit all your changes made so far, by clicking on Commit Changes
- Delete the printer, by clicking on Delete Printer

If you need to modify parameters not shown on this page, click the Advanced View button and modify the appropriate parameters.

When you have made all the changes you need, click Commit Changes and they are made to the share. Samba immediately makes the changes you choose.

Obtaining Status Information

When you select the Status icon, SWAT returns a Web page that provides status about Samba, as well as enabling you to stop and restart the Samba daemons. It also enables you to disconnect active users. The Web page SWAT returns is shown in Figure 9.8.

FIGURE 9.8

The SWAT status page.

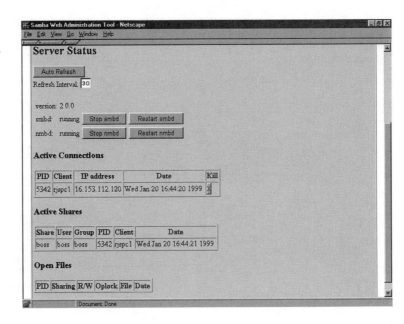

The status page also provides a means of having it refreshed on a continual basis. Simply specify the refresh interval and click Auto Refresh.

Viewing the Complete `smb.conf` File

When you select the View icon, SWAT returns a Web page that displays the whole `smb.conf` file. The page returned is shown in Figure 9.9.

SWAT lists the Samba config as it appears in the `smb.conf` file. If you want a listing that includes the values of all the parameters that Samba maintains, simply click the Full View button.

Changing Your Password

If you select the Password icon, SWAT returns a Web page where you can modify your password on the Samba server that SWAT is running from or change your password on another CIFS/SMB server elsewhere in your network. You can also add users, disable users, or enable users. The page returned is shown in Figure 9.10.

FIGURE 9.9

The smb.conf *file.*

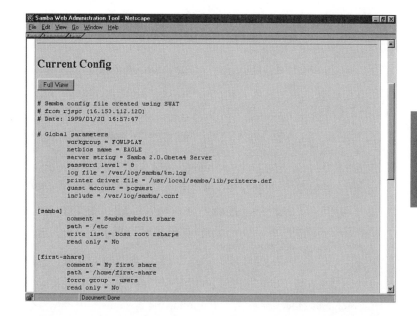

FIGURE 9.10

Changing your password with SWAT.

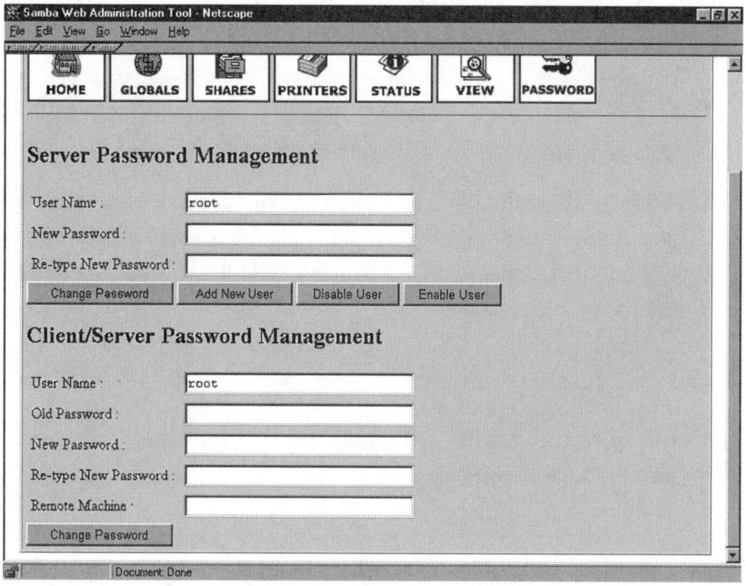

SWAT operates only on your `smbpasswd` file, not on your normal UNIX password files.

Webmin

Webmin is a Web-based system administration package for UNIX systems. It provides facilities for managing Samba, as well as setting up accounts, configuring DNS, configuring Apache, configuring sendmail, and performing many other system administration tasks. Here you concentrate on how Webmin helps with configuring Samba.

Webmin consists of a miniature Web server written in Perl and a set of CGI programs that implement the functions required to provide system configuration over the Web. To use Webmin you must obtain Webmin and install it.

Webmin can be obtained from `http://www.webmin.com/webmin/`. When you have obtained Webmin, you need to break out the gzipped tar file that it is distributed as. A command sequence such as the following does the job:

```
gzip -d webmin-VER_tar.gz
tar -xvf webmin-VER_tar
```

On some systems, simply using `tar -zxvf webmin-VER_tar.gz` does the job as well. In both of the previous commands, replace `VER` with the current version of Webmin. At the time of writing, the latest version of Webmin was 0.65.

After breaking out the distribution, simply change to the directory you just created, usually `webmin-VER`, where `VER` is the version number of Webmin. You should then read the `README` file for installation instructions. At the time of writing, this consists of running the following command:

```
./setup.sh
```

Answer the questions asked by the installation script. During installation, you are asked for a password for the first Webmin user, `admin`. This password is needed when you connect to the Webmin page.

After installing Webmin, you need to modify your system's startup scripts to ensure that Webmin starts on each system boot. Details for how to do this are beyond the scope of this book. You should consult the system administration documentation for your system.

Webmin currently supports the following operating systems:

- RedHat Linux 4.0, 4.1, 4.2, 5.0, 5.1, and 5.2
- Slackware Linux 3.x
- Debian Linux 1.3
- SUSE Linux 5.1, 5.1, and 5.3
- FreeBSD 2.2
- DELIX DLD 5.3
- Solaris 2.5, 2.6, and 2.7
- HPUX 10.01, 10.10, 10.20, and 10.30

For more complete details of the operating systems supported by Webmin, consult the Webmin Web page and installation script.

After installing and starting Webmin, you can access it from your favorite browser (as shown in Figure 9.11) by accessing port 10,000 on the server you installed Webmin on. If you changed the port number that Webmin sits behind from the default of 10,000, you should use your number rather than 10,000.

FIGURE 9.11

Connecting to Webmin.

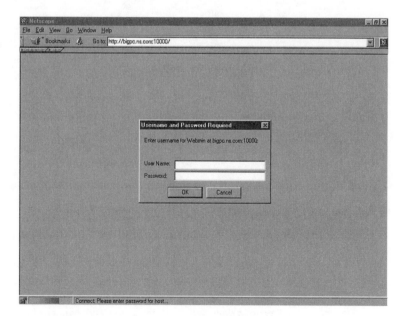

When you have entered the correct username and password, you are presented with the Webmin home page as shown in Figure 9.12. Webmin can administer many aspects of UNIX systems, but you are interested only in its capability to administer Samba. To perform Samba-related configuration, select the File Shares for Windows Networking link on the Webmin main page.

Again, you should be aware that Webmin does not provide support for Secure Sockets Layer (SSL), so you are submitting usernames and passwords in the clear over the network. This is a security problem, and at the very least you should not enable people to administer your Samba servers via the Internet.

FIGURE 9.12

The Webmin main page.

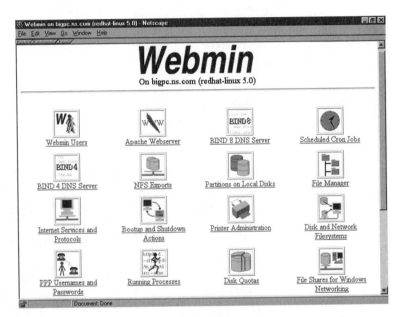

After you select File Shares for Windows Networking, Webmin presents the Samba Exports page, as shown in Figure 9.13. From this page, you can manage file and printer shares, as well as all aspects of the Samba global parameters. You can select global configuration sections by clicking on the icons at the bottom of Figure 9.13.

From these pages, you can perform the same set of functions as you can with SWAT.

Webmin does not create file shares with hyphens (-) in them and does not work with smb.conf files that have include parameters in them.

FIGURE 9.13

The Webmin Samba Exports page.

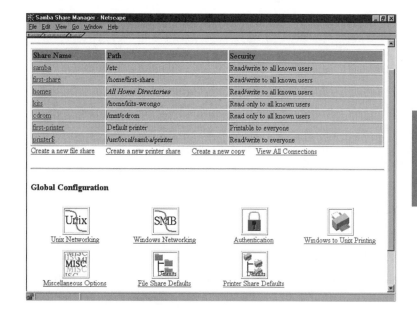

smbconftool

Smbconftool is a Java application that enables you to edit the smb.conf file in a graphical manner. It runs on the machine where the smb.conf file resides. Therefore, whereas smbconftool can run on any machine that supports Java because it uses file IO to access the smb.conf file, it must run on the system where the smb.conf file resides. You can find more information about this tool at http://www.eatonweb.com/samba/.

smb-mode.el

This tool is an Emacs major mode written by Fraser McCrossan that helps administrators edit the smb.conf file. When you have downloaded and configured smb-mode.el, you receive features such as

- Automatic indentation of your smb.conf file
- Editing operations on whole sections of your smb.conf file
- A new mode, outline-minor-mode, which can give you an overview of the whole smb.conf file
- Parameter lookup in the smb.conf manual page
- Parameter completion
- A number of other capabilities

In order to use `smb-mode.el` with Emacs, you should download it from `http://users.gtn.net/fraserm/smbmode.html`. That page also contains instructions on how to install `smb-mode.el`.

The steps you must perform are

1. Download `smb-mode.el` from `http://users.gtn.net/fraserm/smbmode.html`
2. Install `smb-mode.el` in your site-lisp directory
3. Add some Lisp to your `.Emacs` file (or create your `.Emacs` file if it does not already exist)

Instructions for the installation and use of `smb-mode.el` are contained on the aforementioned Web page.

Summary

Configuring your `smb.conf` file can be one of the most difficult aspects of getting Samba to function correctly on your system. The tools that you have explored in this hour make it easier to manage your `smb.conf` file.

Many of these tools, however, are in the early stages of their development, and all of them have problems of one sort or another (for example, many of them remove your comments, some don't like `include` sections, and so on). For experienced administrators, the main use of a tool such as SWAT or Webmin is to make quick changes to the `smb.conf` file via a browser when they are not logged into the server.

> I would also like to stress that the Web-based tools available today for administering Samba do not include SSL support. This means that you submit usernames and passwords in the clear over the network. This causes most security-conscious people a real problem. At the least, you should not allow anyone to administer your Samba servers via the Internet!

In the next hour you will explore the topic of server-side automation, which enables you to use macros and other advanced techniques in your `smb.conf` file.

Q&A

Q I am trying to use SWAT, but I keep getting a message such as: "There was no response. The server could be down or not responding..." What is the problem?

A This sound like SWAT is not listening to connections, or you have used the wrong URL in trying to connect to SWAT.

Swat usually lives behind port 901, so the URL you should use is `http://your.server.dom:901/`, where `your.server.dom` should be replaced with the DNS name of your Samba server.

If you are still having problems, check to see that SWAT is listed in the `/etc/services` file and that `/etc/inetd.conf` has an entry for SWAT as outlined previously.

9

HOUR 10

Server-Side Automation

NEW TERM *Automation* can be defined as the process of designing a solution that can be carried out without human intervention. Automation is closely related to scalability. Your goal for this hour is to develop methods that automate Samba's capability to handle connections from various client machines. Even if you don't manage large numbers of users, computers, or servers, you can still benefit from thinking about automation.

What Is Server-Side Automation?

Server-side automation describes events that the systems administrator has configured to occur on the server as a result of a client connecting to a service, either a file or printer. Perhaps that was a little wordy, but I think the definition will become clearer as look at some examples.

If you think back to previous hours, you have already seen two examples of server-side automation. Do you remember the [homes] service? When a user attempts to connect to his home directory (for example, \\bilbo\joe)—assuming that the [homes] service has been defined—Samba attempts to locate the share name, first in smb.conf and then in the local passwd file. If the name is found in /etc/passwd, Samba automatically creates a copy of the [homes] share and renames it to the name of the connecting user. This occurs transparently to the user and without any human intervention. If you create an account for a new user on the UNIX box, you don't need to change anything in the smb.conf file to enable that user to access his home directory. That's what I mean by server-side automation. The solution is scalable and self-maintaining.

The [printers] service from Hour 8, "Printers," is another example of Samba's built-in automation. You don't need to explicitly define every printer available on the system (although you certainly could if you wanted) in order for the printer to be available. Samba will obtain its list of valid printer names from the defined printcap file. If you create another printer, Samba will be aware of it automatically.

> As a final note before you begin looking at some of the more customizable means of automating client support, remember that these examples are only suggestions and certainly not the only way that the parameters or mechanisms can be used. You should experiment with different combinations. Hopefully, you will be comfortable with the examples and will have ideas of your own to try by the end of the hour. Most of all, make Samba work for you. These examples are here to provide you a basis to work from.

You first examined the variables available in smb.conf in Hour 5, "The smb.conf File: Telling Samba What to Do." Table 5.2 describes the complete list if you need to refer back. Variables provide the foundation for individualizing connections. Some of the more common ones that I'll be using for the rest of this hour are %u, %U, %g, %G, %m, %L, and %d.

preexec and postexec Scripts

Four parameters enable you to specify commands to be executed on the server when a client connects or disconnects to a service:

- preexec
- postexec
- root preexec
- root postexec

preexec and postexec

First, look at `preexec` and `postexec` parameters. Both parameters take a series of commands or a script name that is executed on the server using the uid of %u. If you remember from Hour 5, %u is the username of the current service. I can better explain exactly when the script executes by using output from the `net use` command on a Windows box:

```
C:\users\jerry>net use s: \\bilbo\src
The command was completed successfully.
```

The `preexec` command executes between the time that the `net use` command runs and the time that Windows reports that `The command was completed successfully.` The same is true for `postexec` commands. The Windows client sends the disconnect request (`net use s: /d`). Samba then executes the `postexec` command and tells the Windows machine that the service was disconnected:

```
C:\users\jerry>net use s: /d
The command was completed successfully.
```

What kinds of things can you do with these `preexec` and `postexec` commands? Here is a practical example. More often than once, I have had a user call to report that his UNIX shell account didn't seem to be working correctly. After a few questions, it became clear that the user had accessed his home directory from a PC and deleted several files that didn't seem important. A friend of mine jokingly refers these to as "Those pesky dot files!" By now, you can probably imagine which files the user deleted. Here is an example that will help alleviate some of the help desk calls for this particular problem:

```
[homes]
      preexec = /usr/local/bin/fix_dot_files.sh %H
```

The script itself is very simple.

```
#!/bin/sh

SKELDIR=/usr/local/etc/skel
EXPORT SKELDIR
home=$1

if [ ! -f $home/.login ]; then
   cp -p $SKELDIR/.login $home
fi

if [ ! -f $home/.logout ]; then
   cp -p $SKELDIR/.logout $home
fi

if [ ! -f $home/.profile ]; then
   cp -p $SKELDIR/.profile $home
```

10

```
fi

if [ ! -f $home/.cahrc ]; then
    cp -p $SKELDIR/.cshrc $home
fi
```

This tells Samba to run the `fix_dot_files.sh` shell script when a user connects to her home directory. This particular script will copy default versions of "those pesky dot files!" such as `.cshrc`, `.profile`, `.login`, and `.logout`.

This next example might be a little silly and could get to be annoying for the user. The `preexec` command sends a copy of the `~/todo` file to the user on connection using a WinPopup message. It would probably be better to wrap this command in a script that first checks for the existence of the file:

```
[homes]
    preexec = cat %H/todo ¦ smbclient -M %m
```

The `postexec` parameter is similar to the `preexec` parameter, except that the value executes when the user closes a connection to the service. Here's an example that removes all files in the user's `~/tmp/` directory.

```
[homes]
    postexec = /bin/rm -r %H/tmp/*
```

In this way, a user can store all the temporary files needed during a session in his home directory, thus slightly increasing security in an environment where many people use a machine, such as a student computer lab. I'll leave it up to you whether it is a good idea to delete these files automatically on your server.

These scripts can be extremely hard to debug, because any error messages written to standard error are normally thrown away. My advice is to execute the script manually as a normal user to verify its correctness. A common problem is that a normal user does not have access to read from or write to files necessary to the script. It is also helpful to log all output from the script to a file for later viewing.

root preexec and root postexec

The only difference between the `root preexec` and `root postexec` parameters and the normal `preexec` and `postexec` parameters is that the former ones specify commands that run as root on the server. This can be very helpful for things such as creating directories, setting ownership of files, logging connections to a central file such as `/var/adm/wtmpx`, or mounting and unmounting file devices such as CD-ROMs or floppy disks.

> You should consider the scripts specified by the root preexec and root
> postexec parameters as suid binaries owned by root. This means that secu-
> rity concerns, such as the ability of users to modify the scripts, should not be
> taken lightly. Assuming the user cannot modify the smb.conf file, the para-
> meters that are passed to the script cannot be changed. Therefore, the root
> preexec and root postexec scripts are not as dangerous as root suid binaries
> that can run from a shell prompt.

One of my responsibilities at my current place of employment is to set up, update, and maintain several student-accessible Windows 9x/NT labs. We decided to build the labs as self-sufficient as possible so that we could keep service disruptions to a minimum and localize SMB traffic. All students are issued UNIX accounts that the lab server obtains information about via NIS+ tables. All students have home directory space reserved for their UNIX accounts. The home directory that the students use for the lab, however, is separate from their UNIX home space and local to the lab's server.

Rather than bothering to create a home directory for each user on the lab server at the time of account creation, we chose to create it the first time the user logged into a machine in the lab. Here's how it worked:

```
[homes]
    comment = PC Lab home directories
     root preexec = /usr/local/samba/bin/buildhome %U %G
    path = /export/home/%U
    valid user = %S
    create mode = 0600
    directory mode = 0700
```

You will notice that the path is not the user's home directory from /etc/passwd (that is, %H). The path is set to a local disk, /export/home, and each user has a directory there. Initially the disk is empty.

Now the root preexec script comes into play. The script checks for the existence of the directory name /export/home/*username* and creates it if it doesn't exist. Here is the source for a simple buildhome script:

```
#!/bin/sh
umask 077
user=$1
group=$2

# Does the user's home directory exist ( export/home/$user )?
if [ ! -d /export/home/$user ]; then
   mkdir /export/home/$user
```

```
    chown $user /export/home/$user
    chgrp $group /export/home/$user
fi
```

Here's another fun example of something you can do with postexec scripts. At work, I
have access to an older NCD WinCenter server. If you're unfamiliar with the Cytrix
WinFrame multiuser version of Windows NT, it enables users to access an NT desktop
remotely much in the same way that XDM enables users to network X terminals. Figure
10.1 shows a WinCenter 2.0 desktop side by side with other X applications running on a
Solaris 2.6 machine.

FIGURE 10.1

*NCD WinCenter
Windows NT desktop
displayed on a Sun
Sparc 10 running
Solaris 2.6.*

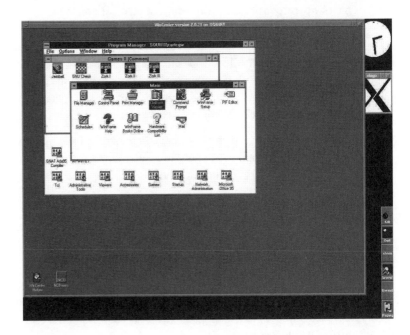

I needed a method to access the SCSI CD-ROM on my Sun workstation from the
WinCenter session, so I set up Samba locally to share the CD-ROM. Here is the
smb.conf service entry:

```
[cdrom]
        comment = 12X CD-Rom
        path = /cdrom/cdrom0
        root postexec = /usr/bin/eject cd
        read only = yes
        public = yes
```

The root preexec is not strictly necessary because I am logged into the console, but it
will basically make no difference.

Now I can insert a CD-ROM (which will be mounted by the Solaris volume manager daemon, `vold`) and execute

```
net use f: \\mymachine\cdrom
```

in the WinCenter session to make the CD-ROM available. When I disconnect from the CD-ROM

```
net use f: /d
```

the CD-ROM ejects automatically.

%U and %u, %G and %g

You have already seen some uses for variables. For example, you used the `%m` variable in the `log file` parameter value to provide logs on a per-machine basis. You could also do the same on a per-user basis with the following:

```
log file = /usr/local/samba/var/log.%U
```

So far, I have not really explained the difference between `%u` and `%U`. Both variables are expanded to a username, but the `%U` variable is expanded to the username sent during the session setup. For example, here is a portion of the `tcpdump` output I showed you in Hour 6, "Security Levels and Passwords." The packet was transmitted from a Windows 95 OSR2 client and contains the password `testpass` and username `boss`:

```
[000] 54 45 53 54 50 41 53 53   00 00 00 00 00 00 42 4F   TESTPASS ......BO
[010] 53 53 00 00 00 00 00 00   42 4F 53 53 00 43 48 49   SS...... BOSS.CHI
[020] 50 53 4E 44 49 50 53 00   57 69 6E 64 6F 77 73 20   PSNDIPS. Windows
[030] 34 2E 30 00 57 69 6E 64   6F 77 73 20 34 2E 30 00   4.0.Wind ows 4.0.
```

The log file created for this connection would be

```
/usr/local/samba/var/log.boss
```

The `%u` variable is expanded to the username of the current service. Normally `%U` and `%u` are the same except under certain circumstances such as when using the `force user` parameter in user-level security.

Here's an example when `%U` and `%u` are different. Let's use this service definition for `[src]`:

```
[src]
        root preexec = echo "%T : U is %U and u is %u" >> /var/log/log.src
        comment = /usr/local/src
        path = /usr/local/src
        create mode = 0644
        directory mode = 0755
        force user = jerryc
```

10

As you can tell, the `preexec` value simply logs the values of `%U` and `%u` to file. This is the easiest way to determine what values Samba is using.

The `smbclient` is a good testing tool for this type of experimentation. I'll simply specify that I want to connect to the `[src]` service using the username `boss`:

```
/usr/local/samba/bin/smbclient //bilbo/src -U boss
Added interface ip=192.168.1.73 bcast=192.168.1.255 nmask=255.255.255.0
Password:
Domain=[FOWLPLAY] OS=[Unix] Server=[Samba 2.0.0beta5]
smb: \>
```

Now if I look at the output that was created in `/var/log/log.src`, I see that `%U` expanded to the username I specified with which to connect, `boss`, and that the actual username I was accessing the service as was `jerryc`:

```
1999/01/09 10:08:02 : U is boss and u is jerryc
```

The `%G` and `%g` variables are directly related to the `%U` and `%u` variables. The discussion of the difference between the two group variables is analogous to the differences between the two username parameters.

`%L`, `%m`, and the `include` Parameters

The `netbios aliases` parameter was mentioned in Hour 5, although at the time it was not explained why anyone would want the same server to appear in browse lists using multiple names. As you remember, the `%L` variable expands to the name the client used in the connection to the Samba server.

The `include` parameter enables you to lexically insert text at any point in the configuration file. It is perfectly valid to use variables in the filename given to the `include` directive. When it's used with the `%L` variable, you can include different settings based on who the client was attempting to connect to. The combination of variables and the `include` parameter provides an extreme amount of flexibility in the server's behavior based on the calling (`%m`) or the called (`%L`) name.

include

If you have ever written a computer program in C, you will be familiar with the `#include` `filename` preprocessor directive. This directive tells the preprocessor to include the entire text of the given file lexically into the source code at the point. Samba's `include` parameter performs the same function.

The parameter's value is a path to a file whose contents will replace the current occurrence of the `include` line. If Samba cannot open the file specified, the `include` parameter has no effect.

Let's use this sample `smb.conf` file:

```
; smb.conf
[global]
     netbios name      = EAGLE
     workgroup         = FOWLPLAY
     security          = user
     password level    = 4
     include           = /usr/local/samba/lib/shares.conf
```

Here are the contents of `/usr/local/samba/lib/shares.conf`:

```
; shares.conf
[foo]
     comment = example disk share
     path = /export/smb/foo
[homes]
     writeable = yes
     valid user = %S
```

The resulting file after parsing would be

```
; smb.conf
 [global]
     netbios name      = EAGLE
     workgroup         = FOWLPLAY
     security          = user
     password level    = 4
; shares.conf
[foo]
     comment = example disk share
     path = /export/smb/foo
[homes]
     writeable = yes
     valid user = %S
```

What difference does this make and why would you want to do something like this? Suppose that you have three departments: Accounting, Personnel, and Administration. Also suppose that each department has a group share that is accessed by its UNIX server through the network file system (NFS) and a central `passwd` file that is distributed using some mechanism such as `rdist` or the network information service (NIS). Each UNIX box also acts as a Samba server for the PCs in that particular department. From time to time, a person from one department needs temporary access to a group share from a machine in another department. The most maintainable solution would be to define all the group shares in one configuration file and then include that at run time into the main `smb.conf` file, as shown in Listings 10.1 and 10.2.

LISTING 10.1   A Sample `smb.conf` File for Each Departmental Server

```
; smb.conf file to manage group shares via the include parameter
[global]
     netbios name = <fill in the machine name>
     workgroup = <fill in the department workgroup name>
     security = user
     password level = 4
[homes]
     comment = <department names> home directory
     writeable = yes
     path = /export/home/%U
; include the group shares
     include = /opt/admin/sys/group_shares.conf
```

LISTING 10.2   Contents of `group_shares.conf`

```
[acctgrp]
     comment = Acccounting departmental share
     Path = /export/acct/acctgrp
     create mode = 0660
     directory mode = 0770
     valid users = @acct
; Personel group share
[persgrp]
     comment = Personel departmental share
     path = /export/personel/persgrp
     create mode = 0660
     directory mode = 0770
     valid users = @personel
; Administration group share
[admingrp]
     comment = Administration departmental share
     path = /export/admin/admingrp
     create mode = 0660
     directory mode = 0770
     valid users = @admin
```

Because I said you had NFS service to all the servers, it's only a small stretch to include NFS automount support as well. Each server uses this `smb.conf` file tailored to its machine settings such as the NetBIOS name and workgroup name. The `group_shares.conf` file is located on an automounted share (Solaris uses `/opt` as the mount on demand point, so I will use that as well by force of habit). This environment enables you to make changes to the group share configuration file and the changes to be seen by all three servers.

Figure 10.2 gives a pictorial explanation of the `smb.conf` file that was previously listed. All three servers, ACCT-1, PERSON-1, and ADMIN-1, have a local configuration file similar to Listing 10.1. The `include` directive at the end tells Samba to insert the text of `/opt/admin/sys/group_shares.conf`, which is shown at the top of the diagram. All the servers will include the same file. Therefore, if a change must be made to a group share definition, it needs be changed only in `group_shares.conf` and will be seen by all three servers as a result.

FIGURE 10.2

Managing group shares by using the `include` parameter.

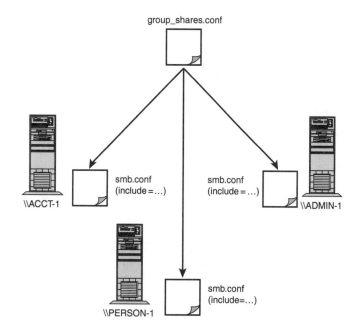

Using Variables in `include`

Although the previous example of using included files was perfectly valid, perhaps a more common scenario is to use variables in the included filename to change the behavior of the server based on the client settings. Here is a simple example that enables you to use encrypted passwords for Windows NT clients and plain text passwords for Windows 95 clients:

```
; smb.conf
[global]
     netbios name = EAGLE
     workgroup = FOWLPLAY
     include = /usr/local/samba/lib/%a.conf
; service definition go next
...
```

Remember that the %a variable expands to the name of the client's operating system. You'll assume that only Windows 9x (win95) or Windows NT (winNT) clients will be connecting. Here are the configuration files needed to support these two clients. The Windows 95 configuration file looks like this:

```
; win95.conf
encrypt passwords = no
password level = 4
```

The Windows NT client uses

```
; winNT.conf
encrypt passwords = yes
smb passwd file = /etc/smbpasswd
```

I hope that the more you use the include parameter, the more the rationalization for using the netbios aliases parameter will become clearer. Remember that the %L variable is expanded to the NetBIOS name of the server that the client used in the session setup request. By using the %L variable in the name of the file to include, the same machine can appear as very different Samba servers.

Return to the previous example using the three departments. Suppose that your company bandwidth increases to enable you to use a central server for all departments. How can you use the include parameter with NetBIOS aliases to make the change transparent to the users and your job easier?

The first thing to do is to configure the Samba server using its primary NetBIOS name:

```
; smb.conf
    netbios name = server1
    workgroup = COMPANY-GRP
    security = user
    password level = 4
; Accounting group share
[acctgrp]
    comment = Acccounting departmental share
    Path = /export/acct/acctgrp
    create mode = 0660
    directory mode = 0770
    valid users = @acct
; Personel group share
[persgrp]
    comment = Personel departmental share
    path = /export/personel/persgrp
    create mode = 0660
    directory mode = 0770
    valid users = @personel
```

```
; Administration group share
[admingrp]
    comment = Administration departmental share
    path = /export/admin/admingrp
    create mode = 0660
    directory mode = 0770
    valid users = @admin
```

Next add the names of the existing departmental servers as `netbios aliases`:

```
netbios aliases = acct-1 person-1 admin-1
```

Then copy the existing configuration files from the departmental servers and name them `acct-1.conf`, `person-1.conf`, and `admin-1.conf` respectively. You still want to keep the home directories separate, so when you move them to the new server's disk, divide them into `/export/acct`, `/export/personel`, and `/export/admin`. Now you need to tell Samba to load the configuration file that matches the name the client used during connection:

```
include = /usr/local/samba/lib/%L.conf
```

The three configuration files are given in Listings 10.3, 10.4, and 10.5.

LISTING 10.3 CONFIGURATION SETTINGS SPECIFIC FOR THE ACCOUNTING DEPARTMENT

```
; acct-1.conf
[homes]
    comment = Accounting home directories
    path = /export/acct/%U
    valid users = %S
[docs]
    comment = department documentation
    path = /export/acct/docs
    writeable = no
```

LISTING 10.4 CONFIGURATION SETTINGS SPECIFIC FOR THE PERSONNEL DEPARTMENT

```
; person-1.conf
[homes]
    comment = Personel home directories
    path = /export/personel/%U
    valid users = %S
[forms]
    comment = personel forms
    path = /export/personel/forms
```

LISTING 10.5   CONFIGURATION SETTINGS SPECIFIC FOR THE ACCOUNTING DEPARTMENT

```
; admin-1.conf
[homes]
     comment = Administration home directories
     path = /export/admin/%U
     valid users = %S
```

Figure 10.3 shows the results of browsing the network. There are physically only two machines available. QUESO is a Windows 95 client and SERVER1 is a Linux box. The other three entries—ACCT-1, ADMIN-1, and PERSON-1—are created by the netbios aliases parameter in smb.conf. Figures 10.4, 10.5, and 10.6 display the shares offered by each server. Notice that each server is slightly different, yet all have the common group shares.

FIGURE 10.3

Browsing each of the three configurations of the Samba server.
QUESO *is the Windows 95 machine used to browse the network.*
SERVER1 *is the primary NetBIOS name of the server.*

FIGURE 10.4

Browsing the shares available on ACCT-1.

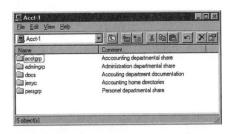

FIGURE 10.5

Browsing the shares available on ADMIN-1.

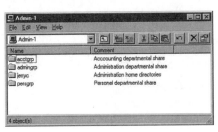

FIGURE 10.6

Browsing the shares available on PERSON-1.

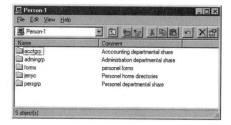

You might have already recognized a glitch. I said that you wanted the transition to be transparent to the user, but we went from three workgroups to one! I admit that I skipped over this. Currently there is no way to make Samba take part in more than one workgroup simultaneously. Therefore, for your example, I assumed that users were accessing their respective server directly using UNC network paths in the form of \\servername\sharename.

%d

I have included this last section in hopes that it will inspire your own creativity. One thing that can be difficult is determining which smbd processes are associated with which users. Hour 4, "Installing and Testing the Configuration," explains how to determine this information by using the smbstatus tool. In this section, I'm going to show you how to use root preexec and postexec scripts to implement the capability to kill all smbd processes that are running in the context of a particular user. The system comprises three basic parts:

- The root preexec and root postexec commands specified in the smb.conf file.
- The directory containing the output files from the root preexec and root postexec scripts.
- The shell script that actually kills the processes.

I'll examine each component one at a time. First, I'll examine the root preexec and root postexec commands. I want to associate a process ID with a username. This information is available in the %d and %U smb.conf variables respectively. The root preexec command creates a file with the name of the process ID for the connection and contains only the username sent by the client:

```
[apps]
    comment = global shared drive
    root preexec = echo %U > /usr/local/samba/lib/proc/%d
    root postexec = /bin/rm /usr/local/samba/lib/proc/%d
    path = /export/smb/apps
```

10

The assumption here is that every client connects to the [apps] share in addition to any other service. This is an easy assumption to work around if you check for the existence of /usr/local/samba/lib/proc/%d before attempting to create it. For now, assume that all clients connect to the [apps] share.

After the files are created, you can create a simple script to grep for the user's login name in the files. The located files will be the process IDs of the associated smbds.

```
#!/bin/sh
# set     the path
PATH=/usr/bin:/bin
export PATH
# set the location for the pid files
SMBD_DIR=/usr/local/samba/lib/proc
# the username should be passed as the single command line parameter
if [ "$1" eq "" ]; then
   echo 'Usage : killsmbd <username>'
else
   username=$1
fi
for pid in `grep $username $SMBD_DIR/*`; do
   echo "Killing $pid"
   kill -9 $pid
done
```

If you want to kill all the smbd processes for the user jdoe, you can simply type

```
killsmbd jdoe
```

You can design a similar system to enable you to terminate smbd processes based on the connected machine name by creating files that contain the %m variable.

Summary

Samba provides many tools for automating activities on the server side of SMB connections. By using the various preexec and postexec parameters, smb.conf variables, and the include directive, you can configure your server to exhibit very dynamic behavior that is able to meet the needs of your clients.

netbios aliases, when used in conjunction with the include parameter, can offer a means of emulating multiple Samba servers using a single machine.

Q&A

Q **Can a share have both a `root preexec` and a `preexec` setting?**

A Yes, it is possible to configure a service to have both a `root preexec` and a `preexec` setting or both a `root postexec` and a `postexec` setting.

Q **Can the %U, %u, %G, and %g variables be used in the `include` parameter?**

A Yes. This would enable you to specify setting on an individual or group basis. An example would to include a departmental share by adding `include = %G.conf` to the configuration, where `%G.conf` would contain the definition for some share.

New Terms

automation   The process of performing a job or task without human intervention.

server-side automation   Those things that occur on the server's end of a network connection that are automated. Examples would be dynamic share creation or reconfiguration based on the client connecting.

10

HOUR **11**

Troubleshooting

"Aaaaarrgghhh!" Have you ever felt like that?

Whether we're configuring Samba for the first time, upgrading from a previous version, or simply unable to make something work, sometimes we all need a little help. Perhaps you think this should be Hour 2 (or maybe you're reading it as Hour 2). I waited to discuss troubleshooting Samba until you had covered enough of the functionality so that I wouldn't have to explain concepts while attempting to explain how to troubleshoot connections or configurations.

The main problem with most chapters about troubleshooting is that they require you to have what I call "a critical mass" of background information. The time when you need troubleshooting the most is before you have the background information to solve things yourself. It seems a variant of the chicken-and-egg problem.

For this reason, I believe that troubleshooting any problem is somewhere between an art and a science. You need to have an understanding of the basics of the problem, but, more often than not, it is a "Eureka!" moment that brings you to jump from problem to solution.

Problem solving often involves viewing the situation from different angles, as shown in Figure 11.1. The information covered this hour comes in snippets or blocks in order to provide you with as many tools and angles as possible. Each method provides a different facet of a larger technique.

FIGURE 11.1

Troubleshooting often involves attacking the problem from different angles in order to narrow down its cause.

One of the wonderful things about an open source project, such as Samba, is that hundreds (or thousands) of people can potentially contribute to the documentation and source code. Although this creates a slight problem of maintaining an organized distribution, it does provide a vast array of experience from which you can draw. Chances are that someone has at least encountered, if not solved, the problem you are facing. Even if someone has not seen your particular problem before, most are willing to help.

In a slightly ironic twist, at the moment that I am writing this chapter, I'm working with another network administrator on a mailing list to track down a configuration problem with his server. This seems like a good way to begin!

Documentation

Generally speaking, the people who write the documentation are very much like you. They are either users or systems administrators and need to be able to find information and answers quickly. For that reason, most of the documentation, aside from man pages, consists of short one-to-two-page explanations of a specific thing and collections of frequently asked questions.

Before sending a barrage of questions and posts to various mailing lists or Usenet newsgroups asking for help, remember this: you will generally get a better response from others if you have invested some time in researching things for yourself. Don't expect others to solve your problems for you. That sounds very much like something a psychiatrist would say, doesn't it?

DIAGNOSIS.txt

When you post a question or plea for help on any type of group communication medium such as a mailing list or newsgroup, your question will normally be answered with another: "Have you completed the steps in DIAGNOSIS.txt?" When someone calls me at work and says that some application or network function isn't working on their PC, my first response is always, "Have you rebooted the PC? If not, reboot it and call me back if things still don't work." There are some general steps that you can follow to help pinpoint the nature of the problem.

The DIAGNOSIS.txt text file is located in the docs/textdocs/ directory for Samba 2.0 and higher distributions. If you are using a version of Samba that was distributed with the operating system--Linux, for example--look in the /usr/doc/samba/ directory. The file outlines a process of ten steps for troubleshooting your server. Each one is incremental and should precede the next.

The purpose for DIAGNOSIS.txt is to troubleshoot connectivity problems between a client and the server. This diagnosis process makes a few assumptions:

- You have Samba installed and have an initial configuration that you want to test.

- You have access to a PC running some version of Windows that has the TCP/IP protocol stack installed. If you're using Windows 95/98, you also need to make sure that the Client for Microsoft Networks is installed. Windows for Workgroups refers to this client as Support for Microsoft Networks, whereas Windows NT installs a Workstation service to handle the SMB client functionality.

- The Samba server has a share name, [tmp], with a path that's set to /tmp. You can create this share by adding the following section to your existing smb.conf:

```
[tmp]
    comment = Temporary Read-only share
    path = /tmp
    writeable = no
```

11

I've decided not to include a complete smb.conf as an example because I believe that you are more interested in testing the configuration for your particular server. Therefore, the described steps and examples enable you to integrate your server into the testing process. For reference, the server name I am using for these examples is BILBO and the client's machine name is QUESO.

Step 1: Testing smb.conf

The first thing you should do is to verify that there are no syntax errors in your smb.conf file by using the testparm utility like you did in Hour 4, "Installing and Testing the Configuration." The testparm tool prints quite a lot of output because it displays the default values of parameters as well as the ones you specifically set. You can view the output a screen at a time with the following:

```
testparm /etc/smb.conf ¦ more
```

You should replace /etc/smb.conf with the location of the configuration file you are testing. If there are any errors, they will be printed at the beginning of the output. Following is the [global] section from a sample smb.conf file that I checked using testparm:

```
[global]
        ; SMB settings
        netbios name = BILBO
        workgroup = FOWLPLAY
        server string = Samba server [%v]

        ; server settings
        security = user
        hosts allow = 192.168.1.
        log file = /usr/local/samba/var/log.%m


        ; password settings
        password level = 4

        ; default service settings
        lcking = no
        case sensitive = no
        public = guest
        writeable = no
```

Here are the first ten or so lines that testparm displayed:

```
[root@bilbo /root]539: /usr/local/samba/bin/testparm smb.conf- ¦ more
Load smb config files from smb.conf-
Unknown parameter encountered: "lcking"
Ignoring unknown parameter "lcking"
ERROR: Badly formed boolean in configuration file: "guest".
```

```
Processing section "[netlogon]"
Processing section "[homes]"
Processing section "[src]"
Loaded services file OK.
Press enter to see a dump of your service definitions
# Global parameters
        workgroup = FOWLPLAY
        netbios name = BILBO
```

The first error reported was the misspelling of *locking* (*lcking*), and the second was the invalid value that I attempted to assign to the `public` parameter.

Step 2: Checking IP Connectivity

After you verify that the `smb.conf` configuration file is correct syntactically, the next step is to verify that the client and server can send packets to each other using IP. First, use the `ping` command to test whether the server can "see" the client. If the `ping` command is not in your normal $PATH, it is normally stored in `/usr/sbin`, `/bin`, or `/usr/bin`:

```
jerryc$ ping queso
PING queso (192.168.1.72): 56 data bytes
64 bytes from 192.168.1.72: icmp_seq=0 ttl=128 time=0.8 ms
64 bytes from 192.168.1.72: icmp_seq=1 ttl=128 time=0.8 ms
64 bytes from 192.168.1.72: icmp_seq=2 ttl=128 time=0.8 ms
64 bytes from 192.168.1.72: icmp_seq=3 ttl=128 time=0.8 ms

--- queso ping statistics ---
4 packets transmitted, 4 packets received, 0% packet loss
round-trip min/avg/max = 0.8/0.8/0.8 ms
```

Some versions of `ping` are more verbose by default that others. The `/usr/sbin/ping` command that ships with Solaris 2.6 simply tells you whether it received any response at all:

```
jerryc$ ping sunspot
sunspot.my.net is alive
```

The type of output you see is not as important as long as you can determine that the server can reach the client.

Next try to use `ping` in the other direction, from the client to the server. The `ping.exe` tool is normally located in the `\windows\system` directory and therefore should be in your path by default:

```
C:\users\jerry>ping bilbo

Pinging bilbo [192.168.1.73] with 32 bytes of data:

Reply from 192.168.1.73: bytes=32 time=1ms TTL=64
Reply from 192.168.1.73: bytes=32 time=1ms TTL=64
```

11

```
Reply from 192.168.1.73: bytes=32 time=1ms TTL=64
Reply from 192.168.1.73: bytes=32 time=1ms TTL=64

Ping statistics for 192.168.1.73:
    Packets: Sent = 4, Received = 4, Lost = 0 (0% loss),
Approximate round trip times in milli-seconds:
    Minimum = 1ms, Maximum =  1ms, Average =  1ms
```

If either machine is having problems resolving hostnames to IP addresses, you should check your DNS settings. UNIX variants normally store the list of name servers in /etc/resolv.conf, whereas Windows clients enable you to set only the IP addresses of the DNS servers using the Network Control Panel. If necessary, you should verify that the name servers are functioning and are reachable.

Step 3: Checking Out smbd

For steps one and two, it was not necessary that the Samba daemons were running (or ready to run if you chose to launch the processes from /etc/inetd.conf). For this and the following steps, you need to start both smbd and nmbd.

After you are confident that the Samba daemons are either started or will launch on connection, use the smbclient tool to obtain a list of shares on the server as you have done previously by executing smbclient -L *servername* -N:

```
jerryc$ smbclient -L bilbo -N
Added interface ip=192.168.1.73 bcast=192.168.1.255 nmask=255.255.255.0
Domain=[FOWLPLAY] OS=[Unix] Server=[Samba 2.0.0]

        Sharename       Type        Comment
        ---------       ----        -------
        src             Disk        /usr/local/src
        tmp             Disk        Tempoary Read-Only share
        IPC$            IPC         IPC Service (Samba server [2.0.0])

        Server                      Comment
        ---------                   -------
        BILBO                       Samba server [2.0.0]

        Workgroup                   Master
        ---------                   -------
        FOWLPLAY                    BILBO
```

If the smbd daemon is not running or cannot bind to TCP port 139 for some reason, you see a message similar to the following:

```
jerryc$ smbclient -L bilbo -N
Added interface ip=192.168.1.73 bcast=192.168.1.255 nmask=255.255.255.0
error connecting to 192.168.1.73:139 (Connection refused)
Connection to bilbo failed
```

If you cannot connect to the server due to a misconfiguration in your host allow or hosts deny parameter, smbclient reports that the server is alive but refusing the session setup:

```
jerryc$ smbclient -L bilbo -N
Added interface ip=192.168.1.73 bcast=192.168.1.255 nmask=255.255.255.0
session request to BILBO failed
session request to *SMBSERVER failed
```

This is not the only possible reason for a session setup failure, but it is the most common one.

If you have problems, you should also verify that the subnet mask and broadcast address are set correctly on both the client and the server. Samba attempts to determine these automatically, but it is possible that it can't. You can explicitly state the address and netmask that Samba should use by setting the interfaces parameter. I'll cover the interfaces parameter more in Hour 20, "Routed Networks and Browsing." The format of the parameter's value is an IP address netmask pair. For example,

```
interfaces = 192.168.1.73/255.255.255.224
```

If you prefer, you can specify the netmask as a decimal number representing the number of bits to use. Remember that a logical AND is performed on the bits of a netmask and the machine's IP address to determine the network address. The following example is equivalent to the previous setting:

```
interfaces = 192.168.1.73/27
```

Step 4: Checking Out nmbd

Now is the time to check whether nmbd is installed correctly. Use the nmblookup utility to attempt to resolve the server's NetBIOS name. The following command should return the Samba server's IP address:

```
nmblookup -B servername _ _SAMBA_ _
```

The -B servername tells nmblookup to use the servername's IP address as the broadcast address and _ _SAMBA_ _ as the NetBIOS name that you want to resolve. This is a special name that only Samba servers will respond to. You should replace the servername argument with the NetBIOS name of your Samba server. For example,

```
jerryc$ nmblookup -B BILBO _ _SAMBA_ _
Sending queries to 192.168.1.73
192.168.1.73 _ _SAMBA_ _<00>
```

If nmblookup does not return your server's IP address, the most likely cause is that nmbd is not installed properly. If you launch smbd and nmbd from inetd.conf, make sure that

11

all the command-line parameters you are passing to nmbd are actually being used at startup. Some inetd implementations limit the number of parameters that can be passed to an application on the command line. If you are having trouble getting nmbd to recognize all the command line parameters, think of writing a script to start nmbd and have inetd launch the script instead.

Step 5: Verifying the Client Software on the PC

Now that you have verified that smbd and nmbd are installed and running, check the status of the client software installed on the PC. This step is very similar to step four. Use nmblookup again to query the NetBIOS interface on the client:

```
nmblookup -B clientname '*'
```

This command uses the IP address of the client machine to broadcast the request for any name. The output displayed should be the IP address of the client PC. If not, recheck that the client's TCP/IP settings are correct and that the Client for Microsoft Networks is installed in the case of Windows 9x and Windows for Workgroups:

```
jerryc$ nmblookup -B queso '*'
Sending queries to 192.168.1.72
192.168.1.72 *<00>
```

If you are using a Windows NT machine, verify that the Server and Workstation services are running and that the NetBIOS interface is bound to the network adapter. If you need more detail on configuring Windows clients, refer to Hour 14, "Windows 9x and Windows NT."

Step 6: Checking the Broadcast Address

Next, verify that the broadcast address that is configured is set properly. Remember that many of the NetBIOS name registration and resolution requests are set by default to broadcast, so you want to make sure that it is correct.

One command-line argument that you have not used in conjunction with nmblookup yet is the -d debug level switch. This parameter performs the same function that it does with respect to smbd and nmbd. The only difference is that the debug output is written to standard output rather than the log files. The wildcard character (*) that is included means that nmblookup should send broadcast requests to any and all names on the local broadcast subnet:

```
jerryc$ nmblookup -d 2 '*'
Added interface ip=192.168.1.73 bcast=192.168.1.255 nmask=255.255.255.0
Sending queries to 192.168.1.255
Got a positive name query response from 192.168.1.72 ( 192.168.1.72 )
Got a positive name query response from 192.168.1.73 ( 192.168.1.73 )
192.168.1.72 *<00>
192.168.1.73 *<00>
```

If the broadcast address is configured correctly, you should see multiple messages saying "Got a positive name query response from..." even if you have only two machines on the network as I do here. The actual number of responses is not important as long as you get one from a machine other than the server.

If you do not see output similar to the example, you might need to experiment with the `interfaces` parameter in `smb.conf` to manually configure the interface and netmask to which `smbd` and `nmbd` will bind. If you have more than one network interface, Samba binds only to the first one by default.

Step 7: Connecting to a Share Locally

Now you are ready to test the security options you have configured in `smb.conf`. By this I mean that you check the password setup to make sure that a user can connect to a share.

If you have not already done so, make sure that the [tmp] share has been added to `smb.conf` and that the /tmp directory exists and is world-readable. Next, using `smbclient` again, attempt to connect to the [tmp] service with a valid account:

```
jerryc$ smbclient '\\bilbo\tmp' -U jerryc
Added interface ip=192.168.1.73 bcast=192.168.1.255 nmask=255.255.255.0
Password: enter password here
Domain=[FOWLPLAY] OS=[Unix] Server=[Samba 2.0.0]
smb: \> dir
  .X11-unix                 DH        0  Tue Jan 12 20:11:12 1999
  log.nmb.nmb                        305  Wed Oct 14 01:03:44 1998
  .ICE-unix                 DH        0  Tue Jan 12 20:21:54 1999
  .X0-lock                  HR       11  Tue Jan 12 20:11:11 1999

        61967 blocks of size 4096. 14548 blocks available
```

> I will make one comment about the use of forward and backward slashes (/ and \). SMB shares are referred by their Universal Naming Convention (UNC) name of \\servername\sharename. UNIX commands normally parse the backslash character (\) as an escape character. Therefore, in order to use backslash characters in the UNC name, you need to enclose the path in either single or double quotes. Alternatively, `smbclient` enables you to substitute forward slashes instead, for example //bilbo/tmp. Which convention you use is your personal preference.

If `smbclient` returns with an error such as "Invalid tree in network connect," make sure that the filename path specified in `smb.conf` for the share you are connecting to is valid. Also verify that the user has permissions (read or write, whichever is appropriate) to access the directory.

If the error returned refers to a bad login name or password, verify that you are entering the password correctly. You might also want to use the -U *username* command-line argument to set the username explicitly that smbclient should use in the session setup request. Other common problems include enabling encrypted passwords but not creating a valid private/smbpasswd entry for the user, incorrect settings in the valid users parameter for the share, or a password level setting that is too low for the number of uppercase letters in the password.

Step 8: Browsing the Server from a DOS Prompt

Next you test whether the PC client can obtain a list of shares from the server. From within a DOS prompt in Windows, try the following command:

```
net view \\servername
```

Replace the *servername* with the NetBIOS name of your Samba server. Here is the output displayed when I performed this step on my test server:

```
C:\users\jerry>net view \\bilbo
Shared resources at \\BILBO

Sharename    Type      Comment
-------------------------------------------------------------------
jerryc       Disk      Linux home directories
src          Disk      /usr/local/src
tmp          Disk      Tempoary Read-Only share
The command was completed successfully.
```

If you are attempting to browse from a Windows NT client but have not enabled encrypted passwords on the server, you will probably see a message that says "Access denied." This is because Windows NT requires encrypted password support to browse the server, and even then this can be problematic. However, this will not prevent you from connecting to a specific share on the server, as you see in the next step.

If you receive an error message such as

```
Error 51: The specified computer is not receiving requests. Make
sure you are specifying the computer name correctly, or try again
later when the remote computer is available.
```

you should verify that you have not restricted access to the server through a hosts deny/allow setting in smb.conf or from a program such as TCP wrappers.

This error message,

```
Error 53: The computer name specified in the network path
cannot be located. Make sure you are specifying the computer
name correctly, or try again later when the remote computer
is available.
```

means that the PC could not resolve the NetBIOS name. This can be corrected by either fixing the nmbd installation on the server or configuring other name resolution mechanisms such as lmhosts files or a WINS server. Hour 18, "Resolving NetBIOS Names Without Using Broadcasts," covers nonbroadcast name resolution in more depth.

Step 9: Connecting to a Share from the PC

If you completed Steps 7 and 8 successfully, this step should work correctly with one possible exception. Before continuing, try to connect to the [tmp] share using the net use command:

```
C:\users\jerry>net use t: \\bilbo\tmp
The command was completed successfully.
```

The command might prompt you for a password if you are logged in to Windows with a different password than your account on the Samba server. If so, enter the correct password and press Enter.

One problem with Windows 9x is that it does not enable you to specify a different user to use in the session setup request as opposed to Windows NT's net.exe command, which contains the /user:username switch. If you are logged in to Windows with a different username than the one you want to use for the connection, you will need to log out of Windows and back in using the correct name. The other possibility is to configure Samba to map the name to a valid account using the username map option.

If you are using the correct username and password and have Samba configured for plain-text passwords but are still unable to connect to any share, you probably need to modify the password level setting in smb.conf. Remember that when Windows 9x transmits passwords in plain text, it converts the password to all uppercase letters first.

Step 10: Browsing from the Network Neighborhood

The final test determines whether network browsing is functioning. I must warn you that browsing can be a "complicated dance" as one of the Samba docs puts it. If you cannot view the Samba server after navigating to the correct workgroup in the Network Neighborhood, hang in there until I can give a proper explanation of network browsing and how to troubleshoot it in Hours 19, "Local Subnet Browsing," and 20.

Other Documentation

Samba's docs/ directory is filled with information. I'm not claiming that it is complete for every question you would ever want to ask, but it does offer quite a lot. If you ever decide that something is missing and you want to write up information on your solution, you can submit it to the Samba maintainers and, I hope, help someone else out with their difficulties.

11

Of this forest of files in the documentation tree, I'll mention only a few more of them here. One that is quite useful is UNIX_INSTALL.txt. This file walks you through the steps of downloading, compiling, and installing the latest source code like you did in Hours 3, "Obtaining the Latest Source," and 4. You are already familiar with most of the information it presents, but it never hurts to hear the same thing from more than one place.

Another file that is helpful if you want to use LanManager and Windows NT encrypted passwords is ENCRYPTION.txt. This file gives a general description of how the password hashes are generated and outlines the steps necessary to enable this support. After reading Hour 6, "Security Levels and Passwords," you should be familiar with the terms and algorithms it describes as well the steps to enable encryption.

I will mention some of the other files in the docs/ directory when I cover WINS support, browsing, and domain control later in the book. For now, feel free to glance over the documentation and know that it is available when you run into a problem.

Working the Problem from Both Ends

I have already talked about the documentation that explains what you should do to attack problems, and now I'll present some tools to help you gather information and hopefully solve your problems.

An old saying is that "It takes two to tango." This saying certainly applies to network connections. I've never been able to have a lot of fun with the loopback network interface (127.0.0.1). You really can't go anywhere with it.

Each network setup comprises at least two machines. To troubleshoot an SMB connection, you have to look at both the client and the server. This is an example of the different angles that are available to probe the problem. I like to visualize it as a warrior who is circling his enemy and poking for soft spots in his opponent's armor. Maybe that's a little too dramatic, but I think you get the idea.

Log Files

One of the best tools for debugging Samba is Samba itself. The amount of information that can be recorded by smbd and nmdb is tremendous. By setting the debug log levels (see debug level parameter in smb.conf or the -d command-line switch), you decide how much information you want to view. Samba defaults to printing level 2 and below debug information. This normally logs connections and any system error messages such as not being able to open the smbpasswd file. Here is an example of entries written by the smbd daemon running at debug level 2.

```
[1999/01/12 23:52:28, 1] smbd/service.c:make_connection(484)
  bilbo (192.168.1.73) connect to service tmp as user jerryc (uid=1009,
➡gid=100) (pid 436)
```

Debug levels range from 0, which is for critical errors, to 10, which is used for development purposes. The breakdown of the various levels appears in Table 11.1. If you need to change the debug level of a specific running process, you can increase the level by sending the process a USR1 signal:

```
kill -USR1 pid
```

Alternatively, you can decrease the log level by sending the process the USR2 signal:

```
kill -USR2 pid
```

TABLE 11.1 DEBUG LEVEL DESCRIPTIONS

Log Level	Description
0	System-critical errors such as a failure to open the system password file.
1–2	General daily logging of connections and user validation.
3–5	Debugging setups, configuration, and source code.
>6	Development.

Here is an example of using the debug logs to correct a problem in the smb.conf file:

```
[src]
        comment = /usr/local/src
        path = /usr/local/sr
        create mode = 0644
        directory mode = 0755
```

The user attempted to connect to the share from a Windows NT 4.0 Workstation using the net use command and received the error "The network name cannot be found." The following entry was found in the smbd debug log:

```
[1999/01/13 16:15:16, 0] smbd/service.c:make_connection(437)
  Can't change directory to /usr/local/sr (No such file or directory)
```

As you can see, the path set for the share did not exist. After correcting this, the user could successfully connect to \\bilbo\src. to put things in perspective. The previous log entry was recorded as a level 0 debug statement.

11

Running Samba at very high log levels results in a very large amount of information being recorded and can quickly fill the disk where the debug logs are located. I do not recommend using debug levels above 2 on normal day-to-day use. If you want to use higher levels, investigate the max log size parameter to control the maximum size in kilobytes of the log files.

To give you an idea about how much information smbd can log, Listing 11.1 shows the output from the same connection to \\bilbo\src at debug level 10. Pretty lengthy, huh? In fact, the listing contains only the steps during the protocol negotiation request.

LISTING 11.1 LEVEL 10 DEBUG OUTPUT RECORDED BY Smbd FOR A PROTOCOL NEGOTIATION REQUEST DURING AN ATTEMPT TO CONNECT TO A DIRECTORY SHARE BY A WINDOWS 95 CLIENT

```
[1999/01/13 16:34:10, 6] param/loadparm.c:lp_file_list_changed(1767)
lp_file_list_changed()
file /etc/smb.conf -> /etc/smb.conf  last mod_time: Wed Jan 13 16:14:54
1999

[1999/01/13 16:34:10, 5] smbd/connection.c:claim_connection(127)
  trying claim /usr/local/samba/var/locks STATUS. 100000
[1999/01/13 16:34:10, 8] lib/util.c:fcntl_lock(2632)
  fcntl_lock 8 7 0 1 1
[1999/01/13 16:34:10, 8] lib/util.c:fcntl_lock(2693)
  Lock call successful
[1999/01/13 16:34:10, 8] lib/util.c:fcntl_lock(2632)
  fcntl_lock 8 7 0 1 2
[1999/01/13 16:34:10, 8] lib/util.c:fcntl_lock(2693)
  Lock call successful
[1999/01/13 16:34:10, 5] smbd/reply.c:reply_special(147)
  init msg_type=0x81 msg_flags=0x0
[1999/01/13 16:34:10, 6] lib/util_sock.c:write_socket(185)
  write_socket(6,4)
[1999/01/13 16:34:10, 6] lib/util_sock.c:write_socket(188)
  write_socket(6,4) wrote 4
[1999/01/13 16:34:10, 10]
lib/util_sock.c:read_smb_length_return_keepalive(445)
  got smb length of 170
[1999/01/13 16:34:10, 6] smbd/process.c:process_smb(564)
  got message type 0x0 of len 0xaa
[1999/01/13 16:34:10, 3] smbd/process.c:process_smb(565)
  Transaction 1 of length 174
[1999/01/13 16:34:10, 5] lib/util.c:show_msg(459)
  size=170
  smb_com=0x72
  smb_rcls=0
```

```
  smb_reh=0
  smb_err=0
  smb_flg=24
  smb_flg2=3
[1999/01/13 16:34:10, 5] lib/util.c:show_msg(465)
  smb_tid=0
  smb_pid=51966
  smb_uid=0
  smb_mid=0
  smt_wct=0
[1999/01/13 16:34:10, 5] lib/util.c:show_msg(475)
  smb_bcc=135
[1999/01/13 16:34:10, 10] lib/util.c:dump_data(2832)
  [000] 02 50 43 20 4E 45 54 57  4F 52 4B 20 50 52 4F 47  .PC NETW ORK
PROG
[1999/01/13 16:34:10, 10] lib/util.c:dump_data(2840)
  [010] 52 41 4D 20 31 2E 30 00  02 58 45 4E 49 58 20 43  RAM 1.0. .XENIX
C
[1999/01/13 16:34:10, 10] lib/util.c:dump_data(2840)
  [020] 4F 52 45 00 02 4D 49 43  52 4F 53 4F 46 54 20 4E  ORE..MIC ROSOFT
N
[1999/01/13 16:34:10, 10] lib/util.c:dump_data(2840)
  [030] 45 54 57 4F 52 4B 53 20  31 2E 30 33 00 02 4C 41  ETWORKS
1.03..LA
[1999/01/13 16:34:10, 10] lib/util.c:dump_data(2840)
  [040] 4E 4D 41 4E 31 2E 30 00  02 57 69 6E 64 6F 77 73  NMAN1.0.
.Windows
[1999/01/13 16:34:10, 10] lib/util.c:dump_data(2840)
  [050] 20 66 6F 72 20 57 6F 72  6B 67 72 6F 75 70 73 20   for Wor kgroups
[1999/01/13 16:34:10, 10] lib/util.c:dump_data(2840)
[060] 33 2E 31 61 00 02 4C 4D  31 2E 32 58 30 30 32 00  3.1a..LM 1.2X002.
[1999/01/13 16:34:10, 10] lib/util.c:dump_data(2840)
  [070] 02 4C 41 4E 4D 41 4E 32  2E 31 00 02 4E 54 20 4C  .LANMAN2 .1..NT
L
[1999/01/13 16:34:10, 10] lib/util.c:dump_data(2840)
  [080] 4D 20 30 2E 31 32 00                              M 0.12.
```

People

People can be the best resource for tracking down problems. You must remember, though, that all the people who you might contact on the various mailings and news-groups help because they want to and not because they are paid to. That includes most of those who develop Samba, commonly referred to as the Samba Team. This means that the ultimate burden for fixing your problems still falls on your shoulders.

When posting to or answering questions on any mailing list or newsgroup, you should follow common Internet etiquette (or *Netiquette*). If you do not, you will find that people will be less than helpful. However, if you are considerate in your postings, someone will normally respond.

You can find out more information about the Samba mailing lists and how to join them at `http://samba.org/listproc`. Some of the available mailing lists are

- `samba@samba.org`—This is the main Samba mailing list for general information about the latest distributed version of Samba (for example, Samba 2.0).

- `samba-technical@samba.org`—This is the mailing list for discussions regarding the development of Samba. If you feel like pitching in, join the list, open up `vi`, and start working through the source code.

- `samba-ntdom@samba.org`—This list focuses on the testing and debugging of Samba's Primary Domain Controller support for Windows NT Domains.

- `samba-bugs@samba.org`—This address is not a mailing list, but rather an address for reporting actual bugs in the Samba applications.

The Usenet newsgroup `comp.protocols.smb` is another good source of information about configuring and testing Samba.

Network Sniffers

As I have told you before, one of my first jobs as a network administrator came as the result of a graduate assistantship. I was working part-time to manage a small network of PCs and a single Sparc IPX mail and Web server running SunOS 4.1.3. After some time, I was able to upgrade the OS on the server to Solaris 2.5 and install a second file server. While trying to locate a problem, another sysadmin who later became a very good friend asked me, "Have you looked at the `snoop` output yet?" (`snoop` is a packet viewing software tool included with Solaris 2.x machines.) I said, "Huh?" and so began my first introduction to packet sniffing. Although it is less harmful than sniffing glue, it can be much more addictive!

NEW TERM A packet (or network) sniffer is a utility that enables you to capture the packets that the host machine sees on the network. If you use a shared media environment, such as Ethernet, the machine network interface sees all the packets on the local subnet. If you use some sort of switched environment, you are able to see only packets sent to and from your machine and those sent to the network broadcast address.

What advantage is there to using a packet sniffer? If you simply want to use Samba and are not curious about what goes on behind the scenes, you can safely skip this last section and proceed directly to Hour 12, "Case Study: Replacing an NT File and Print Server." If you are even slightly curious, I encourage you to read on.

The advantage of using a packet-tracing tool is that you get to see exactly what Samba sees. You also get to see exactly what Samba does. More than once, someone using a packet sniffer has uncovered a bug in Samba, Windows NT, Windows 9x, and [insert your favorite network operating system here]. You get the idea.

I will look at two packet sniffers in this section. One is freely available, and the other is a commercial product.

tcpdump-smb

tcpdump is a freely available network packet analysis tool originally written by Van Jacobson. Parts of the tool were later rewritten by Steven McCanne, and the code is now maintained by the Network Research Group at the Lawrence Berkeley National Laboratory. tcpdump requires the libpcap library, which is a user-level machine-independent interface for capturing packets.

Andrew Tridgell, the original author of Samba, has written a set of patches to enable tcpdump to parse SMB packets. The latest version of tcpdump, the source for libpcap, and the patch set to enable SMB support can be downloaded from ftp://ftp.samba.org/pub/samba/tcpdump-smb.

The advantage that tcpdump has over the other packet-dump utility that you'll examine is that it is entirely command line based. Therefore it runs very nicely in a remote telnet session. When compiled, the binary is self-contained and can easily be copied to the remote machine and executed. There is no need to install special device drivers or other software.

In addition to this, tcpdump is freely available. This means that you can capture a packet trace on an Irix box and send the output file to other administrators who use different platforms. In turn, they can easily view the file when they have compiled tcpdump for their system.

Perhaps it is easier to continue this conversation if you look at some sample output together. To produce the first packet trace, I ran net view \\bilbo from my Windows 95 client. queso. bilbo, a Slackware Linux box, is running Samba 2.0. I captured the packets on bilbo by running

```
tcpdump port 139 and host queso
```

which produces this output shown in Listing 11.2.

11

LISTING 11.2   TCPDUMP OUTPUT FROM A NET VIEW \\SERVERNAME COMMAND ISSUED ON A WINDOWS 95 CLIENT

```
queso.1083 > bilbo.netbios-ssn: P 73:231(158) ack 5 win 8756
>>> NBT Packet
NBT Session Packet
Flags=0x0
Length=154
SMB PACKET: SMBnegprot (REQUEST)

bilbo.netbios-ssn > queso.1083: P 5:87(82) ack 231 win 32736
>>> NBT Packet
NBT Session Packet
Flags=0x0
Length=78
SMB PACKET: SMBnegprot (REPLY)

queso.1083 > bilbo.netbios-ssn: P 231:392(161) ack 87 win 8674
>>> NBT Packet
NBT Session Packet
Flags=0x0
Length=157
SMB PACKET: SMBsesssetupX (REQUEST)
SMB PACKET: SMBtconX (REQUEST) (CHAINED)

bilbo.netbios-ssn > queso.1083: P 87:180(93) ack 392 win 32736
>>> NBT Packet
NBT Session Packet
Flags=0x0
Length=89
SMB PACKET: SMBsesssetupX (REPLY)
SMB PACKET: SMBtconX (REPLY) (CHAINED)
```

I have deleted the portions of the output that display the raw packet information and the SMB flags. A blank line separates each packet. If you look at each line labeled SMB PACKET, you will notice the three steps in an SMB connection to a server in user level security:

```
SMB PACKET: SMBnegprot (REQUEST)
SMB PACKET: SMBnegprot (REPLY)
SMB PACKET: SMBsesssetupX (REQUEST)
SMB PACKET: SMBtconX (REQUEST) (CHAINED)

SMB PACKET: SMBsesssetupX (REPLY)
SMB PACKET: SMBtconX (REPLY) (CHAINED)
```

The first packet is the step during which the client and server decide on the dialect of the SMB protocol to use.

I have not previously mentioned that certain SMB commands can be chained together in one packet. In the request packet, the client sends the session setup request and the tree connection request. The server sends the replies to both requests in one reply packet.

Microsoft's Network Monitor

Microsoft includes a packet-tracing tool with the Windows NT Server CD-ROM and with the System Management Software (SMS) CD-ROM called Network Monitor (a k a netmon). netmon comprises two parts: an agent and the tool itself. Both must be installed for the software to function correctly. Figure 11.2 displays the installation window under Windows NT 4.0 Server.

FIGURE 11.2

Installing the Network Monitor agent and tools on a Windows NT 4.0 Workstation.

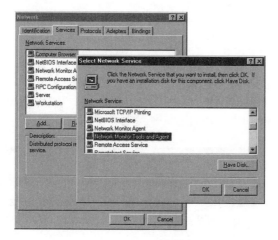

There are two distinct versions of netmon, neither of which are freely available like tcpdump. The version included with the Windows NT 4.0 Server CD-ROM allows only for viewing packets sent to and from the local machine. The version included with the SMS CD-ROM enables the network interface to be put into promiscuous mode where all packets on the shared media can be seen. Both versions can also be run locally on Windows NT Workstations and on Windows 9x clients as long as the Network Monitor agent has been installed.

Although netmon cannot run on a machine using a Telnet window, it is possible to capture packets remotely. The Network Monitor agent must be installed on the remote machine, though. When this has been finished, you can specify the remote network to which you want to connect as shown in Figure 11.3.

FIGURE 11.3

*Connecting to a
remote Network
Monitoring Agent.*

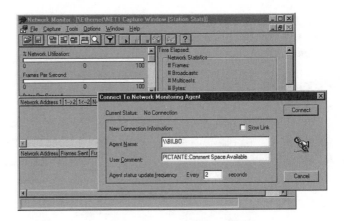

Why would you use netmon if tcpdump is freely available? That is a good question.
Network Monitor does a very nice job of parsing many types of packets from DNS
requests, NFS packets, IPX, and even Microsoft's own implementation of DCE/RPC.
Figure 11.4 displays the same packet trace you saw earlier with tcpdump (see Listing
11.2) when viewed in netmon.

FIGURE 11.4

*Network capture dis-
played in Network
Monitor.*

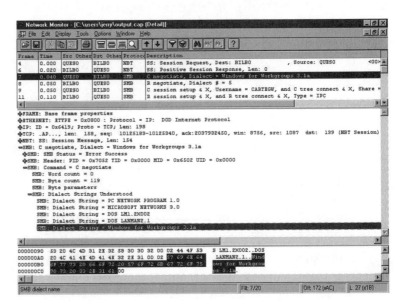

Putting `tcpdump` and `netmon` Together

Network Monitor has a very nice way of displaying output, but what if the only way to capture the packets you need is on a remote UNIX box? Here's an easy way to combine the best of both worlds.

First, use the SMB-enabled version `tcpdump` to capture the packets on the remote network being sure to save them to a file:

```
tcpdump -s 1000 -t -w output.dump host <hostname>
```

Now use the `capconvert` tool to convert the `tcpdump` output file into `netmon`'s CAP format. In case you are wondering, the source file for `capconvert` is also available for download from `ftp://ftp.samba.org/pub/tcpdump-smb/capconvert.c`.

If you are using a Solaris 2.x machine and would rather use Sun's own packet sniffer, `snoop`, you can download a snoop-to-CAP converter from `ftp://ftp.samba.org/pub/tcpdump-smb/snoop2cap.c`.

Now you need to simply copy the converted file to a Windows box where it can be viewed in `netmon`.

Summary

Troubleshooting any problem is somewhere between an art and a science. This hour has provided information on available tools to cover the science portion of your job. Such things as good documentation, log entries, and packet sniffers can provide you with all the information necessary to determine the problem. However, disseminating this information and using it to form a solution can take time, experience, and creativity.

Various mailing lists and Usenet newsgroups can put you in touch with people to help you with the art of troubleshooting. Remember to do your homework and look at the problem from all angles, not simply at the piece that is broken.

Q&A

Q Are there archives for the different Samba mailing lists that I can search to see whether anyone has ever asked my question before?

A Yes. There is a searchable archive for all the mailing lists served by the `samba.org` site. Point your Web browser to `http://samba.org/listproc` for more details.

Q Where can I find out information about commercial support for Samba?

A The main Samba Web site includes a page containing a list of companies that offer commercial support for Samba. An "official" Samba support structure is being organized and will be in place in the near future.

New Terms

packet sniffer   This is a common name for a class of network tools, either software or hardware, that are able to display the raw data being transmitted across a network. These utilities are also called network tracers or packet tracers. Some also provide the capability to parse the packets and display the information in a format more readable to humans.

Hour 12

Case Study: Replacing an NT File and Print Server

I have grown to hate meetings like these. I start going over my slide presentation in my head once more. If only I had a network connection under the table, I could be doing something useful now like checking my email or something.

I can tell that my boss is getting ready to introduce me soon. "…and now with the cost analysis of replacing the server, here is our resident expert network administrator." My boss always likes to throw in that *expert* line. I take another sip of coffee as I make my way to the head of the room to stand by the projector. I press the Spacebar to bring my notebook out of Sleep mode as I speak. "What we want to look at today are some figures that compare the cost of the services that we offer to our users on the network," I begin. I can hear my notebook's hard disk spinning up and the first slide appears as if on cue…

"...so the bottom line is this. By using a combination of Linux and Samba running on commodity PC hardware, we can replace the existing file server with a newer machine that is twice as fast for about half the cost. Second, there will be no per-seat or per-connection client licensing fees associated with the server. And finally, the change will be transparent to the end user." I breathe a silent sigh of relief as I sit back down only to find my coffee cold by now.

"If this solution is as good as it sounds, why didn't we do this the first time?" one of the department heads asks.

I shrug my shoulders a little, remembering the person who installed the last batch of Windows NT servers for the company. "Times change," I explain. "Regardless of the rationale for the plan that got us to here, the solution I presented is the best one for us today, and one that I believe will serve us well in to the future."

"Well done," my boss says as the two of us walk back to the office from the meeting. "I'll have Mike get out the purchase orders for the new hardware by the end of the day."

"She's always overly optimistic about those purchase orders," I smile and think to myself. "Sounds good," I reply as I turn the corner to the lab and beginning walking away. I begin to go over in my mind the things I need to do to replace the Windows NT file server with a Linux box. "Now where did I put that coffee cup?" I mutter...

So far, I have looked at the capabilities of Samba and how to set up the `smb.conf` file. Now it's time to get practical with what you've learned. In this hour, I will walk step by step through the process of replacing a Windows NT 4.0 Server with a Linux box running Samba. The Windows NT machine offers disk and printer shares. The Samba server simply takes over the responsibility of serving these resources. If all goes well, the end users will never know that the NT server has been replaced.

The Existing Network

First, I need to assess what requirements my Samba server will need to meet. I'll make a list:

- All Domain users should be able to access the new shares on the Samba server without requiring a synchronized UNIX account on the machine. This means that the existing NT domain account should provide access to the new server's shared resources.
- The Samba server should appear in the same workgroup and use the same NetBIOS machine name as the existing server in order to minimize confusion for the users.

- Access control mechanism to files should be kept the same so that a user who has access to a file on the existing server should have access to the same file on the Samba server. Also, a user who does not have access to a file on the existing server should not be able to access that file under the new configuration.

Satisfying the first two needs is straightforward, but satisfying the final requirement will take a little work on my part.

Here are the network resources that the current Windows NT server is providing. I have simplified this list somewhat so that I can spend time looking at each service individually.

- [users]—This share contains the home directories for the users in the domain.
- [docs]—A common disk share for group collaboration. All users can create directories within the share, but when a file is created, access is controlled via the standard NTFS ACLs.
- [canon]—A network printer available for all users in the domain.

Finally, Figure 12.1 illustrates the current setup. I will be working within a single domain model with one Primary Domain Controller (PDC) that handles all user authentication. The number of client machines is not important for my purposes here. In order to test the new server, I need the PDC to perform the authentication, the new server, and one Windows NT client machine.

FIGURE 12.1

An overview of the network that contains the Windows NT Server to be replaced.

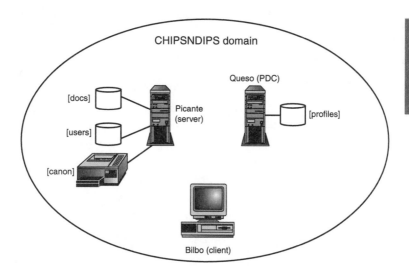

12

The Linux Server

To provide some background and make sure that we are all working from the same page, I will use a server built with the Slackware Linux 3.5 distribution, which is based on the Linux kernel 2.0.34. Here is the output from uname -a:

```
Linux picante 2.0.34 #2 Thu Jun 4 22:36:07 PDT 1998 i586 unknown
```

The machine itself is a Dell Pentium 233 with an 8GB IDE hard disk and 128MB RAM.

The Samba installation is version 2.0, which I downloaded in source form, compiled, and installed using the following three commands:

```
./configure
make
make install
```

The Replacement Process

To replace the Windows NT server with the newer Linux box, I will go through five steps:

1. Deal with existing NT Domain accounts and any necessary mappings within the Linux box.
2. Move the files and print spools from the Windows NT Server to the Linux box.
3. Configure the appropriate parameters in the Samba configuration file (smb.conf).
4. Add the Samba server to the NT Domain.
5. Test the new server.

Step 1: Users and Groups

When I first talked about the services that my Samba server would need to provide, I decided that all the existing domain users should be able to connect to the new server without explicitly knowing of a second account. Creating and maintaining a separate account, even one with a password synchronized to the Domain account, is not an acceptable option. The fact that users will not have a valid shell on the Linux machine makes this decision possible. If Samba can use the Windows NT PDC for user authentication, that's one fewer thing to have to worry about.

NT's Relative IDs and UNIX's uids and gids

Before looking at specific issues related to user accounts, I want to provide some background for those of you who are familiar with how Windows NT represents an account internally. I think it helps justify some of the decisions I need to make later.

Windows NT uses a numeric number to represent accounts internally like UNIX does. However, UNIX does not make the distinction between a domain account and a local account. If you are familiar with Sun's network information service (NIS), it is helpful to think of the PDC as the NIS master and domain accounts are those listed in the NIS `passwd` map. If an account with the username `jdoe` exists in both the local `/etc/passwd` file and the NIS `passwd` map, only one of those accounts is seen, depending on the lookup order defined in `/etc/nsswitch.conf`: files or NIS. This is why previously I stated that UNIX does not allow for the distinction between local and global accounts.

NEW TERM Another difference between the two operating systems is that Windows NT group and user accounts exist in the same number space. It is very possible, if not common, to see a UNIX machine with a group that has an ID of 0 (`wheel`) and a user account that has an ID of 0 (`root`). There is no clash in this case because UNIX gids and uids exist entirely separate from each other. Windows NT groups and user accounts exist side by side. It is therefore impossible to have a group with an ID of 1002 and a user account with an ID of 1002. Windows NT groups and users are created in a monotonically increasing order beginning at 1000. This ID number is called a relative ID or rid. A rid is appended with either the local machine's ID or the domain ID to fully qualify the account and thus provide the distinction between domain and local accounts. These machine IDs are called security identifiers, or sids.

Perhaps you wonder whether groups and users exist in the same number space. How then can you determine whether ID 1002 is a group or a user? Windows NT associates an account-type flag that is stored with each object. The rid alone is not enough to indicate the type of account.

Now that I understand how Windows NT and UNIX represent users and groups, how do I get from one to the other and back again? The easiest method when the Samba server is a member of an NT controlled domain is simply to match the username for the NT account with a username on the UNIX machine.

Wait a minute! Didn't I say that I didn't want users to worry about a second account on the Samba server? Here's the solution. I'll create accounts for the users on my Linux box, but all authentication is passed off the PDC. In this way I can disable all the password fields in `/etc/passwd`, and the users will have only one account to maintain.

So what then is the point of the UNIX account in the first place? One thing that is not currently implemented in Samba is support for Windows NT access control lists on shares that Samba serves. Therefore, I use the standard UNIX file permissions, which means that each user must have a UNIX uid and gid for this to work. Make sense?

12

Creating the Linux User Accounts and Groups

Now that you understand why I need to create accounts for the domain users on the Linux box, I can choose two options. The first is to have Samba create them automatically, if necessary, when a user connects. The second solution is to create the users and groups manually. By manually, I am not ruling out automation via scripts, rather I mean that the accounts will be created without Samba's intervention.

I am choosing the second option for this reason: the existing NT server already has files created and owned by domain users. This is probably the more common circumstance. I can create Linux user accounts on-the-fly, but getting existing group membership correct can be difficult. I think this will become more apparent the farther along I get.

First, I need to get a listing of the user accounts from the PDC. The Windows NT version of the net.exe command has another option that I have not talked about yet. The user option enables me to gain information about local and domain accounts. If I execute the following command, I will get a listing of all the domain users. The machine SALSA is my Windows NT 4.0 PDC.

```
E:\users>net user /domain

User accounts for \\SALSA

-----------------------------------------------------------------------
Administrator          daphnie                dot
freddie                Guest                  jerryc
scooby                 shaggy                 velma
wacko                  yacko
The command completed successfully.
```

If I need to get information about a specific user account, I can add an additional argument to the user option to indicate what user to look up. For example, to find out more information about a user named scooby, I run net user scooby /domain. The output from this is shown in Listing 12.1.

LISTING 12.1 DOMAIN USER ACCOUNT INFORMATION RETURNED FROM net user COMMAND

```
E:\users>net user scooby /domain
User name                 scooby
Full Name
Comment
User's comment
Country code              000 (System Default)
Account active            Yes
Account expires           Never
```

```
Password last set          1/21/99 7:48 AM
Password expires           1/22/99 7:48 AM
Password changeable        1/21/99 7:48 AM
Password required          Yes
User may change password   Yes

Workstations allowed       All
Logon script
User profile               \\salsa\users\scooby\profile
Home directory             \\picante\users\scooby
Last logon                 Never

Logon hours allowed        All

Local Group Memberships
Global Group memberships   *Domain Users        *Accounting
The command completed successfully.
```

Now I need to find some information about the Domain groups. There is an analogous parameter to the user option for the net.exe command for displaying the list of domain or local groups and the associated information:

```
E:\users>net group /domain

Group Accounts for \\SALSA

-------------------------------------------------------------------
*Accounting            *Dept Heads          *Domain Admins
*Domain Guests         *Domain Users        *Web Developers
The command completed successfully.
```

If I need to view current membership, the group option accepts a group name to look up:

```
E:\users>net group "Dept Heads" /domain
Group name      Dept Heads
Comment

Members

-------------------------------------------------------------------
freddie                velma
The command completed successfully.
```

Now that I have access to all the information I need, I now want to create the accounts. I have included a simple Perl script on the CD named nt2passwd that accepts the output from the net user /domain command and produces valid /etc/passwd entries. The script also creates a home directory for each user. If I decide not to do this, the

12

corresponding field in the `passwd` entry is set to `/dev/null`. Here is the output when I ran my list of domain users through the script. First I captured the output from `net user /domain` and piped it to a file:

```
E:\users>net user /domain > users.txt
```

Then I transferred the `users.txt` file to my Linux box and ran the `nt2passwd` script:

```
# ./nt2passwd users.txt
Enter the uid to start with : 1000
Enter the gid to use : 100

Do you want to create a home directory for the users? (y/n) y
Please enter the base directory for the users home : /export/home
Do you want me to make the home directories for you? (y/n) y
Please enter a username for [administrator] of 8 characters or less: ntadm
```

You have probably already noticed that Linux doesn't support usernames longer than eight characters. If the `nt2passwd` script locates one, it prompts for a valid username. If the new username already exists, the script asks whether the user wants to try another name. The user can skip the account altogether by responding with an n. A file containing entries in the form of

UNIXusername=NTusername

is created and named `username.map` to record these mappings. I can use this file with `smb.conf`'s `username map` parameter so that Windows NT usernames are correctly matched with a valid UNIX account. The mapfile created in my example is as follows:

```
ntadmin=administrator
```

`nt2passwd` creates a file named `passwd.new`, which contains all the newly created accounts. All that is necessary is to append the file to my existing `/etc/passwd` file. `nt2passwd` checks for uid conflicts when the accounts are created so that this is not an issue:

```
# cat passwd.new >> /etc/passwd
```

Next I need to create entries in `/etc/group` for the NT domain groups. Again, I use the output from the `net.exe` command to create the entries. First I pipe the output from net group `/domain` to a file:

```
net group /domain > groups.txt
```

Next, I pass the output from the `net group` command to the Perl script named `nt2group`. This script takes an additional parameter, which is the name of a file that contains the mapping from the Windows NT domain group name to the name of a Linux group. Mappings are entered one per line with a colon (:) separating the two names. Here is the sample mapping file I use. The NT group name is listed on the left and the Linux group name is listed on the right:

```
accounting:acct
dept heads:dptheads
domain users:users
web developers:webdev
```

After running the nt2group script

```
# nt2group groups.txt group.map
Enter the gid to start with : 200
```

the following entries are created in a file named group.new. The reason that there is no entry for the users group is that it already existed on my Linux box.

```
acct:*:200:
dptheads:*:201:
webdev:*:203:
```

I append these entries to the existing /etc/group file on the system to create the groups

```
cat group.new >> /etc/group
```

At this point, the users and the group have been created. The final step is to populate the groups with the appropriate usernames. To do this, I again turn to the useful net.exe utility. Remember that I can find out the members of a group by executing net group *groupname* /domain. There is another Perl script named add2group included on the CD that takes this output and prints the updated version of the /etc/group file to standard output.

Look at an example. Here is the output from net group Accounting /domain for the CHIPSNDIPS domain:

```
Group name      Accounting
Comment

Members

- - - - - - - - - - - - - - - - - - - - - - - - - - - - - - - - - - - - - - - - - - - - -
daphnie              scooby                  velma
The command completed successfully.
```

Using the same group mapping that I did previously with the nt2group tool, here is the sample execution for the Linux group named acct. The first parameter is the output from the execution of net group Accounting, the second argument is the group mapfile I used in conjunction with the nt2group Perl script, and the final command line parameter is the file containing the username mappings created by the nt2passwd script.

12

The script actually displays the unmodified entries as well, but the output has been shortened here for display purposes:

```
# add2group accouting.txt group.map username.map
[...output deleted...]
acct:*:200:daphnie,scooby,velma
[...output deleted...]
```

I repeat the same step for each domain group. Here are the results for the four group entries:

```
users::100:games
acct:*:200:daphnie,scooby,velma
dptheads:*:201:freddie,velma
webdev:*:203:freddie,jerryc,shaggy
```

Notice that there are no names listed in the users group. That is because I have no need to add the user to the entry in /etc/group if that is the user's primary group ID as defined in /etc/passwd. The script bypasses any usernames that cannot be located in /etc/passwd. For example, if I choose not to create an account for Administrator, if it had been a member of the Accounting group, it would have simply been skipped.

Finally I have the user accounts created, the groups have been created, and users have been added to the necessary secondary groups. Whew! That was a lot of work! Fortunately, this is the hardest part of replacing the Windows NT server.

I stated before that it was possible for Samba to, if necessary, automatically create user accounts for you when a particular user connected. I do this by defining a script for smbd to run when a user should be added or deleted. These two global parameters, add user script and delete user script, are new to version 2.0. They are part of an effort to create what is called "appliance mode." Support for this enables Samba box deployment in a Windows NT network with minimal configuration, which mostly consists of network address parameters. All users and groups can be created on-the-fly as they are needed. Keep watching as there will be continued development in Samba to support this type of operation.

When you are transferring existing files that have associated access control lists, it is better to configure things apart from Samba as I have done.

Step 2: Moving the Files and Print Spools

Moving files from a Windows NT server to my Linux server could be an absolute nightmare! However, some good systems management techniques can help to smooth things out. By organizing the directory tree to group files with common ownership and common ACLs together, I can minimize the amount of work necessary.

[users]

To start with, I'll take a deeper look at the [users] share provided by the NT file server. The way that the share is set up, it is the equivalent of exporting the /home/ directory to other UNIX machines via NFS and placing the users' home directories one level below. In other words, \\PICANTE\users contains a directory for each domain user. A user's home directory is actually \\PICANTE\users*username*.

The directory permissions for folders contained in the [users] service are very straight-forward. Every user owns and has full control of their respective directory. Only an Administrator (for example, PICANTE\Administrator) can create directories in the top level of the share. This translates to the UNIX permissions:

```
drwx------     username       groupname      username/
```

To transfer files in home directories, I simply need to copy the user's files to the location specified in /etc/passwd. I can then set the permissions using the chown command:

```
chown -R username homedir
chgrp -R groupname homedir
chmod -R 700 homedir
```

I replace *username* with the appropriate string and *homedir* with absolute path to the user's home directory. The *groupname* is the user's primary group ID from /etc/passwd.

Now I define the [users] share in smb.conf to provide the equivalent service as before:

```
[users]
    comment = home directories for domain users
    path = /export/home
    create mode = 0600
    directory mode = 0700
```

[docs]

The [docs] share is slightly harder to transfer due to the variances in the file and directory ACLs. I must deal with two possibilities. One is when a single user or group is used in the access control list. This can map the directory onto the UNIX permission bit model, but the second possibility does not map so nicely. The problem arises when multiple users or groups are included in the ACL.

First, examine the possibility of access from a single user or a single group and how to deal with it.

12

FIGURE 12.2

A diagram of the directory access control lists in the [docs] *share.*

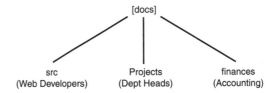

Figure 12.2 represents the various ACLs on directories within the [docs] tree. I assume that, although various directories are owned by differing groups, this access is fairly localized. For example, the Accounting group owns the \\PICANTE\docs\finances directory and everything below it, and the Web Development group controls the \\PICANTE\docs\src directory tree. This type of access control can be represented using the UNIX owner and group permission bits. I will also set the group ID bit so that the group ownership cascades down into the given directory:

```
drwxrws---    root    acct        finances/
-rw-rw----    root    acct        finances/department.xls
drwxrws---    root    webdev      src/
-rw-rw----    root    webdev      src/calendar.html
```

UNIX does not allow for ownership by more than one user or group at a time. Windows NT does not either, for that matter, but the UNIX permission model is based solely on ownership. There is no means for allowing members of only two groups to a file. It is either one group or world-accessible. Windows NT separates ownership from permission by using access-control lists that allow multiple user and group entries, each with a unique set of permissions. The only way to work around this without proper NT ACL support is to use some combination of the valid users, write list, read list, and force user smb.conf parameters. In essence, the first three parameters become the file or directory ACL. The force user parameter can be useful but all "CREATOR OWNER" information is lost.

My example assumes a single user or group in the ACL. I don't believe that this assumption decreases the usability of Samba in this particular setup; rather, it simply creates the need for a more organized directory structure. Although NT ACLs are not currently supported in version 2.0, work is underway to implement the necessary mechanisms.

Prior to moving the files, make notes regarding the current directory ownership and related ACL information. Then I can manually set the appropriate permissions on the Linux server. For example, if \\PICANTE\docs\Projects were owned by the "Dept Heads" group and had at least "Change" permission on the directory (that is rwxd if you aren't familiar with Windows NT ACLs), I would set the equivalent permissions on the Linux box by executing a series of chown, chgrp, and chmod commands:

```
# chown -R root /export/docs
# chgrp -R dptheads /export/docs
# chmod -R 770 /export/docs
# chmod -R g+s /export/docs
# ls -ld /export/docs
drwxrws---     root     dptheads     /export/docs/Projects/
```

To enforce this, I configure the [docs] share in smb.conf to always set the group read-write bits on files and read-write-execute on directories:

```
[docs]
    comment = domain group share
    path = /export/docs
    create mode = 0660
    directory mode = 0770
```

[canon]

I will not go into a lot of detail about Windows NT clients and printing to a Samba server. However, there are two things of which you should be aware.

A Windows NT client uses special mechanisms to print to another Windows NT machine. These are different from the call it makes to print to a Windows 9x server or a Samba server. This means that it is not yet possible to swap a Samba server for a Windows NT print server without a little bit of legwork. This normally involves some slight reconfigurations to the client's network printer connection. The problem with implementing true NT printing is that when you support part of the functionality, Windows NT expects you to support it all. Support for this should be available in Samba in the near future. Portions of the code have already been written, and the rest is on the way.

The second issue, which is actually related to the first problem, is that Samba does not support the downloading of printer driver files when a client first connects to a printer. See Hour 8, "Printers," for a refresher on this if you need to. Again, you can expect this functionality soon.

When transferring a printer spool from an NT server to a Samba server, you should be aware that Samba does not support domain administrative groups such as the "Printer Operators" in the truest sense of the word. If necessary, you can implement a type of support by using the valid users service parameter. Other than these things to be aware of, configuring your printer is exactly what was presented in Hour 8. Here is the printer service definition I will use:

```
[canon]
    print command = lpr -P%p %s; rm %s
    comment = domain printer
    printable = yes
```

12

```
    writeable = no
    public = no
```

Of course, I must correctly configure the printer in the local /etc/printcap file as well.

Step 3: Configuring the smb.conf File

I am almost finished. Next, I need to configure the [global] section of the smb.conf file. First, I cover the parameters that I am already very familiar with: netbios name and workgroup:

```
[global]
    netbios name = PICANTE
    workgroup = CHIPSNDIPS
```

This enables me to meet the second requirement I gave at the beginning of this hour: The machine should appear the same as the NT server when viewed through a network browsing mechanism such as the Network Neighborhood.

Next, I must configure the security level. For lack of space and time, I will not go into the detail of how domain security is implemented on the network wire. Instead, simply believe that in this mode of security, Samba is able to function as a full domain member and participate in trust relationships:

```
    security = domain
```

For Samba to work in domain-level security, I must define a server that validates authentication requests much like in server level security. The password server parameter works exactly as it does when used in conjunction with security = server. The password server should be set to the PDC for my domain. If I had multiple BDCs (Backup Domain Controllers), I could enter them into the list as well:

```
    password server = QUESO
```

Finally, I must specify that I will use encrypted passwords even though maintaining an additional smbpasswd file is not necessary. This parameter turns on the flag in the negotiate protocol reply that indicates whether I support password encryption:

```
    encrypt passwords = yes
```

Unless you are absolutely positive what you are doing, it is better to add the following parameters to your [global] section of smb.conf as well:

```
os level = 0
domain master = no
local master = no
preferred master = no
```

The reason is that a Windows NT PDC must be the domain master browser. This will become more apparent in Hour 19, "Local Subnet Browsing."

Step 4: Getting the Samba Server to Join the NT Domain

Adding a Samba server to an existing Windows NT domain is a two-step process. Currently Samba does not support the option to create a machine account in the domain when joining, so I must create an account on the PDC using the Server Manager for Domains. Figure 12.3 shows the process of adding a new server to the domain. If you wonder why I could not simply use the existing machine account for PICANTE, it is because the Samba box has no idea of what the password for the account would be. Although it could be possible to gain this information, re-adding the server to the domain is the easiest solution.

FIGURE 12.3

Creating a machine account in the CHIPSNDIPS domain using the Server Manager for Domains.

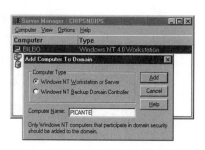

12

When the account has been created, I can join the domain using the smbpasswd tool. It is very important that neither smbd nor nmbd are running while I attempt to join the domain. I should also verify that the directory /usr/local/samba/private exists, because this is where smbpasswd will record the Samba server's current machine password. To actually join the domain, run the following command:

```
# /usr/local/samba/bin/smbpasswd -j CHIPSNDIPS
➥1999/01/21 22:43:38 : change_trust_account_password:
➥Changed password for domain CHIPSNDIPS.
Joined domain CHIPSNDIPS.
```

Of course, you should replace CHIPSNDIPS with the name for your domain. Now it is time to start smbd and nmbd, and try things out.

Step 5: Testing the Configuration

The best way to verify that everything is working correctly is to log in to an existing NT client and see whether everything looks the same. After logging in to a Windows NT Workstation, I first check to make sure that my home directory is accessible. Figure 12.4 shows that the network share \\PICANTE\users is mounted at drive H:. Figure 12.5 shows that even my command prompt starts in the correct directory!

FIGURE 12.4

My Computer display-
ing the current net-
work drive
connections.

FIGURE 12.5

Windows NT Command
Prompt starts in the
user's home directory
by default.

Next, I check network browsing. The server PICANTE appears in the browse list in Figure 12.6 as it should. After verifying that the server is displaying the correct service list (see Figure 12.7), I simply wait to see whether anyone notices the change in servers.

FIGURE 12.6

FIGURE 12.6

Network Neighborhood displaying the current machine for CHIPSNDIPS.

FIGURE 12.7

Share list displayed for PICANTE.

Summary

Although not supporting the entire gambit of NT features, Samba can effectively replace a Windows NT file and print server in an existing network. Samba meets the three requirements necessary that I set forth:

- All Domain users should be able to access the new shares on the Samba server without requiring a synchronized UNIX account on the machine.

  The existing Windows NT domain controller will perform all logon validation.

- The Samba server should appear in the same workgroup and use the same NetBIOS machine name and the existing server in order to minimize confusion for the users.

  The `netbios name` and `workgroup` smb.conf parameters enable us to assume the identity of the previous server.

- Access control mechanism to files should be kept the same so that a user who has access to a file on the existing server should have access to the same file on the Samba server. Also, a user who does not have access to a file on the existing server should not be able to access that file under the new configuration.

  By creating valid /etc/passwd and /etc/group entries, I can use the standard UNIX permission bits to control access.

12

Q&A

Q Why is `security = domain` better than `security = server`?

A There are two reasons why the `security = domain` is better. The first is because this method enables the Samba server to participate in domain trust relationships. This is impossible with server-level security. The second reason is that, under server-level security, each `smbd` process must keep an open connection with the authentication server. This can drain a Windows NT PDC quickly. Under domain-level security, this connection is necessary long enough to perform the validation, thus conserving valuable resources.

New Terms

sid   Security identifier composed of a string of numbers used to differentiate between NT machines and accounts.

rid   A 32-bit number that Windows NT uses to represent a user ID with a relative identifier. The rid is appended to the machine or domain sid to fully qualify the account.

BDC   A Backup Domain Controller is a machine that replicates domain account information from the Primary domain controller in order to distribute the load of authenticating connections.

ACL   An Access Control List is a attribute associated with files, directories, and printers that allows for restricting or granting the capability to manipulate a given object.

PART III

Using Samba

Hour

HOUR 13

UNIX (smbclient, smbfs, smbwrapper, and Various Utilities)

by Richard Sharpe

Many people think of SMB clients as being available only for DOS- and Windows-based systems. It comes as a complete surprise to some people that there might even be UNIX-based SMB clients. After all, what possible use would it be to be able to access SMB servers from a UNIX machine?

It turns out that there are many potential uses for SMB clients from UNIX machines, and Samba provides several of them, while other developers have provided others. These clients include

- smbclient, a standard part of Samba that provides a command-line utility to access SMB servers. It can be used to copy files between UNIX and Windows machines as well as to back up files from an

SMB server, but it is used by a number of other utilities, such as smbprint and smbtar.

- smbfs, a virtual file system for Linux that allows Windows file systems to be mounted on UNIX systems.

- smbwrapper and smbsh, the newest utilities that allow users to browse file systems on Windows systems from within the UNIX shell.

- Sharity, another virtual file system product that also has SSL support.

- various utilities that use smbclient to perform their function, such as smbprint and smbtar.

In addition, other open source packages use Samba clients such as smbclient to provide part of their functionality. A notable example is the network backup utility Amanda, which uses smbclient to back up Windows clients.

This hour explores many of these clients and examines what they can be used for, looks at how they are used, and compares their uses.

smbclient

smbclient is a CIFS/SMB client program for UNIX. It is a command-line utility that is similar to the well-known FTP utility. The following shows an smbclient session where the user has connected to a Windows 95 system and listed all the files in the top level directory:

```
[root@eagle samba-book]# smbclient //eagle/first-share
Added interface ip=16.153.112.110 bcast=16.153.112.255
➥nmask=255.255.255.0
Password:
Domain=[FOWLPLAY] OS=[Unix] Server=[Samba 2.0.0beta4]
smb: \> ls
  file-1.txt                              69  Mon Jan 11 15:35:14 1999
  file-2.txt                              59  Mon Jan 11 15:35:14 1999
  New Folder                       D       0  Sat Jan 16 12:21:56 1999
          55729 blocks of size 16384. 3516 blocks available
smb: \> ^D
```

Here, you have connected to \\eagle\first-share and listed the files in it. You could as easily have connected to any Windows system, however. Notice that you did not use the standard DOS/Windows naming scheme of \\eagle\first-share. Typing the correct DOS/Windows style name would have required us to double all the back slashes (\) because UNIX treats them as an escape. Because smbclient understands either forward or back slashes, therefore, it is easier to use the first.

For the purists, however, the correct form of the smbclient command is

```
smbclient \\\\eagle\\first-share
```

smbclient then tells us that it is adding an interface and asks us for a password. It always asks for a password, but one is not always needed. Because you connected to Eagle, a UNIX machine with Samba running in User level security, a password was needed. smbclient always sends the username of the logged in user (unless you entered the -U *username* on the command line), and you should enter the password on the remote machine (Eagle) for the logged in user. If a password is not needed for the user on the remote machine or the remote machine is using share-level security and no password is on the share, simply press Enter.

When smbclient can connect to the remote machine and access the appropriate share, you are presented with a prompt and can type a command. You entered **ls** and were presented with a detailed listing of the files on the share, which you have seen before. For each file and directory, a line is printed showing its name, whether it is a directory (the D flag), its size, and creation date.

Of course, smbclient can do many more things, including copying files in either direction. To find out more about smbclient commands, enter **help** at the command line. Later, I will go through all the commands that can be entered in smbclient, but first you must look at smbclient's command-line options.

smbclient Command-Line Options

The general form of the smbclient command is

```
smbclient servicename [password] [options]
```

Here, *servicename* is in the form //*server*/*service* (or the alternative DOS/Windows-style service name as discussed previously), *password* is the password for the share or the user logging into the server, and *options* are any of those listed in this section.

[-s smb.conf]

13

smbclient uses the Samba configuration file, smb.conf, to control some aspects of its functioning. This optional parameter allows you to specify an alternative smb.conf file.

This option was not documented prior to Samba 2.0.0.

[-B *IP address*]

To look up the IP address of the server specified, smbclient broadcasts NetBIOS name service requests. This option allows you to specify the broadcast address to be used.

> This option was not documented in the man pages prior to Samba 2.0.0.

[-O *socket options*]

This option allows you to set TCP level socket options for the TCP connection placed to the server. See the socket options parameter in the smb.conf(5) man page for more details of the values allowed for this option.

[-R *name resolve order*]

smbclient can use a number of facilities to resolve server names into IP addresses. This option allows you to specify which facilities are used and in what order. The resolve options are lmhosts, host, wins, and bcast.

The default resolve order is lmhosts, host, wins, and bcast.

Each is tried in the specified order until an IP address is obtained or until no more resolution methods are available, in which case a connection cannot be placed to the server.

The meaning of each of these options is

lmhosts	looks up an IP address in the Samba lmhosts file, which is usually stored in the same directory as the smb.conf file.
host	looks up an IP address in the /etc/hosts file, NIS, or DNS, depending on system settings for your operating system.
wins	looks up an IP address by sending a query to the Windows Internet Name Service (WINS) server listed in the smb.conf file. If a WINS server has not been specified, this method is ignored.
bcast	looks up an IP address by broadcasting a NetBIOS name query on all the known interfaces listed in interfaces parameter in the smb.conf file. If there is no interfaces parameter in the smb.conf, broadcast on all known interfaces.

[-M *NetBIOS name*]

This option allows you to send messages to other computers. smbclient uses the WinPopup protocol and attempts to resolve the NetBIOS name into an IP address using the resolve order specified or the default resolve order.

> You can send messages only by NetBIOS name.

The message to be sent is typed in on STDIN and terminated with a Control-D (^D).

An example is

```
echo "Backup starting" ¦ smbclient -M Controller
```

[-i *scope*]

This option allows you to set the NetBIOS scope that smbclient uses when generating NetBIOS names. This is rarely used, and for more details of NetBIOS names, you should consult RFCs 1001 and 1002.

> This option was not documented in the man pages prior to Samba 2.0.0.

[-N]

This option allows you to suppress the password prompt when smbclient connects to a server. It is most useful when accessing a service that does not have a password.

[-n *NetBIOS name*]

This option allows you to specify a NetBIOS name that the client uses as the local system's NetBIOS name. By default, smbclient uses the uppercase version of the local machine's hostname.

[-d *debug level*]

This option allows you to specify the level of debug messages that is printed out. By default the parameter is 0. The higher the level, the more information is printed out by smbclient about its activities. At the higher levels, it prints out voluminous details,

13

including protocol messages set, most of which is cryptic and only of interest to the developers.

At level 0, only critical errors and serious warnings are logged.

[-P]

In versions of Samba prior to 2.0.0, this option allowed you to specify that you were connecting to a printer share.

This option is no longer needed in Samba 2.0.0 and above (and is silently ignored), because the server is now allowed to decide the device type.

[-p port]

This option allows you to change the TCP port that smbclient connects on when connecting to a server. The default port number is the well-known TCP port number for CIFS/SMB, also known as the NetBIOS Session Service, or port number 139. You should never need to use this option.

This option was broken in Samba 2.0.0 but is fixed in 2.0.1 and beyond.

[-h]

This option allows you to print the usage message for smbclient. The usage message is also printed if an error is found in any options.

This option was not documented in the man pages prior to Samba 2.0.0 but it is kind of obvious.

[-I dest IP]

This option allows you to specify the IP address of the server to connect to.

Normally, smbclient uses the NetBIOS name resolution procedure outlined earlier this hour to resolve a NetBIOS name to an IP address. By using this option, you can force smbclient to connect to the nominated server. However, be aware that most Microsoft clients require that the NetBIOS name in the session request match the server's NetBIOS name. This generally means that you must specify both the -I and -N options.

[-E]

This option specifies that smbclient should write messages and debugging output to STDERR rather than STDOUT.

By default, smbclient sends messages and debugging information to STDOUT.

[-U *username*]

This option allows you to specify the username that is used to log in to the server after a connection is made.

If this option is not specified, smbclient defaults to using an uppercase version of the USER or LOGNAME environment variables, in that order. If neither environment variable exists, the username GUEST is used.

If the USER environment variable contains a percent character (%), everything after it is treated as a password. This allows you to specify *username%password* in the USER environment variable and avoid passing passwords on the command line (where the ps command can see it and display it to other users).

If the server that you are connecting to supports an older version of the SMB protocol and does not support usernames, this option is ignored.

Some servers require that the user name be in uppercase, and some require that it be a valid NetBIOS name (fewer than 16 characters, all uppercase, and so on).

[-L *NetBIOS name*]

This option allows you to get a list of all the services supplied by a server. You might need to specify the -I option if you are trying to reach a host on another network or your NetBIOS names do not match your host names.

[-t *terminal code*]

This option allows you to specify how smbclient interprets filenames coming from the server. This is required because UNIX typically uses different multibyte character sets than Windows does. Setting this option lets smbclient convert from SMB filenames to Windows filenames and vice versa.

Values for the terminal codes include sjis, euc, jis7, jis8, junet, hex, and cap. These are all multibyte character encoding systems, with the following meanings:

sjis	Shift JIS (Japanese Industrial Standard) encoding system
euc	Extended UNIX Coding system
jis7, jis8	7- and 8-bit JIS encoding systems
junet	Japanese UNIX network encoding system
hex, cap	Other multiple byte encoding systems

This option was not documented in Samba prior to version 2.0.0.

13

[-m *max protocol*]

This option is ignored in Samba 2.0.0 and above. Now, smbclient always tries to connect at the maximum protocol level the server supports.

In versions prior to Samba 2.0.0 (for example, 1.9.18p10) this option was not documented. It allowed you to set the maximum protocol level that was negotiated by smbclient, and allowed you to avoid some features (such as the insistence on logging into the server).

[-W *workgroup*]

This option allows you to specify the workgroup that smbclient uses in looking up NetBIOS names and thus in setting up connections to servers. You might need this in connecting to some servers.

[-T *tar options*]

This option allows you to create tar compatible backups of files on CIFS/SMB servers. It takes a series of secondary flags (described later in this hour) that control its behavior.

[-D *directory*]

This option allows you to change to an initial directory before starting whatever operation you want to perform. Mainly of use with the -T (tar) option.

[-c *command string*]

This option allows you to specify a series of commands to be executed by smbclient instead of prompting from STDIN. If this option is used, -N is implied.

This option is mainly used in scripts and to set some parameters with the -T (tar) facility.

The tar form of the smbclient command (smbclient *service name* -T...) has the options found in Table 13.1.

TABLE 13.1 -T OPTIONS

Option	What It Does
c tar file	Specifies that a tar file is to be created by copying files from the service specified on the smbclient command line, modified by the -c option, if any. It must be followed by the name of the tar file to create, which can be a file, a tape device (for example, /dev/st0) or - for standard output (which allows you to pipe the tar file into some other command).

Option	What It Does
x *tar file*	Specifies that a tar file be restored by copying files to the server and service specified on the smbclient command line, modified by the -c option, if any. It must be followed by the name of the tar file to restore, which can be a file, a tape device, or - for standard input. Only one of c and x can be specified at a time.
I *include expression*	Includes files and directories as specified in the expression. Filename globbing (sometimes known as wildcards) is implemented if the r option is also included. If extra names are included at the end of the tar options, smbclient assumes they are the names of directories and files to include in the tar archive.
X *exclude expression*	Excludes files and directories as specified in the expression. Filename globbing (sometimes known as wildcards) is implemented if the r option is also included. (See Note following this table.)
b *blocksize*	Allows you to specify the block size used on the tar file. Requires a valid block size greater than zero, in which case the tar file is read or written in blocksize*512 byte blocks.
g	Specifies incremental mode, in which case, only files that have the archive bit set are backed up. Can be used only with the c suboption
q	Specifies quiet mode, where it refrains from printing diagnostics as it processes files.
r	Specifies that whatever filename globbing has been built in to smbclient should be used in interpreting the include or exclude expression described previously.
N *file*	Allows you to specify that only files newer than *file* should be backed up. Can be used only with the c suboption.
a	Causes smbclient to reset the archive bit on all files that are backed up. Can be used only with the g and c suboptions.

13

Filename globbing works in one of two ways.

If Samba has been built with HAVE_REGEX_H, the expression can be a regular expression, and regular expression matching is used to select the files to include in the tar archive. Note that regular expression matching can be very computationally expensive. You will really notice how much slower smbclient is if you build in REGEX support and you use the -r option.

If Samba has been built without HAVE_REGEX_H, limited filename globbing is supported, where * and ? are treated as wildcards in the expression. This achieves about as much as most people want, and it is much faster as well.

These options are specified immediately after the `-T` option. For example,

```
smbclient //server/service -Tc server.tar
```

creates a backup tar file called `server.tar` that is obtained by copying all files from `//server/service`.

The tar component of smbclient handles all Windows long filenames, but has an internal restriction that the full pathname must be fewer than 1,024 characters. Because Windows 95 has a restriction of 256 characters in the fullpath name and Windows NT 4 has the same restriction, smbclient's `tar` command can fully handle Windows files of any type.

As always, you should consult the man pages on smbclient for the definitive word on its options and functioning.

smbclient Output

smbclient handles informational output (to the user) in the following way.

All informational output is printed to the same file that debug output is sent to. Normally, this is STDOUT, but if smbclient is sending its output to STDOUT (perhaps because the user has specified `-Tc -`, that is, tar to STDOUT), informational and debug output is sent to STDERR.

Another way to force output to STDERR is to specify the `-E` option to smbclient.

smbclient Expressions (Wildcards or Masks)

In many commands, smbclient accepts an *expression* (or *mask* in the smbclient man pages). This expression is used to retrieve matching filenames from the server for further processing by the command.

These expressions can contain standard Windows wildcards, such as `*` and `?`. Only files matching the expression are processed by the commands that accept such an expression.

For example, *dir* `*a*` returns all files with an *a* somewhere in their names.

smbclient Commands

After smbclient has connected to the requested server and service and has logged on, it presents the user with the following prompt:

```
smb:\>
```

Here, \ represents the current directory. It changes as you move about in the remote file system.

At this point you can issue any of the smbclient commands. The following sections describe each of these.

If you need to specify files with spaces in their names, enclose the filename in double quotes (for example, `"a file with a long name"`).

In what follows, optional parameters are shown in square brackets, for example `[optional]`. Required parameters are shown in angle brackets, for example `<required>`.

? [command] ¦ help [command]

These commands provide help on all commands. They take an optional parameter that is the name of the command help is required for. If the parameter is not given, a list of available commands is provided.

```
 An example of this command is:smb: \> ? mkdir
HELP mkdir:
<directory> make a directory
smb: \>
```

This syntax asks for help on the `mkdir` command. You see the results of this command as well.

! [shell command]

This command allows you to run a shell command or run a shell from within smbclient. It might be used to look at the contents of files retrieved from the remote system without exiting from smbclient.

The following shows an example of using this command to look at a file retrieved from the remote server without exiting from smbclient:

```
smb: \> ! cat test.txt
A file with some characters in it.
smb: \>
```

Here you used *cat* to list the file *test.txt*.

archive [level]

This command allows you to control the behavior of `mget` commands with respect to the handling of the archive bit on DOS/Windows files. If *level* is not given, the command simply reports the current value of the archive setting.

13

If level is specified, it must be a value between 0 and 3 and has the following meaning:

0   Retrieves all files regardless of the archive bit and leaves the archive bit alone

1   Retrieves only files that have the archive bit set and leaves the archive bit alone

2   Retrieves only files that have the archive bit set and resets the archive on those files

3   Retrieves all files regardless of the archive bit setting and resets the archive bit on all files

This command is not documented in the man pages but is documented in smbclient's help facility.

The following shows two examples of using the `archive` command:

```
smb: \> archive
Archive level is 0
smb: \> archive 3
smb: \> archive
Archive level is 3
smb: \>
```

Here you use `archive` to check what the current archive level is, set it to 3, and then check that it was set to 3.

blocksize <blocksize>

This command allows you to specify the blocksize to be used with smbclient's `tar` command. The parameter must be an integer greater than 0.

When used, causes the tar command to read or write blocks of *blocksize**TBLOCK (currently, TBLOCK is set to 512) bytes.

An example of using this command is

```
smb: \> blocksize 40
blocksize is now 40
smb: \>
```

which sets the blocksize to 40, that is, 40 512-byte blocks, or 20480 byte blocks.

cancel <jobid>

This command cancels the job *jobid* in the print queue.

This command is not documented in the man pages but is documented in smbclient's help facility.

```
An example of using this command is:smb: \> cancel 7
Job 7 cancelled
smb: \>
```

This shows you canceling a print job. To do this, you must have connected to a printer share that has such a print job pending.

cd [*directory*]

This command allows you to change and print the current working directory on the server.

When a directory is specified, the current working directory on the server is changed to that specified.

If no parameter is given, the current working directory is printed on whatever device debug output goes to.

An example of using this command is

```
smb: \> cd "New Folder"
smb: \New Folder\>
```

which shows you changing to the directory "New Folder".

del <*expression*>

This command allows you to delete files from the working directory on the server. All files matching *expression* are deleted.

```
An example of using this command is:smb: \> ls
  file-1.txt                          69   Mon Jan 11 15:35:14 1999
  file-2.txt                          59   Mon Jan 11 15:35:14 1999
  New Folder                     D     0   Sat Feb  6 10:51:47 1999
  609913.doc                     A 431104  Mon Jan 18 22:25:20 1999

      55729 blocks of size 16384. 6871 blocks available
smb: \> del file-1.txt
smb: \> ls
  file-2.txt                          59   Mon Jan 11 15:35:14 1999
  New Folder                     D     0   Sat Feb  6 10:51:47 1999
  609913.doc                     A 431104  Mon Jan 18 22:25:20 1999

      55729 blocks of size 16384. 6871 blocks available
smb: \>
```

This shows us deleting the file *file-1.txt*. First you list the files that are there, then delete *file-1.txt*, and lastly, check that the file is gone.

13

dir [*expression*] ¦ ls [*expression*]

These commands allow you to get a directory listing of files in any directory on the server.

If an *expression* is supplied, only files and directories matching the expression are listed.

If an *expression* is not given, all files and directories in the current directory are listed.

See also the ls command later.

An example of using this command is

```
smb: \> dir
    file-2.txt                          59  Mon Jan 11 15:35:14 1999
    New Folder                    D      0  Sat Feb  6 10:51:47 1999
    609913.doc                    A 431104  Mon Jan 18 22:25:20 1999

        55729 blocks of size 16384. 6871 blocks available
smb: \>
```

du

This command allows you to get the space occupied by all files in the current directory. If recurse mode is on, it recurses down all directories to calculate the space occupied; otherwise, it only does it for files in the current directory.

This command is not documented in the man pages but is documented in smbclient's help facility.

```
An example of using this command is:smb: \> recurse
directory recursion is now off
smb: \> du

        55729 blocks of size 16384. 5912 blocks available
Total number of bytes: 431163
smb: \> recurse
directory recursion is now on
smb: \> du

        55729 blocks of size 16384. 5912 blocks available
Total number of bytes: 15979461
smb: \>
```

Here you made sure that recurse was off before using the du command. In line 5, you see that only 431,163 bytes are reported, but after switching on recurse at line 6, you see that 15,979,461 bytes are reported at line 10.

exit ¦ quit ¦ q

These commands allow you to exit from smbclient. Before doing so, smbclient terminates its connection to the server. It is the same as issuing Control-D (^D).

get <remote file> [local file]

This command allows you to copy a file from the server to the local machine. The remote filename must be supplied, and if the user specifies a local filename, the remote file is copied and given the local filename.

If a local filename is not provided, the remote file is copied and given the same name.

If lowercase mode is on, all local filenames are created as lowercase versions of the same remote files.

All files are copied in binary mode, unless translation is on, in which case CRLF pairs are mapped to LF on the local machine.

An example of using this command is

```
smb: \> get file-2.txt
getting file file-2.txt of size 59 as file-2.txt (0.414512 kb/s)
➥(average 0.414512 kb/s)
smb: \>
```

Here you used the get command to get file-2.txt. When the file is retrieved, smbclient prints out a number of statistics about the transfer.

lcd [directory]

This command allows you to change your local directory. If a directory is given and is valid, smbclient changes to that directory on the local machine. If no directory is specified, smbclient prints out the current local working directory onto the output file.

An example of this command is

```
smb: \> lcd ..
the local directory is now /
smb: \> lcd /usr/local/sbin
the local directory is now /usr/local/sbin
smb: \>
```

Here you use the lcd command twice, and smbclient reports where you are on each occasion.

13

lowercase

This command allows you to control the case of local filenames when files are copied from CIFS/SMB servers using the get and mget commands. It toggles the current value of lowercase, which is OFF by default.

If lowercase mode is ON, local files' names (where not specified by the user) are created as the lowercase version of the same remote files. This is very useful in copying MS-DOS files from a server, as UNIX filenames are normally in lowercase.

mask <expression>

This command allows the user to specify an expression that is used to filter files in recursive (discussed later this hour) mput and mget operations.

With recursive mput and mget operations, two sets of selection need to be performed. First all the relevant directories need to be selected. Second all the relevant files need to be selected. These two selection operations are usually different. The mask command allows you specify an expression that is used to select which files are processed in recursive operations.

A separate *expression* is specified on the mget and mput commands which select the directories that are processed when in recursive mode.

The mask starts out blank by default, which means that all files are selected. When you change the mask, it stays that way until you change it.

For an example of this command, see the mput and mget commands later this hour.

md <directory> ¦ mkdir <directory>

These commands allow you to create new directories on the server in the current directory as long as you have the privilege to do so. The new directory has the specified name.

An example of this command is

```
smb: \> ls
  file-2.txt                      59  Mon Jan 11 15:35:14 1999
  New Folder                 D      0  Sat Feb  6 10:51:47 1999
  609913.doc                 A 431104  Mon Jan 18 22:25:20 1999

        55729 blocks of size 16384. 5909 blocks available
```

```
smb: \> md new-dir
smb: \> ls
  new-dir                       D        0  Thu Feb 11 01:44:32 1999
  file-2.txt                             59  Mon Jan 11 15:35:14 1999
  New Folder                    D        0  Sat Feb  6 10:51:47 1999
  609913.doc                    A   431104  Mon Jan 18 22:25:20 1999

        55729 blocks of size 16384. 5909 blocks available
smb: \>
```

Here you check the current directory on the remote server, create the directory *new-dir*, and check again to ensure that the directory was created.

mget <expression>

This command allows you to copy all files matching *expression* from the server to the local machine.

However, when recursion is turned on, *expression* selects the directories that are processed, whereas the mask command specifies the files to be processed. When retrieving files using mget, if recurse is on and the mget command recurses into directories, it creates the directory structure on the local machine. That is, it preserves the directory structure of the matching files and directories for the files it copies.

An example of using this command is

```
smb: \> ls
  new-dir                       D        0  Thu Feb 11 11:57:48 1999
  file-4.txt                             59  Mon Jan 11 15:35:14 1999
  2nd-dir                       D        0  Thu Feb 11 11:57:57 1999

        55729 blocks of size 16384. 6887 blocks available
smb: \> prompt
prompting is now off
smb: \> mget *.txt
getting file file-4.txt of size 59 as file-4.txt (1.2259 kb/s)
➥(average 1.2259 kb/s)
smb: \> recurse
directory recursion is now on
smb: \> mask *.txt
smb: \> mget *dir
getting file file-1.txt of size 59 as file-1.txt (0.789275 kb/s)
➥(average 0.960286 kb/s)
getting file file-2.txt of size 59 as file-2.txt (1.25254 kb/s)
➥(average 1.04127 kb/s)
getting file file-3.txt of size 59 as file-3.txt (1.15234 kb/s)
➥(average 1.06698 kb/s)
smb: \>
```

13

Here, for the first mget command, you managed to retrieve only one file. But setting recurse mode on and setting a mask on the second mget command, you managed to get more files. These files were in the subdirectories new-dir and 2nd-dir.

more <file>

This command allows you to retrieve a remote file and view it with your default pager.

This command is not documented in the man pages but is documented in smbclient's help facility.

mput <expression>

This command allows you to copy all files matching expression from the local machine to the server.

However, when recursion is turned on, expression selects the directories that are processed, whereas the mask command specifies the files to be processed.

An example of using this command is

```
smb: \> prompt
prompting is now off
smb: \> mput *.txt
putting file browse.txt as \browse.txt (20.2602 kb/s)
➥(average 20.2602 kb/s)
putting file evi.txt as \evi.txt (37.6367 kb/s) (average 30.4219 kb/s)
putting file file-2.txt as \file-2.txt (2.05775 kb/s)
➥(average 26.431 kb/s)
putting file file-4.txt as \file-4.txt (5.76166 kb/s)
➥(average 25.442 kb/s)
putting file nmblookup.txt as \nmblookup.txt (5.55096 kb/s)
➥(average 23.7844 kb/s)
smb: \>
```

newer <file>

This command allows you to specify that mget commands retrieve only files that are newer than the specified local file.

This command is not documented in the man pages but is documented in smbclient's help facility.

An example of using this command is

```
smb: \> newer log.log
Getting files newer than Sun Jan 17 12:33:26 1999
smb: \>
```

print *<file>*

This command allows you to print a *file* on the local machine via a printable service on the server.

Because a file can also be printed by copying it to a printable service (using put), this command is redundant and should no longer be used, but it is retained for scripts that might be already in service.

An example of using this command is

```
smb: \> print log.log
putting file log.log as log.log (19.3522 kb/s) (average 19.3522 kb/s)
smb: \>
```

Here you can see that the file was actually sent using the put command.

printmode *<mode>*

This command is obsolete in Samba 2.0.0 and has no effect on any other command. It is retained for compatibility with scripts that might already be in use in the field.

In versions of Samba prior to 2.0.0 (for example, 1.9.18p10), printing was implemented by opening a spool file on the server and copying the file to be printed to the spool file. When the spool file was opened, the value of print mode was passed in on the open. However, most modern servers ignore the print mode in any case.

prompt

This command allows you to specify whether you are prompted to allow file transfer for each file during mget and mput operations or whether these commands silently do the transfers.

The initial value of prompt is ON, and this command toggles the current value. When ON, you are prompted to confirm each transfer. When OFF, all transfers occur without any input from you.

put *<local file>* *[remote file]*

This command allows you to copy files from the local machine to the server. The *local file* name must be specified and if the *remote file* name is given, the *remote file* is created and the contents of the *local file* are copied to it.

13

If the remote filename is not given, a remote file with the same name as the *local file* is created and the contents of the *local file* are copied to it.

An example of using this command is

```
smb: \> put log.log
putting file log.log as \log.log (329.792 kb/s) (average 329.793 kb/s)
smb: \>
```

pwd

This command prints the current remote directory.

This command is not documented in the man pages but is documented in smbclient's help facility.

queue

This command allows you to list the jobs on a remote queue, but you must have connected to a printable service in order to do this.

rd *<directory>* ¦ rmdir *<directory>*

These commands allow you to remove a directory on the server. It removes the specified directory from the current directory, as long as you have access, and the directory is empty.

If you try to remove a directory that is not empty, you get an ERRDOS - ERRnoaccess (Access denied.) error return.

recurse

This command lets you force mput and mget commands to recurse into subdirectories when transferring files. By default, recurse is OFF. It also forces the du command to recurse into directories.

When recurse is toggled to ON, the mput and mget commands recurse into all subdirectories that match the expression supplied with the mget or mput commands. The files that are actually processed by these commands are specified with the mask command. If no mask command has been given, all files are processed.

For example,

```
smb: \> mask *.txt
smb: \> mget *dir
```

recurses into each directory on the server that matches *.dir, and retrieves all files that match *.txt.

When recurse is toggled OFF, only files from the current working directory are processed, and only those which match the expression given on the mget or mput commands.

See also mget and mput earlier this hour.

rm <expression>

This command allows you to remove all files that match expression in the current working directory on the server.

setmode <file> <[[+¦-]][r¦s¦h¦a]>

This command allows you to set attributes on files on a server. It is similar to the DOS attrib command. It allows you to set or remove DOS attributes such as read-only (r), system (s), hidden (h), or archive (a). You can specify more than one of these at a time. You can also specify both attributes to add and attributes to remove at the same time (for example, r-s).

An example of using this command is

```
smb: \> setmode log.log +hs

perm set 6 0
smb: \>
```

tar <c¦x>[IXbgNarq parameters]

This command allows you to backup files from the server to a local tar file, tape, or STDOUT. The suboptions and parameters are the same as described under smbclient tar options. You must include one of c or x, which mean create a new archive or extract an existing archive, respectively.

This command can be used to backup remote Windows systems. Examples of using the command-line version of this command are shown in Hour 23, "Tips and Tricks."

tarmode <[no]<full¦inc¦reset¦noreset¦hidden¦quiet¦verbose>>+

This command allows you to control a number of aspects of the tar command's behavior. The parameters to tarmode have the following meaning:

full	do a full backup
inc	backup those files with the archive bit set

13

`reset`	reset the archive bit on all files backed up
`system`	back up only those files with the system bit set
`hidden`	backup only those files with the hidden bit set
`verbose`	print out backup information while operating
`quiet`	don't print any information while operating

Placing a no on the front of the parameter negates its meaning, and more than one parameter can be specified at a time, separated by spaces.

The default values for tar mode are full and verbose.

An example of using this command is

```
smb: \> tarmode nosystem hidden
tarmode is now full, nosystem, hidden, noreset, verbose
smb: \>
```

Here you have specified that you don't want system files and that you do want hidden files. smbclient tells us that the tarmode also contains `noreset` and `verbose`.

translate

This command is not documented in the man pages in any version of Samba. It can be used to control the handling of the different end of line sequences between DOS/Windows and UNIX.

If `translate` is toggled to `ON`, when copying files from a CIFS/SMB server to the local machine, all occurrences of CRLF are translated to `LF`. Similarly, when copying files from the local machine to a CIFS/SMB server, all occurrences of `LF` are translated to `CRLF`.

If `translate` is `OFF`, no modifications are made to any files transferred.

By default, translate is `OFF` in smbclient.

smbclient Examples

Now that you have looked at all the smbclient command-line options and commands, here are some examples of using smbclient.

Utilities such as smbtar and smbprint are also good sources of examples as they use smbclient to perform their functions.

Obtaining a List of Services on a Server

One of the first debugging steps to take in checking why you cannot access a service on a server is to obtain a list of services on that server. Although you can fire up Network Neighborhood under Windows 9x or Windows 95, an easier way is with smbclient. Here is an example:

```
[root@eagle]# smbclient -L eagle -N
Added interface ip=16.153.112.110 bcast=16.153.112.255
➥nmask=255.255.255.0
Domain=[FOWLPLAY] OS=[Unix] Server=[Samba 2.0.0beta4]

        Sharename       Type        Comment
        ---------       ----        -------
        samba           Disk        Samba smbedit share
        first-share     Disk        My first share
        kits            Disk        Kits Area
        cdrom           Disk        CDROM, automounts where connected to
        first-printer   Printer     My first printer
        printer$        Disk
        IPC$            IPC         IPC Service (Samba 2.0.0beta4 Server)

        Server                      Comment
        ---------                   -------
        EAGLE                       Samba 2.0.0beta4 Server

        Workgroup                   Master
        ---------                   -------
        FOWLPLAY                    EAGLE
        NCINET                      RJSPC1
[root@eagle]# exit
```

Here you see that EAGLE is a Samba 2.0.0beta4 server running under UNIX in the workgroup FOWLPLAY. You also see all the services that EAGLE is running, along with the workgroups it knows about.

Printing a File

To print a file, you simply copy the file to a print share. This can be done on one command line with the following:

```
[root@eagle]# cat log.smb ¦ smbclient //eagle/first-printer XXXXXXX \
➥ -N -c "put - fred"
```

13

Here is a successful result:

```
Added interface ip=16.153.112.110 bcast=16.153.112.255
➥nmask=255.255.255.0
Domain=[FOWLPLAY] OS=[Unix] Server=[Samba 2.0.0beta4]
putting file - as \fred (13.8289 kb/s) (average 13.8289 kb/s)
[root@eagle]#
```

Here you cat the file out STDOUT, and in smbprint, you put the file from - to a remote filename you made up. You might want to use something such as $$ (translates to the PID in most shells) in the destination filename to prevent name collisions.

The password has been entered as XXXXXXX. You should use the correct password for the remote account.

If you are not a longtime UNIX user, you might be wondering: what type of file is -? This is a standard UNIX convention that allows programs to obtain their input from STDIN or send their output from STDOUT. Using this approach, programs such as smbclient can be used in a UNIX pipeline and do sensible things.

Let's take a closer look at the command used earlier this hour. It consists of cat log.smb followed by the pipe symbol (|) followed by the smbclient command. By default, cat sends its output out STDOUT, and the pipe symbol connects two programs together such that the STDOUT of the first is connected to the STDIN of the second program. To get smbclient to pick up the file, you need to tell it to copy from STDIN until it sees an End-Of-File (EOF). That's what you did previously. You told smbclient to copy from - which the program treats as a reference to STDIN in this case.

In a similar way, smbclient can retrieve files and send them to STDOUT. For example,

```
smbclient //eagle/first-share XXXXXX -N -c 'get file-1.txt -' ¦ \
    lpr -Pmyprinter
```

retrieves a file called file-1.txt and sends it out STDOUT to the next command in the pipeline, which is the UNIX print command, lpr.

Obtaining a List of Files in a Directory

Although you can use smbclient interactively to obtain a directory listing, the following example shows how to obtain it all from the command line

```
[root@eagle]# smbclient //rjspc1/c -N -D csw -c dir
```

which gives us the following result:

```
Added interface ip=16.153.112.110 bcast=16.153.112.255
➥nmask=255.255.255.0
```

```
Got a positive name query response from 16.153.112.120 ( 16.153.112.120 )
  .                                     D        0  Thu Dec 18 20:20:52 1997
  ..                                    D        0  Thu Dec 18 20:20:52 1997
  METER.DLL                             A     5216  Mon Nov  6 10:35:58 1995
  CSWPROMO.EXE                          A  1314816  Tue Jul 30 12:17:44 1996
  CSHDOC.WRI                            A    22528  Tue Jul 30 12:18:16 1996
  HOSTDSK.WRI                           A     5120  Wed Jan 15 09:28:54 1997

        45035 blocks of size 32768. 735 blocks available
[root@eagle]# exit
```

In this example, you use -N to stop smbclient from prompting us for a password, *-D csw*
to specify an initial directory, and -c dir to specify that you wanted a directory command executed.

Listing the Jobs in a Print Queue

You can list all the jobs in a print queue on a CIFS/SMB server by entering this at the
command prompt

```
[root@eagle]# smbclient //eagle/first-printer XXXXXXX -c queue
```

which produces this result:

```
Added interface ip=16.153.112.110 bcast=16.153.112.255
➥nmask=255.255.255.0
Domain=[FOWLPLAY] OS=[Unix] Server=[Samba 2.0.0beta4]
1285     12228        rjspc1.a00652
1286     12228        rjspc1.a00972
[root@eagle]#
```

Here you again have used -c to specify the command to be executed. You can see that
there are two jobs in the queue.

Copying a File from the Remote Machine

Although you can use an interactive approach for copying files, here you show how a file
can be copied from a CIFS/SMB server in one command-line operation

```
[root@eagle]# smbclient //rjspc1/c -N -D csw -c "get meter.dll"
```

and you receive this result:

```
Added interface ip=16.153.112.110 bcast=16.153.112.255
➥nmask=255.255.255.0
Got a positive name query response from 16.153.112.120 ( 16.153.112.120 )
getting file meter.dll of size 5216 as meter.dll (69.7773 kb/s)
➥(average 69.7774 kb/s)
[root@eagle]#
```

Here you again have used the -D option to set up an initial directory, and the -c option to
specify the command to execute.

13

smbfs

Imagine simply mounting a CIFS/SMB file system on a UNIX machine. Under Linux, this can be done with smbfs, a file system that understands the CIFS/SMB protocol.

In order to use smbfs, you need two things:

- A Linux kernel with smbfs support
- Utilities to allow you to mount and unmount smbfs file systems

Linux kernels have included smbfs for some time now, and you can build smbfs into the kernel, or you can use it as a loadable module. Because teaching you how to build new kernels or configure loadable modules is beyond the scope of this book, you should consult a book on Linux to find out how to do these things. A number of current Linux distributions have out-of-the-box smbfs support.

When you have a kernel with smbfs support, you need the utilities to allow you to mount and unmount smbfs file systems, because the standard Linux mount and umount commands do not support the smbfs file system. There are two choices here.

Firstly, Samba 1.9.18p10 and Samba 2.0.0 come with the utilities smbmount, smbumount, and smbmnt. These utilities allow you to mount and unmount file system from CIFS/SMB servers.

Secondly, the package smbfs-2.0.1-4 contains equivalent utilities to these, including smbmount and smbumount (different code bases to those mentioned previously). They also allow you to mount and unmount file systems from CIFS/SMB servers.

The big factor in choosing between these two packages in that the Samba 2.0.0 version of the smbmount utilities compile only on Linux kernels greater that 2.1.70 and the new Linux 2.2 kernels.

When you have an smbfs file system mounted under Linux, it looks very much like any other file system. However, it has to make some compromises in areas where a CIFS/SMB file system does not provide functionality that UNIX does. The following shows what such a file system looks like when mounted under Linux:

```
Filesystem          1024-blocks  Used Available Capacity Mounted on

/dev/hdb3               876101  430377   400465     52%    /

/dev/sda2               991124    5626   934298      1%    /home

/dev/hdc                572804  572804        0    100%    /mnt/cdrom

//rjspc1/c             1441120 1409344    31776     98%    /mnt/smb
```

Here you can see that the file system from `//rjspc1/c` is mounted on `/mnt/smb`. What does a long listing of a directory within that file system look like? Here is one of `/mnt/smb/Samba`:

```
[root@eagle]# ls -al /mnt/smb/Samba

total 773

drwxr-xr-x 1 root root     512 Jan 17 19:48 .

drwxr-xr-x 1 root root     512 Jan  1  1970 ..

drwxr-xr-x 1 root root     512 Jan 18 01:04 Fol1-2

drwxr-xr-x 1 root root     512 Jan 18 01:05 Fol2-1

-rwxr-xr-x 1 root root   15391 Nov 27 10:50 log.ulysses

-rwxr-xr-x 1 root root  770141 Jan 17 19:48 samba-1.9.18p10-source.tar.gz
```

As you can see, they look like regular UNIX files, but looks can be deceiving. The machine from which the file system was mounted is a Windows 95 system and has no concept of users or groups as far as file ownership is concerned. smbfs is faking up the user and group information based on information (or defaults) given to smbmount. In addition, the permissions do not tell the full story as well, as smbfs picks that information up from other information (or defaults) given to smbmount.

Without care, it could very well be that a file appears to be deletable by the listed owner, whereas the server won't actually allow that file to be deleted.

However, smbfs can be a very convenient way for a system administrator to gain access to file systems from CIFS/SMB servers for backup or administration purposes.

The following sections explore the ways in which the two different sets of utilities mentioned earlier work. In general each of them has to solve similar problems and go about it in slightly different ways because of their heritage.

Samba smbmount Examples

In order to use these utilities, Samba must be built with smbmount enabled. You do this by running configure and passing the `--with-smbmount` option and then completing the build as outlined in Hour 3, "Obtaining the Latest Source." They can only be built on a 2.1.71 or better kernel.

The Samba smbmount utility was developed by deleting unnecessary code from smbclient and adding the capability to perform a mount of a remote CIFS/SMB file system. This is done by executing the smbmnt utility, having it do all the needed work after

13

building all the command-line parameters needed by smbmnt, and performing some checks on the parameters collected.

As a result, this version of the smbmount utility is very similar to smbclient in its use of command-line parameters. Refer to the section "smbclient" for a discussion of the command-line parameters smbmount accepts.

An example of using smbmount is

```
smbmount //rjspc1/c -c 'mount /mnt/smb -u 123 -g 456'
```

which mounts //rjspc1/c on /mnt/smb and gives it a local UID of 123 and a local GID of 456. You can see here the use -f -c. too.

Please refer to the manual pages on smbmount, smbmnt, and smbumount for more information on these utilities.

smbfs smbmount Examples

In order to use this set of utilities, you must have installed the smbfs package. You are likely to find the package on your distribution as smbfs-2.0.1-4. It is beyond the scope of this book to explain how to install such packages. Please refer to the documentation that came with your Linux distribution for instructions on how to install packages.

After you finish this, you can use smbmount for mounting remote CIFS/SMB file systems on your Linux machine and smbumount to unmount them.

An example of using this version of smbmount is

```
smbmount //rjspc1/c /mnt/smb -u 123 -g 456
```

which mounts //rjspc1/c on /mnt/smb and gives a local UID of 123 and a local GID of 456.

Please refer to the manual pages on smbmount and smbumount for more information on these utilities.

smbwrapper

This is an experiment in providing access to CIFS/SMB file systems for existing executable files. It uses the capability of a number of systems to preload shared libraries that override the standard system libraries. smbwrapper provides its own versions of many of the standard system library routines. These routines check to see whether the operation is being applied to a file on a CIFS/SMB file system and, if so, calls an appropriate routine that understands the SMB protocol to perform the operation. However, if the operation is not being applied to a file on a CIFS/SMB file system, the standard system version of that operation is called.

The smbwrapper facility is new to Samba 2.0.0 and is not built by default. To build it you must configure Samba with the `--with-smbwrapper` option and then rebuild and reinstall Samba. Please refer to Hour 3 for details of how to do this.

This facility has been tested on a range of systems, including

- Linux 2.0 with glibc2 (Red Hat 5.1)
- Linux 2.1 with glibc
- Solaris 2.5.1 with gcc
- Solaris 2.6 with gcc
- SunOS 4.1.3 with gcc
- IRIX 6.4 with cc
- Digital UNIX 4.0 with gcc

When smbwrapper is compiled and installed, you can run it by typing **smbsh**. When smbsh starts up, it prompts you for a username and password, which are the username and password you want to use to access the workgroup or domain you are in.

The following shows an example of using smbwrapper:

```
[root@eagle]# smbsh
Username: boss
Password:
```

Here you have started smbsh and have supplied a username of `boss`, with the appropriate password for that account. The username and password details are submitted to any server that is operating with `security=user`:

```
[root@eagle]# ls /smb/rjspc1
c
```

Here you have asked for a file listing of the directory `/smb/rjspc1`. The `/smb` portion tells smbwrapper that you are referring to a CIFS/SMB file system, and the `/rjspc1` pseudo directory tells smbwrapper you want to list the services on the server `rjspc1`. As you can see, `rjspc1` only has the one share available:

```
[root@eagle]# ls /smb/rjspc1/c/samba
Fol1-2                    log.ulysses
Fol2-1                    samba-1.9.18p10-source.tar.gz
```

13

Here you have asked for a listing of the files in a directory called samba in the one share rjspc1 has available. You see a listing of the files in that directory. This demonstrates that standard UNIX programs work with CIFS/SMB file systems accessed via smbsh:

```
[root@eagle]# more /smb/rjspc1/c/samba/log.ulysses
doing parameter lock directory = /opt/samba/var/locks
doing parameter share modes = yes
doing parameter default case = lower
doing parameter case sensitive = no
doing parameter preserve case = yes
doing parameter short preserve case = yes
Processing section "[homes]"
doing parameter comment = Home Directories
doing parameter browseable = yes
```

Here you see that another standard UNIX program can work with CIFS/SMB file systems accessed via smbsh.

Indeed, smbsh has been tested with a large number of UNIX programs and utilities and works quite well with all of them.

However, several operations are known not to work with smbsh:

- Executing any file from a share
- Using any program that uses mmap
- Redirecting to files on a share

Although smbsh offers many of the facilities of smbclient in a more UNIX-friendly way and can be used as a replacement for smbclient in many situations, smbsh still does not work under some operating systems and does not yet support some operations that smbclient supports. Thus, you are likely to see both smbclient and smbsh on future distributions of Samba for some time to come.

smbprint

smbprint is a simple shell script included with Samba that allows a UNIX system to print to printers on other CIFS/SMB servers. Although smbprint has already been discussed in some detail in Hour 8, "Printers," it is worth while exploring some of the details of smbprint.

smbprint uses smbclient to get its job done via its command-line facilities and its capability to handle STDIN to process the file to be printed all in one simple pipeline. For example,

```
(
    echo translate
```

```
    echo print -
    cat
) ¦ smbclient "\\\\$server\\$service" $password -U $server -N -P
```

This syntax is not exactly the same as what smbprint uses, but illustrates the same principles:

1. In a subshell, two `echo` statements tell smbclient to translate all input and to print from STDIN (`-`). You execute these commands in a subshell (surrounded by parentheses) so you can send a stream of commands into smbprint via STDIN.

2. The `cat` command copies from STDIN to STDOUT, but STDOUT is connected to the next stage of the pipeline, and STDIN is connected to the file to be printed by lpd. This command is also executed in the subshell that the previous two are executed in.

3. smbclient runs, connects to the server specified in `$server` on the service specified in `$service` (where `$server` and `$service` are set up by smbprint), using the other parameters passed to it, and processes STDIN.

4. However, because STDIN is connected to the subshell mentioned previously, it receives the `translate` command, then the `print -` command, and finally, the file to be printed, all on STDIN.

smbtar

To make life easier for system administrators, Samba includes a shell script to make tar backups of remote CIFS/SMB servers. This script is smbtar, which uses smbclient to perform its function.

The general format of the smbtar command is

```
smbtar options files
```

smbtar gets all the information it needs from the command line, and takes the following command-line parameters:

`-s server`	This mandatory parameter specifies the server that the share you are backing up resides on.
`[-p password]`	This optional parameter specifies the password for the remote share or the user password on the server. There is no default password.
`[-x service]`	This optional parameter specifies the service to connect to. If not specified, it defaults to a service called backup.

13

`[-X]`	This optional parameter indicates that any filenames included on the command line are to be excluded from the tar create or restore.
`[-d directory]`	This optional parameter specifies the initial directory to change to before restoring or backing up any files.
`[-u user]`	This optional parameter specifies the user name to connect to the server as. If not specified, it defaults to the login name of the user executing the `smbtar` command.
`[-t tape]`	This optional parameter specifies the tape device or file to backup to or restore from. If not specified, smbtar uses the TAPE environment variable, and if that is not set, uses `tar.out`.
`[-b blocksize]`	This optional parameter specifies the tape blocking factor. If specified, must be an integer greater than 0. If not specified, defaults to 20.
`[-N filenames]`	This optional parameter specifies that smbtar should backup only files that are newer than *filenames*.
`[-i]`	This optional parameter specifies that an incremental backup should be performed. That is, only files with the DOS archive bit set are backed up.
`[-a]`	This optional parameter specifies that the archive bit on all files backed up should be reset. The default is to not touch the archive bit.
`[-r]`	This optional parameter specifies that a restore is to be performed, rather than a backup.
`[-l log level]`	This optional parameter specifies the debug level to operate in, and is passed to smbclient via the `-d` flag. The default log level is 0.
`[-v]`	This optional parameter specifies that smbtar should operate in verbose mode.
[filenames]	This optional list of files is included or excluded depending on whether the `-X` option has been included.

On some systems, where the `getopts` function is not properly implemented in the standard system shell (for example, Digital UNIX), you should change the first line of the smbtar script from `#!/bin/sh` to `#!/usr/bin/ksh`. Without this change, smbtar does not function properly and gives error messages about `OPTIND`.

Other Clients

You'll likely encounter other CIFS/SMB clients than those mentioned earlier this hour. One that you are aware of is Sharity, a product for many variants of UNIX that is similar to smbfs in some ways, but has the capability to use SSL to connect to servers. This provides considerable improvements in security. Further information on Sharity can be found at the following Web page: `http://www.obdev.at/Products/Sharity.html`.

Summary

In this hour you have explored in detail many of the UNIX clients available with Samba or related to the CIFS/SMB protocol. These clients all provide a relatively UNIX-friendly approach to CIFS/SMB file systems.

In Hour 14, "Windows 9x and Windows NT," you will look at the various SMB clients for Windows and in Hour 15, "Other SMB Clients," you will look at other clients, such as those for the Mac OS, OS/2 Warp, and MS-DOS.

Q&A

Q How would you provide the translate function of smbclient within smbsh?

A Pipe the file through `fromdos` or `todos` depending on which direction the file is going.

Q I have just installed Amanda at my site, use Samba 1.9.18p10, and my backups are corrupt. Why does Amanda have so many problems with Samba?

A A bug was introduced into Samba 1.9.18p7 or thereabout, where both the tar output and informational messages about the progress of the backup were sent to STDOUT, thus corrupting the archive.

There are several fixes to this problem. The Amanda folks have distributed a patch on their Web site to fix the problem. You can also add the `-E` option to the `smbclient` command that Amanda uses. Finally, a patch has been included in both the 2.0 source tree and the 2.1 source tree to stop this behavior and direct informational output to STDERR when STDOUT is being used for the tar archive. It is available in Samba 2.0.1 and beyond.

13

Q When I restore files to a Win 95 machine, smbclient sometimes fails after telling me that it could not update the creation time on a file. What do I do?

A Windows 95 and Windows NT behave differently when asked to change the creation date on a file. Windows NT performs the requested operation without any problems, whereas Windows 95 performs the requested action and returns an error response. The version of smbclient in Samba 2.0.0 contains a fix for this problem (it ignores the response from the server when changing the creation date), so you should upgrade to 2.0.0.

Hour **14**

Windows 9x and Windows NT

Accessing SMB servers from newer Windows operating systems is fairly easy to configure. Up to this point, I have not mentioned any of the configuration details, but you have more than likely already installed the basic necessary components.

In this hour, I will look at how to install, configure, and use the SMB client included with Windows 9x and Windows NT. I am including Windows 95 and Windows 98 clients together because both are almost identical. There is very little change in the network configuration between the two versions. Windows NT is an altogether different OS and therefore will be covered separately.

The Windows Network Redirector

Before looking at the details of how to configure the Windows network client, I want to take a few moments to explain a little about the Windows network architecture. Be warned that the Windows 9x network redirector and the one that is a part of Windows NT differ significantly, but the basic theory behind them both is similar.

Figure 14.1 shows a simplified version of how Windows handles access to remote network shares. I will assume for my description that I am referring only to disk shares. The explanation for remote printers is similar.

FIGURE 14.1

A general implementation of the network redirector.

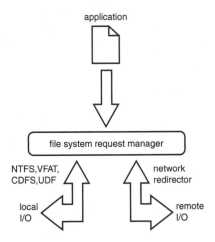

There are three basic parts to the implementation:

- The application requesting the disk I/O.
- Some type of file system request manager. Windows 95 and 98 implement this using an Installable FileSystem Manager. The Workstation service handles the user-level requests in Windows NT.
- The network redirector.

The process works something like this:

1. The application requests some disk I/O.
2. The request is sent to the file system request manager.
3. The file system request manager then forwards the request to the appropriate file system device driver. If the requested I/O is local, the local file system driver (NTFS, VFAT, CDFS, UDF, and so on) will service it. If the request is for I/O on a network share, the information is translated to an SMB packet and sent out on the network.

4. The requested I/O is returned to the application through the file system request manager.

I concede that it is a possibly oversimplified view of the network redirector, but at least when I say, "The network redirector...," you will have a general idea what I am talking about.

Windows 9x

Windows 98 is the latest evolution in the line of Windows operating systems designed for personal use. As with the FAT16 file system, it has expanded beyond its original intention and capacity. However, one of the greatest improvements between Windows 95 and the previous 16-bit versions is in the networking department. The networking code is more robust and more stable. I am not claiming that it is perfect, but it is light years ahead of, say, Windows for Workgroups. (I still have about 125 WfWg 3.11 clients to support where I work.)

Configuring the Client

I will focus on three components to configure the Windows 95 client:

- The network interface adapter driver
- The TCP/IP protocol stack
- The SMB client (a k a Client for Microsoft Networks)

These are shown in the Network control panel in Figure 14.2.

FIGURE 14.2

The necessary network components for connecting to shares on a Samba server.

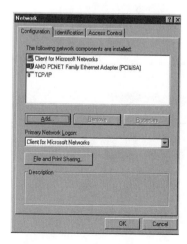

14

The Network Interface Adapter

The network adapter driver is usually the first item that you will install. It is beyond the scope of this book to provide detailed instructions for every network adapter card you could possibly install, but Windows 9x automatically detects and configures most modern network cards. If you are using older 16-bit ISA cards, you will probably have to configure the card manually and install the software drivers yourself. Network cards are usually distributed with a floppy disk that contains instructions for installation and the latest drivers. However, checking the manufacturing company's Web site to verify that you have the most recent version of the drivers disk is always a good idea.

On the initial installation of a network card, Windows 9x automatically adds four networking components in addition to the network card device driver. This occurs regardless of whether Windows locates and installs the network adapter drivers automatically. The four components are

- Client for Microsoft Networks
- Client for NetWare Networks
- IPX/SPX–compatible network protocol
- NetBEUI network protocol

Figure 14.3 shows the Network control panel after installing a new Allied Telesyn 2450 PCI card. Windows matched the chipset on the card rather than the exact make and model, which is why the network adapter driver says AMD PCNET Family Ethernet Adapter.

FIGURE 14.3

The default network components installed by Windows 9x.

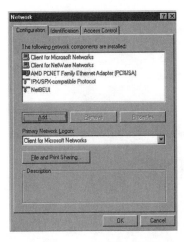

You should remove the following two network protocols by selecting the item in the list and clicking the Remove button:

- IPX/SPX–compatible network protocol
- NetBEUI

This will also remove the two clients. You will read one of them later, but don't worry about that right now. The resulting list should contain only the network adapter driver for your particular card as shown in Figure 14.4.

FIGURE 14.4

Windows 95 Network control panel with the default entries removed.

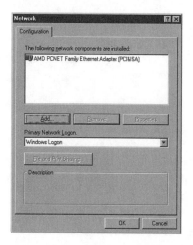

The TCP/IP Network Protocol Stack

After you correctly install the network card, the next step is to add the TCP/IP network protocol stack. To do this, simply click the Add button in the Network control panel and select Protocol from the list in the window that appears. Now select the Add button in this window. The window that appears contains two lists. The list on the left contains a breakdown of the available protocols by company name. When you select a company, the list on the right displays the network protocols that are available from that manufacturer. You should select Microsoft in the left list and TCP/IP in the right list. These three windows are shown in Figure 14.5.

14

FIGURE 14.5

Installing the Microsoft TCP/IP network protocol.

When you click the OK button in the Select Network Protocol window, the TCP/IP protocol is added to the list of installed network components (see Figure 14.6). You can configure several options for TCP/IP on the PC by selecting the TCP/IP protocol from the list and clicking the Properties button.

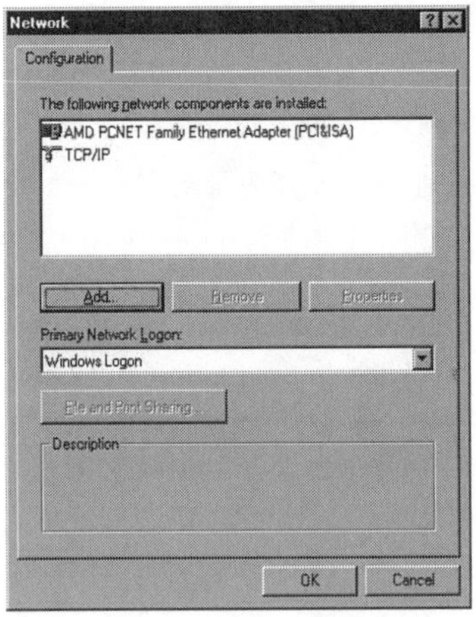

FIGURE 14.6

List of installed network components after adding the TCP/IP protocol.

The first settings page appearing in the resulting window enables you to set the local IP address and subnet mask. There are two possibilities. The first enables you to obtain an IP address from a DHCP (Dynamic Host Configuration Protocol) server, and the second lets you manually configure the two settings. For this example, you will manually configure the IP address and subnet mask (see Figure 14.7).

FIGURE 14.7

IP address settings in TCP/IP Properties window.

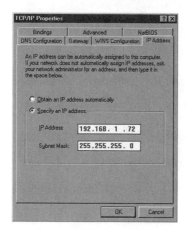

Figure 14.8 displays the next TCP/IP settings tab. You have already seen the WINS Configuration tab in Hour 2, "Windows Networking." This page allows you to enable WINS resolution and to specify the IP addresses of your WINS servers. If WINS resolution is enabled, you can also define a Scope ID string. The third possibility is to obtain the IP addresses for the WINS servers from the DHCP server. For now, you simply disable WINS. More information about WINS can be found in Hour 18, "Resolving NetBIOS Names Without Using Broadcasts."

FIGURE 14.8

The WINS Configuration tab in the TCP/IP Properties window.

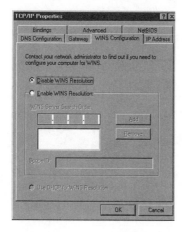

14

If your subnet has a default gateway for traffic destined to another IP network, you can specify the IP of the router in the Gateway tab (see Figure 14.9). For the small network I have installed at home, I do not use a default gateway and so this field is empty.

FIGURE 14.9

Setting the default gateway in the TCP/IP Properties window.

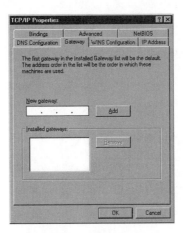

The final TCP/IP settings that I will discuss are the DNS settings for the PC (see Figure 14.10). You have the choice of either enabling or disabling DNS. If you enable DNS, you can define the IP addresses of your DNS servers, the domain suffix search order, and the PC's hostname and domain. Again for my small network at home, these are unnecessary. As a side note, it is possible to set the DNS server's IP addresses using DHCP if you so choose.

FIGURE 14.10

The DNS Configuration tab in the TCP/IP Properties window.

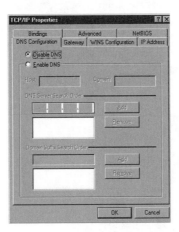

The Client for Microsoft Networks

The final network component to install is the SMB client. As I mentioned in previous hours, Microsoft chose to use the SMB protocol as the resource-sharing mechanism in their network model. Therefore, the SMB client is named Client for Microsoft Networks.

To install the Microsoft Network client, click the Add button in the Network control panel as you did when you added the TCP/IP network protocol. Then select Client from the list of Network Component types, and click the Add button in that window. You see a window that appears very similar to the one you used to select the network protocol to install. This time the list of manufacturers on the left side of the window represents the ones that have developed network clients rather than protocols. First select Microsoft in the list on the left, and then select Client for Microsoft Networks from the list on the right. Finally select the OK button in the Select Network Client window to add the chosen client. Figure 14.11 displays the three windows necessary to add the correct client.

FIGURE 14.11

Selecting the Client for Microsoft Networks for installation.

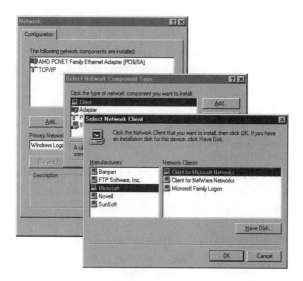

The Network control panel should now show the three network components that you need (as shown in Figure 14.12).

14

Figure 14.12

The Network control panel after installing the network adapter, TCP/IP network stack, and the Microsoft Networks client.

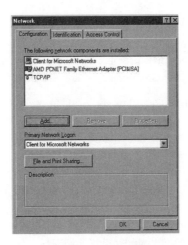

Setting the Machine Name and Workgroup Name

The final step for configuring a Windows 9x PC to access shares located on an SMB server is to set the NetBIOS machine name and workgroup name. You can refer to Hour 2 for a reminder of what constitutes a valid NetBIOS name. In order to define these two strings, you must have installed the Client for Microsoft Networks. The Identification page (see Figure 14.13) is unavailable in the Network control panel unless the correct client is installed. The Comment field on the Identification page enables you to set the text string that is displayed next to the machine name if you have enabled file and print sharing on the PC. This setting is the equivalent of Samba's `server string` parameter in `smb.conf`. After you have set the desired values, you can click the OK button. Windows begins copying the necessary files from the installed `*.cab` files or from the Windows CD-ROM. When the OS is finished copying files, it prompts you to reboot your computer. When you have done so, you can move to the next step of logging in to the network.

Figure 14.13

Setting the NetBIOS machine name, workgroup name, and comment string for a Windows 95 OSR2 client.

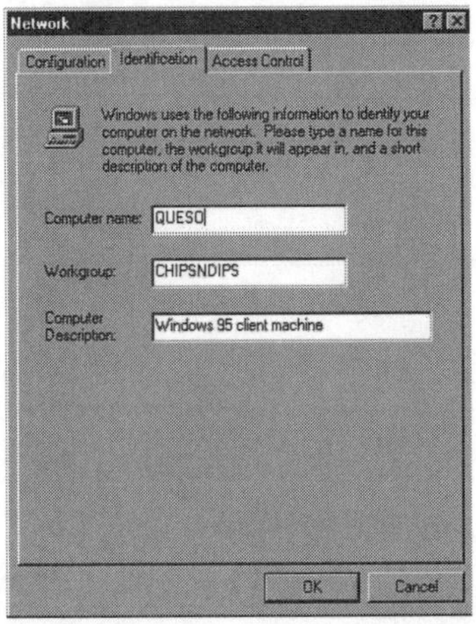

Logging In to the Network

When the PC has rebooted, you will be prompted to log in to the network (see Figure 14.14). There are a few points to remember about logging in to the network:

FIGURE 14.14

Logging in to a Microsoft network.

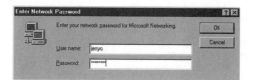

- The username and password you specify in the login box are the defaults used by Windows to connect to remote servers. Windows 9x does not enable you to specify a different username to use in connections to different servers. However, if the username and password that you entered in the login box fails to connect to a server, Windows uses the same username but prompts you for a new password.

- The username and password you enter are not validated at login, but rather when you connect to a server.

- You must log in to access nonguest shares on an SMB server.

Encrypted and Plain-Text Passwords

The original distributions of Windows 95 used plain-text passwords as the default for SMB connections. When an SMB server responds to a negotiate protocol request, the response packet contains a bit to indicate whether the server supports the challenge or response encryption described in Hour 6, "Security Levels and Passwords." With the release of the network redirector update for Windows 95 (vrdrupd.exe), Microsoft changed the default so that Windows 95 clients would not send the plain-text password to a server that did not support encryption. This means that if you attempt to use a Windows 95 client with the following files installed (or later versions) to connect to an unencrypted SMB server

```
windows\system\vredir.vxd     4.00.1114 6/2/97 11:14a 156,773
windows\system\vnetsup.vxd     4.00.1112 6/2/97 11:12a  17,595
```

you are continually prompted for a password even though you are entering a password valid for the account. There are two possible solutions:

- Set up the Samba server to use encrypted passwords using the steps outlined in Hour 6.

- Enable the Windows 95 client to use plain-text passwords.

14

If you choose the second solution, you need to add the following registry key and reboot the client:

```
[HKLM\System\CurrentControlSet\Services\VxD\VNETSUP]
"EnablePlainTextPassword"=dword:00000001
```

 Editing the registry can render your system unusable. Proceed with extreme caution when using the Registry Editor (regedit.exe).

So far I have not mentioned Windows 98 in relation to this. Windows 98 behaves in the same manner as Windows 95 with the redirector update installed. The same two solutions are available for you and the same registry enables plain-text passwords on the Windows 98 client if you so choose.

Connecting to Shares

Windows supports two interfaces for connecting to remote SMB disk shares. One is a command line interface via the net.exe command, and the other is a graphical interface contained in Windows Explorer. You can also use the File Manager to establish drive connections, but this is less popular.

First you use the command line net.exe tool. If you want to view all the options available with the net command, you can execute

```
C:\WINDOWS> net /?
```

In order to see the options available for a particular command—the use argument, for example—you can execute

```
C:\WINDOWS> net option /?
```

The basic syntax of the net use command is

```
net use X: \\servername\sharename
```

where X: is the drive letter to the share and \\servername\sharename is the UNC network path to the share. If the connection is successful, you should see output similar to the following:

```
C:\WINDOWS>net use h: \\eagle\jerryc
The command completed successfully.
```

At this point the share \\eagle\jerryc has been connected to the drive letter H:, and any files contained within it can be accessed in the same manner as files and directories located on the local disk, C:.

It is also possible to make a connection to an SMB share without mapping it to a drive letter by typing

```
net use \\servername\sharename
```

The connection is essentially the same as when it is mapped to a drive letter. The difference is that you must use the UNC name rather than a drive letter, such as H:, to access files. Other than that, there are no major differences.

As I mentioned in the section about logging in, Windows attempts to use the username and password supplied at login time to connect to the remote share. If the session setup fails for authentication reasons, Windows allows you to enter another password but uses the same username. If this occurs, you see a prompt such as this one:

```
C:\users\jerry>net use h: \\eagle\jerryc
The password is invalid for \\EAGLE\JERRYC. For more information, contact
your network administrator.
Type the password for \\EAGLE\JERRYC:********
The command was completed successfully.
```

If you would like to see statistics about a current connection, use the command

```
net use X:
```

where X: is the drive letter for the connection you want to view. Here is the information for the connection I made previously to \\eagle\jerryc:

```
C:\users\jerry>net use h:
Local name        H:
Remote name       \\EAGLE\JERRYC
Resource type     Disk
Status            OK
# Opens           0
# Connections     1
The command was completed successfully.
```

When you are ready to disconnect from a share, you can type

```
net use X: /d
```

to delete the connection. You should replace X: with the appropriate drive letter.

The net use command can also display a list of all the current share connections. If you execute net use without any other command line arguments, the output shows you all the current share connections, even those that are not connected to a drive letter:

14

```
C:\users\jerry>net use

Status          Local name      Remote name
- - - - - - - - - - - - - - - - - - - - - - - - - - - - - - - - - - - - - - - - - - - - -
OK              H:              \\EAGLE\JERRYC
OK                              \\EAGLE\SRC
The command was completed successfully.
```

The other available interface for establishing network resource connections is the set of dialog boxes provided by the Windows Explorer. The GUI interface does not provide as much flexibility as the command line tools, in my opinion, but it does enable you to set persistent share connections. By this I mean that Windows attempts to reconnect the shares for you every time you log in to the network.

Figure 14.15 displays the Map Network Drive dialog box, which you can access by right-clicking either the My Computer desktop icon or the Network Neighborhood desktop icon and selecting the Map Network Drive option. The window provides a popup menu for selecting the available drive letter to connect to. The Path field lets you manually define the path to which to connect and the Reconnect at Logon check box enables you define whether Windows should remember this connection next time you log in. Notice that Windows forces you to select a drive letter from this interface. If you connect to a share using the Explorer interface, you must assign it a drive. There is also no field to enter an initial password to use. Windows again first uses the username and password entered at login, and prompts for a new password only if there is an authentication failure.

FIGURE 14.15

The Map Network Drive dialog box.

When you are ready to disconnect from the network drive, right click the associated drive letter icon in the My Computer window to bring up the Disconnect menu option (see Figure 14.16). Selecting this option informs Windows that you want to disconnect the network drive.

FIGURE 14.16

*Disconnecting a net-
work drive.*

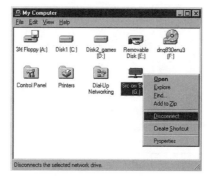

You can freely swap between both interfaces. Drives that are connected using the GUI interface can be disconnected using the net use command and vice versa.

Connecting to Printers

How you connect to a network printer depends on the applications that need the capability to send jobs to it. If you have older DOS programs that require access the printer, the best solution is to map an available LPT to the network printer location, install the appropriate printer driver, and set it to print to the mapped port. If only Windows applications need access to the network printer, you can connect the network printer to the UNC network path only.

The difference in setups stems from the fact that DOS programs tend to print directly to the LPT port (some are even hard coded to print to LPT1 only) and bypass the Windows print drivers. By mapping the LPT port to a network location, all data sent to the port is redirected to the network printer. Look at the details for both setups beginning with the one that supports DOS application printing.

Figure 14.17 shows the basic idea behind DOS printing to a network location. Notice that the diagram looks similar to the explanation of the Windows network redirector in Figure 14.1. The reason is that the logic is basically the same. Rather than printing directly to the port, the output from the DOS application goes through the Windows redirector that either sends the output to a local LPT port or to the network location.

14

FIGURE 14.17

Printing to a mapped LPT port.

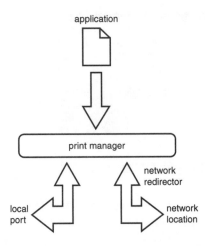

There are two ways to map a network printer UNC path to a local LPT port. These are almost identical to the methods used to map network drives.

> The LPT you use doesn't actually have to exist for you to use it as an attachment point for the network printer. Windows enables you to use LPT1 through LPT9 regardless of whether the ports are present on the local system.

The `net.exe` command enables you to map LPT port as you do drive connections. The syntax is very similar:

```
net use LPTn: \\servername\printername
```

You should replace *n* with an available port between 1 and 9. The `servername` and `printername` compose the UNC path to the remote printer.

If you prefer to use the graphical interface, you can launch the Capture Printer Port dialog box (see Figure 14.18) by right-clicking the printers icon in an open My Computer window and selecting the Capture Printer Port option from the resulting menu.

FIGURE 14.18

*The Windows 95
Capture Printer Port
dialog box.*

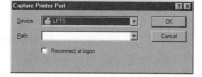

Regardless of which method you use to map the port, if successful, you will be able to
see the connection by executing the net use command with no arguments as you did
before:

```
C:\users\jerry>net use

Status          Local name      Remote name
-------------------------------------------------------------------------
OK              M:              \\EAGLE\FILES
OK              LPT5            \\EAGLE\CANONBJC
The command was completed successfully.
```

You can now set the local printer driver to print to the mapped LPT port. The Print to the
Following Port setting is normally found on the Details tab of the printer's properties as
Figure 14.19 illustrates.

FIGURE 14.19

*Setting the local print-
er to print to the
mapped LPT port.*

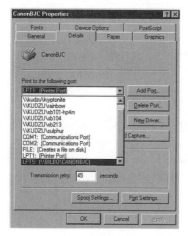

14

There is one more possibility for mapping the network printer to a local port. If you are installing the printer for the first time, Windows 95 enables you to choose whether you want to allow DOS applications to print to this printer. If you select Yes, the Capture Printer Port window appears and, when connected, Windows sets the printer to send its output to captured printer port for you. Figure 14.20 shows the screen that prompts you to choose DOS support or not.

FIGURE 14.20

The Windows 95 Add Printer Wizard enables you to define the network printer's UNC pathname and choose whether to allow DOS programs to access it.

If all the programs that are required to print are native Windows applications, including Windows 3.1 software, it is easier for you simply to connect to the printer's UNC network path during installation. If you designate that the printer is a network printer during installation, Windows presents an editable field where you can either browse for the printer or manually define the network path (see Figure 14.20).

Windows NT

Although it shares the same user interface as Windows 95 and 98, Windows NT is an entirely different operating system from the ground up. The advantage of having the same GUI is that many of the steps for using the Windows NT SMB client are similar to the steps for using the Windows 9x client. Begin by installing the necessary network components.

Configuring the Client

One area where the internal differences between Windows NT and Windows 9x show on the outside is in the networking code. Both operating systems use a type of network redirector such as I described in the first part of this hour. Under Windows NT, the Workstation service does this. The other two components that you need are the network adapter and the TCP/IP network protocol stack, as you did in Windows 9x.

Installing the Network Adapter

Again, you start by installing the software drivers for the network interface card. Unlike Windows 9x, Windows NT requires that you manually add and configure the network adapter drivers. This means that you must know some precise details about your particular card. Again, walking through all the possible steps for installing every network card is beyond the scope of this book, so I will mention only some points that are common to all.

Before you begin, make sure that you have the latest drivers from the hardware manufacturer. I have never seen a case where the plain-vanilla Windows NT drivers were better than those produced by the card's developer. For some newer cards, you might find that the only available drivers are those from the manufacturer.

When you have physically installed the card in the PC and arrive at the Windows NT Network control panel, you should notice that the adapters, protocols, and services are all listed on different pages. Remember when I said that this was one of the places where you can see the difference on the inside. Granted that you cannot equate a new interface with stability, but I think you get the idea.

First navigate to the Adapters tab (see Figure 14.21). Now select the Add button and locate the appropriate driver for your card. If you need to install a custom driver, pressing the Have Disk button will prompt you for the location of the files.

After Windows NT copies the necessary drivers files from the Windows NT installation CD-ROM or drivers disk, if you installed custom software drivers (see Figure 14.22), you are ready to move to the next step where you install the TCP/IP protocol stack.

14

FIGURE 14.21

Installing a new network adapter.

FIGURE 14.22

The newly installed network card driver for an ATI 2450 PCI Ethernet card.

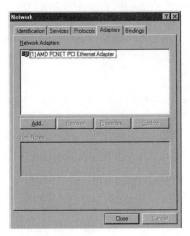

Installing the TCP/IP Protocol

Windows NT, like Windows 9x, automatically adds two protocols for you when the first network adapter is installed. Figure 14.23 shows the two NWLink entries and the one for the NetBEUI protocol. The NWLink NetBIOS entry depends on the NWLink IPX/SPX protocol and is installed with it, so I refer to both as one item.

FIGURE 14.23

Default network proto-cols installed by Windows NT.

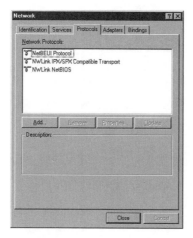

First, you add the TCP/IP network stack by clicking the Add button and selecting the protocol's entry from the list as shown in Figure 14.24. Then you remove the NWLink entries and the NetBEUI protocol from the installed list so that only the TCP/IP network protocol remains.

If you remove the IPX/SPX protocol, Windows NT automatically removes the NWLink NetBIOS entry as well (see Figure 14.25).

FIGURE 14.24

Selecting the TCP/IP protocol to be installed.

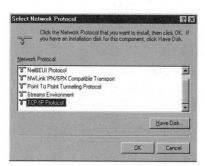

14

FIGURE 14.25

The installed network protocols after removing the NWLink and NetBEUI protocol entries.

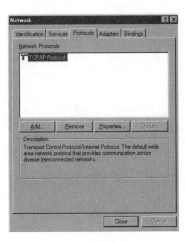

Don't worry about configuring the TCP/IP settings at this moment. Figure 14.26 shows what happens when you choose to close the Network control panel. Windows NT checks the adapter and protocol bindings and prompts you for the necessary TCP/IP settings. The only information that I have chosen to specify at the moment is the IP address of the machine and the subnet mask. If your setup requires setting a default gateway or indicating the IP addresses of your DNS servers, you should do so now.

FIGURE 14.26

TCP/IP Properties window.

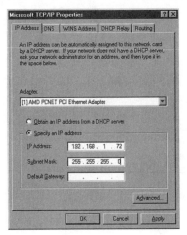

The Workstation Service

I stated at the beginning of this section that the Workstation service implemented the Windows NT SMB redirector. The complementary service that allows a Windows NT machine to share files is named the Server service.

The workstation service requires no configuration and is installed by default when you set up networking under Windows NT. I guess Microsoft assumed that even Windows NT machines would run in some sort of Microsoft network environment. Remember that Microsoft chose the SMB protocol to implement file and printer sharing in its network model. That was probably a fairly safe assumption.

Figure 14.27 shows the other Workstation and other services that are installed by default. You simply accept the entries that are set up in the Services tab.

FIGURE 14.27

The default network services installed by Windows NT including the Workstation service.

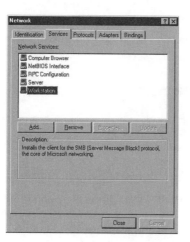

Setting the NetBIOS Machine Name and Workgroup Name

The final thing that you do before accepting the changes you have made by closing the Network control panel is to set the NetBIOS machine name and workgroup name. The machine name is defined during the installation of the operating system; the workgroup is not. The first tab in the Network control panel window is the Identification tab. If you select the Change button, you are able to modify the values as shown in Figure 14.28. For my purposes at the moment, I'm making the client a member of a workgroup. The workgroup I use on my home network is named CHIPSNDIPS because most of the machines are named after some type of corn chip dip such as QUESO, SALSA, and PICANTE.

14

FIGURE 14.28

Setting the workgroup name in the Network control panel.

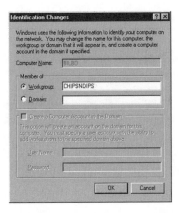

When you click the OK button to apply the workgroup change, you will see a window saying, "Welcome to the CHIPSNDIPS workgroup" (see Figure 14.29). Of course, your message welcomes you to whatever workgroup you enter on your machine. Now you can close the Network control panel and reboot.

FIGURE 14.29

Welcome to the CHIP-SNDIPS workgroup.

Time to Reboot

After you define all the necessary TCP/IP settings, set the workgroup name, and close the Network control panel, Windows NT prompts you for a reboot. Accept the reboot, grab a cup of coffee, and wait for things to come back up.

After the machine has rebooted, you should log in using whatever account has been set up for you. One of the best quotes I ever heard about Windows 95 was that "It gives you all the security you deserve!" Basically there is not real security. Sure some things can give you the feeling of security, but nothing that would keep out any junior-high kid with a few extra minutes on his or her hands.

Windows NT was designed with security in mind. There are many mechanisms to help control access to local resources on a machine. One of these is the requirement that all users log in using some account, whether it is a local account or a domain account, before being given access to a useable desktop.

Now that you're logged in and everything is installed, let's look at connecting to some remote shares.

Service Pack 3 for Windows NT 4.0

Before you attempt to connect to the Samba server, I should mention that Microsoft made the same decision regarding Windows NT and encrypted passwords that they did about Windows 95. You can refer back to the section "Encrypted and Plain-Text Passwords," about the network redirector update for Windows 95 that restricts the client from transmitting the plain text of the user's password over the network if the SMB server does not support encrypted passwords.

Service Pack 3 for Windows introduced the same issue with unencrypted SMB servers. If you attempt to connect to a unencrypted SMB server from a Windows NT client (server or workstation) with Service Pack 3 installed, the network redirector replies

```
System error 1240 has occurred.
The account is not authorized to login from this station.
```

The same two possible solutions for the problem with the Windows 95 redirector update exist for Service Pack 3:

- Set up the Samba server to use encrypted passwords using the steps outlined in Hour 6.
- Enable the Windows NT client to use plain-text passwords.

If you choose the second solution, you need to add the following registry key and reboot the NT client:

```
[HKLM\System\CurrentControlSet\Services\Rdr\Parameters]
"EnablePlainTextPassword"=dword:00000001
```

> Editing the registry can render your system unusable. Proceed with extreme caution when using the Registry Editor (regedit.exe or regedt32.exe).

Connecting to Shares

I will not be quite as verbose in this section as I was in the corresponding section about connecting to shares from a Windows 95 client because there is a great deal of overlap in this area. Rather I will mention only the major difference that you will see.

As does Windows 9x, Windows NT supports a command line and a graphical interface for connecting to remote SMB file shares. There is one major difference found in the methods when compared to Windows 9x. Windows NT supports the capability to connect to a server using a username other than the one used to log in to the local machine console. When executing the net use command to mount a drive, you can specify an

14

additional switch for the username to use in the connection. If I log in to the PC console
with the username jcarter, I can tell Windows NT to send the username jerryc for the
session setup by typing

```
net use h: \\bilbo\jerryc /user:jerryc
```

You will also notice in Figure 14.30 that the Map Network Drive dialog box has an extra
field when compared to the Windows 95 version. The Connect As field is the graphical
equivalent of the /user: switch available with the net use command.

FIGURE 14.30

The Windows NT ver-
sion of the Map
Network Drive dialog
box.

The Windows NT connection GUI also supports connecting to a UNC path by specifying
a drive letter to which the connection should be attached. To do this, you simply choose
(none) in the Drive popup menu (see Figure 14.31).

FIGURE 14.31

Connecting to a net-
work file share without
using a drive letter.

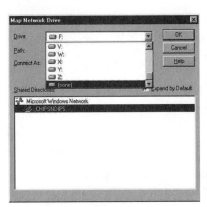

Whereas both Windows 9x and Windows NT enable you to create persistent connections that the operating system attempts to reestablish on login to the PC console, only NT enables you to do this by using the net use command. You can globally set the default behavior of whether or not to remember connections at the next login by executing

```
net use /persistent:option
```

The option is either yes or no. You can override the default behavior by adding the /persistent:option switch to the actual command to map the resource like this:

```
net use h: \\eagle\jerryc /persistent:yes
```

The NT SMB redirector has one small deficiency: you cannot connect to the same server name using multiple usernames. For example, suppose that I have an SMB server named SERVER1, which is either Windows NT, Window 9x, or Samba and provide the following shares: [docs] and [forms]. First I connect to \\server1\docs using the valid account named sysadmin:

```
net use p: \\server1\docs /user:admin
The command completed successfully.
```

Next I try to connect to \\server1\forms using my normal account named jerryc:

```
net use p: \\server1\forms /user:jerryc
System error 1219 has occurred.

The credentials supplied conflict with an existing set of credentials.
```

The way to work around this problem is to make NT think that you are connecting to a different server. The easiest way to do this is to use the IP address of the server rather than its name. For example, to connect to the [forms] shares I run

```
net use p: \\192.168.1.75\forms /user:jerryc
The command completed successfully.
```

This time, Windows NT can connect successfully. You can also use Samba's NetBIOS aliases capability to enable clients to connect to the same server using multiple names rather than using an IP address.

Connecting to Printers

Connecting to a network printer under Windows NT is, for practical purposes, no different that connecting to one under Windows 9x. Because few people are likely to run DOS applications that need to print under Windows NT, I will talk only about directly connecting to the network printer server. If you need the capability to print from DOS programs, you can map an LPT port using the same procedure as you do for Windows 9x.

14

Figure 14.32 shows the first step installing a network printer on an NT 4.0 client. After selecting that the connection is to a network printer server rather than to the local computer, the OS prompts you for the network path as Windows 9x does. You can either manually specify the network path or browse for it in the lower part of the Connect to Printer window.

FIGURE 14.32

Connecting to a printer on a network server.

If you connect to a Samba server or other server that does not have the printer drivers available for download, you are prompted to select the make and model of the printer so that Windows NT can copy the driver files from the installation media.

Summary

Configuring Windows 9x and Windows NT client to connect to a remote SMB server such as Samba on a TCP/IP network requires three components:

- A working network interface card.
- A correctly configured version of the TCP/IP network protocol stack.
- Some type of SMB network redirector. Windows 9x calls this the Client for Microsoft Networks whereas Windows NT implements this in the Workstation service.

Although both appear similar, two operating systems have one major difference that is visible to the end user. Windows 9x doesn't enable you to connect to a server using a username other than the one used for the initial login, whereas Windows NT does support this functionality.

Q&A

Q Can I install both the IPX/SPX network protocol and TCP/IP on my computer?

A Yes, but some postings on the Samba mailing lists indicate that this can cause problems with respect to network browsing. Some people have reported not being able to locate servers on the network when both protocols are installed.

Q Why does Windows NT complain and print the error message 2138 when I try to map network drives?

A The Workstation service must be started in order for you to access the network. You can manually start the service by typing `net start workstation` in a command prompt window.

14

HOUR 15

Other SMB Clients

As you have already seen in Hour 13, "UNIX (smbclient, smbfs, smbwrapper, and Various Utilities)," Windows clients are not the only operating systems that can connect to SMB servers. This hour examines two more SMB clients: one for DOS and one for the Macintosh.

You might believe that with the initial release of Windows 95, and later Windows 98, DOS has become a thing of the past. Perhaps it would only be referred to in a story told by older college professors about their graduate work on an Intel 8086 box running Disk Operating System version 1.0. After all, who in their right mind would still want to use an OS that can only do one thing at a time and has a memory limit at 640KB?

To be truthful, I still use DOS quite often. DOS fits nicely onto a single floppy that can be used to boot a system. You can then proceed to use things that Windows 9x tends not to (such as disk editors).

I have also found these boot floppies to be very helpful when used in conjunction with disk imaging software such as Symantec's Ghost product. By using a SMB client on a DOS floppy, I can boot in to the network, mount any necessary drives, and load the machine from an image file located on a

Samba server. The entire process takes about 15–20 minutes to get a working Windows 95 machine up and on the network. Of course, a few other small details make this possible, such as the use of DHCP and identical hardware on all lab machine. Another useful situation is when you need to install Windows on a machine that does not have a CD-ROM drive. It can take seemingly forever to load Windows 95 off of floppies, but mounting a shared CD-ROM and loading the software across the network is extremely fast in comparison. This hour shows you how to create network boot floppies using Microsoft's DOS network client.

Other SMB clients also exist that can help integrate non-Windows machines into your Samba infrastructure. Perhaps the graphics department at your job uses a lot of Macintoshes, but the large files they produce need to be transferred to another department that uses PCs. You will examine a SMB client named DAVE for Macintosh systems that allows them to access shares on a Samba server and store files there. This creates a central point of distribution for all your users.

Microsoft Network Client Version 3.0 for MS-DOS

This section explains how to create a bootable DOS floppy that allows you to mount SMB shares. You will examine three basic steps:

1. Obtaining the client software
2. Installing the network client software on to the local hard disk
3. Creating the network boot disk from the files installed in step 2

Obtaining the Software

Microsoft freely distributes its network client for DOS. If you have a copy of the Windows NT 4.0 Server CD-ROM, you can save yourself the download time by accessing the two disk set in

`X:\clients\msclient\disks`

where `X:` is the drive letter of your CD-ROM drive.

If you do not have a copy of the CD-ROM, you can download the DOS client install disks from `ftp://ftp.microsoft.com/bussys/Clients/MSCLIENT/`

The directory has two files:

```
DSK3-1.EXE
DSK3-2.EXE
```

Download both files into a temporary directory (for example, c:\temp) and extract each disk by executing

```
C:\> mkdir c:\temp\disk1
C:\> cd c:\temp\disk1
C:\> c:\temp\dsk3-1.exe
C:\> mkdir c:\temp\disk2
C:\> cd c:\temp\disk2
C:\> c:\temp\dsk3-2.exe
```

At this point, no matter what method you use to obtain the network client files (CD-ROM or FTP), you should be ready to copy the files onto two 1.44MB floppies and install the client.

Installing the Client

To create a network boot floppy, first go through the steps for installing the DOS network client onto a hard drive. Then copy only the files required onto the boot floppy. Practice has shown me that it is easier to get things up and running under normal conditions before attempting to create the boot floppy. For reference sake, I will use MS-DOS 6.22 as the operating system.

After you copy the files onto two disks, you are ready to install the software. In this example, I assume that your floppy drive letter is A:. Insert the first disk into the client computer and type **C:\> a:\setup.exe**.

What results should be the screen displayed in Figure 15.1.

FIGURE 15.1

Installation screen for Microsoft's Network Client 3.0.

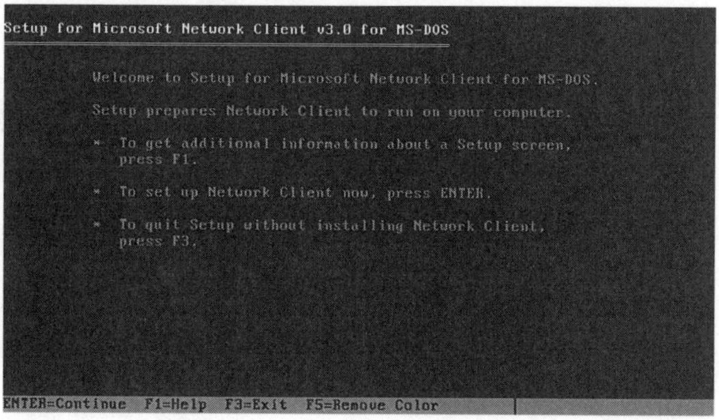

Continuing to the next screen, you accept the default install location of C:\NET. After examining the system for a few seconds, the setup program returns with a list of possible network adapter drivers to install (see Figure 15.2).

FIGURE 15.2

Selecting a network adapter driver to install.

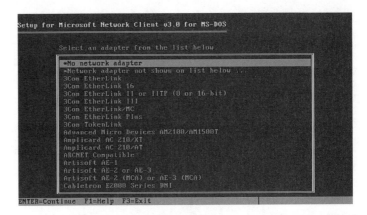

NEW TERM This can be the trickiest part of the setup. If you do not see your particular network adapter listed—and chances are you won't—locate the MS LanMan for DOS drivers for your card. I normally use the standard NDIS2 drivers shipped with the network card. The network client's setup program attempts to locate a file named OEMSETUP.INF in the directory designated as containing the card's drivers. If the setup program does not find this file, it complains that it could not find any legitimate drivers. This can be a hassle. It can take a few tries, but you should be able to select your card from a list of drivers that were located. My network adapter is shown in the list in Figure 15.3.

FIGURE 15.3

Selecting a custom network adapter driver to install.

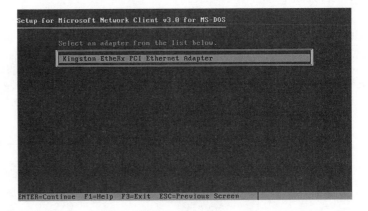

The next step is to specify a username that will be used by default. This is really more for convenience because you can always specify another when actually logging in to the network.

The next screen (see Figure 15.4) allows you to change setup options before installation. The Names setting allows for changing the NetBIOS machine name and the workgroup name used for browsing and the domain name used for validation if the Logon to Domain option is enabled. Figure 15.5 displays the defaults for these three values. Change these to QUESO, CHIPSNDIPS, and CHIPSNDIPS respectively.

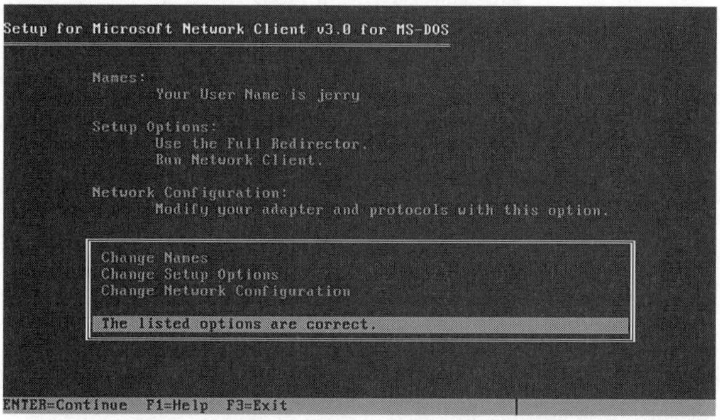

FIGURE 15.4

The general configuration screen for the network client.

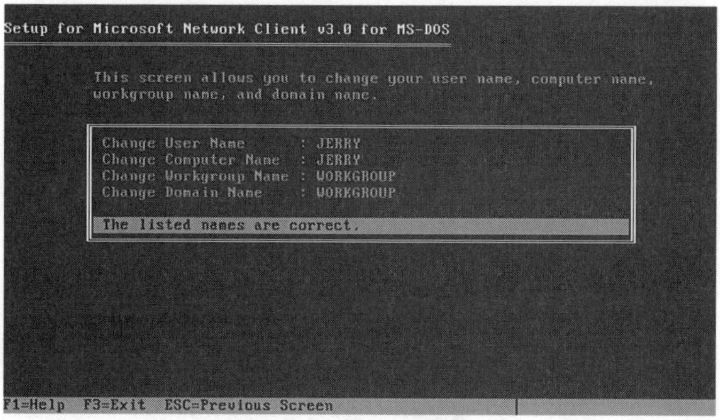

FIGURE 15.5

NetBIOS name settings screen.

The Setup Options probably needs a little clarification. The setting shown in Figure 15.6 says that you are configured to use the Full Redirector. There are two options available to you. The full network redirector allows for domain logins—and, yes, you can get login scripts as well—and uses about 100KB of memory. The basic redirector uses considerably less memory but only allows for mounting printer ports and network drives. The basic redirector also requires that you enable password encryption on your server. The full redirector supports plain-text and encrypted passwords. Choose the Full Redirector for now. If you later discover that you need to reduce the amount of memory in use, you can run the setup program again to modify your settings.

FIGURE 15.6

The network client's detailed network configuration screen.

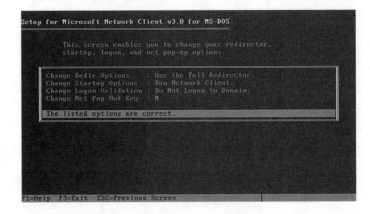

Figure 15.7 displays the installed network components. This is where you choose what network protocols should be installed. As usual, install only the TCP/IP stack, and as usual, the default is to install something else. You have already selected your network adapter, so you should not need to change that setting now.

FIGURE 15.7

Installed network components.

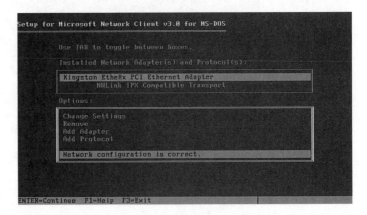

First, add TCP/IP. Figure 15.8 shows the list of available network protocols. After adding the TCP/IP protocol, use the Tab key to select the NWLink entry shown in Figure 15.9 and delete it by using the Remove option listed on the screen. Before returning to the previous screen shown in Figure 15.4, manually configure settings for your IP address and subnet mask. Figure 15.10 shows the default values for the network addresses. The only ones you should concern yourself with now are the Subnet Mask, the IP Address, and Disable DHCP (set to the value 1). If you need to access hosts across a router, you can also specify a default gateway to use.

15

FIGURE 15.8

Listing of available network protocols to install.

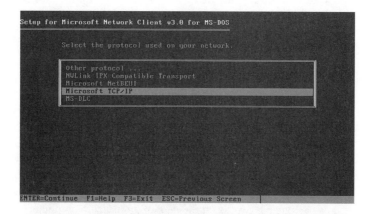

FIGURE 15.9

Installed network components after adding the TCP/IP protocol.

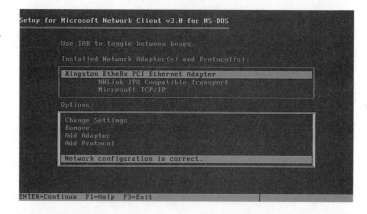

FIGURE 15.10

Listing of default values for network addresses.

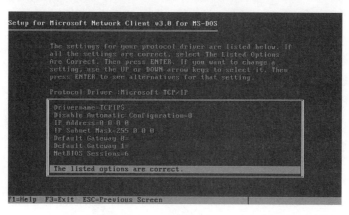

Now the network configuration is correct, and so you return to the screen shown in Figure 15.4 again. After copying the necessary files, setup informs you that everything completed successfully and that you should reboot for the new configuration to take effect.

When the machine comes back up, you will be asked to log in to the network. You'll receive a prompt similar to mine:

```
Type your user name, or press ENTER if it is JERRY:
```

After pressing the Enter key, you are prompted for your password:

```
Type your password:*******
```

Following this, the DOS network client looks for a password cache file to verify the entered password against. Because this is your first time logging in, of course it does not find one. Therefore, it asks whether you want to create one. Given my natural animosity towards caching passwords on the disk of an insecure computer, I decline:

```
There is no password-list for JERRY.
Do you want to create one? (Y/N) [N]:
```

After being informed that `The command completed successfully`, you can use the basic set of options with the `net.exe` command to access drives and browse the network. For example, you can use the `net use` command to mount a shared Zip drive from a Windows NT 4.0 Server or a Samba server for that matter:

```
C:\> net use z: \\picante\zipdisk
The command completed successfully.
```

The DOS network client does suffer from the same problem as the Windows 9x client, however. All connection attempts to servers will use the login name named entered when the client was started on the PC. There to way to work around this.

Making the Network Boot Disk

Now that you have a working setup on the local disk, begin creating the network boot floppy. First create a simple boot disk by executing

```
C:\> format a: /s
```

After the system files have been transferred to the disk, make two directories, one named DOS and one named NET. The first directory will contain any required DOS utilities, such as memory managers, and the second will contain the necessary files for the DOS network client.

If you examine the \NET directory located on the hard disk, you will find approximately 1.6MB of files. Finding the right files to copy to the floppy disk can be a process of trial and error. For that reason, the files you use on the boot floppy are given in Listing 15.1. The disk's `config.sys` file in Listing 15.2 and its `autoexec.bat` in Listing 15.3 follow the directory listing.

LISTING 15.1   FILES LOCATED ON THE NETWORK BOOT DISK

```
Volume in drive A has no label
Volume Serial Number is 2629-09D8

Directory of A:\

dos          <DIR>         02-01-99   2:20a
net          <DIR>         02-01-99   2:20a
autoexec bat          245  02-01-99   2:40a
command  com       54,645  05-31-94   6:22a
config   sys          132  02-01-99   2:39a
        5 file(s)         55,022 bytes

Directory of A:\DOS

.            <DIR>         02-01-99   2:20a
..           <DIR>         02-01-99   2:20a
format   com       22,974  05-31-94   6:22a
sys      com        9,432  05-31-94   6:22a
emm386   exe      120,926  05-31-94   6:22a
fdisk    exe       29,336  05-31-94   6:22a
vi       exe       46,130  01-24-96   2:23p
himem    sys       29,136  02-13-94   6:21a
        8 file(s)        257,934 bytes

Directory of A:\NET

.            <DIR>         02-01-99   2:20a
..           <DIR>         02-01-99   2:20a
hosts                715  08-31-94   7:37p
lmhosts              817  08-31-94   7:36p
networks             395  08-31-94   6:52p
protocol             795  08-31-94   6:52p
services           5,973  05-08-95   2:34p
wfwsys   cfg         840  02-01-99  12:54a
netbind  com       8,513  08-31-94  12:00a
umb      com       3,325  08-31-94  12:00a
connect  dat          40  02-01-99   2:44a
ktc40    dos       49,057  07-21-95   7:31p
protman  dos       21,940  08-31-94  12:00a
nemm     dos        2,619  08-31-94  12:00a
tcpdrv   dos        4,174  08-31-94  12:00a
protman  exe       13,782  08-31-94  12:00a
```

continues

LISTING 15.1 CONTINUED

```
emsbfr   exe       4,294 08-31-94   12:00a
nmtsr    exe      22,826 08-31-94   12:00a
ping     exe      66,460 08-31-94   12:00a
tcptsr   exe      71,040 08-31-94   12:00a
tinyrfc  exe      37,024 12-01-94    7:39p
net      exe     450,326 02-07-95   12:40p
system   ini         497 02-01-99    2:42a
protocol ini         356 02-01-99    1:51a
tcputils ini         233 08-31-94   12:00a
net      msg      76,234 03-03-95    7:11p
neth     msg     123,066 03-03-95    7:12p
shares   pwl         622 02-01-99   12:54a
ifshlp   sys       4,644 08-31-94   12:00a
        29 file(s)       970,607 bytes

Total files listed:
        42 file(s)     1,283,563 bytes
                          18,432 bytes free
```

LISTING 15.2 `config.sys` FILE FROM NETWORK BOOT FLOPPY

```
device=a:\dos\himem.sys
device=a:\dos\emm386.exe noems
dos=high,umb
files=99
buffers=45
lastdrive=z
device=a:\NET\ifshlp.sys
```

LISTING 15.3 `autoexec.bat` FILE FROM NETWORK BOOT FLOPPY

```
@echo off
set prompt=$p$g
set dircmd=/l/oe/p
set copycmd=/v
set PATH=a:\NET;a:\dos

a:\NET\net initialize
a:\NET\netbind.com
a:\NET\umb.com
a:\NET\tcptsr.exe
a:\NET\tinyrfc.exe
a:\NET\nmtsr.exe
a:\NET\emsbfr.exe
a:\NET\net start
```

I'll let you determine what to do with this floppy. I will relate the circumstances that motivated me to first create one of these disks.

As I have said before, one of my responsibilities where I work is to manage several public computer labs. Each lab is set up to contain machines with homogenous hardware. Therefore I can clone the disks and simply place them in another machine without too much disruption. Many software packages are available for cloning hard disks. You can even use the xcopy command to some extent. The particular package I use allows an entire hard disk to be dumped to a single file. These files can be fairly large and can change often due to updates and fixes in the lab.

Originally I used a writable CD-ROM drive to place the image file on a CD, but this proved to be bothersome. After stumbling across the necessary software I can simply pull an image from the server across the network to each machine in the lab at the same time (see Figure 15.11)! Given that a standard configured machine loads the image in about 20 minutes and one lab has close to 50 machines, my roll-out time was cut substantially as you can guess.

FIGURE 15.11

Loading all machines in the lab from the server concurrently via a network connection.

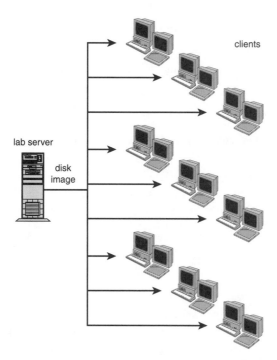

DAVE 2.1 for the Macintosh OS

DAVE is an SMB client developed and sold by Thursby Software Systems
(http://www.thursby.com). It allows your Macintosh to connect to SMB servers. DAVE
sells for a retail price of US$149 currently and works with Windows NT, Windows 95,
WfWg 3.11 (with the TCP/IP) stack, and Samba.

First let me say that I don't use a Mac everyday, so getting a chance to play with DAVE
was fun. I was very impressed with the overall ease of installation and connectivity
options. That's enough of the glossy brochure. You can find product reviews of Thursby's
client on the company's Web site. Now it's time to look at some configuration specifics.

The minimum hardware and software requirements for running DAVE are

- A Macintosh computer with a 68020 processor or higher
- Mac OS version 7.5 or later
- 8MB of RAM
- Apple's MacTCP or Open Transport TCP/IP 1.1 or later
- Any hardware necessary to run TCP/IP (for example, a working network adapter
  card)

Prior to installing DAVE, you should verify that your TCP/IP configuration is correct and
functional.

Installing DAVE

For this example, I downloaded an evaluation copy of DAVE v2.1 from
http://www.thursby.com/. The client system is running Mac OS 7.6 on 16MB of
RAM. You can complete a form on Thursby's Web site to obtain a temporary registration
key. You can also download the user's manual (~172 pages) in Adobe Acrobat reader format. I found this to be fairly helpful as well.

After you have downloaded and extracted the client software and have the registration
key ready, you can install DAVE by executing the installer icon, shown in Figure 15.12,
located in the Dave 2.1 folder.

After launching the installation program and working your way through the license
agreement, you arrive at the DAVE Installer windows show in Figure 15.13. In this
example, use the Easy Install. This screen also provides the choice of installing specific
portions of the client as well removing the software. In addition to containing a client,
DAVE includes SMB file- and printer-sharing support so that the relationship is two-way.

FIGURE 15.12

Installer icon.

FIGURE 15.13

*DAVE Installer
Window for selecting
options.*

Configuring NetBIOS

When DAVE is installed, the client system reboots. After it comes back up, you are ready
to configure the NetBIOS interface. Selecting the NetBIOS option located under the
Control Panels menu off the Apple menu accesses these settings. If you have not entered
registration information for the software prior to this, you will be prompted to enter your
name, organization, and license number. When you finish this, you should see the screen
shown in Figure 15.14.

FIGURE 15.14

*DAVE NetBIOS set-
tings window.*

At this point, this should start to look very familiar. The Name field is for the computer
name, not a username. The Workgroup will be the one used for browsing purposes. This
does not have to be the same as the domain you will later to log in to. The optional

Description field is equivalent to Samba's server string parameter. Also manually define your WINS server's IP address. This information could also be obtained from a DHCP server.

One thing that DAVE does provide is an expansive amount of control over the NetBIOS settings. The Info button, available on the NetBIOS control panel, performs a similar function to Windows nbtstat.exe command (see Figure 15.15). It allows you to view such things as which names are cached locally, which ones the client has registered, and which NBT sessions are active. The Admin button allows you to set things such as ScopeID, node type, and various times and retry settings for name registration and resolution (see Figure 15.16).

FIGURE 15.15

Viewing registered names.

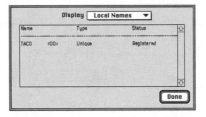

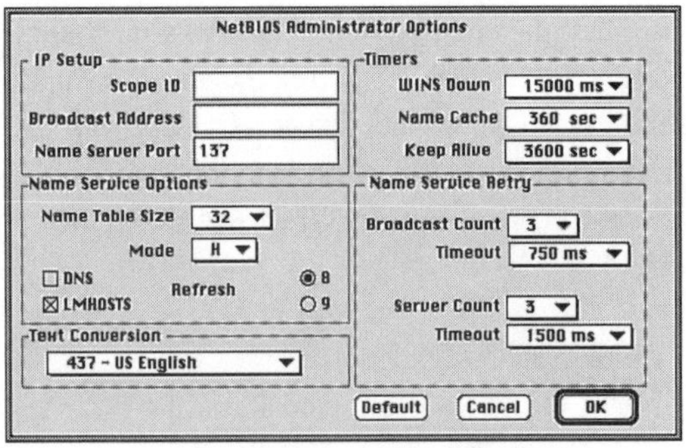

FIGURE 15.16

Setting NetBIOS parameters.

When you are finished, close the window. The OS prompts you to save your changes. If you are a Windows person, you might be surprised that you don't have to restart the computer after defining these settings. Any time you change any information in the Identification page of the network control panel in Windows 9x, you are forced to reboot before the changes take effect.

Logging On and Accessing Servers

When accessing shares, DAVE acts more like Windows NT than Windows 9x because DAVE allows you to specify an alternative user name and password to use when connecting to a share. However, first you must log on using the DAVE Access program, which can be started from the Apple menu. Figure 15.17 shows the Network Logon dialog box, which is accessible by electing Log On from the Access menu. I have chosen to log in to a domain controlled by a Samba server. Of course, it would not make sense for the login script to be executed, but DAVE does support the AppleScript language.

FIGURE 15.17

Using DAVE to log in to a Samba controlled domain.

After you log in successfully, DAVE allows you to mount shares from SMB servers. Figure 15.18 shows the window launched by selecting the Mount a Volume option from the Access menu. The example shows the settings I use to connect to the home directory at work.

FIGURE 15.18

Mounting a SMB disk share using DAVE.

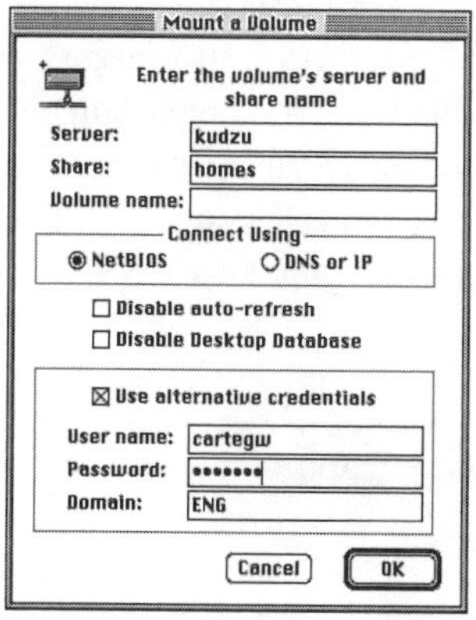

If you prefer to browse for shares using a Windows Network Neighborhood–type interface, the Chooser window (see Figure 15.19) allows browsing using both AppleShare and SMB if you have them installed. After you locate the server and share you want, DAVE supports an option to reconnect the share at login (see Figure 15.20), much like a Windows NT persistent connection.

FIGURE 15.19

Browsing the Entire Network in the Mac Chooser window.

FIGURE 15.20

Mapping a share to be reconnected at login.

Printers are selected in much the same way as disk shares. Figure 15.21 shows the window displayed when connecting to a remote printer. It is necessary to configure the printer in the Chooser window under the LaserWriter entry in order for the network connection to accept spooled print jobs. Figure 15.22 shows the list of printers. The entry named KUDZU Kryptonite is the printer I'm accessing using DAVE. You should note that the documentation for DAVE states that only PostScript printers are supported at the moment.

FIGURE 15.21

Using DAVE for connecting to a remote printer.

FIGURE 15.22

Selecting the mapping printer to configure.

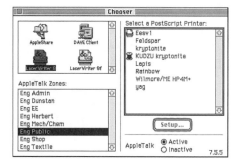

15

Summary

This hour has presented two very different SMB clients. Microsoft's DOS network client is distributed free from various locations. Thursby Software Solutions' DAVE product is a commercial solution for integrating Macintosh clients into a SMB-based network.

Q&A

Q When I try to mount a drive from a Samba server using the MS-DOS network client with the basic redirector, I keep getting an error message saying that the password is invalid. Why is this?

A The DOS client basic redirector transmits only the LanManager 24-byte hash. If your Samba server does not have password encryption enabled, you need to either use the DOS full redirector or enable encrypted passwords on your server.

Q I seem to be having problems using DAVE 2.1 and Samba 2.0. None of the files on the Samba server show up.

A The reason for this is that Samba is reporting its file system to be of type NTFS. Setting `fstype = Samba` in `smb.conf` should solve your problem.

New Terms

NDIS2   Version 2 of the Network Desktop Interface Specification. This creates a defined interface between the hardware and upper-level network protocol that vendors can use to write compliant device drivers for network components. There also exists a version 3 of this specification, referred to as NDIS3.

PART IV
Samba Security

Hour

HOUR 16

Password Synchronization

In previous hours, you looked at how a wide variety of clients can access file and print services offered by a Samba server. You also looked at how Samba associates a local user account name with all file accesses. In most cases, users provide a username and password in order to access a resource on a Samba server. If you administer a complex environment in which you have NT servers, UNIX servers (some running Samba), and perhaps some Windows 9x systems as well, you probably have a password synchronization problem.

This hour

- Explores what this password synchronization problem is
- Provides an overview to some of the approaches to password synchronization
- Examines Samba-based password synchronization
- Looks at PAM-based password synchronization
- Mentions some Windows NT approaches to the problem
- Examines LDAP as a potential solution
- Checks out the problems that remain

Some of the solutions to this problem are based on encrypted password support and the new PDC support included in Samba 2.0.0 and later. It might be appropriate to preview Hours 21, "Windows 9x Domain Control," and 22, "Experimental PDC Support," prior to reading this hour.

What's the Problem?

What is the problem? Suppose you are about to log in to a Windows 9x system and are faced with the login dialog box shown in Figure 16.1.

FIGURE 16.1

The Windows 9x login dialog box.

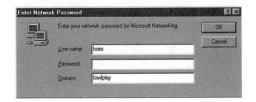

Enter your username (here shown as boss) and your password, log in to the network, and obtain access to your files. Where is your password maintained? If you then change your password (which you access from the Control Panel), where is that password changed?

When you have logged in, you might be given access to a home directory where you can store files and directories. Figure 16.2 shows an example of the home directory provided on a Samba share for the user boss.

FIGURE 16.2

The home directory when logged in to the network.

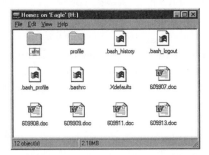

Now, you also happen to need to log in to UNIX machines in your network and have access to the same account name that you use to log in to your Windows 9x systems. The following shows a sample login session where you log in to a Linux system with the account name boss and are given access to the same files that you accessed from Windows in Figure 16.2:

```
Red Hat Linux release 5.2 (Apollo)
Kernel 2.0.36 on an i686
login: boss
Password:
[boss@eagle]$ ls -al
total 2261
drwx------    4 boss     boss        1024 Jan 19 18:34 .
drwxr-xr-x   21 root     root        1024 Jan 19 16:41 ..
-rw-r--r--    1 boss     boss        3768 Jan 10 12:59 .Xdefaults
-rw-r--r--    1 boss     boss          24 Jan 10 12:59 .bash_logout
-rw-r--r--    1 boss     boss         220 Jan 10 12:59 .bash_profile
-rw-r--r--    1 boss     boss         124 Jan 10 12:59 .bashrc
drwxr-xr-x    2 boss     boss        1024 Jan 10 12:59 .xfm
-rwxr--r--    1 boss     boss      551424 Jan 13 00:46 609907.doc
-rwxr--r--    1 boss     boss      309248 Jan 12 15:29 609908.doc
-rwxr--r--    1 boss     boss      945664 Jan 21 02:14 609909.doc
-rwxr--r--    1 boss     boss       48640 Jan 13 00:10 609911.doc
-rwxr--r--    1 boss     boss      431104 Jan 18 22:25 609913.doc
drwxr-xr-x    5 boss     boss        1024 Jan 22 14:28 profile
```

16

Which password has been used to authenticate you in each of the these commands?
When you change your password from one environment, is it changed for both environments? Is it possible that only one password is involved?

To understand the problem and to appreciate the nature of some of the solutions, you
need to know more about where Windows NT and UNIX store passwords for their users
and the way in which passwords are stored.

First, neither NT nor UNIX store plain-text passwords in their respective password files.
Each of them performs an irreversible calculation on the plain-text password a user submits when changing a password. The resulting value is stored in the password databases
each system keeps. When a user wishes to log in, the same irreversible calculation is performed again, and the result is compared with what is stored in the password database. If
they match, the user has submitted the correct password. Both of these processes are
shown in Figure 16.3.

Although both operating systems perform an irreversible calculation on the passwords
and store the result, they both use different algorithms. Windows NT performs an MD4
hash on the user's password and stores that, whereas UNIX uses the user's password as
the key for a modified DES algorithm and stores that. Because each of these operations
is irreversible in a practical time frame, it is not possible to convert one password type
from the other. That is, being given a Windows password hash does not allow the system
to generate a correct UNIX password hash for the same user, and vice versa.

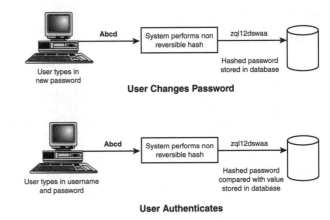

FIGURE 16.3

Changing passwords and authentication.

Windows NT stores passwords in the SAM (Security Account Manager) database, which is part of the registry. In a Windows NT domain, passwords are stored on the Primary Domain Controller and replicated to Backup Domain Controllers. Although each NT machine can also have its own local SAM database, these allow only local logins. When logging in to the domain, the SAM on the Domain Controllers is consulted. Because Backup Domain Controllers receive a copy of the SAM database, there is essentially one source of authentication information in a Windows NT domain.

UNIX stores passwords in the password file (/etc/password) or the shadow password file for extra security (because the password file is world-readable, and it is possible to mount an effective dictionary attack if one has access to the encrypted passwords for a machine). In a networked environment, several schemes have been used to provide a single source of authentication information for UNIX. The most popular of these is a scheme developed by Sun Microsystems called the network information service, or NIS. More recently, Sun has introduced an upgraded version of NIS called NIS+, which addresses a number of issues with NIS, especially security issues. However, NIS+ is not implemented under as many versions of UNIX as NIS is.

If you have both Windows NT and UNIX in your network and if you have a large network, chances are that you have two sets of passwords in your network, one for Windows NT and one for UNIX. Also, Samba can use and maintain Windows NT–style passwords when configured to use encrypted passwords. If you are using Samba under

UNIX to supply file and print services to Windows 9x and Windows NT systems while using encrypted passwords, you have two sets of passwords as well, one for the Windows clients and one for UNIX.

That is, the account called boss has a password for Windows and a password for UNIX.

This creates a problem: How do you keep the passwords synchronized, because users do not like to remember two different passwords, nor do they like to have to change a single password in two different places. If you take the simple approach to setting up Samba in a UNIX environment (or a mixed Windows NT and UNIX environment), you have a password synchronization problem, because your users will have passwords in two places and will have to manually synchronize them. In some cases, the problem might not be noticeable, but if your Windows users use a UNIX-based POP server, RADIUS server, and so on, your Windows users will definitely notice it.

In the following sections, you look at approaches for managing this password synchronization problem.

Password Synchronization Approaches

Password synchronization presents two different questions you have to answer:

- Do you attempt to have only one password format, or do you maintain multiple password formats, one for each environment (for example, Windows NT, UNIX, and so on)?

- Do you attempt to keep one master copy of the password database (perhaps with backup copies that are refreshed from the master copy), or do you allow each environment to keep its own password database(s) and make sure that passwords are updated in each environment when a user changes passwords?

If you use only one password format, you can generate the password hashes on client systems when users change their passwords. However, if you use multiple password formats, you must either generate multiple password hashes at the client when a password is changed (which means that clients must be changed if a new password format is added to the environment) or you must send the clear-text password to a server to allow it to generate the appropriate password hashes.

In either case, you had better encrypt the data sent to the authentication server to prevent anyone who is in a position to snoop on the password-change transaction from obtaining either passwords or password equivalents. (A *password equivalent* is something that attackers who can write their own client programs can use.)

16

If you can keep a single authentication database (even if you keep multiple password hashes in that database), life will be much simpler when updating the database—for example, when the users change their passwords. However, keeping multiple authentication databases means that you must take extra care to ensure that updates are committed to each database, and there will always be opportunities for the databases to get out of synch with each other. The problems are compounded if these databases keep password hashes in different formats, because plain-text passwords must be kept around on the system somewhere until all the databases have been updated.

The solutions that are available to solve the password synchronization problem span these approaches, and include the following:

- Set up Windows NT to use NIS on UNIX machines for authentication. This approach allows you to keep all your passwords in one place under NIS, but it does mean that your NT systems are standalone devices that do not participate in a domain. This solution involves using a piece of software called NISGINA, which can be obtained at `http://www.dcs.qmw.ac.uk/~williams/`. This solution has nothing to do with Samba and will not be discussed further.

- Set up Samba as a logon server (and possibly a Primary Domain controller if you have NT devices), and use encrypted passwords in Samba. You can then configure Samba to push password changes out into whatever UNIX password system you are using. Unfortunately, this solution by itself does not allow password changes from the UNIX side to find their way into the Samba password system.

- Augment the previous solution with Pluggable Authentication Modules (PAM: available for Solaris and Linux, and part of the OSF DTE shipped by most UNIX vendors today, but unfortunately not exposed on most of them) to allow UNIX authentication to be performed against the Samba password database. In some cases, it also allows password changes on UNIX systems to find their way into the Samba password file. This is mentioned more later in the hour.

- Use PAM to perform all UNIX authentication against an SMB server of some sort, either Samba or a genuine Windows NT Primary Domain Controller. This solution currently does not allow UNIX-side password changes to make their way into the password database.

- Use something such as LDAP (Lightweight Directory Access Protocol) for centrally maintaining authentication information and making all systems query the LDAP server. This would have to be augmented on the UNIX side to use PAM for LDAP access and would depend on LDAP support in Samba. At the moment, the LDAP support in Samba is preliminary and should not be used for production environments, but it is clear that LDAP is one of the best approaches for the future.

SWAT can also be used to change passwords for users. However, SWAT does suffer from a number of problems, including that it does not support SSL, so all passwords sent by the user are viewable by anyone snooping.

Samba-Based Password Synchronization

16

Samba can be set up to authenticate Windows 95 and Windows NT clients. To do this (especially the Windows NT systems) requires that Samba use encrypted passwords and the smbpasswd file.

You must add the following parameters to the global section in your smb.conf file:

```
encrypt passwords = yes
smb passwd file = /usr/local/samba/private/smbpasswd
```

Of course, your smbpasswd file can reside in other locations depending on the version of UNIX you are using. On Linux distributions such as Red Hat and TurboLinux, it resides in /etc.

You must also create the smbpasswd file and populate it with any accounts you want pre-loaded into the smbpasswd file. The smbpasswd file is where Samba keeps the NT password hashes for all Windows users and has a very similar format to the UNIX password file.

To populate the smbpasswd file initially, you must execute a command such as

```
cat /etc/passwd ¦ mksmbpasswd.sh > /usr/local/samba/private/smbpasswd
```

or, if you use NIS for UNIX authentication

```
ypcat passwd ¦ mksmbpasswd.sh > /usr/local/samba/private/smbpasswd
```

The mksmbpasswd.sh script can be found in the Samba source directory in the script sub-directory in Samba 2.0.0.

Because of the sensitivity of the information kept in the smbpasswd file (such as the encrypted passwords in the passwd file, which you can keep in a shadow password file), the directory that the smbpasswd file is stored in should be owned by root. Also, the directory should not be accessible to anyone other than root. Finally, the smbpasswd file itself should also not be accessible by anyone other than root. The following commands set the correct permissions on the smbpasswd file when you have created it:

```
chown -R root.root /usr/local/samba/private/
chmod 500 /usr/local/samba/private
chmod 600 /usr/local/samba/private/smbpasswd
```

When you have created the smbpasswd file and restarted Samba, your Windows users can change their passwords and the smbpasswd file is updated. However, the UNIX passwords for their accounts on the Samba server are not modified, unless you set up some more global parameters in the smb.conf file.

You *can* set up Samba to change a Windows user's UNIX password when that person changes one's Windows password. To set this up you must use the unix password sync parameter, and you might need to set the passwd chat, passwd chat debug, and passwd program parameters.

This functionality is available because Samba now implements the password change API call and has access to the plain-text version of the user's new password. It should be noted, however, that the new information is carried across the network encrypted.

Because the appropriate information is available, Samba can organize to run a command for the user that pushes the password change into the UNIX environment as well. This command might simply be /bin/passwd, or it might be /bin/yppasswd or whatever local password command is appropriate.

The following sections explore the smb.conf parameters that relate to password synchronization.

unix password sync

This global parameter specifies whether Samba attempts to synchronize a user's UNIX password when that person's Windows password is being changed in the smbpasswd file. If the parameter is set to true, the program specified in the passwd program parameter is called as root to change the user's password under UNIX. The passwd program must be called as root, because Samba has no access to the plain text of the user's old password. The default value for this parameter is

```
unix password sync = False
```

To have Samba synchronize password changes, change this parameter to True.

passwd chat

This global parameter specifies the password chat sequence that Samba uses to change the user's password under UNIX when that person changes his or her Windows password. This string takes the form of a sequence of send/receive pairs that smbd uses to figure out what to send to the passwd program and what it should get back. If smbd does not receive the expected response, the user's password is not changed.

The chat sequence is usually very specific to your site and depends on the form of the messages output by your system's passwd or yppasswd commands, or whichever command you use to change passwords on your site.

The chat sequence can contain the macros %o and %n, which are replaced with the old password and new password respectively. It can also contain the usual macros \n, \r, \t, and \s, which mean line feed, carriage return, Tab, and Space respectively. If the string contains the asterisk character (*) in a response, it matches any sequence of characters. In addition, double quotes (") can be used to specify strings with embedded spaces. Finally, a period (.) in any part of the chat sequence means that that no string is sent if the period occurs in a send sequence, or no response is expected if the period occurs in a response sequence. The default value for this parameter is

```
passwd chat = \
➡*old*password* %o\n *new*password* %n\n *new*password* %n\n *changed*
```

passwd chat debug

This global parameter specifies whether the passwd chat script is run in debug mode. If switched on, the strings received and sent to the passwd program are logged with a debug level of 100. To see the string, you need to set your debug level to 100.

> This option is dangerous, as it allows plain-text passwords to be seen in the passwd file.

The default value for this parameter is

```
passwd chat debug = False
```

passwd program

This global parameter specifies to smbd what program is run to change a user's UNIX password. Any occurrence of %u is replaced with the user's name on the command line. The default value for this parameter is

```
passwd program = /bin/passwd
```

You should not need to change this parameter.

PAM-Based Password Synchronization

Although setting the unix password sync and passwd chat parameters allows password changes that originate on Windows systems to be reflected in your UNIX password system, what about UNIX password changes?

NEW TERM One of the approaches available for managing authentication and synchronization in a UNIX environment is *PAM*, or *Pluggable Authentication Modules*. PAM is a technique developed at Sun Microsystems and implemented in Solaris and Linux. There is also support in the OSF CDE (Common Desktop Environment), which is widely supported by UNIX vendors for their workstations. However, it is not clear whether PAM in these environments is accessible to system managers.

PAM works by ensuring that all authentication decisions are implemented via shared libraries with well-defined entry points. The libraries to use for each type of authentication are specified in a set of configuration files for PAM. The system administrator can then change the appropriate PAM configuration file to change the way in which authentication is performed. PAM specifies entry points for authentication, password changing, and many other security related functions. For more information on PAM, consult your system administration documentation, or check the following Web pages:
`http://www.sun.com/software/solaris/pam` or
`http://parc.power.net/morgan/Linux-PAM/`.

At least three PAM shared libraries allow UNIX systems to authenticate against SMB servers (either Samba or Windows NT). One of them allows users to change both their UNIX and their SMB passwords in limited circumstances. They are

- `pam_smb` by David Airlie. This module allows UNIX systems to authenticate against SMB servers but does not support password updating. Thus, it can be used to authenticate against a Samba server or a Windows NT server.

- `pam_ntdom` by Luke Leighton. This module allows UNIX systems to authenticate against Domain Controllers. It can authenticate against a Samba server running as a Primary Domain Controller, as well as against a Windows NT PDC. However, this module does not support changing the user's password.

- `pam_smbpass` by Stephen Langasek. This module allows UNIX systems to authenticate against SMB servers and, in limited circumstances, allows UNIX users to update their passwords in Samba's `smbpasswd` file.

You will now explore the configuration of each of these modules for use with Samba.

`pam_smb` Configuration and Installation

You can obtain `pam_smb` from the following Web site: `http://www.csn.ul.ie/~airlied/pam_smb/`.

When you have pulled the kit over to your system, you need to break the kit out into a local directory and then build it and configure it for use. To break out the kit, use the following command if your system's version of `tar` supports gzipped archives:

```
tar zxvf pam_smb-1_1_tar.gz
```

If your system's version of `tar` does not support gzipped archives use the following:.

```
gzip -d pam_smb-1_1_tar.gz
tar xvf pam_smb-1_1_tar
```

When you have untarred the source distribution, you should then `cd` to the directory containing the pam_smb source and build the package. The steps involved are

```
cd <source directory>
./configure
make
```

16

which should leave you with a file called `pam_smb_auth.so`. You must copy this file to the PAM modules directory, which is `/lib/security` under Linux and `/usr/lib/security` under Solaris.

Your next step is to configure PAM to use the new module you have created. This involves editing the various PAM configuration files and creating the `pam_smb.conf` file in `/etc`.

The changes you need in the PAM configuration files are as follows. For Linux, you need to edit `/etc/pam.d/login` and add the following line

```
auth      required      /lib/security/pam_smb_auth.so
```

which should be added before the line for `pam_pwdb.so`, but after the line for `pam_securetty.so`.

This tells PAM that it should check security requirements first and then should authenticate with `pam_smb_auth.so`.

For Solaris, you need to change the other line in `/etc/pam.conf` to

```
other     auth required     /usr/lib/security/pam_smb_auth.so.1
```

For both Linux and Solaris, you can include parameters on the command line including:

- debug, which switches on debug information via syslog
- use_first_pass, a standard PAM command-line option that tells this module not to prompt for a password but to use a previously typed password
- nolocal, which allows authentication of a username/password pair which are not in the local password file

pam_smb_auth works in the following way when a user is logging in to a UNIX system:

1. The user's account must be in the UNIX password file to allow the user to log in. However, if `nolocal` is specified on the module command line, the user does not need to have an account in the local password file, but there are security issues with doing this.

2. If users has a valid password entry in the password file, they are authenticated using that information. That is, they are not authenticated via an SMB server.

3. If the user does not have a password in the password file (that is, a * or !! in their password field), `pam_smb_auth` uses the contents of the file `/etc/pam_smb.conf` to authenticate the user against the specified SMB server.

The `pam_smb` configuration file (`/etc/pam_smb.conf`) is a simple text file containing three lines:

```
Domain Name
Primary Server
Backup Server
```

For example, in the environment you have set up in this book, this file might look like:

```
FOWLPLAY
EAGLE
EAGLE2
```

 Because `pam_smb` is based on `SMBlib`, which does not do NetBIOS name lookup, all names in the `pam_smb` configuration file must be in your hosts file or in the DNS.

This module does not allow users to update their passwords on remote SMB servers, so users cannot change their SMB passwords from UNIX machines. They must do so from a Windows system.

`pam_ntdom` Installation and Configuration

You can obtain `pam_ntdom` from the directory `/samba/ftp/pam_ntdom/` at your favorite mirror of the Samba Web site. To get there, go to your favorite mirror and select the download link that takes you to the HTTP site. You must perform essentially the same steps as in `pam_smb` to get `pam_ntdom` working, because the build environment for `pam_ntdom` is based on that from `pam_smb`. That is,

1. Unpack the distribution

2. Configure the package (`./configure`)

3. Build the package (`make`)

When you have built `pam_ntdom`, you should have a file called `pam_ntdom_auth.so` in the source directory. You must move this file to the appropriate directory as described previously (`/lib/security` for Linux systems and `/usr/lib/security` for Solaris systems).

The next step is to configure PAM in a similar manner to that described for `pam_smb` previously.

For a Linux system, add the following line to `/etc/pam.d/login`:

```
auth      required      /lib/security/pam_ntdom_auth.so
```

This line should be added after the `auth` line for security and before that for `pwdb` if included in your PAM configuration.

For a Solaris system, change the other line in `/etc/pam.conf` to:

```
other      auth required      /usr/lib/security/pam_ntdom_auth.so.1
```

This module supports the same options that `pam_smb` supports, which have the same meanings as they do for `pam_smb`. (Indeed, the code for `pam_ntdom` is essentially the same code as `pam_smb`, with only the validate routine changed.)

Finally, you must set up the `pam_ntdom` configuration file, which is called `/etc/pam_smb.conf`. The entries in this file are exactly the same as those for `pam_smb` and have the same meaning. A sample configuration file would be

```
[root@remote1] ls /etc/pam_smb.conf
FOWLPLAY
EAGLE
EAGLE2
```

This file specifies that the domain to authenticate against is FOWLPLAY, the primary authentication server is EAGLE, and the secondary is EAGLE2.

`pam_ntdom` supports only authentication against Domain Controllers, so the authentication servers specified previously must be Windows Domain Controllers (PDCs or BDCs) or a Samba server configured as a Primary Domain Controller.

In order for a UNIX system running `pam_ntdom` to authenticate in a domain, that UNIX system must be added to the domain. This is achieved in two different ways, depending on whether you are authenticating against Windows NT Domain Controllers or against Samba running as a Domain Controller.

For a UNIX system to authenticate against a Windows NT Domain Controller, you must manually add each such UNIX system to the domain using Server Manager for Domains. Figure 16.4 shows an example of adding a computer to a domain. You must add the UNIX system as a Windows NT Workstation or Server.

FIGURE 16.4

Adding a UNIX system to a Windows NT domain.

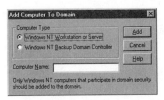

To authenticate against a Samba server running as a PDC, you must manually add each UNIX system wishing to authenticate to the Samba Domain. This is described in the NTDOMAIN.txt file in the Samba documentation (docs/textdocs) directory.

pam_ntdom does not currently allow UNIX users to change their passwords from UNIX. They must make the changes from a Windows system. Password-changing functions will likely be added to pam_ntdom in the near future.

pam_smbpass Installation and Configuration

You can obtain pam_smbpass from the following Web site: ftp://ftp.netexpress.net/pub/pam. It is available as both a source distribution (pam_smbpass-0_5.tgz) or as a Red Hat rpm. You should choose the distribution that suits you, but here I will assume you choose the source distribution. This module is specific to Linux and possibly to those that support PAM.

The steps you need to take with this package are

1. Unpack the distribution. This might involve using gzip if your system's tar command cannot handle compressed tar files.

2. Build the distribution. This package comes with a make file, so simply invoke make in the source directory.

When you have built the distribution, you must copy the resulting module to /lib/security:

cp pam_smbpass.so /lib/security

The next step is to modify the correct PAM configuration file in ways similar to those listed previously for pam_smb and pam_ntdom. To do this, add the following line to /etc/pam.d/login:

auth   required   /lib/security/pam_ntdom_auth.so

This line should be added after the auth line for security and should replace the line for pwdb if included in your PAM configuration file.

This module accepts the following PAM command line options:

- `debug`, which causes it to log debugging information
- `audit`, which causes it to log even more debugging information
- `use_first_pass`, which causes it to use the password already prompted for by previous modules, if possible
- `try_first_pass`, a variation of the previous command (see the PAM documentation for more information)
- `use_authtok`, similar to `try_first_pass`, but it fails if the new `PAM_AUTHTOK` has not been previously set
- `not_set_pass`, which tells the module not to set `PAM_` items with passwords used by this module
- `nodelay`, which prevents failed authentication from causing a delay of approximately one second

The advantage of the `pam_smbpass` module is that it can update both the `passwd` file and the `smbpasswd` file on a Samba server. This gives users a way to change their passwords from UNIX and have both their UNIX and Windows passwords changed. In this regard, it is superior to all the other PAM modules you have considered so far.

However, `pam_smbpass` can update the `smbpasswd` file only on the machine on which it is running. This means that it cannot be used in an environment where you have multiple UNIX systems and where users can log in to any UNIX system and want to change their passwords.

LDAP-Based Approaches

If your environment is large and consists of many UNIX systems with a large number of Windows systems, none of the approaches presented so far are likely to be of use to you. This is mainly because, currently, there is no widely implemented single standard for password repositories or databases.

Over the last few years, a standard called Lightweight Directory Access Protocol, or LDAP, has been developing that promises to reduce the problems you currently have with password synchronization by keeping passwords in one place. Samba currently has embryonic support for LDAP, and all versions of UNIX are expected to interact with LDAP, as will future versions of Windows.

When all the systems in your environment use LDAP for storing and changing passwords, a password synchronization problem will no longer exist.

Hour 24, "Samba's Future," has more to say about future support for LDAP in Samba.

16

Problems

The problems that remain with the majority of the password synchronization approaches you have explored until now are that they work from Windows to UNIX but do not work from UNIX to Windows. Future versions of some of the modules, such as pam_smb and pam_ntdom, will include the same code that Samba currently has for changing passwords remotely in a Windows environment, and thus will alleviate this last problem.

Ultimately, however, the solution is to move to LDAP.

Summary

You have explored the facilities available to system managers to ensure that user's passwords are synchronized between their Windows and UNIX environments. Unfortunately, at present there are still some gaps in what can be done, but if your environment consists of a single UNIX system with a number of Windows systems served from it, life will be easy for you.

In the next hour, you look at the support that Samba has for SSL, which allows you to provide access to Windows File and Print resources over insecure networks.

Q&A

Q Our site has one large Samba server and a large number of Windows 9x systems accessing it. However, some of the users need to access their UNIX accounts as well. What is the best way to ensure that whatever password changes they make are visible from both environments?

A If you do not have any other UNIX system apart from your Samba server, the best way to achieve what you ask is to use encrypted passwords in Samba and to use pam_smbpass for UNIX authentication. This way, your Windows users' password changes get into the Samba smbpasswd file, and any changes that are made by UNIX users are also made in the smbpasswd file.

However, if you have more than one UNIX system, users of UNIX machines other than your Samba server are unable to update their Windows passwords from systems other than the Samba server. On these other UNIX systems, you can still authenticate against the smbpasswd file by using pam_smb, but password changes will not get into the smbpasswd file.

Q Can we use something like `pam_smb` to authenticate against a Samba server running as a Primary Domain Controller? If we do so, what are the limitations?

A Yes, `pam_smb` can authenticate against Samba running as a PDC. The limitations are that such users cannot update their passwords from UNIX. They must do it from Windows.

Q Are there any other ways to change users' passwords other than using the standard Windows facilities or using UNIX facilities?

A Yes, SWAT can change passwords by using the standard Windows NT password change API. However, when you communicate with SWAT your old and new passwords are sent over the network in the clear.

16

New Terms

PAM Pluggable Authentication Modules. PAM was developed by Sun Microsystems and taken up by the Linux community and is used extensively in Linux distributions.

Hour **17**

SSL

by Richard Sharpe

In previous hours, you have looked at how to get Samba up and going on your UNIX server and talking to clients. Clients can even connect to your Samba server over the Internet. The big question arises: What about security?

With clients connecting to your Samba server over the Internet, anyone in a position to snoop the traffic can reconstruct the files that remote users might be working on. With the right programs, these people might even be able to insert data into files that remote users are working on.

NEW TERM The best way to prevent these sorts of problems is to encrypt the data travelling between clients and your Samba server. Does Samba support encryption? Indeed it does. In fact, Samba includes support for the *Secure Sockets Layer*, or *SSL*, which is the same encryption specification used by Web browsers to communicate securely with Web servers over the Internet.

This hour looks at how to build Samba with SSL support and how to configure SSL support into Samba. You will also look at which SMB clients support SSL and how you might set up secure access from Windows clients over the Internet.

Along the way, you will explore concepts such as what certificates are, how to get them, and how to install them so that clients and Samba servers can use them.

Using SSL with Samba

SSL is a standard and a protocol that allows two parties to communicate securely with each other over an insecure network. SLL uses public key cryptography and digital certificates to authenticate one or both parties. It uses symmetric cryptography with random session keys chosen during the authentication phase to allow both parties to communicate information securely for the duration of a session between them.

The SSL support in Samba is based on SSLeay, the freely available SSL source code library from Eric Young (which is where the *eay* comes from in the name).

To build Samba with SSL support, you must perform the following general steps:

1. Obtain, build, and install SSLeay. The latest version of SSLeay can be obtained at http://www.cryptsoft.com. The SSLeay FAQ is also available at this site. This step must be performed before going on to configure Samba with SSL support, or Samba will not build.

2. Build Samba with SSL support switched on and install it.

3. Obtain or create X509 certificates for at least your Samba servers and, depending on your needs, client machines that will access your Samba server over an insecure network.

4. Configure Samba to use SSL, tell Samba where its server certificate and private key are, and set other needed parameters.

5. Understand and set up an environment that allows SSL-enabled SMB clients to access Samba.

In order to use SSL with Samba, then, both Samba and your clients must have SSL support in some way. All you need to do is find some SSL-enabled clients, and you are in business. Unfortunately, few SSL-enabled clients are available. The clients that appear to be available are

- Sharity, a product from Object Development that allows Linux and other operating systems to mount CIFS/SMB file systems

- Smbclient, when compiled with SSL support
- sslproxy, a piece of software available under the GPL, which allows non-SSL clients to have access to SSL-enabled servers

Figure 17.1 shows how an SSL-enabled Samba might be used to provide secure remote file and print access over the Internet. The cloud represents an insecure network, such as the Internet, where people might be able to snoop on all your traffic travelling over it.

FIGURE 17.1

Using SSL-enabled Samba.

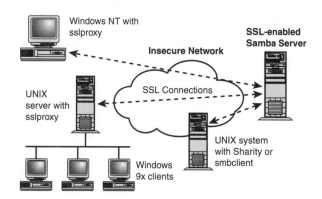

17

Without SSL support, CIFS/SMB clients place simple TCP connections to the server and gain access to files over that TCP connection. However, the commands and data being sent are in clear view for anyone to see. Here you use sslproxy for systems such as Windows NT, Windows 9x, and Sharity or smbclient for UNIX systems. This ensures that when commands and data from remote users travel over an insecure network, they are encrypted and therefore protected from being viewed by anyone who can snoop the data.

By default, the SSL support in Samba is not compiled in; nor could it be, because SSLeay is not supplied with Samba. This is for U.S. export control reasons. If Samba came, by default, with SSL switched on and included SSLeay, it would be very difficult to make it available for download from United States–based Web sites. However, when you obtain SSLeay, build it, and then build Samba with SSL support switched on, you get full 128-bit symmetric key cryptography, not the crippled 40-bit support that current U.S. export controls allow.

Obtaining and Building SSL

The source code for SSLeay is available at http://www.cryptsoft.com. At the time of writing, the latest version was SSLeay-0.9.0b. This site is located in Brisbane, Australia, so there should not be any problems with downloading this software from anywhere in the world. In any event, copies of SSLeay are maintained at other sites around the world. If you have already followed the instructions in Hour 3, "Obtaining the Latest Source," you should be able to download SSLeay from the Web site listed previously.

When you have downloaded SSLeay, unpack it into a directory and build the software. The following steps will generally achieve this:

```
gzip -d SSLeay-0.9.0b_tar.gz
tar -zvf SSLeay-0.9.0b_tar
cd SSLeay-0.9.0b
./Configure OS and Compiler
make
make install
```

To determine what OS and Compiler combination you should indicate, simply type ./Configure, which spits out a list of all the supported combinations.

If you receive an error message like

```
[ba]sh: ./Configure: No such file or directory
```

when you try to execute ./Configure, your Perl interpreter is probably not in the location that Configure expects it to be. Configure is actually a Perl script, and it expects Perl to be in /usr/local/bin/perl. If your Perl interpreter is in another location, simply edit Configure and change the first line (#!/usr/local/bin/perl) to reflect the actual location of Perl on your system.

In addition, many systems have a tar command that supports gzipped files directly. In that case, you can unpack SSLeay with the command

```
tar _zxvf SSLeay-0_9_0b_tar.gz
```

When you have built and installed it, you can go on to the next step, which is building Samba with SSL enabled. However, please note that the subsequent instructions assume that you installed SSLeay in the default location, which is /usr/local/ssl. If you need to install SSLeay in a different location than the default, you need to take careful note of how to do it in the next section.

Building Samba with SSL

When you have built and installed SSLeay, you can proceed to build Samba with SSL support, but you should first note that SSL support in Samba 2.0.0 is broken. You will need to obtain the latest version of Samba (2.0.3 or greater). Please refer to Hour 3 for instructions on how to download the latest version.

When you have obtained Samba version 2.0.3 or greater, you should use the following steps to build it with SSL support:

```
./configure _with-ssl
make
make install
```

If you have installed SSL in a location other than /usr/local/ssl, you will need to change the first line to

```
./configure _with-ssl --with-sslinc=location of ssl
```

You are now ready to build an smb.conf file that allows Samba to accept connections from SSL clients, but first you must look at the SSL protocol a little more, what certificates are, and how SSL uses them.

> When Samba is built with SSL support and SSL mode is switched on, the parameters ssl server cert and ssl server key must have valid values, and smbd requests the passphrase used to encrypt its server key, if it has been encrypted.

Certificates and All That Jazz

The SSL protocol relies on public key cryptography to allow two communicating parties to set up an encrypted communications channel between each other. During the SSL handshake, a random key is generated for use with the chosen symmetric encryption method that will be used for actual communication of information on the SSL-enabled connection. That is, when the SSL handshake is over, public-key algorithms are no longer used. Rather, algorithms such as triple-DES, IDEA, and so on are used with the randomly chosen key communicated during the SSL handshake. Symmetric encryption is used because it is faster than public key technology (100 or more times faster—see, for example, Bruce Schneier, Applied Cryptography).

However, SSL goes further than that because it allows one or both parties to verify that they are communicating with who they think they are communicating with.

An overview of the SSL protocol is shown in Figure 17.2 and is abstracted from `http://home.netscape.com/products/security/ssl/howitworks.html`.

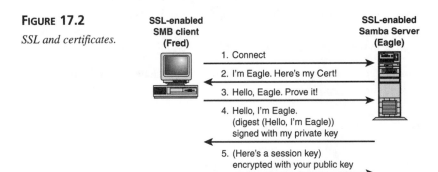

FIGURE 17.2

SSL and certificates.

In step 1, the client connects to the server via TCP. After some initial handshake during which the parties determine that SSL is in use and which version, the server sends back its certificate in step 2. The certificate contains Eagle's public key, and is signed by a certifying authority.

In step 3, the client requests that Eagle prove its identity, which it does by generating a message (Hello, I'm Eagle), computing a digest (MD5) of that message, and then signing the digest (that is, encrypting the digest with its own private key). When the client receives the message, it also computes the digest of the plain text message and decrypts the signed digest sent by Eagle with Eagle's public key (from the certificate). If the decrypted digest matches the computed one, only Eagle could have sent it.

Finally, in step 5, the client generates a random session key, encrypts it with Eagle's public key, and sends it to Eagle. Only Eagle should be able to decrypt the session key, and the client and Eagle can now use symmetric encryption to exchange information from this point on, secure in the knowledge that no one else can decrypt their messages.

If Eagle wants to verify the identity of the client, it can ask the client for a certificate in a similar manner. In this way, both parties can prove their identity to each other and be assured that they are talking to who they think they are.

This protocol depends on the fact that the public key Eagle has offered to client Fred can be verified as belonging to Eagle. How is this achieved? With the certificate that Eagle offered during step 2. Here is how the procedure works:

1. Eagle, or the system administrator on Eagle, generates a key pair (public and private keys) for Eagle. Because the private key is so important and must never be divulged to any other party, it usually is encrypted with a passphrase.

2. The system administrator then generates a Certificate Signing Request (CSR) that binds identifying information about Eagle to Eagle's public key as a certificate and sends it to a Certifying Authority (CA) for signing. This identifying information includes things such as the distinguished name of the server (that is, its DNS name), its location, email address of the requestor, and so on.

3. The CA you have chosen performs some verification steps to ensure in some way that the public key you have submitted is actually for the entity that will use the public key.

4. The CA signs, or encrypts, your certificate with its private key. It then sends the signed certificate back to you. The certificate is now signed by a CA and attests that the public key it contains belongs to the entity named in the certificate as the distinguished name.

5. You load this certificate on to your server and tell your server where to find both the certificate and the private key that relates to the certificate.

With this procedure, a third party (or parties) attest that the public key presented in the certificate belongs to the entity that is offering that certificate. Now usually, a common name component of the distinguished name in the certificate will be the DNS name of the entity presenting the certificate, and the parties that receive the certificates will verify that the common name in the certificate matches the DNS name (or one of them) of the system presenting the certificate.

 Now, the SSL module in Samba verifies only that the other side presents a valid certificate (if requested). It does not match the common name to any DNS names. This function will be implemented in a subsequent release of Samba.

Obtaining Certificates

Before you can configure Samba to use SSL for connections from clients, you must obtain certificates for all entities that need certificates. At a minimum, when Samba operates in SSL mode, it must have a server certificate. However, unlike a Web server, you probably want client certificates as well.

Why is this so? Well, when a user accesses a Web server and is asked to enter sensitive information, the user really must be sure that the Web server is the machine it claims to be. In the case of a Samba server, however, the clients are usually accessing what might be sensitive information on the server. You really want to be sure that only authorized clients are accessing that information. For that reason, you should obtain certificates for clients that access Samba over an insecure network.

Although you can obtain all the certificates you need from someone such as Verisign or Thawte, that is an expensive option when the certificates you need have very limited applicability. They will be submitted only to your own servers. In this case, you probably want to act as your own CA and sign your own certificates.

SSLeay has all the facilities needed to act as a CA. In acting as a CA, you sign your own certificates, which makes a lot of sense, as you most likely will know the clients who use them.

Although most of the procedures to act as a CA and sign certificates are detailed in the SSLeay documentation and in the SSLeay document in the Samba docs directory (under `textdocs` directory), you repeat them here as well, using the following procedures.

Set Yourself Up as a Certifying Authority (CA)

This involves setting up a database of all the certificates signed by the CA, and the key pair used by the CA. The CA needs a private key at least, in order to sign certificates.

In most of what follows, you need your path set up so that you can easily execute programs from `/usr/local/ssl/bin` or wherever you have installed SSL. So set your PATH environment variable in the appropriate place:

```
PATH=$PATH:/usr/local/ssl/bin
```

The command to do this might be different if you use a different shell (such as csh or tcsh, where you might use `setenv`). Consult the appropriate startup files for your shell.

Next, initialize SSLeay's random number generator. The initialization information is kept in the home directory of the account you are operating from in a file called `.rnd`. To initialize it, use the following commands

```
cat > /tmp/random.txt
```

and then enter some random keystrokes on your keyboard for a minute or two. When you have entered enough, enter a Control-D to terminate the file. Next, initialize the SSLeay random number generator with

```
ssleay genrsa -rand /temp/random.txt
rm -f /tmp/random.txt
```

Delete the `random.txt` file, because it might be possible to recover your private key from it. When the `genrsa` command executes, you will see some output about generating an RSA private key. You can ignore this information.

Next you must set up the database the CA will use. This database would normally live in a directory under /usr/local/ssl (if that is where you have installed SSLeay).

Choose a name for the directory where the CA's database resides, for example, myCA. This location must be entered into the ssleay.cnf file in /usr/local/ssl/lib, as well as in the CA.sh script. First, edit /usr/local/ssl/lib/ssleay.cnf and change the dir entry under the CA_default section from

```
[ CA_default]

dir            = ./demoCA                # Where everything is kept
...
```

to

```
[ CA_default]

dir            = /usr/local/ssl/myCA # Where everything is kept
...
```

Next, modify the CA.sh script in /usr/local/ssl/bin/CA.sh to specify the location of the CA database as well. You will find three lines that define the variables CATOP, CAKEY, and CACERT. Change CATOP to point to the location of the database. For example,

```
CATOP=/usr/local/ssl/myCA
```

Next, create the directory where the database resides and set its mode to 700 (to prevent anyone getting access to private keys):

```
mkdir /usr/local/ssl/myCA
chmod 700 /usr/local/ssl/myCA
CA.sh -newca
chmod -R 700 /usr/local/ssl/myCA
```

As a result of executing the CA.sh command, you will be asked a number of questions relating to the distinguished name of the CA:

```
[root@myca]# CA.sh -newca
mkdir: cannot make directory `/usr/local/ssl/myCA': File exists
CA certificate filename (or enter to create)

Making CA certificate ...
Using configuration from /usr/local/ssl/lib/ssleay.cnf
Generating a 1024 bit RSA private key
...+++++
..................................+++++
writing new private key to '/usr/local/ssl/myCA/private/./cakey.pem'
```

```
Enter PEM pass phrase: ─────────────────────────────────────────1
Verifying password - Enter PEM pass phrase: ─────────────────────2
- - - - -
You are about to be asked to enter information that will be incorporated
into your certificate request.
What you are about to enter is what is called a Distinguished Name or
a DN. There are quite a few fields but you can leave some blank
For some fields there will be a default value,
If you enter '.', the field will be left blank.
- - - - -
Country Name (2 letter code) [AU]:AU ─────────────────────────────3
State or Province Name (full name) [Some-State]:South Australia ───4
Locality Name (e.g., city) []:Adelaide ──────────────────────────5
Organization Name (e.g., company) [Internet Widgits Pty Ltd]:NS Widgits ─6
➥Pty Ltd ────────────────────────────────────────────────────────6
Organizational Unit Name (e.g., section) []: ───────────────────7
Common Name (e.g., YOUR name) []:myserver.mydom.com.au───────────8
Email Address []:rsharpe@ns.aus.com─────────────────────────────9
[root@myca]#
```

Note the following with respect to the marked points with the preceding listing:

1. Enter your passphrase for the CA's private key here.

2. Verify your passphrase here. Do not forget this passphrase; otherwise, you will have to regenerate the CA's private key.

3. The remaining points relate to the Distinguished Name of the entity you are defining. Enter your ISO two letter country code here.

4. Enter your state or geographic subdivision here if applicable, for example, South Australia as shown earlier, or California, Quebec, and so on.

5. Enter your locality name here, for example, Adelaide, Fremont, Montreal, and so on.

6. Enter your organization name here, for example, NS Widgits Pty Ltd. Note, Pty Ltd is a legal designation for a company in Australia.

7. Enter your organization unit name here, for example, Production. Here it has been left blank.

8. Enter your common name here, for example, `myserver.mydom.com.au`. This will often be the name that will be checked against the DNS name of the entity presenting the certificate.

9. Enter your email address here.

Generating Certificates for Each Entity

Next, you need to generate certificates for each entity that needs a certificate. The steps involved are

1. Generate a key pair for the client:

   ```
   ssleay genrsa -des3 1024 > client1.pem
   ```

   This requests that a keypair with 1,024-bit keys be generated. The private key is encrypted using triple-DES with a passphrase you specify.

2. Generate a certificate signing request (CSR)

   ```
   ssleay req -new -key client1.pem -out client1-csr.pem
   ```

   which requests that client1.pem be turned into a CSR.

When you generate the CSR, you are asked to enter all the information for the Distinguished Name of the entity the certificate is for. The information you supply should be for the client you are generating a certificate for. In particular, the Common Name should be the DNS name of the client.

17

Signing the Certificates

When you have generated the CSR, you need to sign it. To do this, use the following command:

```
ssleay ca -policy your policy -days 365 \
➥-infiles client1-csr.pem > client1-cert.pem
```

Now you have a certificate. You need to give the private key (client1.pem) and the certificate to the client to place in an appropriate place on his or her machine. They will usually go in the SSLeay directory /usr/local/ssl/certs. However, if you installed SSLeay in another location, place it in the certs directory of that location. If you are using a package other than SSLeay, the documentation for your package should tell you where certificates must be placed.

Ensure the CA's Certificate Is on Each Machine Using SSL

To check the offered certificate, SSL needs the certificate of the CA. This is usually put in a known place, although most of the applications can be told where these areas are as well.

One of the files generated when we created the CA earlier was a file called `cacert.pem`. This is the CA's certificate. The following steps put the CA's certificate in the appropriate directory and create a hashed name for it:

```
cp /usr/local/ssl/myCA/cacert.pem /usr/local/ssl/certs/myCA.pem
cd /usr/local/ssl/certs
ln -s myCA.pem `ssleay x509 -noout -hash < myCA.pem`.0
```

By creating a hashed name, you can have certificates for more than one CA in the certs directory, and SSL can try the appropriate one to verify an offered certificate.

In general, you would use these steps on any client machine that verifies certificates, except that `cacert.pem` comes from another system.

Configuring Samba to Use SSL

When you build Samba with SSL support, you will notice a whole new bunch of `smb.conf` parameters appear in the man pages for `smb.conf`. To have Samba use the SSL support that you have built in to it, you need to set a number of these parameters appropriately.

The minimum `smb.conf` parameters you need to set to have Samba use SSL are `ssl`, `ssl server cert`, and `ssl server key`.

These parameters all go into the global section of your `smb.conf`. Here is an example of how these parameters might be set:

```
ssl = yes
ssl server cert = /root/keys/real-cert.pem
ssl server key = /root/keys/key.pem
```

These entries switch on SSL support, specify where the CA's certificates are kept, and tell Samba where its server certificate and private key are.

The following sections explore all the SSL-related parameters. None of these parameters are available unless SSL support has been compiled into Samba.

ssl

This global parameter switches on the SSL support compiled into Samba. When you enable SSL with this parameter you must set the parameters `ssl server cert` and `ssl server key`. By default, SSL is disabled, even though you have compiled it into Samba.

Here is an example showing how to switch SSL support on:

```
ssl = yes
```

ssl CA certDIR

This global parameter specifies the location of the directory containing certificates for all the Certifying Authorities trusted by your site or system.

The filename of each CA's certificate in this directory actually hashes over the distinguished name contained in the certificate. For details on how to generate these hashes, see the section earlier this hour on ensuring that the CA's certificate is on each machine that uses SSL. Another way to set the required information is to use the `ssl CA certFile` parameter. You would normally use one or the other of these parameters, not both.

You do not need to use this parameter if you do not verify client certificates.

By default, this parameter has no value.

The following example shows how to set the directory containing CA certificates to `/usr/local/ssl/certs`:

```
ssl CA certDir = /usr/local/ssl/certs
```

When a certificate is received from a client, Samba searches for the CA's certificate in this directory.

ssl CA certFile

This global parameter is an alternative way of specifying the certificates of trusted CAs. With this parameter, you specify a file containing all the certificates of the trusted CAs, which are concatenated.

Use this parameter if you have only one certificate and do not want to generate hash values for CA certs.

Another way to set the required information is to use the `ssl CA certDir` parameter. You would normally use one or the other of these parameters, but not both.

You do not need to specify this parameter if you do not need to check client certificates.

By default, this parameter has no value.

The following example shows how to set the certificate file to `/usr/local/ssl/certs/myCAcert.pem`:

```
ssl CA certFile = /usr/local/ssl/certs/myCAcert.pem
```

When a certificate is received from a client, Samba uses this file to search for the CA's certificate.

ssl ciphers

This global parameter allows you to tell Samba which ciphers it can use. You should only use this parameter if you need to override the default ciphers SSLeay offers during negotiation, and know what you are doing.

Values that can be used with this parameter are

DEFAULT

DES-CFB-M1

NULL-MD5

RC4-MD5

EXP-RC4-MD5

RC2-CBC-MD5

EXP-RC2-CBC-MD5

IDEA-CBC-MD5

DES-CBC-MD5

DES-CBC-SHA

DES-CBC3-MD5

DES-CBC3-SHA

RC4-64-MD5

NULL

For more details on these, see the SSLeay source or the SSL spec
(http://www.netscape.com/info/SSL.html).

An example of using this parameter is

Ssl ciphers = DEFAULT

ssl client cert

This global parameter tells smbclient which certificate to use if the server requires a client certificate. This is the only way to specify a certificate to smbclient currently, so if you have multiple certificates for smbclient, you will have to edit the `smb.conf` file to use them.

The default value for this parameter is

```
ssl client cert = /usr/local/ssl/certs/smbclient.pem
```

ssl client key

This global parameter tells smbclient where the private key for smbclient is. This is needed only if the server requires a client certificate and one has been specified for smbclient.

The default value for this parameter is

```
ssl clien key = /usr/local/ssl/certs/smbclient.pem
```

ssl compatibility

This global parameter specifies whether SSLeay should operate in a bug-for-bug compatible mode with other SSL implementations. Because there are no clients at present using other SSL implementations, this is probably not needed. The default value for this parameter is

```
ssl compatibility = no
```

ssl hosts

This global parameter specifies those hosts for which SSL mode connections are required when SSL mode is on. It can list hosts by IP address, address range, net group, or name.

This parameter is related to `ssl hosts resign`, in that if neither parameter is set and SSL mode is on, SSL mode connections are required for all client connections. There is no default value for this parameter.

An example of using this parameter is

```
ssl hosts = host1 host2
```

This specifies that SSL connections are required only for the hosts listed in the parameter (for example, `host1` and `host2`). All other hosts will be able to establish non-SSL connections.

17

ssl hosts resign

This global parameter specifies those hosts for which SSL mode connections are not required when SSL mode is on. It can list hosts by IP address, address range, net group, or name.

This parameter is related to `ssl hosts`, in that if neither parameter is set and SSL mode is on, SSL mode connections are required for all client connections. By default, the parameter is not set.

An example of using this parameter is

```
ssl hosts resign = host1 host2
```

which specifies that SSL mode connections are not required for `host1` and `host2`. All other clients will be required to use SSL.

ssl require clientcert

This global parameter specifies whether the server requires clients to present certificates. If set to yes, clients must present valid certificates, and the server uses the information given in the parameter `ssl CA certDIR` or `ssl CA certFile` to check the CA that issued the client certificates presented.

If a client's certificate cannot be verified, the connection is terminated.

If this parameter is set to no (the default), clients do not need certificates.

ssl require servercert

This global parameter specifies whether `smbclient` requests a certificate from the server. If set to no (the default), smbclient does not request a certificate from the server when it connects. If set to yes, smbclient requests a certificate from the server and uses the information given in the parameter `ssl CA certDIR` or `ssl CA certFile` to check the CA that issued the certificate presented.

ssl server cert

This global parameter specifies the location of the Samba server's (smbd) certificate. This parameter *must* be set if SSL mode is on (it is not set by default).

The file containing the server's certificate might also contain its private key as well.

An example of using this parameter is

```
ssl server cert = /root/keys/samba-cert.pem
```

This tells Samba that its server certificate can be found in the file /root/keys/samba-cert.pem. When a client places an SSL connection to Samba, it hands out the contents of the file as its certificate.

ssl server key

This global parameter specifies the location of the Samba server's (smbd) private key. This parameter *must* be set if SSL mode is on (it is not set by default). Also, the public key in the certificate must match the private key.

When smbd starts in SSL mode, it fetches the private key specified by this parameter. If the private key is encrypted with a passphrase, smbd does not continue until the passphrase has been entered. For security reasons, it is a good reason to encrypt the server's private key, but it does create some difficulties when restarting the server.

An example of using this parameter is

```
ssl server key:   /root/keys/samba-key.pem
```

This tells Samba that its private key is in the file /root/keys/samba-key.pem. You usually are required to enter a passphrase to decrypt this file.

ssl version

This global parameter specifies the version of SSL that Samba uses if SSL mode is on. The values this parameter can take are

ssl2	Results in SSL V2 being used
ssl3	Results in SSL V3 being used
ssl2or3	Allows negotiation of SSL V2 or SSL V3
tls1	Results in TLS V1 being used

The default value of this parameter is

```
ssl version ssl2or3
```

sslproxy

sslproxy is a proxy that sits between a non–SSL-enabled client and an SSL-enabled server. It provides SSL access for the non–SSL-enabled client and has two modes of operation:

- Transparent mode, where it transparently provides SSL services and encryption/decryption for the non–SSL-enabled client

17

- NetBIOS mode, where it detects that the client is talking to a NetBIOS server and initiates SSL mode in the way that Samba expects it.

Figure 17.3 shows how sslproxy might be used. Note that sslproxy could be placed on either the client or the server machine (with the appropriate setup), but I have shown it here on a separate system. If sslproxy were placed on the client system, client programs would generally connect to 127.0.0.1.

In using sslproxy, non-SSL clients connect to the system running sslproxy, rather than the SSL-enabled server.

sslproxy was written by Christian Starkjohan and comes in source form. You can obtain sslproxy from http://www.obdev.at/Products. You can build it on UNIX machines and Windows NT. To build sslproxy, simply uncompress and untar the source file and run the make command while in the source directory.

FIGURE 17.3

Using sslproxy.

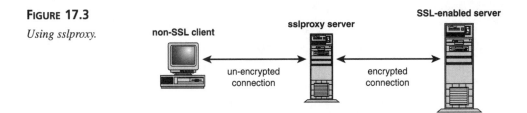

Examples

You have now looked in great depth at configuring Samba with SSL support, how to configure SSL under Samba, how to create certificates, and so on. However, how do things change when SSL support is in use? This section looks briefly at the changes.

The following shows an example of starting Samba when SSL mode has been switched on and configured correctly:

```
[root@bigpc]# /etc/rc.d/init.d/smb start
Starting SMB services: smbd Enter PEM pass phrase:─────────────1
nmbd

[root@bigpc]# ps ax ¦ grep mbd───────────────────────────────2
  446  ?  S    0:00 smbd -D
  455  ?  S    0:00 nmbd -D
[root@bigpc]#
```

You should notice the following:

1. smbd asks for the passphrase for the private key specified in the `ssl server key` parameter. You must enter it before smbd will continue any further. Generally, this causes your system startup to hang, and you might want to use other methods to start Samba if you have enabled SSL mode and don't want your system to hang during startup.(What if no one is watching when your system restarts?)

2. You check to see whether smbd started, and it has.

At this point, Samba with SSL support has started. What does it look like if you try to connect from smbclient on the same machine?

```
[root@bigpc]# smbclient //bigpc/fred ───────────────────────────────1
Added interface ip=16.153.112.65 bcast=16.153.112.255 nmask=255.255.255.0
SSL: Certificate OK: /C=AU/ST=South Australia/L=Adelaide/O=NS Widgets ──2
➡/CN=Richard Sharpe/Email=rsharpe@ns.com.au ──────────────────────2
SSL: Certificate OK: /C=AU/ST=South Australia/L=Adelaide/O=NS Widgets
➡/CN=Richard Sharpe/Email=rsharpe@ns.com.au
SSL: negotiated cipher: DES-CBC3-SHA ─────────────────────────────3
Password: ────────────────────────────────────────────────────4
Domain=[FOWLPLAY] OS=[Unix] Server=[Samba 2.0.0]
smb: \> ls
  smb.conf                              501  Sun Jan 24 21:21:08 1999

        61945 blocks of size 16384. 58392 blocks available
smb: \>
```

You should notice the following points:

1. You start up smbclient in the same way as usual.

2. When smbclient connects to the server, it presents a certificate, which is presented to the user.

3. The SSL routines also tell us which cipher has been selected.

4. From this point on, everything is the same.

Finally, to use sslproxy to allow non–SSL-enabled clients to access Samba via SSL, the following setup must be performed:

1. Start sslproxy on the system you want to run it on, with at least the following command line options:

   ```
   sslproxy -l 139 -R server -r 139 -n -c certificate-file
   ```

   You might need to specify the full path to sslproxy.

2. Use your client to connect to the sslproxy system rather than the SSL-enabled server. This might require that you enter the name of the sslproxy system in your lmhosts file so that you can translate the NetBIOS name of the sslproxy system to its IP address.

17

Summary

You looked in some detail at how to implement SSL support in Samba. This support allows you provide secure access to Samba servers over insecure networks, but if you do not need to provide such access over insecure networks, you are probably better off leaving out SSL support.

Part V, "Advanced Topics," looks at such topics as WINS support, local subnet browsing, and browsing in routed networks.

Q&A

Q If Microsoft does not ship any SSL-enabled CIFS/CMB clients, how can I use the SSL support that Samba has?

A You would use smbclient for simple command-line access to Samba over SSL. For Windows NT clients, you can compile up sslproxy and use that between your Windows NT server and Samba. For Win 9x clients, you need to run sslproxy on a separate server. Examples are shown in Figure 17.3.

Q Would you normally need client certificates when using SSL mode with Samba?

A Yes, you would. In fact, the server certificate that Samba offers is much less important than client certificates. This is because you would generally want to be certain that only authorized users could use Samba over an insecure network. By issuing certificates to clients and requiring their use, you can gain a level of assurance that only authorized users are accessing your server (they must have a certificate). Note that with the current implementation of SSL in Samba, if client certificates are required, only a valid certificate is required. There is no checking that the client is who her certificate claims her to be.

Q Do we need to obtain certificates from a CA such as Verisign (http://www.verisign.com) or Thawte (http://www.thawte.com)?

A It is not clear that any of the Certifying Authorities are signing certificates for Samba. In any case, you really do not need a certificate from one of the commercial certifying authorities, because you will not allow connections to the general public.

Because you will hand out certificates to the clients that will be allowed to access your Samba server, you can easily sign your own certificates and install your CA certificate on all systems that need it.

PART V

Advanced Topics

Hour

Hour 18

Resolving NetBIOS Names Without Using Broadcasts

It finally happened. My boss finally agreed to hire another person to help run the network.

"Maybe now I can do some improvement rather than putting out fires all day long," I think to myself as the plane touches down. My boss thought it would be a good idea to send me and my new officemate to the latest UNIX and Windows Integration conference. I tend to look forward to these conferences. They are fairly interesting, and I always manage to see some old friends who are in attendance as well.

The next morning, the two of us are walking up a flight of stairs leading to the ballroom where the first session is being held when I hear a voice from behind yelling my name. As I turn around, I recognize the familiar face of Ian.

"Good to see you Ian," I say with excitement as we shake hands vigorously. "How have you been?"

Ian replies, "Good. Busy as always. Still at CMU. How 'bout yourself?"

"Same here, except the CMU part," I smile. "Ian, let me introduce you to Gary Danz. Gary came on board a few weeks ago."

Gary holds out his hand and says some polite greetings.

"Nice to meet you Gary," replies Ian. "Hey, we'd better get going. I want to get a seat close to the coffee pot and bagels." The three of us walk toward the ballroom door laughing about some bad joke that we're sure we've heard before somewhere.

I've often thought it would be wonderful to have a photographic memory and be able to associate faces with names flawlessly. Or maybe have a pair of glasses that perform a visual search through some online database for the faces of people I've met before but whose names I can't seem to remember. Such a *name service* would almost surely be popular among the socially challenged. If you think about it, in the previous story I acted as a type of name service by introducing Gary to Ian.

As a general rule, people address other people with a name, but it is impossible to learn and remember the names of everyone in the world. Machines on a network deal with the same problem. Although it is possible to know all the machines on the Internet, searching a single global hosts file in real time would be impractical and inefficient. Also, administrators tend to change the names of machines, so keeping the information up-to-date is also a problem.

This hour focuses on name servers and the services they provide. I will focus primarily on how Samba uses the Windows Internet Name Service (or WINS) and its implementation of a NetBIOS name server. In closing, I will discuss how DNS affects NetBIOS names resolution and what parameters are available in Samba for configuring this behavior.

WINS

NEW TERM
In Hour 2, "Windows Networking," I mentioned the concept of a NetBIOS name server (NBNS) during the discussion on NetBIOS names and how clients resolve the names to network addresses. This idea is presented in RFC 1001 where the theory of NetBIOS over TCP is defined.

NEW TERM
The RFC presents two types of name servers. The first type acts as a bulletin board for clients to post and remove names without performing any validation on the names themselves. At the other end of the spectrum, the server might choose to pro-

vide full validation for any name registration requests. This validation ensures that no name collisions occur by acting on behalf of the requesting client. I'll explain more about this in a minute. WINS is an implementation of the latter type of NBNS.

Windows NT 4.0 Server ships with a WINS server that can be installed. Samba also has the capability to act as a WINS server. However, Samba does not currently implement the protocol for replicating a WINS database with another WINS server, either Windows NT or Samba.

The implications of this are that if you choose Samba as your WINS server, you will have no fail over capabilities should the Samba server crash. In a practical sense, I use Samba as the sole WINS server at one site that has over 400 clients spread across at least 15 to 20 subnets. Each client requires the WINS server to be available in order to function correctly. The Samba box is incredibly stable. So although calling this a "single point of failure" is technically accurate, I don't want you to associate this with instability.

> As you will see in Hour 19, "Local Subnet Browsing," a WINS server is not the same thing as a browse master, although people often confuse the two.

18

Why Is It Needed?

From Hour 2, you will remember that a NetBIOS client registers and resolves names using two methods: broadcast (sent to every machine on the subnet) or unicast (sent to a particular machine). One problem that was already mentioned is the amount of broadcast traffic that a large number of NetBIOS clients can generate. Another problem is that broadcasts are, by default, isolated to a logical subnet. This means that hosts on different subnets cannot communicate with each other.

WINS was designed to address both these problems. First, by configuring clients to register and resolve a name with a single machine, broadcast traffic is substantially reduced (see Figure 18.1). Second, because name queries are now sent directly to a machine, NetBIOS clients on different subnets can register and resolve names in the same name space. Figure 18.2 illustrates how this works. First, the client NACHO registers its name with the WINS server. Then, QUESO asks the WINS server to resolve the name NACHO for it. The server replies with the IP address previously registered by the first machine. In order for any type of consolidation of multiple subnets, whether for browsing or to access remote servers, WINS becomes a requirement.

FIGURE **18.1**

Name registration via (a) IP broadcasts and (b) point-to-point with a WINS server.

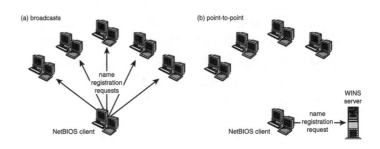

FIGURE **18.2**

Using a WINS server allows clients on multiple IP subnets to exist in the same name space.

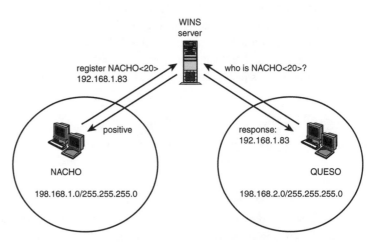

To better understand both these issues, let's see how NetBIOS clients interact with a WINS server. First let's look at name registration.

When a WINS-enabled client boots on to the network, it sends a name registration request directly to the WINS server, as shown in Figure 18.3. This name registration request is essentially the same as a broadcast name request with the exception that it is transmitted point-to-point from the client to the WINS server.

The WINS server might choose one of three responses:

- No response—The server is disabled or otherwise configured to ignore packets from the host.

- Positive—The server finds no matching records in its database that indicate a name collision with another client. Therefore the client is allowed to successfully register the name and the record is stored in the WINS database.

- Negative—If the WINS server locates a name in its database that matches the name used in the registration request, it issues a name query request to the IP in the located record. It attempts this multiple times. If there is no response from the client who owns the names, the new client is allowed to register the name successfully. If the name's owner does respond, however, the requesting client is sent a negative response and is not allowed to register the name.

FIGURE 18.3

Name registration request packet sent from a client to a WINS server.

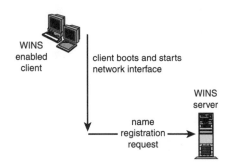

Name resolution works much in the same fashion. A client sends the name to be resolved in a packet to the WINS server. The server then searches its database for the name and, if found, responds with the appropriate IP address. Otherwise the server sends a negative response.

wins server

Now that you have a basic understanding of what WINS is and why it is needed, I'll examine how to configure Samba to use a WINS server. Perhaps you are wondering why Samba would want to use another WINS server when it can act as one itself.

When implementing your NetBIOS network, you should install only one WINS server. You can have multiple servers if they are able to synchronize databases with each other such as the Windows NT 4.0 WINS server. The reason for this is that the purpose of using a WINS server is to combine the name spaces from all the IP subnets into one. In Figure 18.4, two different hosts attempt to combine into the unique name NACHO. In the absence of a WINS server, this is possible because the two machines are located on different subnets. However, with the introduction of a WINS server, the name space of the two subnets is combined (for WINS-enabled clients at least). The client on the right is unable to register the name with the server because the client on the left already owns the name.

18

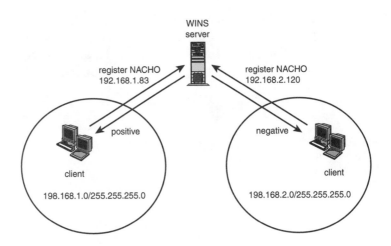

FIGURE 18.4

Unifying the NetBIOS name space by installing a WINS server.

If you use multiple unsynchronized WINS servers, the name space remains fragmented. Therefore, if you have an existing WINS server installed on your network and you want to participate with other NetBIOS clients that have registered with it, you need to register with the WINS as well.

To do this, you need to use Samba's `wins server` setting. This parameter accepts the IP address of your existing WINS server as a value. It is possible to use the DNS name of the WINS server instead, but using the IP address is the preferred method. The default is to not use a WINS server:

```
wins server = none
```

Assuming that you have configured some machine (possibly another Samba server) at IP address 198.162.1.80 as a WINS server, you can specify that the current machine use this server for name registration and resolution by entering the following value in your `smb.conf` file:

```
wins server = 192.168.1.80
```

wins support

The `wins support` parameter accepts a Boolean value to either enable or disable Samba's WINS server capability. The default action is to not act as a WINS server at all:

```
wins support = no
```

To enable Samba as a WINS server, simply enable this parameter

```
wins support = yes
```

and configure the necessary settings on the client. For Windows clients, this was covered in Hour 14, "Windows 9x and Windows NT."

The database used by nmbd when acting as a WINS server is in the form of a flat text file named wins.dat, which is located in the lock directory, /usr/local/samba/var/locks/ in the default installation. You needn't worry about all the information represented in each WINS entry. Some fields, however, are obvious. Here is a sample listing:

```
"CHIPSNDIPS#00" 919228124 255.255.255.255 c4R
"CHIPSNDIPS#1b" 919228124 192.168.1.72 44R
"CHIPSNDIPS#1c" 919228124 192.168.1.72 c4R
"CHIPSNDIPS#1e" 919228124 255.255.255.255 c4R
"QUESO#00" 919228124 192.168.1.72 46R
"QUESO#03" 919228124 192.168.1.72 46R
"QUESO#20" 919228124 192.168.1.72 46R
```

You should recognize the hexadecimal number following the # character in the name. This is the same syntax that nmblookup uses to indicate the NetBIOS resource byte.

If Samba is enabled as a WINS server, it queries itself when it obtains a name that needs to be resolved. In this way, Samba acts simultaneously as a WINS server and a WINS client.

> Your naturally tendency might be to set
>
> ```
>     wins support = yes
> ```
> and set
> ```
>     wins server = YourIPaddress
> ```
> This would be wrong. The wins support and wins server parameters are mutually exclusive. They should not both be set at the same time.

wins proxy

If the TCP/IP settings on your PC clients are set manually, you might have a hard time implementing WINS without paying a visit to every machine in order to update the necessary settings. One possible option would be to set a Samba server up on each subnet to act as a proxy agent for broadcast name resolution queries. Figure 18.5 illustrates this idea.

FIGURE 18.5

Using a WINS proxy agent to help name resolution.

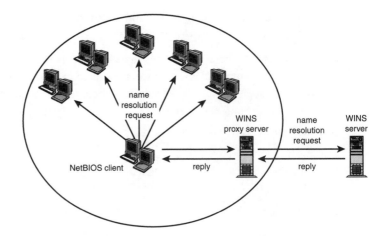

The wins proxy Boolean parameter controls whether nmbd responds to broadcast queries on behalf of other hosts. The default is no:

```
wins proxy = no
```

If you enable this setting, nmbd forwards name queries, both registration and resolution, to the WINS server specified in smb.conf (possibly itself in the case of wins support = yes) as well as forwarding the reply to the requesting client.

dns proxy

When Samba is configured as a WINS server (wins support = yes), it is possible to tell nmbd that all attempts to resolve names should be queried in DNS if they are not located in the local WINS database. The dns proxy parameter controls this behavior. Samba defaults to querying DNS if a name cannot be located in WINS:

```
dns proxy = yes
```

With dns proxy enabled, nmbd spawns another nmbd process to perform the DNS queries. The reason for this is that the standard gethostbyname() function in UNIX is a blocking call. The extra process allows this without penalizing normal NetBIOS name service.

If you do not have a dedicated link to your DNS servers, you might choose to disable the dns proxy behavior. This prevents Samba from initiating an uplink to your name servers every time someone queries a nonexistent name:

```
dns proxy = no
```

This would be the case if you were connected to your DNS servers via a dial-up connection.

lmhosts

NEW TERM One method of name resolution that I have not really talked about much is looking up a name in a local lmhosts file. The LanManager hosts file is the functional equivalent of UNIX's /etc/hosts file except that it matches IP addresses to NetBIOS names other than hostnames. The format for Samba's lmhosts file and one used by Windows clients is slightly different, so I will mention them both.

Information on the syntax of Samba lmhosts file can be found by reading its man page (man lmhosts). Each entry looks like

```
IPaddress          MachineName
```

For example, the entry for my Samba server I am currently using is

```
192.168.1.73      queso
```

Remember than NetBIOS names are not case sensitive, so I could have as easily used the name QUESO. The *MachineName* entry can be any valid name accepted by the nmblookup tool. For example, I can specify a particular name type by appending a NetBIOS tag onto the name.

```
192.168.1.73      queso#20
192.168.1.73      chipsndips#1b
```

The first entry refers to the server resource queso. Remember that <20> is the tag used to indicate share points. The second entry is used to locate the domain master browser for the group chipsndips.

Normally Samba's lmhosts file is located in the same directory as its configuration file, /usr/local/samba/lib. It is possible to specify another location when starting nmbd by using the -H filename flag. The follow example starts nmdb as a daemon using /etc/lmhosts as the default:

```
/usr/local/samba/bin/nmbd -H /etc/lmhosts -D
```

One final note about Samba's use of a lmhosts file. The contents of the file affect name resolution from the Samba hosts only. Samba does not use any entries to resolve requests that it receives from other hosts.

18

Windows's `lmhosts` file format is a little more extensive, but basically is the same thing. In its simplest form, an `lmhosts` file entry looks the same as Samba's:

```
IPaddress          MachineName
```

However, Microsoft's format allows for inserting other files by using a `#include` directive. This gives the possibility of using a central `lmhosts` file for all clients:

```
#include \\publicserv\global\lmhosts
```

Of course it is necessary to define a mapping for `publicserv` prior to the `#include` for things to work. More information about Microsoft's `lmhosts` file can be found by reading the `lmhosts.sam` file that is installed with the TCP/IP protocol.

name resolve order

Although the `name resolve order` parameter was mentioned in Hour 5, "The `smb.conf` File: Telling Samba What to Do," I would like to revisit it now after having covered all the possible methods. Particularly, I would like to point out that this parameter affects only how Samba resolves its own name queries and not those received from others. Therefore, if the following order is defined, Samba itself would not broadcast name queries and not attempt to resolve the name via DNS:

```
name resolve order = lmhosts wins
```

It would only search the local `lmhosts` file and then query the configured WINS server. If the WINS server that is contacted is another Samba server (or possibly itself) and that server has the `dns proxy` setting enabled, it is possible that the name would eventually be resolved via DNS. Figure 18.6 illustrates how this might happen. SAMBA1 attempts to resolve a name. After failing to find the host in its own `lmhosts` file, the server queries WINS. The WINS server, SAMBA2, attempts to locate the name in its internal WINS database. On failing to find the name, SAMBA2 contacts the domain's DNS server. This time the name is found and the resulting IP address is forwarded back to SAMBA1.

Even though the name is eventually resolved via DNS, it was not SAMBA1 that queried the Domain Name Server. This example is still valid if SAMBA1 and SAMBA2 are the same machine. This is the subtle distinction I referred to when I stated earlier that Samba can act as a WINS client and a WINS server simultaneously.

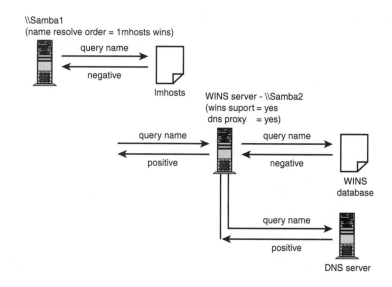

FIGURE 18.6

An example of the
name resolve order
parameter.

WINS and Windows 2000

You might have heard some of the hype about the next release of Windows NT (now referred to as Windows 2000). One of the main differences between the new OS and current versions of Windows NT is that "WINS will be going away in NT 5." I cannot count the number of times I have heard people say this.

Windows 2000 will have the capability to use the CIFS (SMB) protocol without layering it on top of NetBIOS. This NetBIOS-less implementation will allow for using DNS for all name resolution. However, you can only take advantage of this feature in a homogenous Windows 2000 environment. If older Windows NT or Windows 9x clients still exist on the network, WINS will still be necessary. Therefore, despite all the discussion of WINS disappearing with the next release of Microsoft's flagship operating system, you can expect NetBIOS and WINS to remain for at least several more years.

Summary

The Windows Internet Name Service (WINS) allows for managing NetBIOS names across multiple IP subnets. By registering all client names with a single WINS server, it is possible to implement such things as cross subnet browsing (see Hour 20, "Routed Networks and Browsing") and domain logons across a router (see Hour 21, "Windows 9x Domain Control"). If you use NetBIOS clients in a multiple subnet environment or if you want to decrease the number of broadcast packets related to name registration and resolution, you should install a WINS server on your network.

18

Q&A

Q **Can NetBIOS clients still resolve names if the WINS server is unavailable in the event of a crash?**

A If the client is configured as an H-node as most Microsoft clients are that register with using WINS, the client resorts to using broadcast queries to register and resolve names if it cannot contact the WINS server. Only if the name being resolved is owned by a machine on the logical subnet (that is, can be reached via broadcast mechanisms), does the client get a positive response. Refer back to Hour 2 for complete explanations of the different NetBIOS node types.

Q **Technically, can I run multiple WINS servers at the same time?**

A Yes, it is possible. The NetBIOS name space, however, remains segmented. Only clients registered with the same WINS server are able to see each other across routers.

Q **How does WINS relate to Dynamic DNS?**

A WINS and DNS, dynamic or not, are two entirely separate beasts. Dynamic DNS (DDNS) is essentially an implementation of DNS that allows for automatic updating of zones whenever changes are made to the domain. Microsoft's DNS server queries its WINS server if a DNS lookup fails, but the two are still different services. DNS deals with IP names; WINS handles NetBIOS names.

New Terms

NetBIOS Name Server (NBNS)   A server defined in RFC 1001 that allows for point-to-point NetBIOS name registration and resolution.

Windows Internet Name Service (WINS)   Microsoft's implementation of an RFC 1001/1002–compliant NBNS.

lmhosts   An ASCII file containing mapping from IP addresses to NetBIOS names. This is the NetBIOS functional equivalent of UNIX's /etc/hosts file.

HOUR 19

Local Subnet Browsing

In previous hours, you have looked at how to configure Samba for file and printer servicing, how to administer Samba, and how to access it via SSL if that is needed. However, many Windows users use network browsing to locate the resources you have configured for their use. In this hour you explore how Samba supports local subnet browsing. Hour 20, "Routed Networks and Browsing," explores how Samba supports browsing across a WAN.

In this hour:

- Present a brief introduction to browsing
- Look at all the Samba parameters that affect local subnet browsing in any way
- Provide some examples of Samba's support for browsing
- Suggest ways of troubleshooting browsing issues

Introduction to Browsing

Windows users browse the network to find servers and services that they need to use. Under Windows 9x and Windows NT this is achieved using Network Neighborhood. However, browsing is supported by systems in the network operating as browse servers. These browse servers can be systems running Windows NT Server, Windows NT Workstation, Windows 9x, Windows for Workgroups, or Samba (and possibly also LMU- and ASU-based servers). Figure 19.1 shows a network with browse servers and clients.

FIGURE 19.1

Browsing in a Windows network.

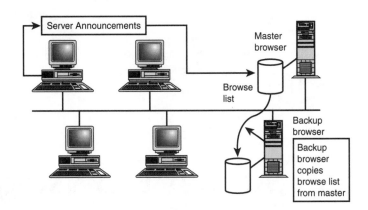

When Windows users browse the network, Windows

1. Sends a `QueryBrowserServers` request to the network to obtain the list of browser servers for the workgroup or domain it is a member of

2. Chooses a random server from the list and sends a `NetServerEnum2` (or `NetServerEnum`) call to that server asking for the browse list

The browse list is a list of all servers in the master browse server's workgroup or domain and all domains on the network. The browse list is built up by the master browser over a period of time as it listens to the *server announcements* and *domain announcements* made by all servers and domain master browsers (explained later in this hour) in the network. Figure 19.2 shows the results of browsing a network containing the `Fowlplay` domain/workgroup along with another domain/workgroup called `Nsdom`. When users click one of the domains or workgroups, they are shown all the servers in that domain or workgroup. An example is shown in Figure 19.3.

FIGURE 19.2

Browsing the network shows two domains/workgroups.

FIGURE 19.3

Browsing a domain or workgroup shows the servers.

In order to provide redundancy and distribute the browsing load across multiple systems, a Windows network will usually have several backup browsers as well as a master browser. Samba can operate as either a master browser or a backup browser, depending on the values of a number of parameters in the smb.conf file.

By using this browsing architecture, Windows clients obtain two important benefits:

- They do not have to devote CPU and memory resources to processing server announcements and maintaining browse lists.

- They do not have to build up browse lists slowly as they see each announcement. Rather, they can simply contact a browser, which most likely has been up for considerably longer than they have.

In addition to maintaining the browse list for a workgroup or domain, the master browse server (or master browser) maintains a list of all the browse servers (or backup browsers) in the local subnet. This list is provided to clients when they issue a QueryBrowserServers request (in response to the user wanting to browse the network).

A backup browser contacts the master browser every 15 minutes to obtain the latest copy of the browse list. It caches this list of servers and domains and uses it to respond to NetServerEnum[2] requests from browse clients.

NEW TERM However, if a backup browser cannot contact the master browser, it forces an *election*. An election is the process used by all browsers on the network to determine which one should be the master browser and which ones should be backup browsers.

NEW TERM When a system in a Windows network wants to force a browser election, it sends out an election request. Contained in each election request is a four-byte field called the *election criteria*. The structure of the election criteria field is shown in Figure 19.4, along with the fields you can control.

FIGURE **19.4**

Election criteria field.

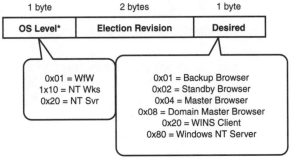

When the current master browser receives an election request, it examines values in the OS level (or OS Summary) field, as well as election revision and election summary to determine what to do. You can control Samba's behavior with regard to browser elections by setting the os level parameter along with other parameters appropriately (see the section, "Samba Browsing Parameters," later this hour).

If its own OS level is higher than that of any other browser, a browser enters the running election state. While in this state, it sends up to four more election requests at intervals of 200 or 400 milliseconds, depending on whether it is a master browser or backup browser, respectively. If a browser wins each election four times in a row, it becomes the master browser for that workgroup or domain. If its OS level matches that of another browser in the network, it checks other fields such as the election revision and desired to determine who should win the election.

If a master browser receives an election request that indicates another system will win the election, it demotes itself to a backup browser.

When a system becomes the master browser, it broadcasts a RequestAnnouncement request to machines on the subnet. Systems respond to the RequestAnnouncement request by sending a ServerAnnouncement after a random time within the subsequent 30 seconds. This helps to reduce the load on the master browser.

When a Windows user clicks a server listed in a browsing view (from Network Neighborhood, for example), Windows sends a NetShareEnum request to the selected server and displays the results. An example is shown in Figure 19.5. Although this last step does not involve interacting with either a master or backup browser, a number of Samba parameters control the information presented. Technically, the Samba server that you are seeking a list of shares from can also be either the master or a backup browser. However, this function is independent of its function in listing shares and providing file and print services.

FIGURE 19.5

Browsing the shares on a server.

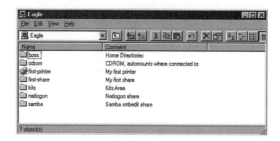

Samba Browsing Parameters

The behavior of Samba with respect to browsing is controlled by a number of `smb.conf` parameters. These parameters affect such things as

- Whether Samba provides browsing services
- Whether Samba seeks to become a master browser or becomes a backup browser
- Which services show up when a Samba server is being browsed by a client Windows system

The following sections describe each of these parameters.

19

announce as

This global parameter specifies what type of server Samba announces itself as. The valid options are

NT	Announce us as an NT server during a host announcement. This is the default.
Win95	Announce us as a Windows 95 system during a host announcement.
WfW	Announce us as a Windows for Workgroups system during a host announcement.

In general, you should not need to change this parameter from the default of

```
announce as = NT
```

announce version

This global parameter specifies the version numbers Samba (nmbd) will use when sending a host announcement. By default, Samba currently uses a version number of 4.2 (major version of 4 and minor version of 2), which is larger than the value of 4.0 that Windows NT 4.0 uses.

In general you should not need to change this value from the default of

```
announce version = 4.2
```

auto services

This global parameter provides the list of services you want automatically added to the browse list. This parameter is most useful for adding specific homes and printers services that would not normally be visible. For example:

```
auto services = boss      lp postscrip
```

would specify to Samba (nmbd) that the services lp and postscript should be made available for browsing. Please note, however, that this affects only what people can see when they click the icon for your server in Network Neighborhood.

If you simply want to be able to browse all printers in your printcap file, use the load printers option.

browsable

This service-level parameter specifies whether individual services appear in browse lists. By setting this parameter to No for a service

```
browsable = No
```

you can hide it from clients, because the default is yes:

```
browsable = Yes
```

This parameter has a synonym of browseable.

browse list

This global parameter specifies whether Samba serves browse lists to clients at all. You should generally not need to change this parameter from its default:

```
browse list = Yes
```

comment

This service-level parameter specifies which text field appears next to a service when a client browses the server. Here is an example:

```
comment = My first share
```

interfaces

This global parameter specifies that Samba should set up and use multiple network interfaces for browsing and other activities. By default, Samba operates only on the primary interface of a system.

This parameter takes a list of IP/NETMASK pairs, either in CIDR format (a.b.c.d/prefix-bits) or the more classical NETMASK format (a.b.c.d/e.f.g.h). Here is an example:

```
interfaces = 192.168.1.0/24 192.168.2.0/255.255.255.0
```

lm announce

This global parameter specifies whether Samba (nmbd) produces LanManager-style host announcements, such as those needed by OS/2 and other clients, so that the Samba server can appear in their browse lists.

The values this parameter can take are

true	Send LanMan-style host announcements at the frequency set by the lm interval parameter.
false	Never send LanMan-style host announcements.
auto	Do not send LanMan-style host announcements until one is seen on the network. After that point, send them at the frequency set by the lm interval parameter.

This is the default:

```
lm announce = auto
```

lm interval

Used in conjunction with lm announce, this global parameter specifies the frequency in seconds with which LanMan style host announcements will be made if the lm announce parameter is set to true or auto.

If this parameter is set to 0, no LanMan host announcements are made, despite the setting of the lm announce parameter. By default, this parameter is set to 60, which means that LanMan host announcements are made every 60 seconds:

19

```
lm interval = 60
```

load printers

This global parameter specifies whether Samba loads all printers in the printcap file for browsing. However, this works only if you have a [printers] section defined. If you do not have a [printers] section defined, this parameter does nothing. By default, the parameter is set to Yes:

```
load printers = Yes
```

local master

This global parameter specifies that Samba should try to become the local master browser on the subnet on startup. If set to No, Samba does not participate in elections but can force them if it detects a local master does not exist.

If this parameter is set to Yes, the default, Samba participates in elections for the local master browser:

```
local master = Yes
```

Whether it becomes the local master browser depends on the value of other parameters in the smb.conf file and a number of other parameters. That is, this Samba instance has to win a browser election to become the local master browser.

netbios aliases

This global parameter specifies the additional NetBIOS names that Samba advertises as aliases for itself. This allows a single system to appear under multiple names in browse lists.

If the system is acting as a browse server or a logon server, none of the aliases are advertised as either a browse server or a logon server.

By default, Samba does not define any netbios aliases. An example of this command is

```
netbios aliases = bald money pinkfloyd
```

This specifies that Samba registers the NetBIOS names bald, money, and pinkfloyd as aliases for the Samba server.

netbios name

This global parameter sets the NetBIOS name that Samba is known by on the network. By default, this is set to the first component of the server's DNS name. If this machine is a browse server or a logon server, these services are advertised under the NetBIOS name specified (and only under that name, not under any aliases). The default is the first component of the server's hostname.

To force the `netbios name` of your server to `eagle`, use the following:

```
netbios name = eagle
```

os level

This global parameter specifies the value of the OS Level or OS Summary that Samba uses in election requests. The value used determines whether Samba becomes a master browser on the local network.

Windows NT Server uses a value of 32, Windows NT Workstation uses a value of 16, and Windows 95 and Windows for Workgroups use a value of 1. During an election, the system with the largest OS Level wins. (If there is a tie, other factors are used to determine which system wins.)

Setting this value to 33 ensures that a Samba server always wins, whereas setting it to 0 ensures that Samba always loses. Setting it to a value such as 17 ensures that Samba always wins elections with Windows NT Workstation but loses to Windows NT Server.

The default value of this parameter is 0, which means that Samba always loses elections to any other browser. The following command forces your server's OS Level to 33 and makes sure it always wins elections:

```
os level = 33
```

preferred master

This global parameter specifies whether Samba is the preferred master browser for its workgroup. On startup, if this parameter is set to `Yes` (the default is `No`), Samba forces an election. Its chances of becoming a master browser then depend on the value of a number of other parameters (for example, `os level`).

This parameter should be used with care because, if several systems are the preferred master browser, they will periodically have browser wars with each other.

A synonym for this parameter is `prefered master`.

server string

This global parameter specifies what descriptive string appears beside a Samba server's name in browse lists. It can be any string you want to appear in browse lists and can have the following macros in it:

19

%v   This macro is replaced with the Samba version number, for example, 2.0.0.

%h   This macro is replaced with the hostname of the Samba server.

%L   This macro is replaced with the NetBIOS name of the Samba server.

The default value for this parameter is

```
server string = Samba %v
```

To include more information in your server string, such as the DNS hostname, try the following command:

```
Samba %v on host %h
```

workgroup

This global parameter specifies the workgroup that a Samba server will appear in. Samba (nmbd) places the name specified on this parameter in host announcements as the workgroup. It is also used as the domain name of the Samba server when in domain-level security or Samba is operating as a Primary Domain Controller. The default is

```
workgroup = WORKGROUP
```

To change your workgroup to FOWLPLAY, add the following to the global section of your smb.conf file and restart

```
Samba:workgroup = FOWLPLAY
```

Browsing Examples

So far, I have looked at what browsing is and the meaning of all the smb.conf parameters that affect local subnet browsing. In this system I present an sample smb.conf file and see how it affects browsing the network.

First, here is the relevant entries from the global section of the smb.conf file for your test server, eagle:

```
[global]
  workgroup = FOWLPLAY
  server string = Samba %v on host %h, NetBIOS %L
  guest account = pcguest
  netbios name = EAGLE
  netbios aliases = BALD MONEY PINKFLOYD
  os level = 33
  preferred master = yes
```

The following notes apply to these parameters:

1. The workgroup/domain selected is FOWLPLAY.

2. The server advertises a string of Samba 2.0.0 on host *hostname*, NetBIOS eagle because the version of Samba running on the machine is 2.0.0 and I set its NetBIOS name to eagle later in this hour.

3. The server announces itself as eagle, and if it is operating as a browser or a logon server, it provides these services under the name eagle.

4. The server also announces itself under all the names provided in this parameter.

5. The server wins elections against all Windows systems, because its level is higher than that which any Windows operating system uses.

6. The server is a preferred master browser and forces an election when it starts up.

Figure 19.6 shows the result of browsing this server.

FIGURE 19.6

Browsing the FOWLPLAY workgroup.

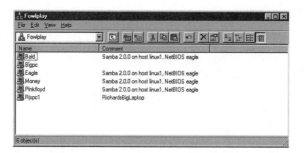

In Figure 19.6, you can see the result of the netbios name and netbios aliases parameters. The browse list for the workgroup FOWLPLAY shows a server called Eagle, as well as servers called Bald, Money, and Pinkfloyd. In each case, the comment associated with these servers is Samba 2.0.0 on host linux1, NetBIOS eagle, which is a direct result of the server string parameter you set. You can infer from the comment that the hostname for each of these machines is linux1.

What you cannot see here is which system is the master browser. However, a few quick checks with nmblookup on a Samba server can find that out for us:

```
[root@eagle]# nmblookup -S eagle
Sending queries to 16.153.112.255
16.153.112.110 eagle<00>
Looking up status of 16.153.112.110
received 18 names
        EAGLE           <00> -          M <ACTIVE>
        EAGLE           <03> -          M <ACTIVE>
        EAGLE           <20> -          M <ACTIVE>
```

19

```
      .._MSBROWSE__.  <01> - <GROUP> M <ACTIVE>
      BALD             <00> -         M <ACTIVE>
      BALD             <03> -         M <ACTIVE>
      BALD             <20> -         M <ACTIVE>
      FOWLPLAY         <00> - <GROUP> M <ACTIVE>
      FOWLPLAY         <1b> -         M <ACTIVE>
      FOWLPLAY         <1c> - <GROUP> M <ACTIVE>
      FOWLPLAY         <1d> -         M <ACTIVE>
      FOWLPLAY         <1e> - <GROUP> M <ACTIVE>
      MONEY            <00> -         M <ACTIVE>
      MONEY            <03> -         M <ACTIVE>
      MONEY            <20> -         M <ACTIVE>
      PINKFLOYD        <00> -         M <ACTIVE>
      PINKFLOYD        <03> -         M <ACTIVE>
      PINKFLOYD        <20> -         M <ACTIVE>
num_good_sends=0 num_good_receives=0

[root@eagle]# nmblookup -S bigpc
Sending queries to 16.153.112.255
16.153.112.99 bigpc<00>
Looking up status of 16.153.112.99
received 6 names
      BIGPC            <00> -         M <ACTIVE>
      FOWLPLAY         <00> - <GROUP> M <ACTIVE>
      BIGPC            <03> -         M <ACTIVE>
      BIGPC            <20> -         M <ACTIVE>
      FOWLPLAY         <1e> - <GROUP> M <ACTIVE>
      ADMINISTRATOR    <03> -         M <ACTIVE>
num_good_sends=0 num_good_receives=0
```

In the output from nmblookup against the names eagle and bigpc, you see that eagle has the name FOWLPLAY registered as a <1d>-type name. This means that eagle is the local master browser for the workgroup FOWLPLAY. It is also possible to use nmblookup -M to find the master browser as well:

```
[root@linux1 /root]# nmblookup -M fowlplay
Sending queries to 16.153.112.255
16.153.112.110 fowlplay<1d>
```

Here you see that the master browser is 16.153.112.110. By rerunning nmblookup in the following way, you can find the master browser:

```
nmblookup -S -A 16.153.112.110
```

Another way to find out the identity of the master browser is by adding the -T flag to nmblookup:

```
nmblookup -T -M fowlplay
```

This tells nmblookup to translate IP addresses back into DNS names and print them as well as the IP addresses shown previously.

Browsing Problems

Most browsing problems can be resolved by carefully setting up the relevant parameters in your smb.conf file. However, when master browsers go down and elections occur, you might see messages such as The list of servers for this workgroup is not currently available. You might also see large parts of the network disappear if there are not enough backup browsers on the network.

You can use nmblookup on a Samba server to investigate which nodes are in the workgroup/domain and which node is the master browser, if any.

Some browsing-related problems to watch out for include the following:

- Not having a guest account configured on your system or not having a guest account entry in the smb.conf file. Either of these can result in clients being unable to browse servers to find out the list of services available.
- Windows NT systems requiring passwords in order to browse Samba servers.
- Large parts of the network disappearing and reappearing at random. This is caused by excessive elections in the network. Two browsers are fighting to become the master browse server.

Finally, Samba keeps several important files that are useful for tracking down browsing problems. You have already come across them in previous hours, but here they are again:

browse.dat	This file contains the browse list. It consists of one line per server in the browse list.
wins.dat	This file contains all the entries that nmbd keeps in its WINS database.

19

Summary

This hour explores local subnet browsing in some depth and looks at all the smb.conf parameters that affect browsing in any way. You should now be equipped to resolve most issues surrounding browsing in a Windows network where Samba is offering SMB services.

In the next hour, you will explore browsing in routed networks and how you can configure Samba to synchronize browsing information across subnets.

Q&A

Q We can't browse our Samba server. That is, none of its shares show up when we click the server's icon. How can we fix this?

A This might be because you have not made the shares browsable. By default, shares in Samba are not browsable. To make them browsable, add the following line to those shares that you want to be browsable:

```
browsable = yes
```

Q We are planning to move our Samba server to another machine, but would like to enable our users to see the new machine in their browse lists as the current server, which is called HOBBIT.

A You need to have the new server advertise a NetBIOS alias or give the NetBIOS name of the old server. In fact, it is worthwhile giving a Samba server a NetBIOS name that relates to the service it performs, rather than letting it default to the first component of the server's DNS address. You can give a Samba server a NetBIOS name with the following:

```
netbios name = hobbit
```

You can give a Samba server a NetBIOS alias in the following way:

```
netbios aliases = hobbit
```

Q How can I make sure that my Samba server becomes the master browser in our workgroup? Sometimes we find that a Windows 95 PC becomes the master browser, which is not so good.

A To ensure that Samba becomes the master browser, you need to make sure it wins browser elections. To do this, give it an OS Level that is higher than any other potential browse server on the network—for example, 33. You can do this with the following in the global section of your smb.conf file:

```
os level = 33
```

Q We have a lot of printers defined on our Samba server in the printcap file. These all show up in the browse lists when users browse the server, but they are of little use to users, because they mostly do not have drivers for the printers. We have defined the printers that are of interest to PC users in our smb.conf file. How do we stop Samba from displaying all these unnecessary printers?

A By default, Samba loads all printers in your printcap file. To switch this behavior off, simply add the following to your smb.conf file in the global section:

```
load printers = no
```

HOUR 20

Routed Networks and Browsing

by Richard Sharpe

Samba supports browsing in local subnets as well as across routed networks. The previous hour explores browsing in the local subnet in some detail. This hour explores the ways that Samba supports browsing in routed networks or across subnets.

First, you look at the differences between local subnet browsing and browsing across routed networks. Next, you look at how Samba can be configured to support browsing in routed networks. Then, you look at a sample configuration, and finally, you look at some troubleshooting techniques in relation to browsing in routed networks.

Browsing Across Subnets

Recall from the previous hour that CIFS/SMB servers send host announcements to inform master browsers of their presence. In addition, domain master browsers send workgroup/domain announcements to inform other master browsers of the presence of their workgroup/domain on the network.

However, all these announcements are sent UDP broadcasts to the broadcast address for the subnet the sender is in. For example, if your subnet is 172.16.1.0/24, these announcements are sent to the address 172.16.1.255. Although all nodes on your subnet should see these broadcasts, in general, nodes in other subnets do not see these broadcasts. Figure 20.1 shows this situation in more detail.

FIGURE 20.1

Announcements are broadcast on the local subnet.

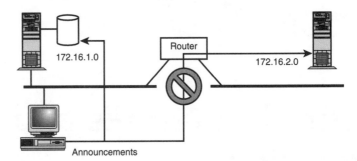

The concern in a network consisting of multiple subnets that are connected via routers, then, is to ensure that all subnets can receive enough information so that they can browse the servers available in the network. Samba provides several ways to accomplish this:

- Remote announcement from a Samba server to a subnet
- Remote browser sync from one subnet to another
- Normal Windows Networking browser synchronization

However, you need to distinguish between workgroups and domains in what follows. With standard Microsoft Windows Networking, workgroups cannot span subnets. That is, if the workgroup FOWLPLAY exists in the two subnets 172.16.1.0/24 and 172.16.2.0/24, they are actually two separate workgroups. This is shown in Figure 20.2.

Windows Networking treats this as two separate workgroups because host announcements in any subnet do not reach the other subnets, so browse servers do not see the presence of servers of any type in other subnets.

In a Windows NT Domain on the other hand, one machine, the Primary Domain Controller, is designated as the Domain Master Browser. In addition, each subnet contains a local master browser as well as backup browsers. A local master browser collates the browse list for that subnet and tells the domain master browser of its presence with a `MasterBrowserAnnouncement`. A local master browser finds its domain master browser by translating the name *Workgroup*<1b> using WINS, as the domain master browser registers that name with WINS. Thus, in the domain FOWLPLAY, the domain master browser would register the name FOWLPLAY<1b>.

FIGURE 20.2

A workgroup split across two subnets.

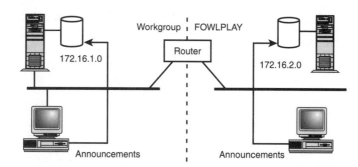

The domain master browser sends a `NetServerEnum` request to the master browsers in each subnet every 15 minutes and merges the server list from each local master browser into its own server list. This allows the domain master browser to build a complete list of all the servers in the domain.

In addition, the local master browser in each subnet sends a `NetServerEnum` request to the domain master browser every 15 minutes as well to obtain a list of all the servers in the domain. In this way, each subnet has available to it a browse list that includes the whole domain. This is shown in Figure 20.3.

FIGURE 20.3

Browsing in an NT Domain.

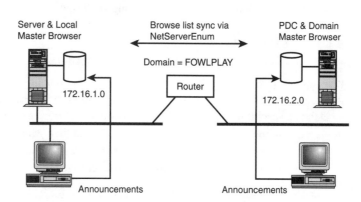

20

In a workgroup, then, you set up Samba to broadcast host announcements into the remote subnets it is connected to; if you have Samba servers on each of your subnets, you might also set them up to synchronize browse lists with each other. In an NT Domain setup, you configure one machine in the domain as the domain master browser with a server in each subnet becoming the local master browser.

Samba separates the function of Primary Domain Controller and Domain Master Browser. That is, Samba has separate parameters that control whether Samba operates as a Primary Domain Controller and a Domain Master Browser. Under Windows NT, the same machine must provide both these functions. It is possible to confuse a Windows NT domain if you set up a Samba server to operate as the domain master browser. You might find clients trying to log in to the Samba server.

In each case, however, a WINS server generally is needed because the browse lists that browse servers collate contain only the names of servers seen in host announcements. That is, they do not contain the IP addresses of the servers. To translate from NetBIOS names to IP addresses, some form of WINS support is needed.

Samba Configuration for Browsing Across Subnets

The following are all the `smb.conf` parameters that affect the provision by Samba of browsing support across subnets. Some of these are repeated from the previous hour because they affect both local subnet browsing and browsing across subnets.

domain master

This global parameter specifies whether Samba is a domain master browser. When this parameter is set, it tells Samba (nmbd) to start collating domain-wide browse lists (or workgroup-wide browse lists if you have workgroup-spanning subnet). Samba (nmbd) also claims a special domain specific NetBIOS name (*Workgroup*<1b>, where *Workgroup* is replaced with the name of your workgroup). Samba then waits for local master browsers in the domain to contact it with `MasterBrowserAnnouncements` and starts collecting browse lists from each local master browser that contacts it.

Local master browsers on other subnets contact Samba for its browse lists and supply their own browse lists when Samba requests those from them. In this way, domain-wide browse lists are maintained.

It is dangerous to set this parameter if you already have a Windows NT system running as a Primary Domain Controller. Large parts of the network are likely to get upset and not be able to find login servers.

The default value for this parameter is

```
domain master = no
```

local master

This global parameter specifies that Samba should try to become the local master browser on a subnet. If set, Samba (nmbd) participates in elections for the local master browser. Samba also sends `MasterBrowserAnnouncements` to the domain master browser. It finds the domain master browser by looking up the name `WORKGROUP<1B>` in WINS, which is registered by the domain master browser.

Samba is not guaranted to become the local master browser; it's guaranteed only to participate in elections for the local master browser. To guarantee that Samba becomes the local master browser, you need to set the `os level` on Samba higher than any other potential browse server in the network.

The default of this parameter is

```
local master = Yes
```

If this parameter is `false`, Samba does not participate in browser elections and thus does not become the local master browser.

netbios aliases

This global parameter specifies the additional NetBIOS names that Samba advertises as aliases for itself. This allows a single system to appear under multiple names in browse lists.

If the system acts as a browse server or a login server, none of the aliases are advertised as either a browse server or a login server.

These aliases appear in browse lists across subnets if the appropriate configuration has been set up.

By default, Samba does not advertise any NetBIOS aliases. An example of using this parameter is

```
netbios aliases = bald money pinkfloyd
```

20

netbios name

This global parameter sets the NetBIOS name that Samba is known by on the network. By default, this is set to the first component of the server's DNS name. If this machine is a browse server or a login server, these services are advertised under the NetBIOS name specified (and only under that name, not under any aliases).

This NetBIOS name appears in browse lists across subnets if the appropriate configuration has been set up.

os level

This global parameter specifies the value of the OS Level or OS Summary that Samba uses in election requests. The value used determines whether Samba becomes a master browser on the local network.

Windows NT Server uses a value of 32, Windows NT Workstation uses a value of 16, and Windows 95 and Windows for Workgroups uses a value of 1. During an election, the system with the largest OS Level wins (if there is a tie, other factors are used to determine which system wins).

Setting this value to 33 ensures that a Samba server always wins, whereas setting it to 0 ensures that Samba always loses. Setting it to a value such as 17 ensures that Samba always wins elections with Windows NT Workstation but loses to Windows NT Server.

preferred master

This global parameter specifies whether Samba is the preferred master browser for its workgroup. On startup, if this parameter is set to Yes (the default is No), Samba forces an election. Its chances of becoming a master browser then depend on the value of a number of other parameters (for example, os level).

This parameter should be used with care because, if several systems are the preferred master browser, they periodically have browser wars with each other causing network congestion resulting in poor performance.

Browser wars, where multiple servers on a subnet are fighting to become the browse master, cause two problems:

- Unnecessary broadcast traffic on your subnet, which could result in poor performance; and

- Reduced browsing capabilities, as the master browser is continuously rebuilding the browse list for the domain.

A synonym for this parameter is `prefered master`.

remote announce

This global parameter specifies that Samba (`nmbd`) should periodically send host announcements to the specified IP addresses under the specified workgroup name.

This allows you to have your Samba server appear in the browse lists of remote (subnet) workgroups when they normally would not if following the correct Windows Networking rules.

Here's an example of this parameter in action:

```
remote announce = 172.30.0.255/FOWLPLAY
```

This specifies that Samba sends host announcements on the workgroup `FOWLPLAY` into the address `172.30.0.255`.

Many routers do not allow directed broadcasts (for example, an IP datagram to the broadcast address of a subnet, such as `172.30.0.255` where the subnet mask is `255.255.255.0`) to be forwarded by default. You need to enable directed broadcasts in your routers to be able to send remote announcements to the broadcast address in another subnet.

If your router does not allow you to forward directed broadcasts, you need to send remote announcements to the local master browser in the remote subnets.

remote browse sync

This global parameter specifies that Samba (`nmbd`) should periodically request synchronization of browse lists with the specified master browsers on remote subnets. The synchronization mechanism used works only with other Samba servers, but it provides for the synchronization of browse lists between Samba servers across subnets.

Here's an example of this parameter in action:

```
remote browse sync = 172.30.0.255
```

This specifies that Samba requests the master browser on the specified address to synchronize browse lists.

20

server string

This global parameter specifies the descriptive string that appears beside a Samba server's name in browse lists. It can be any string you want to appear in browse lists and can have the following macros in it:

%v   This macro is replaced with the Samba version number, for example 2.0.0.

%h   This macro is replaced with the hostname of the Samba server.

%L   This macro is replaced with the NetBIOS name of the Samba server.

The default value for this parameter is

```
server string = Samba %v
```

To include more information in your server string, such as the DNS host name, try the following command:

```
server string = samba %v on host %h
```

wins proxy

This global parameter specifies whether Samba (nmbd) acts as a WINS proxy: whether it responds to broadcast name queries on behalf of other hosts that do not understand WINS or are not configured for WINS. The default value for this parameter is

```
wins proxy = No
```

You might need to set this for older clients, and you probably need to specify some form of WINS service for remote subnets if you are using remote announce or remote browse sync or are in an NT Domain and have browse list synchronization functioning.

wins server

This global parameter specifies the IP address or the DNS name of the WINS server that Samba (nmbd) should register with. This parameter should be used only if Samba is not providing the WINS function itself.

If you are using cross-subnet browsing, you might need to configure Samba on the remote subnets to point to a WINS server on the more central subnets. Here is an example:

```
wins server = 172.30.0.1
```

wins support

This global parameter specifies whether Samba (nmbd) should act as a WINS server. If set, Samba (nmbd) acts as a WINS server. There should never be more than one Samba

WINS server in your network, and Samba does not yet support the Microsoft WINS replication protocols, so Samba cannot be set up as a WINS server when a Windows system is already performing this function. The default value for this parameter is

```
wins support = No
```

You need a WINS server somewhere in your network if you are using cross-subnet browsing.

workgroup

This global parameter specifies the workgroup where a Samba server appears. Samba (nmbd) places the name specified on this parameter in host announcements as the workgroup. It is also used as the domain name of the Samba server when in domain-level security or when Samba is operating as a Primary Domain Controller. The default value for this parameter is

```
workgroup = WORKGROUP
```

Sample Configurations

In this section, you look at some sample configurations. First, you explore using remote announce to allow a workgroup that is spread across subnets to browse its Samba servers. Then you explore setting up a domain master browser to set up a domain that is spread across subnets.

Workgroups Across Subnets

If you have a workgroup that is spread across subnets, you can use the remote announce command to allow clients in other subnets to keep in touch with those parts of the network that contain the servers. Figure 20.4 shows an example of this.

FIGURE 20.4

Keeping a workgroup in touch across subnets.

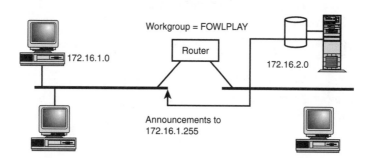

20

The following command would be used to ensure that subnet 172.16.1.0 knew about the server in subnet 172.16.2.0:

```
remote announce = 172.16.1.255/FOWLPLAY
```

This ensures that all nodes within 172.16.1.0 hear about the presence of the Samba servers within 172.16.2.0. However, it does not help the nodes in 172.16.2.0 to find out about the servers that might be in 172.16.1.0.

 You must ensure that your router passes directed broadcasts for something like this to work. If directed broadcasts between the two subnets do not work, you can replace 172.16.1.255 with the IP address of the local master browser in the subnet.

If you have Samba servers in each of your subnets, you can use the remote browse sync parameter to synchronize browse lists between all the subnets. To do this, use the following steps:

1. Nominate one of your Samba servers as the domain master browser. You do this by adding the parameter *domain master = yes* to the global section of the smb.conf file on the machine that is to become the domain master browser

2. Specify the remote networks that Samba synchronizes browse lists with using the remote browse sync parameter.

3. Make sure that the Samba server in each remote network becomes the local master browser.

If your network has subnets 172.16.1.0, 172.16.2.0, and 172.30.3.0 and your domain master browser is in 172.30.1.0 on the Samba server that is to be your domain master browser, you would add the following parameters to the global section of the smb.conf file:

```
domain master = yes
remote browse sync = 172.16.2.255 172.16.3.255
```

If your routers do not forward directed broadcasts, you need to replace the broadcast addresses with the IP address of the Samba server that is the local master browser in each of the subnets listed.

On the Samba server that is to be the local master browser in each of the remote subnets, you should add the following parameters to the global section of the `smb.conf` file:

```
local master = yes
preferred master = yes
os level = 33
```

You can set the os level to any value above 32.

Domains Across Subnets

If you have a domain that is spread across subnets, you might not need to do anything extra on your Samba systems to make everything work correctly. This is because Windows NT domains already handle this situation.

However, if you set Samba up as a primary domain controller, add the following in the global area of your `smb.conf` file:

```
domain master = yes
```

In addition, you might want to ensure that you have the following in the `smb.conf` file of each Samba server in each subnet:

```
local master = yes
```

These statements ensure that there is a domain master browser in the network and that some node is trying to become a local master browser in each subnet.

> If you already have a Windows NT server as a primary domain controller, do not make a Samba system the domain master browser! This confuses a great many clients and they might try to log in to your Samba server rather than the primary domain controller.

Troubleshooting Remote Browsing

20

In debugging problems with browsing, remember that browse lists contain only names—the names of the servers that have sent host announcements in the workgroup or domain, and the names of the domains whose announcements have been seen by the master browser. This means it is very important that WINS is functioning correctly in your network.

If you can see all the servers in Network Neighborhood but you cannot obtain a list of services on a particular server, you should ensure that the WINS servers are functioning

and your clients can access the WINS server. Figure 20.5 shows an example of the sort
of error messages you might see.

FIGURE 20.5

*Errors accessing a
server in Network
Neighborhood.*

You are likely to encounter other problems:

- Being unable to see any nodes in Network Neighborhood, or being unable to see
  nodes that were there before. This problem is due to browsers changing roles and
  having frequent elections. You might need to ensure that Samba is not forcing elections to occur too frequently. One way to check this is to look at the log.nmb file
  in the Samba log directory.

- Being asked for a password to browse a server. This problem is usually due to you
  not having an account on the machine that you are trying to browse, or your password on that machine being different than the password you logged in to the network with.

Summary

In this hour you have explored how browsing works in a routed network. You have seen
that Samba can support both workgroups that are split across subnets as well as NT
domains that are split across subnets.

In Hour 21, "Windows 9x Domain Control," you explore how DOS and Windows
(Windows for Workgroups and Win 9x) clients can log in to a domain managed by
Samba. In subsequent hours you explore the Primary Domain Controller functions that
Samba includes.

Q&A

**Q We have a number of Samba servers in a network that already has a Windows
NT domain with its own Primary Domain Controller. A number of our client
machines seem to want to log in to the Samba server, and thus cannot log in to
the domain. What is the problem and how do we fix it?**

A This is probably caused by Samba being configured to operate as a Domain Master
Browser. If it is up before the PDC is started, the Samba server has registered the

name DOMAIN<1B> (where DOMAIN is replaced with your domain name). Remove any domain master parameters from the smb.conf file on your Samba server and restart Samba. You might also need to restart your Primary Domain Controller.

Q Our workgroup is spread across several subnets, and we have Samba servers in each subnet. We are having problems with browsing. I have read that only a Windows NT domain supports browsing across subnets. Do I have to replace our main Samba server with a Windows NT PDC to provide browsing throughout the whole network?

A Although Microsoft Windows Networking does not support browsing across subnets in a workgroup, Samba does. You do not need to replace your main Samba server. You can simply configure it as a domain master browser, switch on remote browse sync, and make sure that your Samba servers in the remote subnets are local master browsers.

Q We can browse servers in remote subnets in our network, but whenever anyone tries to browse the services provided on a server, they get an error message such as "Network name not found," and it does not work. How can we fix this?

A This is usually caused because you do not have WINS set up correctly in the clients in the remote network. Browse lists provide only the NetBIOS names of servers and domains. Translating a NetBIOS name to an IP address in a routed network requires the use of WINS (or an lmhosts file, but WINS is better). In cases where you have clients that do not understand WINS, you need to set up a Samba server on the local subnet as a WINS proxy.

20

HOUR 21

Windows 9x Domain Control

"No, sir. I'm sorry, sir.…I understand, sir. I know that your bookmarks in Netscape are important. It's just that they were stored on your PC's local hard disk and when it crashed…well sir, there's just nothing I can do about it." I hear a loud click as the other participant in this conversation slams down the phone in disgust.

"There has to be a better way," I sigh. "The best thing to do would be to store his Netscape profile directory on a network drive. That way it would get caught in the nightly backups. No need to save the cache files, though. I could turn caching off…or I could set the cache directory to be on the local disk. In fact, after the preference files were on a network drive, I could change settings and fix problems as needed without walking down to an office somewhere or explain what to do over the phone!"

"I like it," I say with a half grin. It's one of those grins of satisfaction. "Hmmm…but how can I guarantee that the user's home directory will be mounted and that it will be at the right drive letter?" I wonder. "If only I could make sure that everyone was mounting the same shares when they logged in."

Does this sound familiar? If you have managed PCs on any type of network before, you have probably heard all the stories and complaints. In this hour I want to show you how to set up Samba as a domain controller (DC) for Windows 9x clients to help solve some of these problems. The same type of setup also works for Windows for Workgroups and the MS-DOS client, but I will not focus on those.

I hope that after this hour, you will have learned some mechanisms that will make your life a little easier. I know some of these things have really helped me.

Domains Versus Workgroups

Do you remember when I talked about domains and workgroups in Hour 2, "Windows Networking"? I hope that by now, the two concepts make more sense to you if you were not already familiar with them. Let's look at the two figures again (Figures 21.1 and 21.2).

FIGURE 21.1

A sample workgroup.

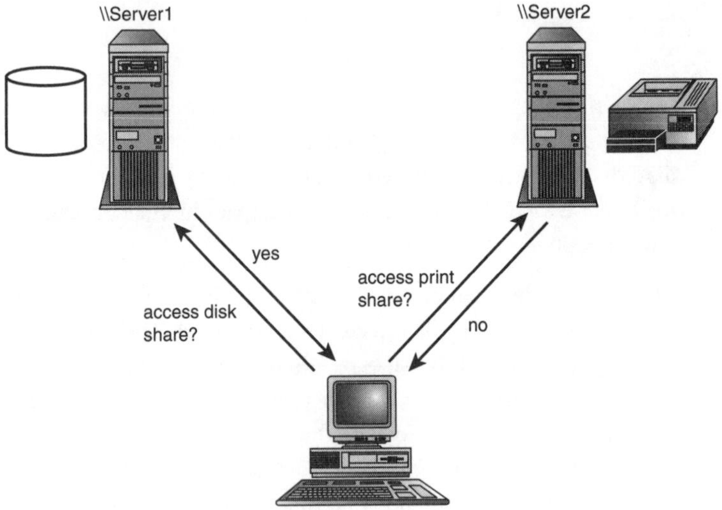

FIGURE 21.2

A sample domain.

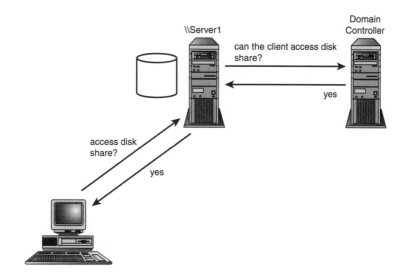

As you look at Figures 21.1 and 21.2, think about the concept of logging in to the network. At this point, *the network* is some vague idea such as when someone says, "Well, you know what they say." Who are *they*? No one really knows.

The difference between logging in to the network in a workgroup environment and logging in to a domain environment is that in a domain, the login is really validated! In a workgroup, the local machine simply caches the user information to transmit to other servers on an actual connection. Now if you refer back to Figure 21.2, you will notice that the same DC that validated the login is validating every connection to a share served by another domain member. This realization brings us to my new illustrations of workgroups and domains in Figure 21.3 and 21.4, respectively.

How does this help us? First, if the user enters an incorrect password or username at login in a workgroup, the Windows 9x system simply accepts it without giving any feedback. Of course without connecting to a server, it is impossible for the local system to return any feedback.

Let me backpedal for a moment. Windows 9x can validate the username and password against a local password cache file. These are found in the \windows directory and have the extension *.pwl. In my opinion, these are evil. Perhaps not so evil that they would cause the world to end, but nonetheless. They use weak encryption algorithms and are sufficiently easy to crack. They, therefore, represent a hole in my sacred network security model and must be dealt with accordingly.

21

FIGURE 21.3

Logging in to the network in a workgroup environment.

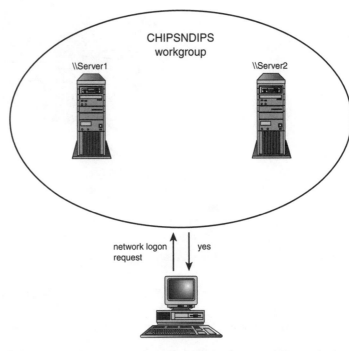

FIGURE 21.4

Logging in to the network in a domain environment.

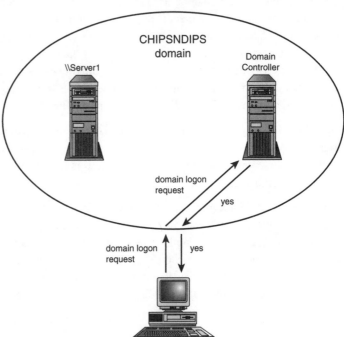

Okay. Maybe I've had too much coffee today, but here's the scoop. Password cache files are easy to crack. They are also an annoyance. If you change your password on the DC, you also have to change your password on the local Windows machine. The main use for a password cache file is to collect all the passwords a user needs for accessing servers in a workgroup. That way if you log in to the system using `pass1` and connect to `\\server-a` using `pass2`, Windows first attempts to connect to the server using `pass1` and then `pass2`, which was cached in your associated `*.pwl` file. Windows unlocks your password cache file by using your login password as a key so that the system uses any passwords found in the file. In a domain environment, a user needs only one password, so the original rationalization for password cache files is gone. Also, if someone could steal and crack one of these `*.pwl` files that contain a domain password, the intruder would have access to every server that grants the right to log in to that account across the network.

For these reasons, I will assume that password caching has been turned off. You can do this by using the Policy Editor, which I'll talk about briefly at the end of the hour, or you can simply delete all the `*.pwl` files in your `\windows` directory, add the following setting to the local system Registry, and then reboot:

```
[HKLM\SOFTWARE\Microsoft\Windows\CurrentVersion\Policies\Network]
"DisablePwdCaching"=dword:00000001
```

> Editing the Registry can render your system unusable. Proceed with extreme caution when using the Registry Editor (`regedit.exe`).

With password caching disabled, I can stand by my original statement with confidence: No validation occurs when logging in to a workgroup until the first SMB connection to a server occurs.

Now I will return to my original point. When a user logs in to a workgroup, the local system can provide no feedback as to the validity of the username/password pair. When a user logs in to a domain, however, the username and proof of identity are sent to the domain controller, which sends a response either accepting or rejecting the login.

So how does this help you? In some sense it is more helpful to the user. Suppose that a user possesses a login name of `beckett`. Now suppose that she logs in to the workgroup but mistypes her username, entering `beclett` instead. Anytime that the user attempts to connect to a network resource during this login session, the local sessions send `beclett` as the session setup username. This would most likely result in phone calls to your help desk complaining that "The network didn't like my password, but I know I'm typing it in correctly." However, if the same scenario occurs in a domain setting, the DC would complain about a bad username/password pair so that the local system could bring this to the user's attention.

That's enough of the theoretical and philosophical explanation of domain control. Let's look at how to implement it and what kinds of tricks and toys I play with.

Setting Up the Samba Domain Controller

The first requirement for configuring Samba as a domain controller is that the server be in user-level security. `security = server` works as well because Samba advertises that it is in user-mode security.

```
security = user
```

That's how it is. Samba cannot be in share-mode security and act as a domain controller.

Next you should make sure that Samba is the master browser for the domain. Remember in Hour 2, when I talked about the NetBIOS resource bytes that were associated with names. A domain controller, whether it is a Windows NT PDC or a Samba box, must be able to register the *domainname*<1b> NetBIOS name successfully. The <1b> resource type indicates the master browser for a domain and is how Windows clients locate the domain's login server. This should be clear from Hours 19, "Local Subnet Browsing," and 20, "Routed Networks and Browsing." For now, the easiest way to configure this is to add the following parameters to your `smb.conf` file:

```
os level = 64
domain master = yes
local master = yes
preferred master = yes
```

The third requirement is that you tell Samba that the server should act as a domain controller by setting the `domain logons` parameter:

```
domain logons = yes
```

Finally, you need to create a share in `smb.conf` named `[netlogon]`. All Windows 9x clients that attempt to log in to a domain connect to this service. The `[netlogon]` share does not necessarily contain any data at all, only that it exists and that users can initiate a successful connection to it. Here is a simple example that you will use:

```
[netlogon]
    path = /export/smb/netlogon
    writeable = no
    public = no
```

I will mention one item here that is optional but one that I have come to depend on greatly. With domain control comes the capability to specify a batch file that is run when a user logs in successfully to the domain. This batch file should be located somewhere in the [netlogon] share and is specified by the logon script parameter in smb.conf. The filename itself can contain any of the standard smb.conf macros, but parameters passed to the batch file cannot. For example, the following setting works exactly as you'd think it would:

```
logon script = %U.bat
```

The login script for a connection is set to a *username*.bat, where *username* is obtained from the session setup information.

If user beckett logs in successfully, the file that the Windows client attempts to run would be

```
\\server\netlogon\beckett.bat
```

However, if you want to pass the current username to the batch file as a parameter, the following would not work. The batch file would actually get %U as a single command line argument:

```
logon script = logon.bat %U
```

For this example, you will use a single batch file for all users. The script performs only one command that mounts the user's home directory. Add the following entry to smb.conf:

```
logon script = logon.bat
```

Now create a text file in \\server\netlogon named logon.bat. Also make sure that the batch file uses DOS-formatted text with a CR and LF character at the end of each line. You can create the file either with the Notepad editor that is shipped with Windows or with vi and appending a Ctrl-V + Ctrl-M sequence to each line. Here is the logon.bat file you will use for these examples:

```
echo Mapping home directory...
net use h: \\picante\homes
```

For completeness, Listing 21.1 shows the entire smb.conf file you have set up for your server. You will notice that you are using plain-text passwords, but Samba's domain control capabilities also works with encrypted passwords. With either method, make sure that you have set up the user accounts correctly. Verify that if you are using plain-text passwords, you have enabled this capability on Windows 98 clients and the necessary Windows 95 clients (see Hour 12, "Case Study: Replacing an NT File and Print Server").

21

LISTING 21.1   SAMBA CONFIGURATION FILE FOR A SIMPLE WINDOWS 9X DOMAIN CONTROLLER

```
;
;         Thu Jan 23 11:00:27 CST 1999
;         jerry carter
;
;         Sams Teach Yourself Samba in 24 Hours
;
;         smb.conf for Windows 9x domain controller

[global]
          netbios name = picante
          workgroup = CHIPSNDIPS
          security = user
          password level = 4
          domain logons = yes
          logon script = logon.bat

          os level = 64
          domain master = yes
          local master = yes
          preferred master = yes

          browseable = yes
          writeable = yes
          locking = no
          case sensitive = no
          default case = lower
          preserve case = yes
          short preserve case = no

[netlogon]
          comment = NETLOGON service
          path = /export/smb/netlogon
          locking = no
          public = no
          writeable = no

[homes]
          comment = Home directories for CHIPSNDIPS domain users
          path = %H
          create mode = 0600
          directory mode = 0700
          browseable = no
          valid users = %S
```

Setting Up a Windows 9x Client

Now that you have configured and started the Samba server, the next step is to configure the Windows client to log in to the domain. Assuming you have already configured the Windows box to access SMB servers, relatively few steps are necessary. Depending on your network topology, there can be as few as one!

Figure 21.5 displays the Client for Microsoft Networks Properties window. To access this, open the Network control panel, highlight the Client for Microsoft Networks entry, and select the Properties button. Select the Log on to Windows NT Domain checkbox in the Logon Validation section and enter the name of the domain you want to use. After you have finished this, you can click OK buttons until you have backed out of the Network control panel. At this point, Windows might want to copy some files from the Windows 95 install CD (why the system needs to copy files when the client was already installed makes no sense to me, but…). After this, you need to reboot the system for the change to take effect.

FIGURE 21.5

Configuring a Windows 95 OSR2 client to log in to the CHIPSNDIPS domain.

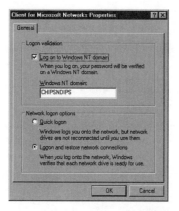

Testing and Troubleshooting

After the PC reboots, you should see the familiar login box except that this time it contains an extra field with the domain name (see Figure 21.6) specified in Figure 21.5.

FIGURE 21.6

Windows network login box containing the domain (CHIPSNDIPS) to validate against.

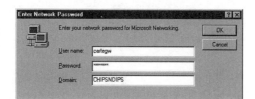

21

No Domain Server Was Available to Validate Your Password...

You might see two common error messages when attempting to log in to the domain. Figure 21.7 shows the first one. This message is Windows's way of telling you, "I asked around to see whether anyone would try to validate this username and password for me but nobody responded one way or the other."

FIGURE 21.7

Windows error message when the client can't locate the owner of the NetBIOS name DOMAINNAME<1b>. *The value of* DOMAINNAME *in this example was* CHIPSNDIPS.

The happened because Windows couldn't locate the owner of the CHIPSNDIPS<1b> NetBIOS name or it was able to resolve the name to an IP address but never received a response either way from the server.

Why would the client be unable to locate the domain server? Remember when I said that depending on your network topology, some configuration steps could be skipped? If your Samba domain controller and your Windows client are on different subnets, the client isn't able to resolve the CHIPSNDIPS<1b> name using the normal broadcast methods because IP broadcast packets are not normally forwarded by routers. In order to locate the domain controller, the Windows client will need to contact a WINS (Windows Internet Name Service) server where the domain controller has registered its names. I would recommend testing your domain controller using a client on the same logical subnet first, but if you must test across routers, you should refer to Hour 18, "Resolving NetBIOS Names Without Using Broadcasts," to see how to administer WINS.

Another possible explanation to the current difficulties is that the Samba domain controller could not register the CHIPSNDIPS<1b> name successfully. You can verify this problem in the nmbd debug log file (that is, /usr/local/samba/var/log.nmb). If Samba could successfully register the name, you would see entries such as these:

```
1999/01/23 10:06:46, 0] nmbd/nmbd_become_dmb.c:become_domain_master_
➡stage2(118)
  *****

Samba server PICANTE is now a domain master browser for workgroup
```

```
    CHIPSNDIPS on subnet 192.168.1.74

    *****
    [1999/01/23 10:07:01, 0] nmbd/nmbd_become_lmb.c:become_local_master_
➡stage2(406)
    *****

    Samba name server PICANTE is now a local master browser for workgroup
    CHIPSNDIPS on subnet 192.168.1.74

    *****
```

I went into this more in Hours 19 and 20, but the fundamental difference between a domain master browser (DMB) and a local master browser (LMB) is you can have only one DMB per domain. However, you should have an LMB for each subnet. Obviously, the DMB should also be the LMB for its logical subnet.

If you want to locate the DMB for a given domain, use the nmblookup tool to resolve the *DOMAINNAME*<1b> name:

```
# nmblookup CHIPSNDIPS#1b
Sending queries to 192.168.1.255
192.168.1.74 CHIPSNDIPS<1b>
```

The output should display the IP address of the Samba domain controller. If not, you should double-check your smb.conf and verify that the os level, domain master, local master, and preferred master parameters are configured as I mentioned before. Also verify that the nmbd daemon is actually running.

The Domain Password You Supplied Was Incorrect...

The second common problem when attempting to log in to a domain is that the server was located but said "Nope!" (see Figure 21.8). There are two main possibilities other than simply mistyping the username or password.

FIGURE 21.8

The domain controller refused to validate your password.

The first is that the server refused the session setup. I have already talked about a few things that could cause this in Hour 4, "Installing and Testing the Configuration." But to refresh your memory, this can occur if the client's IP address was not included in the hosts allow value in smb.conf or was listed in the hosts deny line.

21

Another possibility is that the server is set up to use plain-text passwords but the client will not downgrade to clear text. You should follow the two solutions listed in previous hours:

- Set up the Samba server to encrypted passwords using the steps outlined in Hour 6, "Security Levels and Passwords."

- Enable the Windows 9x client to use plain-text passwords as described in Hour 14, "Windows 9x and Windows NT."

Successfully Logging In to the Domain

If you can successfully log in to the domain, you should see the login script execute in a DOS window as shown in Figure 21.9. The beauty about this is that, with a few small exceptions, the Windows 9x client cannot tell the difference between a Samba-controlled domain and a Windows NT–controlled domain. Therefore, most likely your users will not be able to tell the difference either!

FIGURE 21.9

The Windows NT login script is executed on a successful login.

One advantage of using a login script over using the Windows persistent connection setting to initiate drive connections is that you can make changes to the login script without even sitting at the client machine. You can reassign network connections and even run OS and application patches in the login script. Cool! That's what I like.

Extra Stuff

What you have seen so far is fairly nice. You can make sure that users enter the correct information when they log in, you can be assured that each user has at least some required network drive connections, and you can execute other things on login. What else can you do?

I said before that the beauty of this setup was that the Windows client, for the most part, did not know that it wasn't a Windows NT Server acting as the domain controller. The subjects I want to look at next are not specific to using Samba as a domain controller.

Rather they are part of the Windows 9x network model. Regardless of whether you like the model or not, you have to use the tools you are given to do the best job you can.

Profiles

A user's profile is similar to the collection of dot (.) files that UNIX uses to control login, logout, and application behavior. If your background is rooted more in Windows terminology, you can think of it as a collection of user specific *.ini files and program groups. The bottom line is that profiles allow a user to customize his or her environment without permanently attaching it to an individual machine.

The Windows Registry 101

Consider this section as enough background to put us on the same page. If you're already familiar with the system Registry, bear with me for a few moments.

The Windows Registry is a database composed of two binary files, system.dat and user.dat. The system.dat file is always located in the \windows directory (or whatever directory you used to install Windows). The user.dat file is normally located there as well. However, in the case of roaming profiles, it will be downloaded from somewhere specific to the user.

The two files combine for a treelike structure with six main roots. Figure 21.10 shows the system Registry as displayed by the Windows 95 Registry Editor. I will concern myself with only two of them: HKEY_LOCAL_MACHINE (HKLM) and HKEY_CURRENT_USER (HKCU).

FIGURE 21.10

The system Registry as displayed by the Windows 95 Registry Editor (regedit.exe).

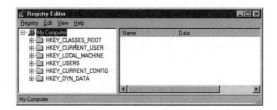

| NEW TERM | The HKLM *hive* (each of the six roots is called a hive) is supposed to contain only information that is local to the machine. This is not always the case, because applications do not always use the Registry they should.

The HKCU hive)contains information related to the currently logged user. Some examples of settings that are stored in the HKCU hive include wallpaper and screensaver settings, recently used file lists for applications, and other user-specific file locations. The local machine can be set to use the same user information for anyone who logs in, or it can keep track of information for each user. The former circumstance is the default

21

behavior for Windows. In this case the HKCU hive is the same as the HKEY_USERS (HKU) hive. You can enable individual profiles with the User Profiles tab of the Passwords Properties control panel (see Figure 21.11).

FIGURE 21.11

Enabling user profiles under Windows 95.

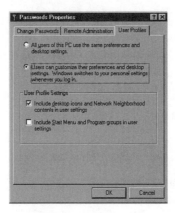

What Else Can Be in a User Profile?

Being able to maintain individual settings in the Registry alone can be very useful, but Windows also allows you to associate the Start Menu and Desktop icons with a user profile.

You can configure individual user profiles in two ways. The first method allows only a single machine to use the user profile that is stored locally. The second method allows the profile to follow the user on the network so that any machine that the user logs in to has access to the profile. The latter is referred to as a roving or roaming user profile.

If the Windows client with user profiles enabled is configured to log in to a domain, the local system automatically attempts to store the profile on the user's home directory. The profile is then cached from the network to the local disk and then back at login and logout respectively. Figure 21.12 shows an example of this.

When using Samba as the domain controller, the location where Windows stores the roaming profile on the network is set by the logon path parameter in smb.conf. The default value for this is a subdirectory in the user's home directory named profile. Many people on the Samba mailing lists have reported that it is a better idea to store the profiles on a separate share. For example, first define a share named [profile]:

```
[profile]
    comment = Windows user profiles
    path = /export/profile
    create mode = 0600
```

```
directory mode = 0770
browseable = yes
writeable = yes
```

Then set the `logon path` parameter to

```
logon path = \\servername\profile\%U
```

FIGURE 21.12

The process of storing profile information in the user's home directory.

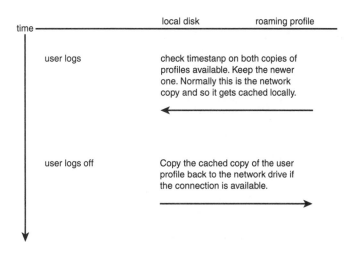

You can find more information about roaming profiles in the Windows 95 Resource Kit, which is available in Windows help format on the Windows 95 installation CD in the `\admin\reskit` directory.

Making Profiles Work for You

I need to give some justification for my explanation of user profiles. How can they really make my job easier instead of worse? Here is one example that I use to manage the Windows 95 student labs that I maintain at work.

Suppose you have a particular shortcut that you need to place on everyone's desktop (or the Start menu for that matter). What are your options?

- You can send out instructions for creating the shortcut. (This is bad.)
- You can go to every machine and add the link manually. (Also bad.)
- You can use the login script to copy the shortcut. (This is okay.)
- You can set a `preexec` script on the user's home directory that copies the necessary files to the user's roaming profile. (This is even better.)

21

Although the third option would work, I favor the last one because I prefer to script in Perl or a shell language as opposed to using batch files. In addition, you can pass smb.conf variables to preexec or postexec scripts and have the variables interpreted correctly.

Let me set the stage. You have defined the logon path as

```
logon path = \\%N\profile\%U
```

You have configured the follow settings for the [profile] service:

```
[profile]
    comment = Windows user profiles
    path = /export/profile
    preexec = /usr/local/bin/buildprofile %U
    create mode = 0600
     directory mode = 0700
     broweseable = yes
```

Now here is the buildprofile script:

```
#!/bin/sh

user=$1
umask 077
if [ !-f /export/profile/$user/desktop/somelink.lnk ]; then
    cp -p /usr/local/samba/lib/somelink.lnk /export/profile/$user/desktop/
fi
```

In this script, somelink.lnk is the name of the shortcut file that you want to distribute to each user's desktop. When Windows connects to the [profile] service to access the user's profile, smbd executes the preexec script that copies the necessary shortcut. You can perform all sorts of elaborate tricks with this type of configuration. Be creative!

Policies

System policies are closely linked to the Windows 95 Registry. The relationship can be explained like this: Policies define what should be allowed and what should be restricted. The Windows Registry contains the current policy settings in the form of Registry keys.

In the beginning of the hour, I used a Registry setting to disable password caching. This is an example of a policy. It is the operating system's responsibility to enforce the policy settings recorded in the Registry.

Just as Windows provides a Registry editor, regedit.exe, it also provides a policy editor named poledit.exe, which is displayed in Figure 21.13. Discussing every detail of policy files and templates is beyond the scope of this book. Rather I will focus on how to configure Windows clients to download the policy files from a server and some possibilities that can be done with system policies.

FIGURE 21.13

*The Windows 95
System Policy Editor.*

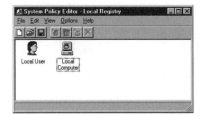

The System Policy Editor can be loaded from the Windows 95 installation CD.
Instructions for installing the tool are located in `\admin\apptools\poledit` in a file
named `poledit.txt`.

The Policy Editor allows you to create a file that can be merged with the local system
Registry during login. You can tell Windows to download the policy file automatically:

`\\server\netlogon\config.pol`

Here, *server* is the NetBIOS name of the domain controller that authenticated the login
by setting the following Registry key:

```
[HKLM\System\CurrentControlSet\control\Update]
"UpdateMode"=dword:00000001
```

Remember the standard warning about using the Registry editor. Alternatively, you can
install the Policy Editor to the local machine and open the Registry. When open, you can
set the update mode as shown in Figure 21.14.

FIGURE 21.14

*Setting the Policy
Update Mode by using
the System Policy
Editor.*

21

Now that you have been exposed to the Policy Editor, Figure 21.15 illustrates the process
of logging in to the network and when the policy file is downloaded if at all.

FIGURE 21.15

Chronological look at logging in to the network.

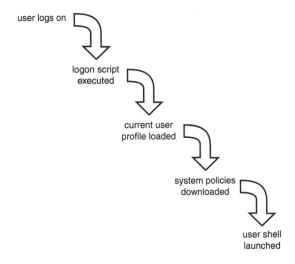

To create a policy file (for example, `config.pol`), start the Policy Editor and choose `New File` from the `File` menu. You can define settings such as

- Restricting access to portions of the control panel
- Removing items from the Start menu and the Desktop such as the Network Neighborhood
- Requiring the client to validate the user login before granting access to the Desktop
- Disabling file and printer sharing

Experiment with the settings available. You can find out more information about system policies in the Windows 95 and Windows 98 Resource Kits. See the Windows installation CD for the available documentation.

When you have created your policy file, save the settings in a file named `config.pol` in the `[netlogon]` share on the DC. Also make sure that you have disabled locking on this service. You might explicitly want to add the following to the service's definition in `smb.conf`:

```
locking = no
```

One last word about policies. Although they do provide a great deal of control, there is no mechanism native to Windows 9x that prevents a local user from changing policy settings in the Registry. You've been warned.

Summary

Samba's domain control capabilities for Windows 95 and Windows 98 clients provide a means to validate network logins and not just resource connections. The four requirements for a Samba DC are

- The server must be in user level security.
- The DC must be configured as the domain master browser for the domain.
- Domain logins must be enabled (that is, `domain logons = yes`) in the `smb.conf` file.
- A share named `[netlogon]` has been correctly configured in `smb.conf` and is accessible to users.

Beyond standard domain logins and login scripts, Samba also supports Windows 9x capabilities to download system policies and store user profiles on network drives.

Q&A

Q I have successfully set up Samba as a domain controller and use login scripts. However, when a user logs in, the batch file runs correctly, but the Window NT Logon Script window hangs there and eventually the user presses the Cancel button. What am I doing wrong?

A You're doing nothing wrong. This little annoyance is caused by the batch file signaling its end of execution by creating a file named `LMSCRIPT.$$$` in the current working directory. The Windows NT logon script window should then clean things up. The problem occurs when the batch file cannot create the `LMSCRIPT.$$$` file. Therefore the NT logon script window never knows that the batch file has completed. Probably you have changed to a drive and directory that the user does not have write permission in. To remedy this, add a line to the end of the script that changes back to the user's local hard disk (for example, `c:`).

21

Hour **22**

Experimental PDC Support

Let me begin this hour by saying that this is a small glimpse of the future. Samba can minimally act as a Primary Domain Controller (PDC) by performing domain logins for Windows NT clients. However, this functionality is currently incomplete and not officially supported. So if you are a little shy of development code (also called *prealpha test code*), beware!

If the support is not official, why do I mention it here? Because it is so cool!

This is so important that I will say it again. There is no currently distributed version of Samba (this includes version 2.0) containing PDC functionality for Windows NT Domains that is *officially* supported. Unofficial support comes in the form of a mailing list (samba-ntdom@samba.org) devoted to debugging and testing the code.

The capability to run a PDC on your UNIX server opens up tremendous possibilities that would not exist otherwise. For example, managing user accounts becomes easier when the information is readily accessible on one machine (or at least the means to do so is known). Another advantage is that you can leverage the same hardware for other UNIX services. Given a sufficiently large server, there is no reason that your Samba PDC could not function as a NIS master as well. Without this, it would be necessary to purchase, install, and maintain a completely different machine with a potentially completely different architecture (consider the case of Sparc versus Intel platforms). In addition, who really wants another server OS to support? Here, it becomes an issue of simply having the people power to correctly administer all the services provided by your network support organization.

For the remainder of this hour, you will examine what Windows NT PDC functions have been implemented in Samba and how to configure it. As in Hour 21, "Windows 9x Domain Control," you will also briefly look at system policies and user profiles. Finally you will explore how this support will be affected by the imminent release of Windows NT 5.0, officially known now as Windows 2000.

What Has Been Implemented and What Has Not

Windows NT domain control and Windows 9x domain control use different mechanisms. As you saw in Hour 21, the Windows 9x domain control is stable and fully supported. The mechanisms to implement Windows NT domain control have only been partially completed and the support is still under development.

So what is different about a Windows NT domain? Well, for starters, the NT domain control protocol is entirely undocumented at this time. The function to implement this in Samba has been done by staring at bits and packets transmitted across a network between domain members and domain controllers. No small feat! Another issue is the amount of functionality that must be supported to simply log in to the domain. If you remember in

Hour 12, "Case Study: Replacing an NT File and Print Server," I said that when you support part of the functionality, Windows NT expects you to support all of it. This becomes strikingly apparent when attempting to implement domain control and the associated administrative tools such as the User Manager for Domains and the Server Manager for Domains.

22

If this is such a large, monstrous project, you are probably asking yourself, "How much of it has been done?" and "How much is left to do?" Because this part of Samba is under active development (very active at the moment), the best place to find information on the current status of support is the on-line NT Domain FAQ. The table of contents page for this can be located under the Documentation link on the Samba home page.

NEW TERM Because the Samba code is such a moving target and there really are no milestones such as a distributed release, it can be hard to convey exactly what version of the development code that I am using other than the date I last downloaded the source files. You will hear people refer to the current development code (also called the HEAD branch), using a prealpha version number. For example, the latest HEAD branch code reports itself as 2.1.0-prealpha when displaying the %v smb.conf variable.

Here is a list of currently or partially implemented features:

- The capability to act as a PDC for Windows NT 3.51 and 4.0 clients.
- The capability to view domain account information stored in the smbpasswd file using the Windows NT 4.0 User Manager for Domains.
- Allowance for the viewing of Samba shares via the Windows NT 4.0 Server Manager for Domains.
- Placement of Windows 9x clients in user-level security. However, the clients are unable to browse a list of domain accounts in order to specify permissions on file and printer shares.
- Windows NT domain members that can change their machine account password periodically. I'll discuss machine trust accounts later.
- The ability for users to change their password recorded in the smbpasswd file while logged into a Windows NT client by using the Ctrl+Alt+Del key sequence and then selecting Change Password.
- The capability to map Windows NT groups and usernames to UNIX equivalents. For example, you can specify that all members of the UNIX wheel group should be members of the Windows NT group Domain Admins.
- Support for including domain users and groups in NTFS ACLs.

That is a fairly long list! Well, here are the things that are not implemented yet and hence missing from the previous items:

- The capability for a Samba PDC to participate in a trust relationship with another PDC, Samba, or Windows NT.

- The capability to replicate the systems account database with a Backup Domain Controller (BDC). This refers to the protocol that a Windows NT PDC uses to send updated user information to a Windows NT BDC.

- Support for true Windows NT–style printing. Currently Samba tricks Windows NT clients into "thunking" down to a lower version of the SMB protocol (for example, LanMan rather than NTLM). Please refer to Hour 2, "Windows Networking," for a refresher on SMB protocol levels.

- The capability to implement Windows NT ACLs on Samba shares rather than the standard UNIX permission bits.

Although the list of things that have been implemented is longer than the one of those items that have not yet been implemented, the NT domain support will continually evolve. Official PDC functionality is tentatively scheduled to be included in version 2.1.

How Do I Get It?

So you have decided to try things out. Okay, the next step is to download the latest HEAD branch source code. The best way to obtain the source code for the HEAD Samba branch is to use CVS, which stands for Concurrent Versions System. CVS enables the Samba developers to check out source much in the same way that you would check out a book from the library. The difference is that a developer checks out a copy of the code. This is different from revision control software, such as SCCS, that enables only one person to modify the code at a time.

When a developer modifies the copy of the source tree, those changes must be committed to the main branch. CVS merges the changes that are being committed with any other changes that others have added since the source code was last checked out. This is very similar to what a diff script or the UNIX patch utility does.

Samba's development source code is available via anonymous CVS for those who do not have write access to the source tree; that is, everyone who is not a member of the Samba Team. In order to obtain use anonymous CVS access, you first need to download and install a copy of the CVS client.

You can find out more information about CVS by navigating your Web browser to http://www.cyclic.com/. The source code for the CVS client is available from ftp://download.cyclic.com/pub/.

22

The CVS client source supports the GNU autoconf tests as Samba 2.0 does, so compilation and installation are straightforward. When the client is installed, you can download the HEAD branch source code by first logging into the Samba CVS server:

```
cvs -d :pserver:cvs@cvs.samba.org:/cvsroot login
```

You should do this in the directory to which you want the source tree to be downloaded. When you are prompted for a password, enter **cvs**.

The next command creates a subdirectory named ./samba and checks out a copy of the HEAD branch source tree:

```
cvs -d :pserver:cvs@cvs.samba.org:/cvsroot co samba
```

When the CVS client source code has completed downloading the source tree, you can compile Samba using the same methods used for version 2.0 (see Hour 3, "Obtaining the Latest Source"). Sorry, but for obvious reasons, there are no binary distributions of this. Because this is development code, the compile process might not be as clean and error free as when you are compiling a distributed, stable version of Samba. By this, I mean that you might see more warning messages or you might experience problems compiling for your platform. Make sure that you report any problems via email to samba-bugs@samba.org. Also join the samba-ntdom@samba.org mailing list to watch for updates, fixes, and changes.

After you have executed configure and make, run make install to create the installation directory and copy the binaries. If you have installed Samba before on your server, you should make a backup of the /usr/local/samba/ directory prior to installing the new version. You should be especially careful of any files located in the /usr/local/samba/private/ directory from this point forward.

How to Configure a Samba PDC for a Windows NT Domain

If you have any background knowledge of administering a normal Windows NT Primary Domain Controller, you find that this step is very similar. The first thing to do is to configure a working smb.conf file. You need to configure the server to be in user-level security and you must enable password encryption. There is no way around either of these settings:

```
security = user
encrypt passwords = yes
```

Assume that you have configured only the following share. This gives you something to test as you progress:

```
[homes]
    comment =  user home directories
    path = %H
    valid users = %S
    create mode = 0600
    directory mode = 0700
    locking = no
```

In addition to these settings, I am choosing the server's NetBIOS name to be BURRITO and the workgroup will again be CHIPSNDIPS:

```
[global]
netbios name = BURRITO
workgroup = CHIPSNDIPS
```

Now, start the Samba processes. The first time that Samba runs as a domain controller, it searches for a file named *DOMAINNAME*.SID in the same directory as the smbpasswd file. *DOMAINNAME* should be whatever the name of your workgroup is set to in smb.conf. For this example, the file would be /usr/local/samba/private/CHIPSNDIPS.SID. If the file does not exist, smbd generates a random domain sid and saves it to this file; otherwise, it reads the contents of the file and uses whatever value is stored there. Remember that a sid is how Windows NT identifies machines and, in this case, a domain.

> Make sure you do not change the sid file created by smbd. If you do, all machines that are currently members of the domain will not be able to log in and must be readded to the domain.

At this point, it might be a good idea to create a user account to be the test case for logging in to the domain and connecting to shares. Use the username speedy. After creating the UNIX account in /etc/passwd using whatever means you need with your OS (Slackware Linux has a command named adduser that works well enough), you need to create an account for the user in Samba's smbpasswd file by running

```
root# /usr/local/samba/bin/smbpasswd -a speedy
New SMB password: enter password
```

```
Retype new SMB password: enter password
Added user speedy.
Password changed for user speedy
```

Using the current development code, Samba must be running on the server and the smbpassword tool must be able to resolve the primary NetBIOS name specified in the local smb.conf file. If Samba is not running you might see an error message such as

```
root# /usr/local/samba/bin/smbpasswd -a speedy
error connecting to 192.168.1.74:139 (Connection refused)
cli_establish_connection: failed to connect to BURRITO<00> (192.168.1.74)
error connecting to 192.168.1.74:139 (Connection refused)
cli_establish_connection: failed to connect to BURRITO<00> (192.168.1.74)
cli_connect_serverlist: Domain password server not available.
get_member_domain_sid: unable to initialise client connection.
Can't setup password database vectors.
```

If smbpasswd cannot resolve the server's NetBIOS name, the following error message is displayed:

```
root# /usr/local/samba/bin/smbpasswd -a speedy
cli_connect_serverlist: Can't resolve address for PICANTE
cli_connect_serverlist: Domain password server not available.
get_member_domain_sid: unable to initialise client connection.
Can't setup password database vectors.
```

When you meet these two requirements, however, you should be greeted with a message indicating that the user was successfully added. Now using smbclient and the test account that you created, make sure that everything is okay so far. Attempt to connect to the user's home directory:

```
root# /usr/local/samba/bin/smbclient //burrito/speedy -U speedy
Added interface ip=192.168.1.74 bcast=192.168.1.255 nmask=255.255.255.0
Password:
Domain=[CHIPSNDIPS] OS=[Unix] Server=[Samba 2.1.0-prealpha]
smb: \>
```

This step gives some confidence that things are working as they should. Next, configure Samba to perform domain logins as you did for a Windows 9x domain controller. In addition to enabling the domain logons parameter, make sure you remember to config-ure the [netlogon] share as well. Here are the relevant entries to add to smb.conf:

```
[global]
    ; previous entries go here...
      domain logons = yes

[netlogon]
        comment = NETLOGON service
        path = /export/smb/netlogon
```

```
            locking = no
            public = no
            writeable = no
```

Although it is not necessary, also specify a login script to be run for users. Setting this option is done as you did in Hour 21:

```
logon script = logon.bat
```

The batch file simply displays a message of the day as an example. As you will soon see, there is an alternative way to mount a user's home directory, so I will not do that in the login script this time. Here is my sample batch file:

```
@echo off
echo ******************************************************
echo *         Welcome to Samba controlled NT domain      *
echo *         Sams Teach Yourself Samba in 24 Hours       *
echo *                  Sams Publishing                    *
echo ******************************************************
pause
```

Now that you have configured the domain controller, add an NT client to the domain.

Adding the Clients

The domain control support for Windows NT clients has been tested for Windows NT 3.51 (Service Pack 5) and Windows NT 4.0 (Service Pack 4). It is also possible to add another Samba server as a domain member. Think of the possibilities!

Adding any type of client to a Windows NT domain follows the same steps:

1. Creating a computer account (also called a machine trust account) on the domain controller for the client.

2. Getting the client to join the domain.

3. Rebooting the client (unless of course, this is a Samba server using `security = domain`).

I'll talk about these steps on at a time. First I'll answer the question, "What is a workstation trust account?"

Machine Trust Accounts

NEW TERM   A *trust account* is really a user account that is used by the domain member machine. UNIX, as a general rule, does not have such a thing as an account for workstations. The exception to this would be some type of secure information distribution systems such as Sun Microsystems's NIS+.

The rationalization for this is that the machine must log in to the domain before the DC allows user logins from the machine. For this reason, Windows 9x clients, even though they might log in to a domain, are not considered to be true members of the domain. By this I mean that the Windows 9x machine has no trust account and cannot really be trusted by the domain controller to be presenting accurate information. There is no way to ensure that someone is really who he says he is when transmitting the information from a Windows 9x client.

Samba does not currently support the Windows NT method of creating a trust account on the PDC when attempting to join the domain (see Figure 22.1). Therefore, you have to create the account manually on the Samba PDC.

FIGURE 22.1

The dialog box used Windows NT 4.0 to specify an administrative account that will be used to create the trust account when attempting to join the domain.

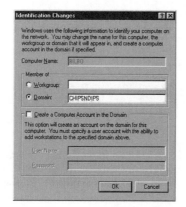

What is the username for a trust account? That's a good question. It turns out to be the machine's NetBIOS name with a $ character appended to the end of it. Therefore if your Windows NT client's name were BILBO, the name used for the trust account would be BILBO$. The initial password of the account is set to the machine's NetBIOS name, this time with no characters added to it, in lowercase letters. So in my pervious example, the initial password for the account BILBO$ would be bilbo. Really secure, huh?

Because each trust account is simply a user account that is used by a machine, each one must also have an associated rid (see Hour 12 if you need a refresher on rid). All user accounts, including trust accounts and groups, exist in the same number space. Therefore, you need some mechanism to ensure that each trust account has a unique rid. How do you do this for users? In the case of users and groups, you generate the rid from the respective uid or gid using a mathematical function.

Why not use the same function to generate a rid for a trust account? Perhaps you see the problem already. Under normal circumstances, a UNIX workstation does not possess a uid. The way to work around this is to create a user account in /etc/passwd using the name of the trust account (BILBO$ in this case). The /etc/passwd entry is simply a placeholder for a uid and not used for authentication. Here is the entry I added to the local password file on my Linux server:

```
bilbo$:*:10000:1000:WinNT trust account:/dev/null:/bin/false
```

You notice that I have disabled the passwd field, set the home directory to point to /dev/null, and specified an invalid shell. Remember that all you need is the real uid for the machine.

Now you can use /usr/local/samba/bin/smbpasswd to create the trust account for the client. The -a switch indicates you are adding an account, and the -m switch tells the smbpasswd tool that the account is a machine trust account:

```
root# /usr/local/samba/bin/smbpasswd -a -m bilbo
Added user bilbo$.
Password changed for user bilbo$
```

This sets the password in the private/smbpasswd file to be the default value for machine accounts, the machine's name in lowercase letters.

> Some versions of UNIX do not support usernames longer than eight charac-
> ters in length. Because a NetBIOS name can be up to 15 characters long, you
> most likely have to deal with this name difference. Make sure you check
> details on your particular system. Although Slackware's adduser utility does-
> n't allow a username longer than eight characters, you can add one to
> /etc/passwd manually.

When a client joins the domain, it changes its trust account password to some random value and sends the new one in an encrypted form to the PDC. The new password isn't used, however, until the machine logs in to the domain again after rebooting.

Joining the Domain (Windows NT 4.0 Client)

If the client machine is another Samba server, use the instructions on joining a domain found in Hour 12. This section examines how to get a Windows NT machine to join a Samba domain. The example uses version 4.0 of the operating system, but the process is very similar for Windows NT 3.51. In fact, the steps are almost identical to joining a domain controlled by a Windows NT PDC.

First you need to open the Network control panel on the Windows NT client and select the Change button on the Identification page. The window shown in Figure 22.1 appears.

After entering the desired domain name and clicking the OK button, you should be greeted by the welcome message shown in Figure 22.2. Simply click the OK button in the message window and then close the Network control panel. Windows NT prompts you to reboot. After the machine has rebooted, you are able to log in to the domain using the test account that you created earlier, speedy.

FIGURE 22.2

Welcome to the CHIP-
SNDIPS domain.

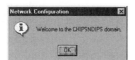

If you receive an error message indicating that the domain controller could not be found, make sure that Samba is running, that the client machine can resolve the name CHIPSNDIPS<1b>, and that the client can actually connect to the server. For example, verify that the machine is not listed in a hosts deny setting on the server.

If the error displayed says that the client could not connect to the domain controller and that you should have the administrator check the client's machine account, make sure that you added the machine account correctly. After all, you are the administrator.

Reboot the NT Client

After rebooting the NT client, you should be able to log in using the valid domain account, speedy. Make sure that you select the CHIPSNDIPS domain rather than the local machine in the domain popup menu. After logging in, press Ctrl+Alt+Del again to bring up the Windows NT Security dialog box. You should notice that the window says you are logged in as CHIPSNDIPS\speedy.

If you receive an error message that says "The CHIPSNDIPS domain is not available" when attempting to log in, make sure that Samba is running and the client machine can resolve the CHIPSNDIPS<1b> name using techniques presented in Hour 11, "Troubleshooting." You might need to use a WINS server depending on your setup. Refer to Hour 18, "Resolving NetBIOS Names Without Using Broadcasts," for a refresher on WINS and why it is needed.

Additional Parameters

Of course there is more to a Windows NT domain than simply logging in. Many security mechanisms are built in to Windows NT that you want to leverage from. For example, an NTFS file system supports access control lists for setting permissions on files, directories, and printers. You need a mechanism for including domain users and domain groups in ACLs on the local disk. Another capability that you examine is supporting roaming user profiles and system policies as you can with Windows 9x.

A basic capability necessary for all these features is mapping UNIX users and groups to ones that Windows NT clients can understand. Let's start with this.

Groups and Users

Figure 22.3 illustrates how Samba maps a Windows NT username to a UNIX username and vice-versa. The general idea is that a username is received in the session setup request first. The username is then filtered through a mapping function, and the resulting username is authenticated against the server's password database. The Windows NT client never knows of the UNIX username and the UNIX machine never knows of the Windows NT username. Samba insulates each operating system from the other.

FIGURE 22.3

Mapping Windows NT users and groups to UNIX users and groups.

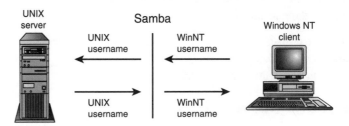

domain group map

Three parameters support this functionality. The first is domain group map. The value it defines is the location to a file that contains mappings between UNIX and NT groups. The groups are treated as domain, or global, groups.

```
domain group map = /usr/local/samba/lib/domain_group.map
```

The syntax of the map file is very simple. Each entry is in the following format:

```
UNIXgroupname = NTgroupname
```

UNIXgroupname is the name of group defined in /etc/group (or network equivalent) on the local system. *NTgroupname* is the name to be displayed on the Windows NT clients. For example, the following entry defines an NT group named Accounting and maps it to the UNIX group named acct:

```
acct = Accounting
```

Here is the output from the command net group /domain:

```
D:\>net group /domain
```

The request will be processed at the primary domain controller for domain
CHIPSNDIPS.

Group Accounts for \\BURRITO

```
-----------------------------------------------------------------
*Accounting          *adm                *bin
*daemon              *disk               *Domain Admins
*Domain Guests       *Domain Users       *dptheads
*floppy              *kmem               *lp
*mail                *man                *mem
*news                *nogroup            *root
*sys                 *tty                *users
*uucp                *webdev             *wheel
*wrks
The command completed successfully.
```

The Accounting group is listed with the other domain groups. Notice that all the UNIX
groups not included in the domain group map files are listed as well. The acct UNIX
group is not listed because it is contained in the map file.

First I create a directory named acct on an NTFS partition, set the ownership to the
Accounting domain group, and grant access to only them. The Windows Explorer
window displays the permissions and ownership shown in Figure 22.4.

FIGURE 22.4

Displaying the permis-
sions on the acct
directory.

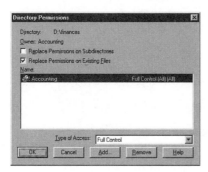

Next I add the user speedy to the acct group in /etc/group. The resulting entry looks
like

```
acct:*:200:daphnie,scooby,velma,speedy
```

If I log in to the NT client and attempt to create a file in D:\finances, because of the
membership in the acct group, I have full control over the directory.

A few global groups always appear: the well-known domain groups such as Domain
Admins, Domain Users, and Domain Guests. In order to configure an account as a

domain administrator, you first need to select an appropriate UNIX group to use in the mapping. I use a group name `ntadmin` and add the account `speedy` to the entry in `/etc/group`:

```
ntadmin:*:16:speedy
```

Now when I view the domain users on the Samba PDC using the User Manager for Domains, I can see that the user `speedy` is a member of both the `Accounting` group and the `Domain Admins` group (see Figure 22.5).

FIGURE 22.5

Displaying the group membership for the user speedy in the User Manager for Domains.

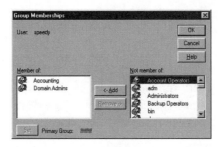

domain user map

The `domain user map` parameter basically works the same way as `domain group map`: It accepts the path to a file as a value. The file contains mapping from UNIX usernames to Windows NT usernames.

```
domain user map = /usr/local/samba/lib/domain_user.map
```

The format of a domain username mapping is

```
UNIXusername = [\\Domainname\\]NTusername
```

UNIXusername is an existing account on the UNIX server; *NTusername* is the name that is mapped. *Domainname* here is optional. If one is not specified, Samba assumes the domain is the value of the `workgroup` parameter. The purpose is to allow Samba to map NT users from other trusted domains. Because trust relationships are not implemented in Samba yet, this is unnecessary for the purposes of this example.

> The `domain user map` is not the same as the `username map`. Do not get them confused. The latter parameter does not relate to Windows NT domains at all.

22

Suppose that you want to create a domain account named `Administrator` that maps to the UNIX `root` account. To accomplish this, you need to perform the following steps:

1. Set the value of the `domain user map` parameter in `smb.conf` as so:

   ```
   domain user map = /usr/local/samba/lib/domain_user.map
   ```

2. Add this entry in `/usr/local/samba/lib/domain_user.map`:

   ```
   root = Administrator
   ```

3. Add an entry for `root` in the `smbpasswd` file if necessary, by executing

   ```
   root# /usr/local/samba/bin/smbpasswd -a root
   New SMB password: enter password
   Retype new SMB password: enter password
   Added user root.
   Password changed for user root
   ```

Now you can log in to the domain from a Windows NT client using the account name `Administrator` and the password you set for `root` in the `smbpasswd` file. The `Administrator` account is also visible in the User Manager for Domains (see Figure 22.6).

FIGURE 22.6

Displaying the available domain user accounts, including `Administrator`, *for the* `CHIPSNDIPS` *domain in the User Manager for Domains.*

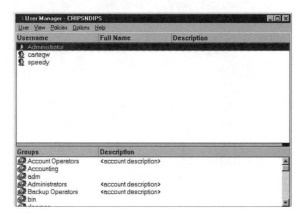

local group map

The third mapping parameter is `local group map`, which enables you to define local groups on the Samba PDC. For this example, it does not come into play much, so I give a cursory glance at it.

First you must specify the location of the file containing the mappings from NT local group names to UNIX group names:

```
local group map = /usr/local/samba/lib/local_group.map
```

The format of the `local group map` file is

UNIXgroupname = [BUILTIN\]*NTgroupname*

Again, the *UNIXgroupname* is the group defined in /etc/group to which the *NTgroupname* is mapped. The BUILTIN\ string should preface all the well-known local group names such as Administrators and Users.

For example, to map the local Administrators group on the Samba PDC to the UNIX group wheel, you need to add an entry in the `local group map` file like this:

wheel=BUILTIN\Administrators

logon home, logon drive, and logon path

Part of a user's account information in a Windows NT domain is the location of and mount point of the user's home directory as well as a location for the roaming user profile (see Figure 22.7). The user's login script is also included with this information. You can associate some of the fields shown in the window with smb.conf parameters.

FIGURE 22.7

*User account informa-
tion as displayed in the
User Manager for
Domains.*

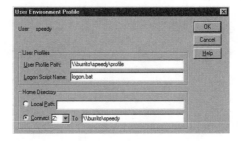

First, examine the settings relating to the user's home directory. The Home Directory section of the window specifies a drive letter to which the network home path should be connected. These are the logon drive and logon home parameters respectively:

logon drive = Z:
logon home = \\%N\%U

These settings, along with those displayed in Figure 22.7, are the default settings for these parameters.

The logon home parameter accepts a path that is mounted as the user's home directory. With Samba, this is easy to do using the [homes] service. If you want, you can also specify things such as

logon home = *server*\users*username*

This assumes that you have defined a share named [users] and that each user has a directory that matches their *username*. *server* is the name of the possibly remote server that provides the [users] share.

The logon drive accepts a drive letter where the Windows NT client mounts the user's home directory. The default is to use Z:. You can specify any letter you want. You should choose a drive letter that you are fairly confident is available on the client. For example, although you could specify C:, that would probably not be a good idea.

Finally, the logon path parameter works as it does for Windows 9x clients: It defines the location on the network that contains the user's roaming profile. The default is to store the profile information in the user's home directory. For reasons stated in Hour 21, you should create a separate share on which all the user profiles are stored. For example, define a share named [profiles] as you did in the previous hour and set logon path as follows:

```
logon path = \\server\profiles\username
```

The [profiles] service does not necessarily need to be located on the Samba PDC.

Profiles and Policies

User profiles and system policies are conceptually the same as they are in Windows 9x, but the importance of the two greatly increases because of the security mechanisms available in Windows NT.

Consider this example: Suppose that you use system policies to remove the Shut Down option from the Start menu. Under Windows 9x, the user can simply change the setting back to include the Shut Down option, kill explorer.exe, restart the shell, and voilà! The Shut Down menu returns.

However, if you set this same policy under Windows NT, you can restrict the user from changing it by using ACL on various Registry keys. Windows NT not only provides the policy options, but also the means to enforce the policy settings, something that is lacking in Windows 9x.

User profiles under Windows NT become more of a necessity than the luxury that they are under Windows 9x. I treat Windows NT clients more like UNIX workstations than PCs in the sense that the machine is generally locked down to prevent changes and the user has a specified location (usually the home directory) in which to save files. This is especially true in the case of public lab environments.

Therefore, it becomes necessary to provide users with an environment that can be set and that follows them from machine to machine. User profiles in a Samba controller domain are, by default, roaming profiles. This should be obvious from the default settings of the logon path parameter.

As a general rule, the management of user profiles in a Samba controlled domain is the same as the case for a Windows NT controlled domain. For example, one possibility is to create a Default User profile on the [netlogon] share of the PDC that will be used for all new users. This method works the same whether your PDC is a Samba server or a Windows NT box.

> Microsoft has provided several good white papers on its Web site regarding user profile administration. You can refer to http://www.microsoft.com/ntserver/nts/techdetails/ for more information.

One issue does arise when using a Samba server for a PDC. If you do not have a copy of the Windows NT 4.0 Server CD-ROM, where can you get the server tools such as the Server Manager, the User Manager for Domains, and the System Policy Editor?

Luckily, you can download these from the Microsoft Web site or its FTP site. The Policy Editor is distributed with Service Packs 3 and 4 for Windows NT 4.0, although it is not installed on workstations by default. The Windows NT 4.0 versions of the Server Manager and the User Manager for Domains are available for download from ftp://ftp.microsoft.com/Softlib/MSLFILES/.

The filename is SRVTOOL.EXE. A version of these tools that can be installed on Windows 9x is available from the same location and is named NEXUS.EXE.

rpcclient

In the beginning days of Samba, Andrew Tridgell needed tools to test smbd, and thus smbclient was born. In the early days of implementing Samba PDC support, Luke Leighton needed a tool to test the DCE/RPC functionality in smbd, and now you have rpcclient

rpcclient is still more of a testing tool than something to get work finished. I mention it simply because it offers the wonderful capability to obtain and set information on Windows NT machines. You'll look at a few examples to see the possibilities. Be warned that the output can be cryptic. The degree of rpcclient's value is your decision.

First I log in to a Windows NT 4.0 Workstation using a local account on the machine:

```
root# /usr/local/samba/bin/rpcclient -S bilbo -U jerry -W BILBO
Added interface ip=192.168.1.72 bcast=192.168.1.255 nmask=255.255.255.0
Enter Password:
smb: \>
```

You can see a list of available commands by typing help at the smb: \> prompt:

```
smb: \> help
help

svcenum        regenum        regdeletekey   regcreatekey   regquerykey
regdeleteval   regcreateval   reggetsec      regtestsec     ntlogin
wksinfo        srvinfo        srvsessions    srvshares      srvconnections
srvfiles       lsaquery       lookupsids     lookupnames    enumusers
addgroupmem    addaliasmem    creategroup    createalias    delgroup
delalias       ntpass         samuser        samtest        enumaliases
enumgroups     samgroups      quit           q              exit
bye            help           ?              !
```

I won't explain all the commands, but you can see that there are functions to add and delete groups, query services, and query registry keys and values.

Next, I simply obtain some information about the server:

```
smb: \> srvinfo
srvinfo

Server Info Level 101:
        BILBO           Wk Sv Din NT PtB
        platform_id   :       500
        os version    :       4.0
```

From this I can determine the server's name (BILBO), which I already knew, and also the server's operating system version, 4.0 in this case.

NEW TERM   You can also find out more internal information if you want. Windows NT contains a service called the Local Security Authority (LSA) that is in charge of verifying things such as object access and user logins. You can obtain information of the machine's sid by querying the Windows NT LSA:

```
smb: \> lsaquery
lsaquery

LSA Query Info Policy
Domain Member     - Domain: CHIPSNDIPS SID: S-1-5-21-123486-344389-124325
Domain Controller - Domain: BILBO SID: S-1-5-21-1842630440-1322791361-
➥134157935
```

As I said, `rpcclient` is not really a production tool. Rather it is a simple testing tool for Samba PDC support. It gives you a glimpse of some methods you can use to find out information, such as Registry settings and user accounts, from remote Windows NT machines while sitting at a UNIX console.

Windows 2000

As you have heard by now, Windows 2000 (formally known as Windows NT 5.0) will change quite a few things. While in a homogeneous Windows 2000 environment, many things will be different. Many people will run Windows NT 4.0 and Windows 2000 side by side. Therefore, things such as WINS will realistically be around for quite some time.

As of this time (Windows NT 5.0 Beta 2), Windows 2000 clients cannot log in to a Samba-controlled domain. This is due to changes in the way that Windows 2000 attempts to communicate with a PDC. Rest assured, though, the push to implement full PDC functionality in Samba will continue, and eventually support for the latest release of Windows NT will be implemented.

Summary

The latest Samba development code contains experimental support for Windows NT domain logins. This is different from Samba's capability to validate Windows 9x domain logins. Currently the Primary Domain Control features are not officially supported. Things will change and improve until the service can be distributed as complete.

Some of the more commonly used features that are implemented are the capability to perform domain logins, support for mapping functions from Windows NT users and groups to UNIX users and groups, and the capability to provide roaming user profiles and system policies.

Q&A

Q Can Samba 2.0 act as a Windows NT domain controller?

A There is some limited functionality for PDC support implemented in Samba 2.0, but it is broken when compared to the latest HEAD branch code. If you are going to experiment with Samba PDC capabilities, I strongly suggest obtaining the HEAD branch source code instead.

Q Where can I get help or report bugs when testing the PDC support?

A The `samba-ntdom@samba.org` mailing list comprises people doing this. Point your Web browser to `http://samba.org/listproc/` for instruction on how to join the list. It will be your best source of information.

Q I can't seem to find a lot of documentation on Samba PDC capabilities. Where should I look?

A A version of the Samba NT Domain FAQ is included on the CD-ROM. The latest version is available online at the Samba Web site. The link is located under the Documentation section.

New Terms

HEAD branch   This is Samba's latest source code. This is what the developers are currently working on and is not the same thing as the latest distributed version, for example, Samba 2.0.

Local Security Authority (LSA)[em]The service in Windows NT responsible for controlling verifying access to local resources such as a console or network login.

HOUR 23

Tips and Tricks

by Jerry Carter with Richard Sharpe

One of the fun things in life is getting something to work in a way that you have never done before. A good friend of mine came into the possession of a hard disk that had almost died. He needed to recover some data off it but the motor that spun the disk platters was very weak. Because the disk was already bad, he figured he had nothing to lose, removed the casing, and spun the disks with a screwdriver until they were rotating fast enough that the motor could take over. That was so cool! Those are the kinds of stories you sit around the table at conferences and tell over and over.

This hour is a melting pot of different tricks and tips that have made my life better (as far as administering Samba servers goes). The purpose is to give you some ideas that you can use to help you as well as sparking some of your own creativity. Although it might sound contradictory, the main reason I got into computers in the first place was the creative prospects. Well, that and the movie *Tron,* which I still have on videotape.

Performance Tuning

Rarely do I find the need to tune the performance parameters of my Samba servers at work. Perhaps that is a blessing of the hardware we run on or the underlying network design. However, every now and then an issue does arise.

Before continuing, let me say that any performance tuning section in a book is simple advice and should be treated as such. There are some good general suggestions, but the main thing to do is experiment. Everyone's network is different, and there are simply too many variables in the problem to solve them all in every situation.

That said, if you want to compare transfer rates via Samba or some other mechanism, a good judge of raw transfer speed is to compare its performance against the FTP protocol. All the TCP/IP stacks distributed by Microsoft for its operating systems come with an FTP client. Simply gauge the transfer rate of a large file, approximately 8MB or so, using FTP and the standard DOS `copy` command. You should find the read and the write rate for a particular method similar.

On the small network I have at home, I was able to download a file via FTP at around 990KBps. Using Windows NT's `copy` command, I was able to copy the file to the local disk from the same server running Samba at approximately 890KBps. This transfer rate was similar for reads and writes. The Windows client was a Dell Pentium 400Mz running Windows NT 4.0 Server. It had 128MB of RAM and an EIDE hard disk. The Linux server was a Pentium 133 with 64MB of RAM and an EIDE hard disk also. The Linux distribution was Slackware 3.5 using version 2.0.34 of the Linux kernel.

Network Bandwidth

When looking at performance, there are multiple sides from which to watch. The most obvious one, although often overlooked, is the network bandwidth itself. If you saturate the network wire, there is not much you can do except either cut traffic or increase bandwidth.

An easy way to check a UNIX machine is to use the `ifconfig` or the `netstat -i` commands. Make sure that you watch the statistics over time to get an idea of the general usage. Both give you the total transmit and receive errors in addition to the number of collisions. Here is some output from Linux's `ifconfig` command taken on my machine at home.

To produce the collisions (denoted by the `coll:` statistics), I flooded a host from my Linux box with `echo` requests and copied a large (around 15MB) file from the host to my Samba server so traffic would be flowing in both directions:

```
eth0 Link encap:Ethernet  HWaddr 00:00:F4:D8:6C:0D
     inet addr:192.168.1.72  Bcast:192.168.1.255  Mask:255.255.255.0
```

```
UP BROADCAST RUNNING MULTICAST  MTU:1500  Metric:1
RX packets:161777 errors:0 dropped:0 overruns:0 frame:0
TX packets:159703 errors:0 dropped:0 overruns:0 carrier:0 coll:21734
Interrupt:10 Base address:0xff40 DMA chan:4
```

If your network traffic statistics seem abnormal, one possible explanation is the existence of a bad adapter card on the network. I have seen cases where a network card in a PC would go bad and begin spewing packets onto the network at random.

Server Tuning

23

If you are confident that the problem does not lie with the network's bandwidth, another angle from which to view things is the side of the server. Generally server side tuning falls into two categories:

- File locking settings
- TCP and socket settings

File Locking Settings

Beginning with release 1.9.18, Samba correctly supports the SMB *opportunistic locking mechanisms*, *oplocks* for short. These allow clients to cache file operations aggressively. This can bring a big performance boost depending on client settings and is enabled by default. It is recommended that for versions of Samba above 1.9.18, you do not disable oplock support. Recent evaluations imply up to a 30 percent increase in performance with oplocks enabled.

Samba also offers the option of enabling strict locking. When enabled, Samba checks the file lock on every access to a file rather than only when a client requests a file lock check. If you enable strict locking, you might experience a hit in performance on some systems. The default action is to not enforce strict locking.

Not necessarily related to locking but to disk I/O in general is the strict sync Boolean parameter. This setting, which is disabled by default, controls whether smbd honors requests from PC clients to sync the data to disk. Often times, what the application wants is to flush the data rather than sync. This is a subtle difference, but on UNIX, a call to sync() blocks until all outstanding data in the kernel buffers have been written to disk. This burns CPU cycles and slows down your file access. The problem was first noticed with the release of Windows 98. The Windows Explorer was writing data in small chunks during a file copy and requesting a sync after each one.

The only danger of data corruption with the default setting is if the operating system that Samba is executing on crashes. Therefore the danger is very low. I believe you will find its benefits outweigh the slight risks.

Socket Settings

The primary means of tuning sockets within Samba is via the `socket options` parameter. The possible values are

- `SO_KEEPALIVE`
- `SO_REUSEADDR`
- `SO_BROADCAST`
- `TCP_NODELAY`
- `IPTOS_LOWDELAY`
- `IPTOS_THROUGHPUT`
- `SO_SNDBUF=integer`
- `SO_RCVBUF=integer`
- `SO_SNDLOWAT=integer`
- `SO_RCVLOWAT=integer`

The last four options accept an integer value. For example, you could specify `SO_RCVBUF=16384`. If you want to enable one of the first six options and define the Default Receive Window, you would add something like this:

```
soket options = TCP_NODELAY SO_RCVBUF=13384
```

The benefits of each option depend on your network topology and server particulars. In order to tune Samba, you are required to have a little background in TCP/IP, such as what is the *Receive Window* and what would be the affect of changing it. Then again you can simply change settings blindly and see what happens. Because such topics are beyond the scope of this book, I would encourage you to read the man pages on the `setsocketopt` function for your system as well as referring to the `smb.conf` man page. The default enables the TCP_NODLAY option and nothing else:

```
Default:    socket options = TCP_NODELAY
```

Client Tuning

This is a difficult category to discuss in any depth because so many different clients and PCs can have any range of network hardware installed. Microsoft has published a list of configurable TCP/IP settings for Windows 9x in the Knowledge base article entitled "Windows TCP/IP Registry Entries" (Q158474). I was unable to locate a similar article for Windows NT, although Dr. Karanjit S. Siyan has written a good reference entitled *Windows NT TCP/IP*, published by New Riders (ISBN 1-56205-887-8).

To access the MS Knowledge base on the Web, go to
`http://support.microsoft.com/support`.

23

One commonly tweaked setting is the size of the advertised TCP default receive window. The default for Windows 9x is 8KB. However, some people have reported better performance by increasing this to 16,384 bytes. You will have to experiment with your clients to be sure.

Other Miscellaneous Settings

A few circumstances can affect your server's performance that really don't apply to the network. One is the current log level for smbd and nmbd. Samba can be very verbose with regards to debug messages written out to the logs. This is good when you are trying to locate a problem, but it can clog disk space and slow the Samba daemons down as they constantly flush output to log files. Consider running the daemons at the default level of 2. This gives you enough information to verify and perform basic troubleshooting without bogging Samba down.

Another possibility of slow response during logon is that settings such as username level and password level are set to a very high value such as 8. Remember that this makes Samba attempt all combinations of case in the string up to the maximum level defined. The higher the level the more strings to compare for authentication.

Multiple Samba Servers on a Single Machine

One thing that most network administrators have in common with PC users is that we always think we need more hardware. The toys are bigger, but the idea is the same. Of course, with us we really do need the hardware!

It is possible to configure multiple Samba servers on a single machine with multiple network interfaces. However, if you can achieve the same objective by using netbios aliases and include settings as presented in Hour 10, "Server-Side Automation," I strongly recommend you do that. The only reason to install more than one Samba server per machine is when you must run multiple versions of the smbd and nmbd binaries. For example, you need to run version 2.0 for file service but also want to install the latest HEAD branch code to act as a PDC.

First you need to have both network interfaces correctly configured on the machine. I have used a virtual network interface for the second Samba server. For example, under Solaris this fictional network adapter is referred to as le0:1.

Next, you need to create a separate `smb.conf` file for each server. Of course, you can use the `include` directive for common settings.

In each `smb.conf` you need to set two parameters. The first is the interface to which Samba should bind. For example, assuming that you have two network adapters with IP addresses `192.168.1.90` and `192.168.1.91` respectively. I will use a subnet mask of `255.255.255.0`. Therefore, each `smb.conf` contains one of the following:

```
interfaces = 192.168.1.90/24
```

or

```
interfaces = 192.168.1.91/24
```

You also need to specify the address on which a given Samba server should listen for connections. By default, connections on any address are accepted. The address you specify using the `socket address` parameter must match the one used in the `interfaces` value. Here is an example for the first network interface.

```
socket address = 192.168.1.90
```

> Using the socket address parameter more than likely breaks standard browsing rules. To work around this, you need to use a WINS server and have the Samba box register with it.

Now when you start the two servers, each one should be bound to only one interface. If you experience problems starting `smbd` and `nmbd`, check the debug logs for error messages such as "not able to bind to address." You might also try starting one server and waiting a few seconds before starting the second server.

This type of setup can be very complex and bugs can become very hard to track down. In one instance, I was running a Samba PDC on a virtual interface and Samba 1.9.18p7 on the real interface. Both servers were set to register with another Samba machine acting as a WINS server, but the PDC was unable to register the *DOMAIN*<1b> name. The reason is that the packets were getting lost at the primary interface and the PDC on the virtual interface was never seeing the response from the WINS server. The fix for this was to start the PDC, wait five seconds and then start the 1.9.18p7 server. If you do decide to run this type of setup, be prepared to dig in a little to make things work.

Backing Up a Remote PC's Hard Disk

One of the biggest problems with PCs is backing up their hard disks. Users never bother, but when they lose something, they come running to the system administration staff asking for their files back. In some sites, it is made clear that the contents of the hard disk on each PC are not saved and any files the users want to save must be stored on the Samba server (perhaps in their homes share).

However, at some sites, it is impossible to take this approach, and other solutions are needed. Here is an approach to solving that problem. This approach uses smbclient to backup the files, plus some shell script glue and maybe cron scripts.

smbclient has already been discussed in Hour 13, "UNIX (smbclient, smbfs, smbwrapper, and Various Utilities." It has a tar mode that allows you to copy files from a remote CIFS/SMB file share and save them as a TAR (GNUtar) file. Here you use this capability to back up PCs. You do not need to run smbclient from your primary Samba server. Indeed, you do not need to run it from a Samba server at all. Simply install the Samba binaries on the system you want to perform backups from.

The steps involved in backing up PCs using smbclient are

1. Decide which PCs you want to back up. This is the easiest step.
2. For each PC that is being backed up, set up a share that provides access to the files and directories you want to backup.
3. Set up the cron scripts and shell scripts that you want to use to back up the files on each PC.

Here you concentrate on steps two and three. smbclient can be used to back up files from Windows for Workgroups, Windows 9x, and Windows NT. To set up a share on a PC, start Windows Explorer (or use your favorite approach) and select the directory that contains all the files you want to back up. An example of doing this is shown in Figure 23.1. You should share only the directory for read access. The procedures are slightly different for Windows for Workgroups. You might want to call the share backup or something else consistent across all the PCs.

> Setting up PCs this way allows anyone to read files on those PCs remotely. If you are connected to the Internet, you should ensure that CIFS/SMB access from the Internet to your internal systems is prevented by a firewall.

FIGURE 23.1

Sharing a directory on Windows 9x and Windows NT.

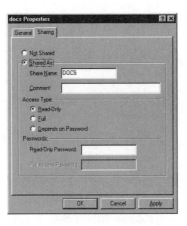

When you have set up file shares on the PCs that you want to back up, you should set up the cron scripts or shell scripts to back up the files on those shares.

Although the scripts likely are specific to your site, the form of the smbclient command is similar to the following:

```
smbclient //$client/backup -Tc device or file
```

Here `$client` is a shell variable that contains the current client being processed, and `<device or file>` is the name of the device or file to put the backup on. It might be

- `/dev/st0`, for a SCSI tape
- `/home/backup/$client.` `date +%d%m%Y` `.tar` to save the backup to a file tagged with the client's name and a Y2K compliant date
- `- ¦ some other command` to pipe the backup to some other facility for processing

If you need to exclude files, you might change the previous command to

```
smbclient //$client/backup -TcX device or file files to exclude
```

where `files to exclude` follows the rules outlined in Hour 13. Briefly, the wildcard characters * and % work here.

You might also want to look at Amanda as a backup tool as it uses smbclient to back up PCs, allows multiple backups to occur in parallel, and provides simple tape handling capabilities. The main Amanda home page is located at http://www.cs.umd.edu/projects/amanda/.

Faxing

Samba can be used to allow users to send faxes directly from their PCs. The basic strategy is

1. Install HylaFAX (www.vix.com/hylafax/) or mgetty+sendfax (ftp://sunsite.unc.edu/pub/linux/system/Serial/mgetty+sendfax) on your Samba system.

2. Set up a printer share under Samba, perhaps called FAX, directing the print jobs to the LPD-style queue FAX. Jobs are submitted to this queue as PostScript.

3. Provide a print filter for the queue FAX that performs the following:

   - Rummages through the PostScript, looking for a string such as Fax-Number: d[d*][-d*]

   - Queue the PostScript file to either HylaFAX or sendfax+mgetty

4. On clients, the queue is configured as a PostScript printer of some sort.

5. A user simply prepares their fax as a word processing document and prints it to the remote queue.

The details of obtaining, installing, and configuring either HylaFAX or mgetty+sendfax for sending handling outgoing faxes are beyond the scope of this book.

Samba Across a PPP Link

Accessing an SMB server across a PPP connection is very similar to accessing a server on a remote subnet. Most of the problems people experience are related to name resolution. If you can successfully resolve names, many of the other issues go away.

For my examples in this section, I will use a notebook running Windows NT 4.0 Workstation. The ideas presented are fundamentally the same for configuring a Windows 95 PPP client. Also, because you are looking at accessing Samba across a PPP link, I will not try to explain how to set up a PPP server. Rather I will distance myself from specifics of the PPP server implementation and control settings on the clients.

The primary thing to define is the IP address of your WINS server. Figure 23.2 displays the PPP TCP/IP Setting windows for Windows NT 4.0. As you can see, I have manually

23

entered the DNS server IP addresses and the single WINS server address. Depending on your server, these addresses can be assigned dynamically on the initiation of a new connection.

FIGURE 23.2

DNS and WINS server settings for a PPP connection under Windows NT 4.0.

If you are using Windows 9x, you should also verify that you have selected to Log On to Network (see Figure 23.3) in the connection properties and that you have installed the Client for Microsoft Network as if you were configuring for a connection to a LAN.

FIGURE 23.3

Windows 9x connection properties. Selecting the Log On to Network option.

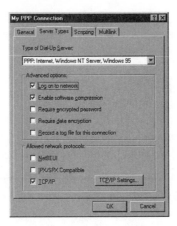

The other detail that I have found to be important is that the client dialing in should be a member of the same NetBIOS workgroup as the WINS server. In my case, the WINS server is also the workgroup's Domain Master Browser. Therefore, I can see all the workgroups that the WINS/DMB server sees. It is not necessary for the WINS server to be the same machine as the PPP server.

Browsing, as usual, is the hardest part to configure of a dial-up link. Assuming you have enabled the Log On to Network option under Windows 9x (this is built-in to Windows NT), you should be able to connect to specific servers even if browsing does not fall into place. All that is required for this is that you have your WINS server entries correct.

All the standard net.exe options function normally. For example, I can access my home directory by executing

```
net use h: \\burrito\jerry
```

It is also possible to perform domain logons across a PPP link by using a either a WINS server or a static LMHOSTS entry to resolve the *DOMAIN*<1b> NetBIOS name. For fun, using this simple setup, I was able to add a Windows NT 4.0 Server to a Samba controlled Windows NT domain using a connection through our modem pool at work. I was also able to log on to the domain using the dial up connection and download my roaming profile. I would not recommend this across a dial-up link due to transfer speeds, but the logon script and drive connections work very well.

Simple Domain Logon Script Tricks

Windows 9x, as opposed to Windows NT, does not provide an easy means of determining the username of the person currently logged in. This annoys me. Here is how I got around this.

First I have a generic logon script for all Windows 9x clients set by

```
logon script = logon.bat
```

The batch file itself (shown in Listing 23.1) is fairly simple. Most of the script is specific for my site. However, the design is very versatile.

LISTING 23.1   LOGON SCRIPT FOR WINDOWS 95 CLIENTS

```
1.   @echo off
2.
3.   rem #
4.   rem #    971007    Jerry Carter - COE Network Services
5.   rem #
6.   rem #    Login script for Windows 95 clients
7.   rem #
8.
9.   echo Executing Windows 95 login script....
10.
11.  rem # Clean up old pcnfsPro 2.0 files if neccessary...
```

continues

LISTING 23.1   CONTINUED

```
12. if exist %winbootdir%\pcnfswin.ini call \\ivy\scripts\delpro.bat
➥%winbootdir%
13.
14. rem --------- Set the PC's system clock
15. net time \\kudzu /set /yes
16.
17. rem --------- Mount the normal network drives
18. echo Mapping I: to \\kudzu\apps
19. net use i: \\kudzu\apps
20. echo Mapping H: to \\kudzu\homes
21. net use h: \\kudzu\homes
22.
23. rem --------- Now the user specific stuff
24. if not exist h:\user.bat GOTO no_user
25. call h:\user.bat
26. :no_user
27.
28. :group
29. rem --------- Mount the default group drive
30. %COMSPEC% /c \\kudzu\netlogon\group.bat %GROUP%
31.
32. rem --------- Mount any office shares
33. if "%MACHINE_GROUP%" == "" goto no_machine_group
34. %COMSPEC% /c \\kudzu\netlogon\off-dirs.bat %MACHINE_GROUP%
35. GOTO end
36.
37. :no_machine_group
38. regedit /s /w \\kudzu\netlogon\update.reg
39. GOTO end
40.
41. :end
42 . m ******* end of logon.bat
```

The first step to notice is that the user's home directory is always mounted as drive H: (line 21). The next thing to notice is that the logon script calls h:\user.bat if it exists (lines 24 and 25). This batch file is specific to the user and is where I will set the USER-NAME environment variable.

When a connection is made to a home directory, I have a preexec script that will create the ~/user.bat file if it does not exist. Here are the settings for the [homes] share:

```
[homes]
        preexec = /usr/samba/lib/netlogon/user.pl %U
        comment = Unix Home Directories
        browseable = no
        path = %H
        writeable = yes
```

```
        wide links = no
        create mode = 0600
        directory mode = 0700
        invalid users = @ugrad
```

Listing 23.2 contains the source code for the Perl script that is defined for the preexec value.

LISTING 23.2   PERL SCRIPT TO CREATE ~/USER.BAT

```perl
#!/usr/local/bin/perl5

$user = $ARGV[0];

# get the user's home directory
( $name, $passwd, $uid, $gid, $quota, $comment, $gcos, $dir, $shell ) =
➥getpwnam($user);
( $group, $passwd, $gid ) = getgrgid ( $gid );

if ( ! -f "$dir/user.bat" ) {

    open ( USERINFO, "> $dir/user.bat" ) ¦¦ die "Couldn't open
    ➥user.bat!!\n";
    print USERINFO "\\\\\ivy\\bin\\winset USERNAME=$user\015\n";
    print USERINFO "set USERNAME=$user\015\n";
    print USERINFO "set GROUP=$group\015\n";
    close ( USERINFO );
    chmod 0600, "$dir/user.bat"

}

exit 0
```

The winset command is a tool included on the Windows 95 CD-ROM that allows you to set a value in the global environment space from a DOS command prompt. After logging on, the information is available in the %USERNAME% variable.

The user.bat can also contain command unique to the person such as mapping an LPT port or copying some files. I have added commands in mine to mount the \\server\ netlogon directory:

```
\\ivy\bin\winset USERNAME=jerry
set USERNAME=jerry
set GROUP=uucp

echo Mapping X: to \\burrito\netlogon
net use x: \\burrito\netlogon
```

23

Both the \\ivy\bin\winset USERNAME and set USERNAME entries are both
necessary. The winset command does not make the variable effective in the
current command shell. Therefore the standard set USERNAME is used so I can
refer to its value from within the login script.

Summary

Samba offers many possibilities for doing things that make your job easier. In the case of
performance tuning, as is the case with smb.conf, you can get into as much detail as you
want. Often Samba's default settings work well enough, but feel free to experiment.

Samba is a tool to be used in any way you can think of. I hope that the examples presented in this hour stir your creativity some more to create your own tips and tricks.

Q&A

Q Where can I find out more information about other tips and tricks?

A The best place to look is on the comp.protocols.smb Usenet newsgroup and the
main Samba mailing list at samba@samba.org. You can search the Samba mailing
list archives by following links off the Samba home page.

Q I just created my own useful tip or trick. How can I tell other people about it?

A Probably the best place is the comp.protocols.smb newsgroup or the various
Samba mailings lists.

HOUR 24

Samba's Future

Now that you are at the end of things, the natural question is "What happens now?" I've said before that Samba is a moving target as far as development is concerned. This hour covers some of the things that are on the To Do list and will hopefully be implemented in the near future. Not only will I look at the future plans for Samba, I'll also examine how these plans could affect you.

One thing to remember is that OSS projects such as Samba work very much on a supply-and-demand method. Features usually are implemented when someone has a sufficient need and the available resources to put into the project. Therefore, the features presented in this hour are the current set of goals for the developers. As things change and demand changes, resources can be apportioned to new features not yet thought of.

Primary Domain Controller Support

One of the main thrusts (I say one and not the only) at the moment is to continue to implement the necessary functionality for Samba to act as Primary Domain Controller for Windows NT domains. The tentative completion date is in time for the release of Samba 2.1. However, given the complexity of details and testing that need to be attended to, this might be optimistic.

An important project is to implement the capability to participate in trust relationships with other domain controllers, either Samba or Windows NT. One of the stated goals of the PDC project is to make Samba appear identical to an NT server when viewed across the network wire. The capability to engage and take part in trust relationships is the one of the last major pieces of the puzzle to be completed.

Domain trusts truly become important only when you are functioning with a multiple-domain model. If you are not familiar with trust relationships and why they are important, imagine the following scenario. Your goal is to provide a set of resources for all users without performing the validation for those users. The corporate network has been divided into three sections based on the functional purpose of the associated department (see Figure 24.1). If network resources need to be shared among two or more domains, the easiest way to administer them is to place them in a single-resource domain that trusts the accessing domains to perform the user authentication for it. Trust relationships are one way. If the ResourceDomain trusts DomainA, the users in DomainA can access items in the ResourceDomain. However, any users in the ResourceDomain cannot access items in DomainA without an account there.

FIGURE 24.1

Multiple domains and a single-resource domain.

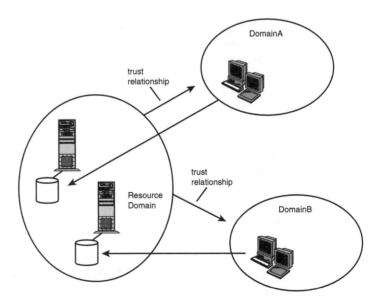

By implementing domain trust relationships, Samba could then function in the multiple-domain topology. As it is now, Samba can control a Windows NT domain, but it does so in an isolated manner.

Although the protocol used to replicate Windows NT SAM databases between primary domain controllers and backup domain controllers has not been decoded, there is very little push to do so in Samba. The reason is that the purpose for replicating account databases between machines becomes pointless when both machines access a shared database from an LDAP server, which I'll discuss next. If you want to replicate the account database for load balancing or fail over purposes, you do not need to implement your own protocol when LDAP allows for replication already.

Account Databases

24

A fitting topic to follow NT domain control support is the subject of user account databases. In Hour 2, "Windows Networking," I mentioned that version 2.0 introduced a password database API and I have already mentioned the use of an LDAP server. Primarily, this API was designed to maintain the necessary information to support Samba's PDC functionality for Windows NT domains. It abstracted the user account information from the routines necessary to access the data and modify it. As a result, several alternative user account databases now exist as opposed to the single flat ASCII file (/usr/local/samba/private/smbpasswd). Without password encryption enabled, Samba functions normally using plain-text passwords, comparing against /etc/passwd. If you want to enable any of these experimental back-ends, you need to enable encrypted passwords and configure Samba compile-time options to include the necessary flag.

First, examine Samba LDAP support. Figure 24.2 illustrates a possible setup using a separate machine as an LDAP server to maintain the user account information. All three Samba servers obtain information for user validation from a single point. Although this inserts a single point of failure into the topology, it also provides for a single point of change that will be seen by all. You can, of course, use replicated LDAP servers as well to balance the load and provide for fail over.

Currently, support for an LDAP database back-end is in experimental testing. This means that at least one person has successfully configured and used an LDAP server for storing user accounts. Although LDAP support has no set release date, chances are that you can expect it to go into production release at the same time that the Primary Domain Controller functionality becomes officially advertised.

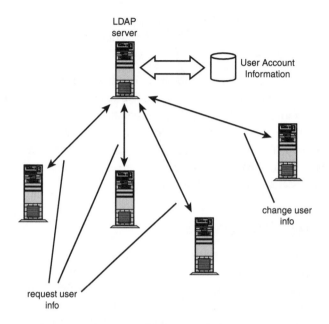

FIGURE 24.2

A single LDAP server provides user account information to multiple Samba servers.

Work has also commenced on using NIS+ tables to serve Windows NT–like user account information. This smbpasswd table is separate from the standard passwd.org_dir and contains information such as a Windows NT list of machines to which the user is granted permissions to log on to and the location of the user's roaming profile. Although code has been written, the NIS+ database back-end is not as far along as the LDAP support.

Another example of how the new password API opens up possibilities is the use of a gdbm table to hold the smbpasswd information. This provides increased lookup speed without the complexity of a network database server.

NTFS Access Control Lists

If you view the properties of a Samba 2.0 disk share, you will notice that the file system type is reported as NTFS. The reason for this is related to long filename support when serving Windows 95 clients. However, actually implementing NTFS access control lists for directories and files stored on Samba shares is on the To Do list. Although the design for this has not been thoroughly fleshed out yet, it could be possible to see this feature sometime during the 2.0 lifetime.

What is the rationalization behind wanting to implement NTFS ACLs on a UNIX file system served over SMB? If you remember in Hour 12, "Case Study: Replacing an NT File and Print Server," one of the problems I ran into was when two or more groups had access to a specific folder. The difficulty in this arose from the fact the UNIX file permission bits are tied to ownership, whether it be a user or a group. There is no means of allowing two groups ownership of a single directory. This, however, is a common occurrence under Windows NT.

The goal is to enable users to set ACLs on a folder or file using the standard methods available under Windows NT, such as the Windows Explorer, and have Samba enforce those permissions. The motivation, other than the one previously mentioned, is to allow Samba to be placed in a Windows NT environment and behave normally given the behavior that the user would expect (for example, NTFS ACLs and the domain security model).

True Windows NT Printing

24

As I described in Hour 12, Samba does not currently support the full gamut of Windows NT printing functionality, but this feature is almost completed. Approximately 75% of the code necessary to support Windows NT print functions has been written, although none of it has committed to the Samba source code tree as of this writing.

Features that will be supported in the final product include

- Printing via the Microsoft DCE/RPC functions that a Windows NT machines uses when printing to another Windows NT machine.
- The capability to download printer driver files from the Samba server as is currently supported for Windows 95 clients.

The Windows NT printing functionality will not include support for the Windows Enhanced Metafile (EMF) format because a Windows NT client that sends a print job to a remote server in the EMF format requires that the server process the job using the Windows printer driver. Because it would be impossible (or at the very least not very fun) to do this on a UNIX machine, Samba only supports print jobs spooled in the RAW format so that they can be simply passed onto the UNIX printing system without any modification.

Most likely, this feature will also be included in the 2.1 release of Samba.

WINS Replication

Microsoft Windows NT Servers are shipped with a WINS server that can be installed from the CD-ROM. This was mentioned briefly in Hour 18, "Resolving NetBIOS Names Without Using Broadcasts." You also know that Samba can act as a WINS server but cannot currently provide any type of automatic replication of its WINS database with another server, Windows NT, or Samba.

There are two approaches to implementing some type of WINS replication protocol within Samba. One approach is to decode yet another undocumented (surprise!) Microsoft protocol. The advantage of this is that Samba could interact with another WINS server running on a Windows NT platform. The disadvantage of this is the work necessary to decode the packets transmitted on the wire during the replication process.

The second approach is to design an entirely new and possibly better protocol for use by Samba. Although protocol design is not trivial, this approach has the advantage of leveraging off of Samba's internal code. The implementation would probably be less complex to design than it would be to decode Microsoft's protocol.

There is, however, a third approach that says Let's do both! This proposal says to implement the Microsoft WINS replication protocol for interoperability purposes but use a more finely tuned protocol for replication between two Samba servers. It is not known at this time which path, if any, will be taken.

Currently Samba is isolated as a WINS server, which is why this replication feature is important. There are no means available for fail over, redundancy, or load balancing. Also, the dynamic nature of NetBIOS names makes it important that Samba handles the replication automatically rather than through some method that attempts to `rdist` the WINS database among servers. This, in fact, would not work because WINS replication should be designed to allow multiple primary servers that update each other as opposed to the model used for primary and secondary DNS servers.

Distributed File System

A person once made a very funny comment to me regarding the remote disk shares in a Windows environment. He said, "What happens when you run out of letters?" He was, of course, using that as example to argue that NFS offers a more unified view of the network than does standard UNC network paths. Of course, I agreed with him.

When compared to NFS, UNC network paths can be very bothersome and hard to change without breaking some application. For example, how do you combine multiple SMB servers into one machine using only one NetBIOS name without causing grief to your users? There needs to be some mechanism to order the network shares in much the same way that directories are ordered on a disk by a file system. This is the approach that NFS takes.

NEW TERM   The *Distributed File System* (DFS) enables an administrator to create a "share of shares". In this manner, users can maintain a few connections to DFS root servers and access all the necessary files. Figure 24.3 illustrates how DFS unifies the name space of servers and enables users to view a single network directory tree.

FIGURE 24.3

Using a DFS server to act as an access point for multiple SMB servers.

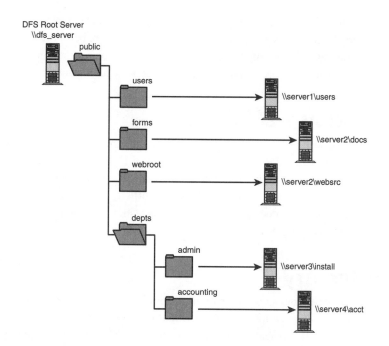

DFS Root Server
\\dfs_server
public
users   \\server1\users
forms   \\server2\docs
webroot   \\server2\websrc
depts
admin   \\server3\install
accounting   \\server4\acct

24

For example, the user can mount \\dfs_server\public to a drive letter, for example N:. When the user accesses a file in N:\users, the actual request is referred to the UNC network path \\server1\users. If you, as the administrator, decide that the [users] share should be located on a server other than server1, the users never need to know. All that needs to be done is to change the referral configuration on the DFS server for the users directory and all clients automatically point to the new server. Likewise any attempts to access N:\dept\admin are referred to \\server3\install.

NEW TERM   A DFS root share acts as a mount point for other shares. The root directory can contain junction points that represent other network disk shares or normal directories. The subdirectories can also contain subdirectories and junction points. It is also possible for a junction point to refer to another DFS root server. This way a department could manage its own name space using DFS and then make that available others within the company by configuring a referral from the main DFS root server.

When used in conjunction with a directory service such as LDAP, multiple servers can be configured to serve a single junction point. If an administrator sets up two servers to replicate a public disk share, DFS would then refer client request to one of the two SMB servers listed in the directory service. DFS does not provide any means to support the disk replication, only the referrals to one of multiple servers.

This brief overview should be enough to spark your interest in Samba's future support for DFS. At this point, some code has been written, but more development needs to be done to make the support portable and manageable. Although there is no expected date for releasing DFS support, it does have a fairly high priority.

Windows 2000

Windows 2000 will offer many new features and change many of the existing ones. Rather than going into details of the Active Directory, Kerberos, and NetBIOS-less file sharing, I will simply say that the Samba will operate with future versions of Microsoft's operating systems as long as there is a sufficient demand for it. It is interesting to note that Microsoft does perform regressions testing of their Window clients against Samba. This is strictly as a file server and not as a PDC, of course.

Summary

The development of Samba will continue as long as there is demand for it. Apparently there is demand for it, or else I would not be writing this book and you would not be reading it! The features listed in the hour (PDC functionality, pluggable user account databases, NTFS ACL support, WINS replication, DFS support, and interoperability with Windows 2000) are only a few of the possibilities. The OSS community can form strong bonds with each other and a given project can become like a family member. If you are interested, join a mailing list, get involved, and send in your wish list.

Q&A

Q Where can I find out about the latest plans for Samba development?

A The best place to start is the Samba Web site, http://samba.org. However, if you really want to find out about what people are thinking, you should check the various mailing lists given in Hour 11, "Troubleshooting."

Q I have an idea for a really cool feature to add to Samba. What should I do with it?

A The preferred thing to do would be to implement it first and then send the patches to samba-bugs@samba.org. If you for some reason are unable to this, send a message to samba-bugs@samba.org with "WISH" as the first word of the subject line.

New Terms

Distributed File System (DFS)   A type of network file system that enables SMB shares to be mounted with the DFS tree and then made available to clients using a single, unified name space.

DFS root share   The root directory of the DFS tree. This is the part that is mounted by users on their local machine just as a SMB share is mounted. The actual network location of a share found within the DFS tree is transparent to the user.

junction points   A directory with a DFS tree that acts as a mount point for a remote disk share.

DFS referral   The act of resolving a junction point to a UNC network path.

Directory Service   A network database used to locate objects such as printers, machines, and users. The DS helps applications resolve names to network locations.

24

INDEX

X

Other Related Titles

GNU GENERAL PUBLIC LICENSE

Version 2, June 1991

Copyright © 1989, 1991 Free Software Foundation, Inc.

675 Mass Ave, Cambridge, MA 02139, USA

Preamble

The licenses for most software are designed to take away your freedom to share and change it. By contrast, the GNU General Public License is intended to guarantee your freedom to share and change free software—to make sure the software is free for all its users. This General Public License applies to most of the Free Software Foundation's software and to any other program whose authors commit to using it. (Some other Free Software Foundation software is covered by the GNU Library General Public License instead.) You can apply it to your programs, too.

When we speak of free software, we are referring to freedom, not price. Our General Public Licenses are designed to make sure that you have the freedom to distribute copies of free software (and charge for this service if you wish), that you receive source code or can get it if you want it, that you can change the software or use pieces of it in new free programs; and that you know you can do these things.

To protect your rights, we need to make restrictions that forbid anyone to deny you these rights or to ask you to surrender the rights. These restrictions translate to certain responsibilities for you if you distribute copies of the software, or if you modify it.

For example, if you distribute copies of such a program, whether gratis or for a fee, you must give the recipients all the rights that you have. You must make sure that they, too, receive or can get the source code. And you must show them these terms so they know their rights.

We protect your rights with two steps: (1) copyright the software, and (2) offer you this license which gives you legal permission to copy, distribute and/or modify the software.

Also, for each author's protection and ours, we want to make certain that everyone understands that there is no warranty for this free software. If the software is modified by someone else and passed on, we want its recipients to know that what they have is not the original, so that any problems introduced by others will not reflect on the original authors' reputations.

Finally, any free program is threatened constantly by software patents. We wish to avoid the danger that redistributors of a free program will individually obtain patent licenses, in effect making the program proprietary. To prevent this, we have made it clear that any patent must be licensed for everyone's free use or not licensed at all.

The precise terms and conditions for copying, distribution and modification follow.

GNU General Public License

Terms and Conditions for Copying, Distribution and Modification

0. This License applies to any program or other work which contains a notice placed by the copyright holder saying it may be distributed under the terms of this General Public License. The "Program", below, refers to any such program or work, and a "work based on the Program" means either the Program or any derivative work under copyright law: that is to say, a work containing the Program or a portion of it, either verbatim or with modifications and/or translated into another language. (Hereinafter, translation is included without limitation in the term "modification".) Each licensee is addressed as "you".

   Activities other than copying, distribution and modification are not covered by this License; they are outside its scope. The act of running the Program is not restricted, and the output from the Program is covered only if its contents constitute a work based on the Program (independent of having been made by running the Program). Whether that is true depends on what the Program does.

1. You may copy and distribute verbatim copies of the Program's source code as you receive it, in any medium, provided that you conspicuously and appropriately publish on each copy an appropriate copyright notice and disclaimer of warranty; keep intact all the notices that refer to this License and to the absence of any warranty; and give any other recipients of the Program a copy of this License along with the Program.

   You may charge a fee for the physical act of transferring a copy, and you may at your option offer warranty protection in exchange for a fee.

2. You may modify your copy or copies of the Program or any portion of it, thus forming a work based on the Program, and copy and distribute such modifications or work under the terms of Section 1 above, provided that you also meet all of these conditions:

   a) You must cause the modified files to carry prominent notices stating that you changed the files and the date of any change.

   b) You must cause any work that you distribute or publish, that in whole or in part contains or is derived from the Program or any part thereof, to be licensed as a whole at no charge to all third parties under the terms of this License.

   c) If the modified program normally reads commands interactively when run, you must cause it, when started running for such interactive use in the most ordinary way, to print or display an announcement including an appropriate copyright notice and a notice that there is no warranty (or else, saying that you provide a warranty) and that users may redistribute the program under these conditions, and telling the user how to view a copy of this License. (Exception: if the Program itself is interactive but does not normally print such an announcement, your work based on the Program is not required to print an announcement.)

   These requirements apply to the modified work as a whole. If identifiable sections of that work are not derived from the Program, and can be reasonably considered independent and separate works in themselves, then this License, and its terms, do not apply to those sections when you distribute them as separate works. But when you distribute the same sections as part of a whole which is a work based on the Program, the distribution of the whole must be on the terms of this License, whose permissions for other licensees extend to the entire whole, and thus to each and every part regardless of who wrote it.

   Thus, it is not the intent of this section to claim rights or contest your rights to work written entirely by you; rather, the intent is to exercise the right to control the distribution of derivative or collective works based on the Program.

   In addition, mere aggregation of another work not based on the Program with the Program (or with a work based on the Program) on a volume of a storage or distribution medium does not bring the other work under the scope of this License.

3. You may copy and distribute the Program (or a work based on it, under Section 2) in object code or executable form under the terms of Sections 1 and 2 above provided that you also do one of the following:

   a) Accompany it with the complete corresponding machine-readable source code, which must be distributed under the terms of Sections 1 and 2 above on a medium customarily used for software interchange; or,

b) Accompany it with a written offer, valid for at least three years, to give any third party, for a charge no more than your cost of physically performing source distribution, a complete machine-readable copy of the corresponding source code, to be distributed under the terms of Sections 1 and 2 above on a medium customarily used for software interchange; or,

c) Accompany it with the information you received as to the offer to distribute corresponding source code. (This alternative is allowed only for noncommercial distribution and only if you received the program in object code or executable form with such an offer, in accord with Subsection b above.)

The source code for a work means the preferred form of the work for making modifications to it. For an executable work, complete source code means all the source code for all modules it contains, plus any associated interface definition files, plus the scripts used to control compilation and installation of the executable. However, as a special exception, the source code distributed need not include anything that is normally distributed (in either source or binary form) with the major components (compiler, kernel, and so on) of the operating system on which the executable runs, unless that component itself accompanies the executable.

If distribution of executable or object code is made by offering access to copy from a designated place, then offering equivalent access to copy the source code from the same place counts as distribution of the source code, even though third parties are not compelled to copy the source along with the object code.

4. You may not copy, modify, sublicense, or distribute the Program except as expressly provided under this License. Any attempt otherwise to copy, modify, sublicense or distribute the Program is void, and will automatically terminate your rights under this License. However, parties who have received copies, or rights, from you under this License will not have their licenses terminated so long as such parties remain in full compliance.

5. You are not required to accept this License, since you have not signed it. However, nothing else grants you permission to modify or distribute the Program or its derivative works. These actions are prohibited by law if you do not accept this License. Therefore, by modifying or distributing the Program (or any work based on the Program), you indicate your acceptance of this License to do so, and all its terms and conditions for copying, distributing or modifying the Program or works based on it.

6. Each time you redistribute the Program (or any work based on the Program), the recipient automatically receives a license from the original licensor to copy, distribute or modify the Program subject to these terms and conditions. You may not impose any further restrictions on the recipients' exercise of the rights granted herein. You are not responsible for enforcing compliance by third parties to this License.

7. If, as a consequence of a court judgment or allegation of patent infringement or for any other reason (not limited to patent issues), conditions are imposed on you (whether by court order, agreement or otherwise) that contradict the conditions of this License, they do not excuse you from the conditions of this License. If you cannot distribute so as to satisfy simultaneously your obligations under this License and any other pertinent obligations, then as a consequence you may not distribute the Program at all. For example, if a patent license would not permit royalty-free redistribution of the Program by all those who receive copies directly or indirectly through you, then the only way you could satisfy both it and this License would be to refrain entirely from distribution of the Program.

   If any portion of this section is held invalid or unenforceable under any particular circumstance, the balance of the section is intended to apply and the section as a whole is intended to apply in other circumstances.

   It is not the purpose of this section to induce you to infringe any patents or other property right claims or to contest validity of any such claims; this section has the sole purpose of protecting the integrity of the free software distribution system, which is implemented by public license practices. Many people have made generous contributions to the wide range of software distributed through that system in reliance on consistent application of that system; it is up to the author/donor to decide if he or she is willing to distribute software through any other system and a licensee cannot impose that choice.

   This section is intended to make thoroughly clear what is believed to be a consequence of the rest of this License.

8. If the distribution and/or use of the Program is restricted in certain countries either by patents or by copyrighted interfaces, the original copyright holder who places the Program under this License may add an explicit geographical distribution limitation excluding those countries, so that distribution is permitted only in or among countries not thus excluded. In such case, this License incorporates the limitation as if written in the body of this License.

9. The Free Software Foundation may publish revised and/or new versions of the General Public License from time to time. Such new versions will be similar in spirit to the present version, but may differ in detail to address new problems or concerns.

   Each version is given a distinguishing version number. If the Program specifies a version number of this License which applies to it and "any later version", you have the option of following the terms and conditions either of that version or of any later version published by the Free Software Foundation. If the Program does not specify a version number of this License, you may choose any version ever published by the Free Software Foundation.

10. If you wish to incorporate parts of the Program into other free programs whose distribution conditions are different, write to the author to ask for permission. For software which is copyrighted by the Free Software Foundation, write to the Free Software Foundation; we sometimes make exceptions for this. Our decision will be guided by the two goals of preserving the free status of all derivatives of our free software and of promoting the sharing and reuse of software generally.

NO WARRANTY

11. BECAUSE THE PROGRAM IS LICENSED FREE OF CHARGE, THERE IS NO WARRANTY FOR THE PROGRAM, TO THE EXTENT PERMITTED BY APPLICABLE LAW. EXCEPT WHEN OTHERWISE STATED IN WRITING THE COPYRIGHT HOLDERS AND/OR OTHER PARTIES PROVIDE THE PROGRAM "AS IS" WITHOUT WARRANTY OF ANY KIND, EITHER EXPRESSED OR IMPLIED, INCLUDING, BUT NOT LIMITED TO, THE IMPLIED WARRANTIES OF MERCHANTABILITY AND FITNESS FOR A PARTICULAR PURPOSE. THE ENTIRE RISK AS TO THE QUALITY AND PERFORMANCE OF THE PROGRAM IS WITH YOU. SHOULD THE PROGRAM PROVE DEFECTIVE, YOU ASSUME THE COST OF ALL NECESSARY SERVICING, REPAIR OR CORRECTION.

12. IN NO EVENT UNLESS REQUIRED BY APPLICABLE LAW OR AGREED TO IN WRITING WILL ANY COPYRIGHT HOLDER, OR ANY OTHER PARTY WHO MAY MODIFY AND/OR REDISTRIBUTE THE PROGRAM AS PERMITTED ABOVE, BE LIABLE TO YOU FOR DAMAGES, INCLUDING ANY GENERAL, SPECIAL, INCIDENTAL OR CONSEQUENTIAL DAMAGES ARISING OUT OF THE USE OR INABILITY TO USE THE PROGRAM (INCLUDING BUT NOT LIMITED TO LOSS OF DATA OR DATA BEING RENDERED INACCURATE OR LOSSES SUSTAINED BY YOU OR THIRD PARTIES OR A FAILURE OF THE PROGRAM TO OPERATE WITH ANY OTHER PROGRAMS), EVEN IF SUCH HOLDER OR OTHER PARTY HAS BEEN ADVISED OF THE POSSIBILITY OF SUCH DAMAGES.

END OF TERMS AND CONDITIONS

Linux and the GNU system

The GNU project started 12 years ago with the goal of developing a complete free Unix-like operating system. "Free" refers to freedom, not price; it means you are free to run, copy, distribute, study, change, and improve the software.

A Unix-like system consists of many different programs. We found some components already available as free software—for example, X Windows and TeX. We obtained other components by helping to convince their developers to make them free—for example, the Berkeley network utilities. Other components we wrote specifically for GNU—for example, GNU Emacs, the GNU C compiler, the GNU C library, Bash, and Ghostscript. The components in this last category are "GNU software". The GNU system consists of all three categories together.

The GNU project is not just about developing and distributing free software. The heart of the GNU project is an idea: that software should be free, and that the users' freedom is worth defending. For if people have freedom but do not value it, they will not keep it for long. In order to make freedom last, we have to teach people to value it.

The GNU project's method is that free software and the idea of users' freedom support each other. We develop GNU software, and as people encounter GNU programs or the GNU system and start to use them, they also think about the GNU idea. The software shows that the idea can work in practice. People who come to agree with the idea are likely to write additional free software. Thus, the software embodies the idea, spreads the idea, and grows from the idea.

This method was working well—until someone combined the Linux kernel with the GNU system (which still lacked a kernel), and called the combination a "Linux system."

The Linux kernel is a free Unix-compatible kernel written by Linus Torvalds. It was not written specifically for the GNU project, but the Linux kernel and the GNU system work together well. In fact, adding Linux to the GNU system brought the system to completion: it made a free Unix-compatible operating system available for use.

But ironically, the practice of calling it a "Linux system" undermines our method of communicating the GNU idea. At first impression, a "Linux system" sounds like something completely distinct from the "GNU system." And that is what most users think it is.

Most introductions to the "Linux system" acknowledge the role played by the GNU software components. But they don't say that the system as a whole is more or less the same GNU system that the GNU project has been compiling for a decade. They don't say that the idea of a free Unix-like system originates from the GNU project. So most users don't know these things.

This leads many of those users to identify themselves as a separate community of "Linux users", distinct from the GNU user community. They use all of the GNU software; in fact, they use almost all of the GNU system; but they don't think of themselves as GNU users, and they may not think about the GNU idea.

It leads to other problems as well—even hampering cooperation on software maintenance. Normally when users change a GNU program to make it work better on a particular system, they send the change to the maintainer of that program; then they work with the maintainer, explaining the change, arguing for it and sometimes rewriting it, to get it installed.

But people who think of themselves as "Linux users" are more likely to release a forked "Linux-only" version of the GNU program, and consider the job done. We want each and every GNU program to work "out of the box" on Linux-based systems; but if the users do not help, that goal becomes much harder to achieve.

So how should the GNU project respond? What should we do now to spread the idea that freedom for computer users is important?

We should continue to talk about the freedom to share and change software—and to teach other users to value these freedoms. If we enjoy having a free operating system, it makes sense for us to think about preserving those freedoms for the long term. If we enjoy having a variety of free software, it makes sense for to think about encouraging others to write additional free software, instead of additional proprietary software.

We should not accept the splitting of the community in two. Instead we should spread the word that "Linux systems" are variant GNU systems—that users of these systems are GNU users, and that they ought to consider the GNU philosophy which brought these systems into existence.

This article is one way of doing that. Another way is to use the terms "Linux-based GNU system" (or "GNU/Linux system" or "Lignux" for short) to refer to the combination of the Linux kernel and the GNU system.

The FreeBSD Copyright

All of the documentation and software included in the 4.4BSD and 4.4BSD-Lite Releases is copyrighted by The Regents of the University of California.

Copyright 1979, 1980, 1983, 1986, 1988, 1989, 1991, 1992, 1993, 1994 The Regents of the University of California. All rights reserved.

Redistribution and use in source and binary forms, with or without modification, are permitted provided that the following conditions are met:

1. Redistributions of source code must retain the above copyright notice, this list of conditions and the following disclaimer.
2. Redistributions in binary form must reproduce the above copyright notice, this list of conditions and the following disclaimer in the documentation and/or other materials provided with the distribution.
3. All advertising materials mentioning features or use of this software must display the following acknowledgement:

   This product includes software developed by the University of California, Berkeley and its contributors.
4. Neither the name of the University nor the names of its contributors may be used to endorse or promote products derived from this software without specific prior written permission.

THIS SOFTWARE IS PROVIDED BY THE REGENTS AND CONTRIBUTORS "AS IS" AND ANY EXPRESS OR IMPLIED WARRANTIES, INCLUDING, BUT NOT LIMITED TO, THE IMPLIED WARRANTIES OF MERCHANTABILITY AND FITNESS FOR A PARTICULAR PURPOSE ARE DISCLAIMED. IN NO EVENT SHALL THE REGENTS OR CONTRIBUTORS BE LIABLE FOR ANY DIRECT, INDIRECT, INCIDENTAL, SPECIAL, EXEMPLARY, OR CONSEQUENTIAL DAMAGES (INCLUDING, BUT NOT LIMITED TO, PROCUREMENT OF SUBSTITUTE GOODS OR SERVICES; LOSS OF USE, DATA, OR PROFITS; OR BUSINESS INTERRUPTION) HOWEVER CAUSED AND ON ANY THEORY OF LIABILITY, WHETHER IN CONTRACT, STRICT LIABILITY, OR TORT (INCLUDING NEGLIGENCE OR OTHERWISE) ARISING IN ANY WAY OUT OF THE USE OF THIS SOFTWARE, EVEN IF ADVISED OF THE POSSIBILITY OF SUCH DAMAGE.

The Institute of Electrical and Electronics Engineers and the American National Standards Committee X3, on Information Processing Systems have given us permission to reprint portions of their documentation.

In the following statement, the phrase "this text" refers to portions of the system documentation.

Portions of this text are reprinted and reproduced in electronic form in the second BSD Networking Software Release, from IEEE Std 1003.1-1988, IEEE Standard Portable Operating System Interface for Computer Environments (POSIX), copyright © 1988 by the Institute of Electrical and Electronics Engineers, Inc. In the event of any discrepancy between these versions and the original IEEE Standard, the original IEEE Standard is the referee document.

In the following statement, the phrase "This material" refers to portions of the system documentation.

This material is reproduced with permission from American National Standards Committee X3, on Information Processing Systems. Computer and Business Equipment Manufacturers Association (CBEMA), 311 First St., NW, Suite 500, Washington, DC 20001-2178. The developmental work of Programming Language C was completed by the X3J11 Technical Committee.

The views and conclusions contained in the software and documentation are those of the authors and should not be interpreted as representing official policies, either expressed or implied, of the Regents of the University of California.

www@FreeBSD.ORG

$Date: 1997/07/01 03:52:05 $